It is a commonplace of modern scholarship that there was no general theory of language available to Renaissance thinkers, and that studies of grammar confined themselves for the most part to the investigation of formal features of language. However, no community can operate without some shared assumptions about meaning and its transmission; and it is manifest from the plethora of works of interpretation at this time – commentaries, translations, paraphrases, editions, epitomes – that the practice of conveying significance was thriving, and giving rise to heated debates about correct interpretation in theology, law, medicine, philosophy and humanistic studies.

This book investigates theories of interpretation and meaning in Renaissance jurisprudence. How do they relate to the institutions of the law, especially pedagogical institutions? What characterizes the most commonly adopted theories of the legal profession? In what form were they published? How do they relate to the principles of interpretation found in the trivium of grammar, dilaectics and rhetoric? In what ways, if any, do they mark a departure from medieval approaches? How do they relate to modern canons of interpretation? And how do they relate to similar issues in modern semantics and the philosophy of language, such as speech act theory or the 'logic of the supplement'? An answer to these questions is sought through an investigation of Renaissance problems concerning the authority of interpreters, the questions of signification, definition, verbal propriety and verbal extension, the problem of cavillation, the alternative interpretative strategies of *ratio legis* and *mens legislatoris*, the performative functions of language, and custom and equity as means of interpretation. The theoretical issues raised are examined in the exemplary case of defamation.

INTERPRETATION AND MEANING
IN THE RENAISSANCE

IDEAS IN CONTEXT

Edited by Richard Rorty, J. B. Schneewind, Quentin Skinner and
Wolf Lepenies

The books in this series discuss the emergence of intellectual traditions and of
related disciplines. The procedures, aims and vocabularies generated will be
set in the context of the alternatives available within the contemporary
frameworks of ideas and institutions. Through detailed studies of the
evolution of such traditions, and their modification by different audiences, it
is hoped that a new picture will form of the development of ideas in their
concrete contexts. By this means, artificial distinctions between the history of
philosophy, of the various sciences, of society and politics, and of literature,
may be seen to dissolve.

Ideas in context is published with the support of the Exxon Education
Foundation.

For a full list of titles in this series, please see end of book.

INTERPRETATION AND MEANING IN THE RENAISSANCE

THE CASE OF LAW

IAN MACLEAN

The Queen's College, Oxford

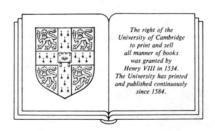

The right of the
University of Cambridge
to print and sell
all manner of books
was granted by
Henry VIII in 1534.
The University has printed
and published continuously
since 1584.

CAMBRIDGE UNIVERSITY PRESS

Cambridge
New York   Port Chester
Melbourne   Sydney

Published by the Press Syndicate of the University of Cambridge
The Pitt Building, Trumpington Street, Cambridge CB2 1RP
40 West 20th Street, New York, NY 10011-4211, USA
10 Stamford Road, Oakleigh, Victoria 3166, Australia

First published 1992

Printed in Great Britain at the University Press, Cambridge

A catalogue record for this book is available from the British Library

Library of Congress cataloguing in publication data applied for

ISBN 0 521 41546 2 hardback

VN

For Isobel

Spéron-Spéroni [1500–88] explique très bien comment un auteur qui s'énonce très clairement pour lui-même est quelquefois obscur pour son lecteur: 'c'est', dit-il, 'que l'auteur va de la pensée à l'expression, et que le lecteur va de l'expression à la pensée.'

Chamfort, Maximes et pensées (1795), no. 462

Contents

Illustrations
(pages 41–8)

Acknowledgements

It gives me great pleasure to record my gratitude for the help and advice I have received from colleagues and librarians. My debts are too extensive all to be recorded here, but I should like to make special mention of those I owe to Angus Bowie, for his generous assistance with Greek and the knottier problems of the Latin, to John Kaye and Geoffrey Marshall for their patient and tactful replies to my naïve enquiries about the law, to Richard Green, Terence Cave, Nigel Smith and Conal Condren for reading parts of the text or its entirety with characteristic care and acumen, to Archie Young and Grahame Lock who arranged for me to deliver part of chapter 4 as a lecture to audiences in Leiden and Western Ontario, to Quentin Skinner who encouraged me to publish the book, and to librarians in Oxford, Paris and Wolfenbüttel (especially Ulrich Kopp and Christian Hogrefe), who deftly steered me to the corpus of texts which forms the basis of this enquiry. I received generous grants from the Deutscher Akademischer Austauschdientst and The Queen's College, Oxford, which permitted me to pursue research in Germany and France. Pat Lloyd, who typed the manuscript, showed almost superhuman patience and palaeographical skills in its decipherment. Iris Hunter copy-edited the text with meticulous care. I am immensely grateful to them, as I am to my family, who have borne with characteristic good humour and kindness my absences and long periods of mental distraction. These agencies, between them, have made this book possible: its defects are solely attributable to its author.

Notes on the presentation of the text

For the Corpus Juris Civilis, I have chosen to quote the text of the Krüger/Mommsen edition; where significant divergences occur, these are indicated. Modern editions of Cicero and other classical authors have also been used, as there are no significant divergences. In Latin quotation, accents have been removed, and i and j, u and v standardized wherever appropriate; the style of author's name (vernacular or Latin) follows the practice of the catalogues of major libraries. References to the Corpus Juris Civilis follow the usual convention (Digest 1.1.2 = D 1.1.2, Codex 1.1. = C 1.1; Institutes 1.1 = I 1.1. etc.).

Introduction

In conscribendo libros scopus est, rei veritas. In explicandis libros aliorum, auctoris sententia. Quatuor igitur sunt munia boni expositoris; auctoris mentem declarare, demonstrare, quod ita sit quod dicitur, amplificare illius doctrinam, et tueri ipsum a calumniatoribus.

> (Cardano [1501–76], *De libris propriis*, in *Opera omnia*, ed. Spon, Lyon, 1663, i.139)

The aim in writing books is the truth of the matter in question; in expounding the books of other writers, it is the writers' meaning. Four duties therefore fall to the good interpreter: to declare authorial meaning; to show that things are indeed as they are said to be by the author; to illustrate his doctrine; and to protect him from unfair criticism.

Any survey of sixteenth-century scholarly and pedagogical writing must take into account the plethora of works of interpretation: translations, commentaries, paraphrases, exegeses, epitomes and critical editions abound in all academic disciplines, not least in the law. But although most of this material involves the construal of texts and much of it is interdisciplinary or pluridisciplinary in approach, no general theory of language emerges from it; indeed, some modern commentators have gone so far as to claim that the Renaissance did not have a concept of language as such, only of words.[1] Questions of grammar, translation and meaning are of course much discussed; but there is nothing resembling a comprehensive study of linguistics. This is also true of semantics; if one takes the twenty-two meanings of

---

[1] Richard Waswo, *Language and meaning in the Renaissance*, Princeton, 1987, p. 87. See also Karl Otto Apel, *Die Idee der Sprache in der Tradition des Humanismus von Dante bis Vico*, 2nd ed., Bonn, 1975.

'meaning' identified by Ogden and Richards,[2] a number of these are debated, but in widely different contexts.

Some of these questions arise in legal studies, which require quite sophisticated semantic distinctions to be made: the concepts of *mens rea*, of verbal assault, of contract, of promise, of the meaning of wills and of statutes, to name but a few, are indispensable to the working of the legal system and to the existence of law as an academic discipline. Indeed, such concepts are closely allied to the specificity of legal studies itself: 'to think like a lawyer' and 'to be trained as a lawyer' are phrases which presuppose a juristic attitude to language in relation to reference and logic as much as anything else. But even for Renaissance writers on jurisprudence, there is not a single, coherent account of the system of language in respect of meaning to which they can all refer, and this lack deprives them of an important resource when they turn to the texts of the law to interpret them.

In general terms, interpretation includes any act of mediation, exposition or elucidation of meaning; in law, this may be done by the legislator (the Emperor, in terms of the Corpus Juris Civilis), the judge, or the jurist who explicates the law for the student or a client. It can be approached in many ways: it may, for example, be categorized by its degree of authority, absolute in some cases, limited in others; it may be described in terms of a procedure or method which requires certain steps to be taken in a given order; it may be distinguished from other, similar, procedures – signification, conjecture, presumption, inference. It may be exercised differently in different sectors of the law. It may be separated into modes, such as 'extensive', 'restrictive', 'declarative'. It may aspire to recover the historical sense of a text or merely to determine what it might mean in contemporary circumstances. Certain problematic topics may be linked to it: the avoidance of cavillation (deliberate misconstruction), the resolution of ambiguity, the determination of a speaker's or writer's intention, the nature of objective meaning. Interpretation may be exercised differently by judges and by legal pedagogues or exegetes; it may take various forms – the resolution of obscurity or ambiguity, of the conflict of laws, of intention and literal meaning, the determination of parallel cases. It is subject in different ways to the constraints of

---

[2] See C.K. Ogden and I.A. Richards, *The meaning of meaning* (1923), London, 1946, pp. 186–7; the most relevant meanings are quoted by Geoffrey Leech, *Semantics*, 2nd ed., Harmondsworth, 1981, p. 1.

history, of language and of logic. It operates differently in statutory law systems and systems based on precedent. It is an awesomely wide-ranging phenomenon.

In setting out to give an account of interpretation and meaning in Renaissance law, my purpose has been twofold: to draw attention to a large, mainly neglected corpus of texts which have interesting things to say about the theory of interpretation and issues in semantics and the philosophy of language, and to show how the discussion of these topics in this corpus can throw light both on the paradigms of Renaissance thought about linguistic issues and on modern debates about the intellectual history of this period. This study aims therefore to be both expository and critical; as such, I cannot claim even to attempt to fulfil the second duty which Cardano ascribes to interpreters. But I hope to be faithful (in so far as this is possible) to his other prescriptions; indeed, the first and third of these account for two features of the approach adopted by this book. First, the copious quotation of obscure texts is, I hope, justified by the need to illustrate adequately the patterns of thought which I have set out to describe; second, I have included two chapters giving the broad historical background and intellectual contexts of my chosen corpus of texts in the belief that, as a number of different disciplines and different genres of writing are at issue, such contexts may not be known to all readers and may therefore be of use to some.

The question of language and meaning in the Renaissance has been at the centre of a recent fierce critical debate to which I must refer before embarking on my own examination of it. Richard Waswo's *Language and meaning in the Renaissance* (1987) is an attempt to show that Renaissance philosophers, grammarians and theologians adumbrate, if they do not actually enunciate, modern, post-Saussurean attitudes to meaning. The author is very careful to state that his own interest in the past is dictated by current linguistic concerns; his is an exercise in self-consciously ideological historical writing. The integrity of his scholarly enterprise is thus guaranteed not only by the usual academic ethics – adequate translation from one language to another, non-fabrication of evidence, regard for the distinction between plausibility and validity in inference, etc. – but also by the willingness on the part of the historian to recognize himself as an active ingredient in the reconstruction of the past. The reaction of traditional scholars to this approach has been strong; it is most clearly expressed in John Monfasani's refutation of Waswo's claims about

Valla in an article in the *Journal of the history of ideas*.[3] According to Waswo, Valla argues that linguistic categories structure our knowledge of reality;[4] this claim is impugned by Monfasani, a dedicated philologist, who shows persuasively that Valla's text is susceptible of a straightforward scholastic construction. In the same issue of the journal, Waswo replies equally persuasively that if all that Valla had done was to restate scholastic linguistic premises, he would not have been attacked so vigorously by contemporaries and near-contemporaries as heterodox.[5] This line of defence raises in turn the broader issue of Foucault's epistemes and Kuhn's conceptual paradigms, and the identification of epistemological breaks; and it requires also that account be taken of the hard relativist argument that the thought of the past is in some radical sense irrecoverable, and cannot be restated in the terms of the present.[6]

To attempt to adjudicate in this debate would be incautious: but as my own preoccupations are very close to it, it would be inappropriate to ignore it completely. One reason for the contentious nature of enquiries into meaning is that their abstract nature has encouraged scholars to treat them unhistorically (in the way in which much of the history of philosophy is treated by analytical philosophers); this may be done either by admitting (as Waswo does) the modernity of one's preoccupations about the past, or by isolating philosophical questions and treating intellectual life as in some sense insulated from social and economic issues of its day. One may, however, be able to go some way towards containing this problem by approaching issues of interpretation and meaning through law rather than, for example, theology or grammar, since the law can be studied historically as the remedy for an existing social mischief: when the French jurist François Baudouin wrote in 1562 'leges bonae ex malis moribus natae sunt' (good laws are born of evil behaviour) he was not only quoting an Erasmian adage, but also alluding to the religious and civil conflict of his own

---

[3] 'Is Valla an ordinary language philosopher?', *Journal of the history of ideas* l (1989), 309–23.
[4] *Language and meaning*, pp. 96ff. This argument may also be found in Donald R. Kelley, *Foundations of modern historical scholarship: law and history in the Renaissance*, New York and London, 1970, pp. 29ff.
[5] Waswo, 'Motives of misreading', *Journal of the history of ideas*, l (1989), 324–32.
[6] For a statement of this argument relevant to this book, see Oswald Ducrot, 'Quelques implications linguistiques de la théorie médiévale de la supposition', in *History of linguistic thought and contemporary linguistics*, ed. Herman Parret, New York and Berlin, 1976, pp. 189–227 (esp. p. 227).

day, and its connection with the social evil of defamation.[7] One is thus able to situate historically his preoccupation with such perennial issues as the following: how may the intention behind an utterance be established? By what criteria may the law determine some words and phrases to be actionable as slander and others not? How are the implications of a given utterance to be assessed? By what criteria may the prevaricative use of language (that is, the use of language to mislead as to intention or truth)[8] be overcome?

All these questions (as well as others) arise not only in the case of defamation, but also in that of contracts, promises, wills and intentions of legislators; and they are discussed both in theoretical and practical contexts; that is, both in the interpretation of written law and evidence, and in its application in the courts. The material available for the study of such topics is practically limitless; to examine theories of interpretation and meaning in Renaissance jurisprudence would thus seem to constitute a hopelessly ambitious task: 'arduum quidem et infiniti laboris opus', as Jean Bodin put it. 'Who', asked one writer on interpretation, 'could think of writing a history of hermeneutics, so defined?'[9] The great German legal historian Helmut Coing offers, it is true, some crumbs of comfort by declaring that in the Renaissance there is virtually no connection between the theory of legal interpretation and the practice of the courts as this is enshrined in *consilia*;[10] his assertion would seem to licence a study of either legal theory or positive law, but not both. In recognition of this, the major part of this book is concerned with theory on the Continent where Roman law (the Corpus Juris Civilis) is authoritative; but I have ventured also to take a sidelong glance at practice in England, because historical and political contexts can be more directly perceived in a system which operates neither solely nor principally with a body of written statutes or rules. The purpose of

---

[7] Baudouin, *Ad leges de famosis libellis et de calumniatoribus, commentarius*, Paris, 1562, p. 5; see also Erasmus, *Adagia*, Frankfurt, 1643, p. 557, citing Macrobius, *Saturnalia*, iii.17.10 ('vetus verbum leges inquit bonae ex malis moribus procreantur').

[8] On prevarication see John Lyons, *Semantics*, Cambridge, 1977, i.5–10, 74–85; Umberto Eco, *A theory of semiotics*, Bloomington, 1976, p. 7.

[9] R.E. Palmer, *Hermeneutics*, Evanston, 1969, p. 37.

[10] In *Studi Koschaker*, I (1954), p. 73; cited by Norbert Horn, *Aequitas in den Lehren des Baldus*, Cologne and Graz, 1968, p. 2; see also O. Gierke, *Johannes Althusius und die Entwicklung der naturrechtlichen Staatstheorien*, Breslau, 1880, p. 27, cited by Samuel E. Thorne (ed.), *A discourse upon the exposicion and understanding of statutes . . .*, San Marino, 1942, 'Introduction', p. 29.

this digression into England is to enquire whether the same conceptual problems are encountered as in the areas in which the Corpus Juris Civilis is authoritative; and, if so, whether these problems arise from a common legal context, or from a common intellectual heritage facing a similar crisis.

To raise the issue, however fleetingly, of the relationship of legal theory to practice prompts the questions: is the law nothing but practice? Are references to interpretative techniques and principles no more than verbal decoration helping to disguise the unpalatable fact that the law reaches context-bound decisions possibly under the influence of politics or ideology? This has been suggested recently by critics of modern legal systems;[11] it accords well with a certain hoary distaste for theorizing commonly attributed to lawyers. After all, it is the function of courts to reach decisions and to show the law to be workable; to do this judges may have recourse to compilations of interpretative rules or definition of terms (such as D 1.3, D 50.16, and D 50.17), but they are not committed to the belief that such compilations are either complete or even internally consistent; indeed, they may well be of more use in providing *ex post facto* justifications for decisions if they are not. That such use of interpretative theory was made in the Middle Ages or Renaissance seems to me clear and undeniable; writers of *consilia* and treatises on interpretation have recourse to a relatively small anthology of references (see below 1.4.5) which contain maxims to support contrary arguments: thus, the legislator's intention may be prized above the literal meaning of the text, or the literal meaning above intention (D 1.3.17, D 50.16.6.1; D 32.25, D 40.9.12); the facts of the case can be prized above the written record, or the written record above the facts (D 33.2.19); laws may be extended in application to *casus omissi*, or all extension disallowed. It is frequently claimed that the Middle Ages and early Renaissance particularly relished the citing of authority in support of argument; but it is still in some sense the case today, for reference is frequently made in decisions to convenient earlier judgements. Does this mean that semantics is no more than a context-bound and pliable pursuit for lawyers? And does this render invalid any conclusions about theories of meaning made on the basis of evidence drawn from legal texts? I venture to argue not; for the law, as

---

[11] See Peter Goodrich, *Legal discourse: studies in linguistics, rhetoric and legal analysis*, London, 1987; *Post-modern law: enlightenment, revolution and the death of man*, ed. Anthony Carty, Edinburgh, 1990.

well as being a practice, is a discipline: it is taught, and its teachers choose not to characterize it as an arbitrary or politically biased practice which has recourse to linguistics only to veil the naked application of interest. There is, moreover, a strong presumption, if not of the rationality, then at least of the reasonableness of the law, which implies that the law can be described according to quasi-objective canons and, above all else, be discussed and argued over, as is only appropriate to an adversarial system. Finally, explanations of language use which are offered and systems of interpretation which are sketched out are testimony to the conceptual parameters of those who proffer them: and one might venture to claim that they are testimony not only to the general problematics of a period but also of the specific problematics of the legal profession at that time.

There are, of course, many excellent histories of Renaissance law, philosophy and grammar available to scholars; on the whole, these have shown scant respect for the theory and practice of interpretation and for Renaissance thinking on language, which has been described as 'jejune and simplistic cliché'.[12] It has become fashionable to argue that Renaissance writers were aware of severe problems about meaning and the construal of meaning, and about the articulation of words and things; but that this awareness emerges most clearly in sceptical or fictional discourses. The articulation of *res* and *verba* is often discussed, though they are given different senses and connotations by different historians: G.A. Padley distinguishes between them, as he distinguishes between semantics and formal grammar; Waswo, as he distinguishes between ontology and epistemology; Foucault analyses this articulation in terms of different modes of similarity (analogy, *convenientia, aemulatio,* sympathy); Terence Cave sees it as the distinction between the humanist yearning for substantial and full meaning (*qua* significance) and empty or inadequate semiosis.[13] Historians of law, however, rarely stray into discussion of the relationship of words to things, although some give excellent and perceptive accounts of the rôle of logical argument and inference in jurisprudence.[14] I have looked to legal texts for a discussion of

---

[12] Waswo, *Language and meaning,* p. 80.
[13] G.A. Padley, *Grammatical theory in Western Europe 1500–1700: the Latin tradition,* Cambridge, 1976; Waswo, *Language and meaning*; Michel Foucault, *Les Mots et les choses,* Paris, 1966; Terence Cave, *The Cornucopian text,* Oxford, 1979.
[14] See especially V. Piano Mortari, *Diritto, logica, metodo nel secolo XVI,* Naples, 1978, and *Dogmatica e interpretazione: i giuristi medievali,* Naples, 1976; Ennio Cortese, *La norma giuridica,* Milan, 1962–4; Gerhard Otte, *Dialektik und Jurisprudenz; Untersuchungen zur Methode der Glossatoren,* Frankfurt am Main, 1971.

interpretation and meaning because it is manifestly indispensable to the practice of the law, and in the Renaissance it formed an essential part of legal training. The medieval trivium of grammar, dialectics and rhetoric is acknowledged as propaedeutic to jurisprudence; throughout the Middle Ages, but especially after the rediscovery of the 'logica nova' and, later, of Quintilian and Ciceronian texts on topics, legal pedagogues and commentators write copiously and sometimes systematically about issues of interpretation and semantics.[15] But as well as being affected by the discoveries of humanists, this writing belongs to an institutional and economic context which affects it in a variety of ways. It is some of these that I have tried to chart in the first chapter. The results of this investigation may well appear meagre, but it seemed to me important to attempt to situate what are by their nature highly abstract texts both institutionally and historically.

In setting out to link abstract theory with institutional and social forces, I have strayed into the battleground of modern intellectual history, on which a war is being waged between those who would seek to reduce the importance of the social vis-à-vis the linguistic or conceptual, and those who conversely seek to make ideas epiphenomena of socio-political forces. This debate is the culmination of a century of fertile developments in this domain; since the positivist methodology of historians such as Stinzing or Paulsen, the intellectual historian has had the choice of such methodologies as Weber's *Idealtypus*, Cassirer's version of the history of epistemology, Lovejoy's history of ideas, opposed by Collingwood, the Annales school's study of *outillage mental* and *conjoncture*, Gadamer's philosophical hermeneutics, opposed by Habermas's notion of critical rationality, Kuhn's paradigm, Foucault's episteme, Skinner's razor to eliminate inauthentic historical construction, Kracauer's notion of undifferentiated historical consciousness, Bourdieu's 'field of cultural production' and finally the 'linguistic turn' referred to above.[16] It is tempting

---

[15] Semantics is sometimes taken to refer only to the system of linguistic communication; I have used the term more loosely here to include the consideration of speaker's meaning, hearer's meaning, questions of intention and logical problems in the language system generally.

[16] For a recent discussion of these issues, see Anthony Pagden, 'Rethinking the linguistic turn: current anxieties in intellectual history', *Journal of the history of ideas*, xlix (1988), 519–29. See also Hans Erich Troje, 'Alciats Methode', in *Der Kommentar in der Renaissance*, ed. August Beck and Otto Herding, Bonn, 1974, pp. 47–61 (esp. p. 54); and Siegfried Wollgast, 'Zur Stellung des Gelehrten in Deutschland im 17. Jahrhundert', *Sitzungsberichte der Sächsischen Akademie der Wissenschaften zu Leipzig*, cxxv.2 (1984), 3–79, for an inflexible application of Marxist analysis to intellectual history.

to begin with a voluminous *pars prima theorica* which would evaluate all these approaches comparatively; such an exercise would seem, however, over-ambitious at best, and at worst presumptuous.

Yet it is not inappropriate to sketch out the broad choices which are open to the intellectual historian in this respect. If he accepts the hard relativist line that we are totally cut off from the past, then he is committed to the view expressed by Waswo that the past is the creation of our questions about it; we may think that we have some objective access to it, but this is a delusion; we are permanently imprisoned in our own conceptual paradigm and are animated by our own ideological concerns. A less severe view (that which might be adopted by the Annales school, or perhaps by Kuhn) would concede that we cannot aspire to a perfect knowledge of the past, but that it is possible to recreate a verifiable if approximate model of past thought which is not merely a reproduction of our own *mentalité*; we are thus able to identify some of the ideological investments of a given period which would have been invisible to those living at the time, and can even hope to expose confusions and contradictions in the thought of past generations. An even more optimistic position is taken by those who would argue that we are no more cut off from the past than we are from each other, because although we all experience different psychic events when we think, we are none the less capable of thinking the same thoughts. This optimistic view implies, if it does not entail, that the more that is known about the past (i.e. the more thoughts of the past that are recovered), the closer we can come to a significant reliving of past *mentalités*. It implies also that access to past thoughts or *mentalités* might best be gained by those who study the same discipline – in our case, the law – as the historical objects of study. It entails furthermore that past thinkers, if confronted with the contradictions in their conceptual schemes or the ideological investments in their view of the world, would be able to recognize these and appraise them as can a modern scholar. To put this in legal terms: a legislator would be able to apply his law to circumstances he did not envisage at the time of legislation if asked to do so. This last view – the view of the intellectual optimist who believes in the accessibility of the past – finally presupposes that as an adequate account of the thoughts of others can be given, the safest means of acquiring those thoughts is to stick to what they explicitly say.

None of these positions is unproblematic. A hard relativist stand may be theoretically irrefutable, but it leaves the historian with the practical problem that no obvious constraints remain to limit or validate any account of the past: one reading of the evidence (whatever that might be) is as good as another. The mediate position appears attractive, but it contains an inbuilt tendency to Whiggish history: by identifying ideological investments and tolerated contradictions in past thought, the historian implicitly assents to his own superiority. But the problems of the third (broadly positivist) position are even greater. It requires the historian to adopt a model of human understanding in which human beings are characterized as potentially fully aware of the limits of the conceptual scheme by which they live; that is to say, they can in some sense or other pass beyond the language system or system of metaphors through which all their knowledge comes to them. The positivist position seems further to commit the historian to the view that for all practical purposes human beings are able to express themselves and understand each other in a logically adequate way, and that failure to foresee all the consequences of an act or a thought is a sign of inevitable human frailty, but not of an intrinsic weakness in the processes of logic or of language. As the present study is designed specifically to call into question the adequacy of the system of communication and language, and to identify (in so far as this is possible) those points where the Renaissance conceptual scheme breaks down, neither the first nor the third alternatives are congenial to it. It must thus, as Montaigne says, 'vivoter dans la moyenne region'; and hope to do this without too much arrogance.

As I have already indicated, interpretation is understood as a broad term comprising various modes of mediation or transmission: it might be the reaffirmation, the recovery or even the correction of a linguistic message (this last being justified by appeal to an authority greater than the text or utterance in question, such as the principle of coherence or the intention of the writer or speaker). Such a determination of interpretation has a very modern ring to it, and is close to the classic questions of hermeneutics: does a reader of a text institute its sense or does he or she recover it? Is it possible to understand an author better than he or she understood himself or herself? In the place of these questions, Renaissance jurists might have asked: who has the authority to interpret the law? What is the nature of that authority? Does the judge who applies the law or the jurist who explicates it extend the law, or change it in any way? Is it possible for laws to change in sense and force without new legislation? In determining the scope of a law, does its intrinsic coherence and the purpose for which it was enacted override the intention of the legislator? I have tried in this study to approach interpretation both in the terms of the problems addressed by the jurisprudential texts themselves, and with regard to the modern understanding of interpretation; in investigating the contemporary distinctions *necessarius/probabilis* (3.1.3), *significatio/interpretatio/proprietas verborum* (3.3.2), *probatio artificialis/inartificialis* (3.2.5), *definitio/descriptio* (3.3.2), *proprietas/improprietas verborum* (3.4.2), *claritas/ambiguitas* (3.2.1; 3.4.3), *mens/ratio* (3.6.1), and in examining such concepts as *usus* (3.4.4), *cavillatio* (3.5.1), *consuetudo* (3.7.1), *aequitas* (3.8.1) and *mens rea* (4.3), I have tried to show both how the distinctions were upheld in the texts, and where in modern terms they might be said to be inadequate or problematic.

In doing this, I have encountered a major difficulty concerning quotation. As will become clear below, it is the practice of legal commentary and pedagogical texts to restate, paraphrase, or allude not only to fragments of the text of the Corpus Juris Civilis itself, but also the views and claims of earlier commentators. The relationship between the quoted text and the text in which the quotation occurs is complex; many borrowings and appropriations are unacknowledged or pass through intermediary texts, others suffer what the Italians elegantly call *resemantizazzione*. Creating a stemma of texts, or attributing sources to quotations in such circumstances is fraught with risks; where I have suggested historical sequences or sources, or attempted to assess the changes made from medieval approaches, it is with great caution and in the hope that the more instructed reader will forgive my misattributions. I have long since learned not to scoff at historians who have failed to identify direct quotation from the Digest, and have attributed it to a jurist as an original statement. The learning, sometimes lightly worn, of Renaissance jurists imposes modesty on their modern readers; especially if they have not had training in the law themselves. But any reader of sixteenth-century scholarly works becomes quickly aware of the interdependence of academic disciplines at that time as well as their autonomy, and may feel that to transgress academic frontiers is encouraged in some sense by Renaissance scholars themselves. This investigation into aspects of Renaissance thought has depended heavily on such encouragement from its sources.

CHAPTER I

Contexts

Quis agit? apud quem agit? pro quo? adversus quem? quibus
praesentibus? quibus obpugnantibus? quibus faventibus?

(Fortunatianus, *De arte rhetorica*, iii.20)

Who is the agent? where? on behalf of whom? against whom? in
whose company? opposed by whom? helped by whom?

1.1.1

To investigate so broad a phenomenon as the interpretation of law
over a period of some 150 years throughout Continental Western
Europe (with some forays into England) is a daunting task; but I
believe that there are good reasons for treating this period as a
meaningful unit, characterized by its own discursive paradigm. The
practice of interpretation is closely linked to the social function of law
faculties and to the discipline which they embody; it shares features
with the other senior university faculties, theology and medicine,
notably in their common rôle of mediation between a body of
knowledge accessible only to experts, and the rest of humanity on
whose behalf it is deployed, and in the need to justify this rôle and
dissociate it from potential accusations or parasitism or self-interest,
such as those rehearsed in Heinrich Cornelius Agrippa's *De incertitudine et vanitate omnium scientiarum et artium*[1] (1530). A famous passage of
Baldassare Castiglione's *Courtier* of 1528 records the bon mot of a
Florentine divine who declared drily that men have only their souls,
their bodies and their material possessions in this world; and that they
are deprived of the free enjoyment of even these by theologians,

---

[1] See esp. chs. 91–5 ('De iure et legibus', 'De iure canonico', 'De arte advocatoria', 'De arte
notariatus et procuratoria' and 'De iurisprudentia').

doctors and lawyers respectively.[2] But as well as being united under this general indictment, professions also attacked each other, and in a world in which precedence was of great importance, squabbled over seniority. Humanism and the advent of printing brought a new dimension to these debates, as well as causing writing to proliferate and to spread; the market for scholarly books became a complex phenomenon in which intellectual, political, confessional and economic interests interacted, although the presence of all these factors is not always immediately apparent. This chapter is intended to provide a context for the investigation of legal interpretation in the light of such issues. A brief history of the evolution of legal studies from the Middle Ages to the Renaissance (1.1.2–6) will be followed by an examination of the status of law faculties in universities (1.2.1–5); the genera of law books relevant to the practice of interpretation, their readership, diffusion and manner of presentation will next be investigated (1.2.1–1.4.5), after which an account will be given of the profession's attempts to circumvent the prohibition placed on interpretation by the Emperor Justinian, and to justify its hermeneutic and pedagogical practices (1.5.1–1.6.3). The chapter will conclude with an assessment of how far the Renaissance marks a paradigm shift from the medieval position with respect to these issues.

THE STUDY OF ROMAN LAW IN THE MIDDLE AGES AND RENAISSANCE

1.1.2

The history of Roman civil law (for our purposes, the Corpus Juris Civilis established by the sixth-century Emperor Justinian) in the Renaissance is not so much a story of substitution as of accumulation. From the late eleventh century, when the glossators (Irnerius (*c.* 1055–1130), Azo (*c.* 1150–1230) and especially Accursius (*c.* 1185–1263), the author of the *Glossa ordinaria*) began their work of explanation and instruction, to the mid-seventeenth century, a steady development of materials, teaching methods, interpretative strategies and practical applications can be traced. The penetration of this

---

[2] See *Courtier*, ii.66. It is of interest that the Inquisition felt it necessary to exclude theologians from this list when the book received a licence for publication from them, having been 'renewed and corrected' by Antonio Ciccarelli da Forgligni, dottore in Teologia, in Venice in 1584 (fols. 99–100).

material into the legal practice and teaching of various parts of Europe is not uniform, but it can be said by the early years of the sixteenth century to occupy an important, indeed often preponderant, place in the legal affairs of Italy, Germany, Iberia and parts of France. The postglossators, notably Bartolus de Saxoferrato (1314–57) and Baldus de Ubaldis (1327–1400), who inherited the *Glossa ordinaria* on the texts of the Digest (or Pandects), Institutes, Code and Novels, enriched this in turn with commentaries informed by revised scholastic interpretative methods based on the 'new logic' (see below 2.2); a group of French scholars known as the 'Ultramontani' or 'Commentatores', who included Jacobus de Ravanis or Raveniaco (Jacques de Révigny) (d. 1296) and Petrus de Bellapertica (Pierre de Belleperche) (d. 1308) had already begun this work, and had developed also the practice of using the Corpus to serve the legal needs of their world. From the earliest times, the work of academic scholars and teachers was allied to practical uses – the struggle between Pope and Emperor, problems of local legislation, the reconciliation and drafting of laws, the assimilation of Roman law with local statute and custom (the product of which came to be known as 'ius commune'); much of this activity is enshrined in the *consilia* written by jurists which offered their clients legal opinions on given issues, and which proliferated in the course of the fourteenth century. Alongside the 'ius commune', canon law regulated those aspects of life which fell under the authority of the Church; unlike its civil counterpart, it was near-universal in Catholic Europe, although its constitutions varied a little from place to place. By the mid-fifteenth century, the text of the Corpus Juris Civilis was quite literally encased in a thick accretion of explanatory legal material which was far more extensive than the text itself. The purpose of this explanatory material was not purely pedagogical; it was of use also to the Continental practitioners who turned to the accumulated wisdom of three centuries for a guide to settle points of law. England, and to some degree northern parts of France, had meanwhile developed their own idiosyncratic forms and institutions of law which were not to influence Continental practice, although, as we shall see, they may offer illuminating sidelights on it.[3]

---

[3] There is a vast literature on the history of law in this period: full bibliographies are given by Vincenzo Piano Mortari, *Dogmatica e interpretazione*, Naples, 1976; Mortari *Diritto, logica, metodo nel secolo XVI*, Naples, 1978, pp. 121–4; Mortari, *Gli inizi del diritto moderno in Europa*, Naples, 1986; Donald R. Kelley, *History, law and the human sciences*, London, 1984; Helmut

1.1.3

Humanism, as is well known, unsettled this relatively steady evolution. Whether it marked a discontinuity or not has been a matter of debate since the sixteenth century; but its disruptive influence and aggressive stance vis-à-vis existing jurisprudence cannot be denied, and this manifested itself in a number of ways. It caused a revision in the teaching methods employed in university law faculties; it highlighted linguistic issues by making accessible the Greek passages of the Digest which had been known previously only in inadequate translations, or not known at all; it led to a switch in introductory courses from study of D 50.17 (*De regulis iuris antiqui*) to D 50.16 (*De verborum significatione*) as a result of Lorenzo Valla's pedagogical initiatives; it focussed attention on the Pandecta florentina – the earliest known manuscript of the Digest – which was eventually (in 1553) to enjoy an authoritative edition. It influenced also the mode of commentary; Andrea Alciato's *De verborum significatione* of 1530 heralded an age of clearly presented, uncluttered secondary literature. Most of all, however, it gave rise to historical study of the legal texts of Justinian and of the fragments of earlier jurists of which they are composed; a study eventually characterized by a strongly censorious attitude to the editorial activity of Tribonian, Justinian's senior jurist and editor.[4] This development, which, like the edition of the Pandecta florentina was slow in coming, is often associated with the names of Ulrich Zäsy [Zazius] (1461–1536), Guillaume Budé (1467–1540) and Alciato (1492–1550), and has come to be known as the *mos gallicus*, as opposed to the *mos italicus* (the approach of the postglossators). The distinction dates from the 1550s, and was

Coing (ed.), *Handbuch der Quellen und Literatur der neueren europäischen Privatrechtsgeschichte*, Munich, 1977. See also John Gilissen, *Introduction historique du droit*, Brussels, 1979, esp. pp. 314–33, and O.F. Robinson, T.D. Fergus and W.M. Gordon, *An introduction to European legal history*, Abingdon, 1985, esp. pp. 71–121, 179–207, 208–334. See also the various writings of Guido Kisch, notably his *Studien zur humanistischen Jurisprudenz*, Berlin, 1972, and Hans Erich Troje, esp. his *Graeca leguntur; die Aneignung des byzantinischen Rechts und die Entstehung eines humanistischen Corpus iuris civilis in der Jurisprudenz des 16. Jahrhunderts*, Vienna, 1971.

[4] See Alberigo Gentili, *De iuris interpretibus*, London, 1582; Troje, 'Die Literatur des gemeinen Rechts unter dem Einfluss des Humanismus', in Coing, *Handbuch*, pp. 615–795; Kelley, 'Civil Science in the Renaissance; jurisprudence in the French manner', in *History, law and the human sciences*, vii. For expressions of hostility to medieval jurisprudence, see Guillaume Budé, *Annotationes in Pandectas*, cited by Kisch, *Gestalten und Probleme aus Humanismus und Jurisprudenz*, Berlin, 1969, pp. 45ff.; Marc-Antoine Muret, *Commentarius in quattuor titulos e primo Digestorum*, Ferrara, 1581, fols. 2–6; François Hotman, *Anti-Tribonian*, Paris, 1567; Kelley, *Foundations*, pp. 54ff. See also the useful summary in Adalbert Erler and Ekkehard Kaufmann, *Handwörterbuch zur deutschen Rechtsgeschichte*, Berlin, 1984, iii.691–8.

invoked at first to distinguish two methods of teaching of which one, the French, was specifically associated with the University of Bourges, where Alciato taught for a short while.[5] But the names of Zazius of Basle and Alciato himself, who returned to teach in Italy, make it clear that the *mos gallicus* was international in character.

1.1.4

The sixteenth-century historical school of Roman law is to a greater degree a French phenomenon, but postdates the first use of the term *mos gallicus*. It produced some remarkable legal historians and scholars – Charles Du Moulin [Molinaeus] (1500–66), François de Connan (or Conan, or Connat) (1508?–51), François le Douaren [Duarenus] (1509–59), François Baudouin (1520–73), Hugues Doneau [Donellus] (1527–91), Jacques Cujas (1522–90); but it occurred in a part of France which had for long not recognized the practical authority of the Corpus Juris Civilis. Whereas in sixteenth-century Germany and Italy the teaching of law was directly connected to its practice, in France a separation took place which was to make of the study of law an intellectual pursuit for its own sake; or rather, an exercise in historical understanding designed to bolster the claims of local customary law against supposed imperial legal uniformity, seen as a threat to the indigenous institutions of the French nation.[6]

1.1.5

In Germany meanwhile the practice of using the Corpus Juris Civilis as part of positive law, together with customary law and imperial edicts – a practice which was to be known eventually as the *usus modernus Pandectarum* – continued throughout the sixteenth and seventeenth centuries, as it did in Italy. In these countries the *mos italicus* continued to flourish. Neither in Germany nor in Italy was the study of pre-Justinian law pursued with the same vigour as in France.

---

[5] According to Troje, 'Zur humanistischen Jurisprudenz', in *Festschrift für H. Hempel*, Göttingen, 1972, ii.110–39 (where the precursors of the *mos gallicus* jurists, notably Tolomeo Socino (1437–1507) are also named; see also Troje, in Coing, *Handbuch*, pp. 718–23). See also Steven Rowan, 'Jurists and the printing press in Germany: the first century', in *Print and Culture in the Renaissance*, ed. Gerald R. Tyson and Sylvia S. Wagonheim, London, Toronto and Newark, 1986, pp. 74–89, esp. p. 85, n. 6. Gilissen (*Introduction historique*, pp. 313–33) offers a different list: viz. Doneau, Nicolas Everaerts (1462–1532), Viglius Zuichem (1507–71), Gabriel Mudaeus (1500–60), Jacques Reyvaert (1535–68) and Matthäus Wesenbeck (1531–86).   [6] See Kelley, *Foundations*.

There, the attempt at palingenesis – the reconstruction of the 'pure', 'simple' originary Roman legal system supposedly encapsulated in the 'Twelve Tables' (D 1.2.2) – gave rise in turn both to attempts to recover the simple ancient law of the Gauls and to ambitious projects to ground a universal science of jurisprudence; elsewhere these developments were not greeted with great enthusiasm. The works of Jean Bodin (1530–90), Doneau, François Hotman (1524–90), Connan and others in this domain were, it is true, cited, but in a way which assimilated them into the *mos italicus*; they were absorbed precisely by being used as additions to the quotable list of authorities of which the most important were the texts of the Corpus Juris Civilis itself, but which encompassed also the gloss, the commentary of the postglossators, and the arguments of modern scholars (the 'doctores nostrae aetatis'). The act of citing authorities (that is, establishing the 'opinio communis doctorum') in constructing legal argument was an important function of *mos italicus* lawyers, who had been given a boost in status by the imperial *Constitutio criminalis carolina* of 1532. In this vernacular code of criminal law, which although not binding throughout the Empire, was very influential, 'Rechtsverstendige' ('those who know the law', i.e., the academic legal profession) were specifically named as persons from whom the courts might seek guidance in matters of interpretation.[7]

Moreover, as had happened in Italy in an earlier century, towns employed academic lawyers such as Ulrich Zazius to draft statutes and whole constitutions; in some cities, the whole university law faculty was involved in producing opinions after the documents and facts of the case had been submitted to them by a process known as 'Aktenversendung'. In the words of Robinson, Fergus and Gordon,

the law faculties were no longer simply producing graduates for legal and administrative posts and studying Roman law in academic isolation. They were using the Roman law they were working on, that is, both the historical pursuit of classical Roman law in the Humanist tradition and the accumulated interpretative knowledge of the *Gloss*, to solve actual disputes, in a sense repeating the work of the Commentators.[8]

A difference, however, should be noted between the *usus modernus Pandectarum* and the *mos italicus*; the latter tended to give priority to logical analysis and to reach conclusions by appeal to *ratio* (see below

[7] See Rowan, 'Jurists', p. 81, and the *Constitutio criminalis carolina*, §28, §219, and *passim*.
[8] *Introduction*, pp. 327–8.

3.6.1), whereas the former, being so closely associated with actual practice, gave greater prominence to authority and decisive argument, and was more overtly political in its application. This political dimension was reinforced by the *Constitutio criminalis carolina* and various associated *Reichsabschiede* which made crime a matter as much for the state as for the victim, even where the crimes involved were *prima facie* concerned only with private damages, such as theft and libel (see below 4.3).

1.1.6

It is difficult to place neat chronological limits on the developments set out above. Some legal historians have suggested that the revival of studies in Germanic local law, heralded by the publication of Hermann Conring's *De origine iuris germanici* (1643), marks an important shift in legal studies and procedures;[9] the fragmentation of the Empire and the independent positions vis-à-vis the law adopted by the various principalities (which even went so far as to debar their local universities from seeking advice from law faculties outside their borders) is another important factor; confessional divisions also play their part. As can be simply demonstrated from the trade in law books, Italian jurists of the sixteenth and early seventeenth centuries were printed in northern Europe, and were read and quoted quite widely; the converse is very rarely the case. This may be due in part to the work of the Inquisition, who placed many protestant legal writers on the Index and even caused their names to be blacked out when cited in books by Italian authors;[10] it may also not be far-fetched to detect in the behaviour of Italian publishers and their authors a sense of cultural superiority, even (pen)insularity. After 1600, the situation in France tends to exaggerate local interests: law developed in relation to the evolving political situation, which did not encourage the pursuit of Roman law studies except where these either served local interests or were engaged in for mainly academic ends. Such factors as these (and no doubt many others might be adduced) have predisposed most historians to identify the period from 1460 to 1630

---

[9] *Ibid.*, p. 329.
[10] See Rowan, 'Jurists'; Hans Jürgen Becker, *Deutsche Juristen auf den römischen Indices*, Berlin, 1970; *Librorum post Indicem Clementis VIII prohibitorum decreta omnia hactenus edita*, Rome, 1642, pp. 70–89. Examples of inking out are found in the holdings of public libraries (e.g. the name of Jean Crespin is made illegible in the Bibliothèque Nationale, Paris, copy of Alessandro Turamini's *De exaequatione legatorum et fideicommissorum disputatio paradoxica*, Naples, 1593, p. 3).

as the heyday in a broad European context of investigations into legal interpretation based on the texts of the Corpus Juris Civilis.[11]

1.2.1

The coherence of this period as a unit of study is confirmed by the development both of universities and of means of communication and distribution of texts. Roderich Stinzing's monumental study of German law faculties in the early modern period has identified the principal jurists and shown how as colleagues, tutors and pupils they are connected to each other;[12] although his work has been accused of ignoring the historical school of law and undervaluing the systematizers, it may be defended from this charge by the claim that the *mos gallicus* did not impinge very far on German practice and indeed met with some hostility.[13] As Franz Eulenberg's tables of attendance at German universities show, student numbers in all faculties rise steadily from the foundation of the new Reformation and Counter-Reformation universities, and drop off sharply after the inception of the Thirty Years War; this curve corresponds very closely to the statistics prepared by Gustav Schwetschke of books on offer at the Frankfurt Book Fair in the same period. Between 1570 and 1630, it is noteworthy that the section of law books advertised in the biennial catalogues varies between 10 per cent and 24 per cent of the total, but that the absolute number of books advertised in the decades 1600–10 and 1610–20 is double that of the decades 1570–80 and 1580–90.[14] Furthermore, this number includes a steady percentage of massive multi-volume folio publications. It seems clear that the book market in all its dimensions – author, printer, publisher, distributor and seller – grew to meet an increasing demand. Similar data are not so conveniently available for France, Spain and Italy, although Jacques le Goff's general study of universities in this period provides evidence

---

[11] Kelley, however, in a recent article ('Jurisconsultus perfectus: the lawyer as Renaissance man', *Journal of the Warburg and Courtauld Institutes*, li (1989), 84–102), makes the case for seeing the early nineteenth century as a more significant break; but the consensus of the historians listed in note 3 above favours the view recorded here.

[12] *Geschichte der deutschen Rechtswissenschaft*, Munich and Leipzig, 1880.

[13] Troje, 'Peccatum Triboniani: zur Dialektik der "Interpretatio duplex" bei François Baudouin', *Studia et documenta historiae et iuris*, xxxvi (1970), 341–58; Rowan, 'Jurists', p. 79.

[14] Eulenberg, *Die Frequenz der deutschen Universitäten von ihrer Gründung bis zur Gegenwart*, Leipzig, 1904; Schwetschke, *Codex nundinarius Germaniae literatae bisecularis*, Halle, 1850–77.

in support of the thesis of a marked expansion in the second half of the sixteenth century.[15] During this period, too, local traditions of law teaching were established by successful lecturers and served by local presses; sometimes these were illicitly published elsewhere from students' notes.[16] In this way, as well as through the legitimate trade in books, traditions intermingled to form a unified cultural pheno-menon, a 'universe of discourse' in sociological terms, or even, in those of Bourdieu, 'a field of cultural production', whose unity is confirmed by the citation indexes to be found in many legal books of this date.[17] As has been already intimated, such citation is rarely infused with a strict historical sense; Hotman is taken to be a contemporary of Bartolus, Cujas of Accursius.[18] The *mos italicus* was thus able to unite in the same intellectual practice divergent, even contrary, ap-proaches, overriding the sense of historical difference in a way which has been already charted by Siegbert Kracauer in another context, and engaging in the reappropriation of materials from the past for use by the present.[19]

1.2.2

Law faculties in universities found their place alongside faculties of theology and medicine as one of the three senior disciplines. The pre-eminence of theology is rarely disputed; the precedence of medicine and law often is. In most German and Italian contexts, the law faculty ranks second to theology, but it is clear that this is not an uncontested position. Many doctors and lawyers earned much more, of course,

---

[15] Le Goff, in *Les Universités européennes du XVIᵉ au XVIIᵉ siècle*, Geneva, 1961, pp. 71–100; also Richard Kagan, 'Universities in Italy 1500–1700', in *Histoire sociale des populations étudiantes*, ed. Dominique Julia, Jacques Revel and Roger Chartier, Paris, 1986–9, i.153–86; see also *ibid.*, ii.25–486 (Julia and Revel, 'Les Etudiants et leurs études dans la France moderne') and iii.487–526 (Lawrence W.B. Brockliss, 'Patterns of attendance at the University of Paris, 1400–1800'). See also Kagan, *Students and society in early modern Spain*, Baltimore, 1974.

[16] See Rowan, 'Jurists', pp. 80 ff.; Kisch, *Studien*, pp. 65–104.

[17] Peter Winch, *The idea of a social science*, London, 1958, esp. p. 115 (where the term 'realm of discourse' is used; 'universe of discourse' belongs properly to logic: see Augustus de Morgan, *On the syllogism and other logical writings*, ed. Peter Heath, London, 1966, xxv); Pierre Bourdieu, 'The field of cultural production or: the economic world reversal', *Poetics*, xii (1983), 311–56; also 'Champ du pouvoir, champ intellectuel et habitus de classe', *Scolies*, i (1971), 7–26. For examples of citation indexes, see the works of a Dassel, Förster, Besold, Matthaeacius and Coras.

[18] See Christoph Hegendorf, *Epitome tyrocinii iuris civilis*, Basle, 1540, p. 34; anon., *Clarissimorum et praestantissimorum iurisconsultorum tam veterum quam recentium varii utilissimi et diu multumque desiderati tractatus*, Cologne, 1585, p. 177 (Pierre Grégoire).

[19] See *Zeugnisse: Theodor W. Adorno zum 60. Geburtstag*, Frankfurt, 1963, pp. 50–64, and *History: the first things before the last*, New York, 1969, pp. 139–63.

outside the university than from their positions within it; but as
academic salaries were fixed to some degree by the prestige of the
subject and its seniority in a given institution, the question was not
one of theoretical precedence alone, although precedence (said by the
glossator Odofredus to be indicated by the academic title 'antecessor'
rather than 'professor' for lawyers in some Italian universities) was
clearly a matter of importance in itself.[20] In the case of law (as, to a
certain degree, of medicine),[21] the central issue was the status of legal
studies: did they constitute a science or an art? This apparently
innocuous question is, however, directly connected by Renaissance
writers with institutional issues: Peter Gilkens (d. 1616) points out
that the motive behind the attack on law by the philosophers Angelo
Tio [Thius] and Giacomo Zabarella of Pavia arose directly from local
rivalries. Their attempt to vilify jurisprudence ('ad deprimendam
auctoritatem tam insignis doctrinae') was prompted by the relatively
low status given to mathematics and philosophy, both considered as
propaedeutic studies for the higher faculties.[22] Criticism of law is
found also in the writings of anti-intellectual satirists such as Heinrich
Cornelius Agrippa, sceptics such as Montaigne, doctors (one remem-
bers Rabelais's trenchant satire of jurists)[23] and others; David
Schmugk, the author of an *Apologeticus contra iuris studiosorum obtec-
tatores* published in 1630 records one not uneducated merchant ('non
ineruditus mercator') as saying that he would prefer to see his son on
the gallows rather than as a lawyer.[24] Not all attacks, however, are

[20] Kelley, 'Vera philosophia: the philosophical significance of Renaissance jurisprudence'
(1976), in *History, law and the human sciences*, iv, 269; Domenico Maffei, *Gli inizi dell'umanesimo
giuridico*, Milan, 1964, pp. 66–80; Troje, 'Die Literatur des gemeinen Rechts unter dem
Einfluss des Humanismus', in Coing, *Handbuch*, pp. 723f. On the *prudentes* and the *responsa
prudentium*, see D 1.2.2 and C 1.21.1.

[21] See Nancy G. Siraisi, 'Medicine, physiology and anatomy in early sixteenth-century
critiques of the arts and sciences' in *New perspectives on Renaissance thought*, ed. John Henry and
Sarah Hutton, London, 1990, pp. 214–29.

[22] See Tio, *Lectiones de praecognitionibus logices*, Paris, 1547; Zabarella, *Liber de naturalis scientiae
constitutione*, Venice, 1586, xxxiii, pp. 120–1; Angelus Matthaeacius, *De via et ratione artificiosa
iuris universi libri duo*, Venice, 1591, i.10, fols. 22ʳ–24ʳ. Gilkens, *Iurisprudentiam nedum constare
ratione, sed esse scientiam proprie dictam contra calumnias Angeli Thii et Iacobi Zabarella Philosophiae
Doctorum . . .*, Frankfurt, 1605, p. 10. Gilkens quotes Tio and Zabarella from Matthaeacius,
his former tutor at Padua, not from the originals. On the interests involved in university
teaching of law, see Coing, *Handbuch*, pp. 16ff.

[23] See M.A. Screech, *Rabelais*, London, 1979, pp. 73ff.; Montaigne, *Œuvres complètes*, ed. Albert
Thibaudet and Maurice Rat, Paris, 1967, iii.13, pp. 1046ff.; Ian Maclean, 'The place of
interpretation: Montaigne and humanist jurists on words, intention and meaning', in *Neo-
Latin and the vernacular in Renaissance France*, ed. Grahame Castor and Terence Cave, Oxford,
1984, pp. 252–72. On Agrippa see above, note 1.

[24] David Schmugk, *Apologeticus contra iuris studiosorum obtrectatores*, Frankfurt, 1630, p. 39: 'Er
wolte lieber/dass sein Sohn am galgen hienge, als dass er Jurist wuerde'.

flippant or interested; and it is pertinent here to consider the arguments for and against the 'science' or 'art' of jurisprudence, as their substance is relevant to the interpretative and linguistic issues which this study addresses, and is seen by Renaissance commentators to be intimately linked to them.

1.2.3

Whether jurisprudence is an art or a science is a perennial question; it was asked by the glossator Azo before being discussed by Renaissance jurists,[25] and it is closely connected with a set of topoi concerning justice, equity, knowledge and wisdom drawn from Aristotle, Cicero and the Corpus Juris Civilis itself. As these topoi will recur throughout this study, it is worthwhile citing them in full. Aristotle is usually quoted in the Latin, but from one of a number of translations or paraphrases, including that of Aquinas; as these can vary quite widely in terminology, it has seemed most convenient to quote the English here:

Aristotle, *Physics* i.1 (184a10–14)   In all sciences that are concerned with principles or causes or elements, it is acquaintance with these that constitutes knowledge or understanding. For we concern ourselves to know about a thing when we are acquainted with its ultimate causes and first principles, and have got down to its elements (cf. *Metaphysics*, ii.2,993b24).

Posterior analytics ii.11 (94a20–5)   We only think we have knowledge of a thing when we know its cause. There are four kinds of cause: the essence, the necessitating conditions, the efficient cause which started the process, and the final cause (cf. *Physics*, ii.3 194b24, where the four causes (αἰτίαι) are named as material, formal, efficient and final).

Politics, ii.5 [ii.8] (1269a7–14)   Even written codes of law may with advantage not be left unaltered. For just as in the other arts as well, so with the structure of the state it is impossible that it should be framed aright in all its details; for it must of necessity be couched in general terms, but our actions deal with particular things.

Nicomachean Ethics, v.10 [v.14] (1137b 11–33)   Equity (ἐπιείκεια), though just, is not legal justice (δικαιοσύνη), but a rectification of legal justice. The reason for this is that law is always a general statement, yet there are cases which it is not possible to cover in a general statement . . . When therefore the law lays down a general rule, and thereafter a case arises which is an exception to the rule, it is then right, where the lawgiver's pronouncement because of its absoluteness is defective and erroneous, to rectify the defect by deciding as the lawgiver would himself decide if he were present on the

---

[25] See Piano Mortari, *Dogmatica*, pp. 158ff.; Kelley, 'Jurisconsultus perfectus', p. 89.

occasion, and would have enacted if he had been cognizant of the case in question . . . The equitable . . . is a rectification of the law where law is defective because of its generality . . . What is itself indefinite can only be measured by an indefinite standard, like the leaden rule used by Lesbian builders; just as the rule is not rigid but can be bent to shape of the stone, so a special ordinance is made to fit the circumstances of the case (cf. *Magna moralia*, ii.1 (1198b24)).

Ibid., vi.3–7 (1139b15–1141b16)   Let it be assumed that there are five qualities through which the mind achieves truth in affirmation or denial, namely art or technical skill, scientific knowledge, prudence, wisdom and intelligence. Conception and opinion are capable of error . . . An object of scientific knowledge exists of necessity. It is therefore eternal . . . All art deals with bringing something into existence . . . Prudence (practical wisdom) is not science, because matters of conduct admit of variation, and not art, because doing and making are generically different . . . Prudence is a truth-attaining rational quality concerned with action in relation to things that are good and bad for human beings . . . first principles must be apprehended by intelligence . . . Wisdom must be a combination of intelligence and scientific knowledge . . . Prudence must take account of particular facts, since it is concerned with action, and action deals with particular things.

Rhetoric, i.13 (1374a–b)   Omissions [in the law] are sometimes voluntary, sometimes involuntary, on the part of legislators; involuntary when it may have escaped their notice, voluntary when, being unable to define for all cases, they are obliged to make a universal statement, which is not applicable to all, but only to most, cases, and whenever it is difficult to give a definition owing to the infinite number of cases . . . Actions which should be leniently treated are cases for equity . . . and it is equitable to pardon human weaknesses, and to look, not to the law but to the legislator; not to the letter of the law but to the intention of the legislator; not to the action itself, but to the moral purpose; not to the part, but to the whole . . .

Cicero, *De finibus*, iii.7.24   Sola enim sapientia in se tota conversa est, quod idem in caeteris artibus non fit.

For wisdom alone is entirely self-contained, which is not the case with the other arts.

Disputationes Tuscalanae, iv.26   Sapientiam esse rerum divinarum et humanarum scientiam cognitionemque, quae cuiusque rei causa sit.

Wisdom is the knowledge of divine and human things and the cause of each of them.

De officiis, i.43.153.   Princepsque omnium virtutum illa sapientia, quam σοφία. Graeci vocant – prudentiam enim, quam Graeci φρόνησις dicunt, aliam quandam intelligimus, quae est rerum expetendarum fugiendarum scientia; ulla autem scientia, quam principem dixi, rerum est divinarum et humanarum scientia . . .

The foremost of all virtues is wisdom – what the Greeks call sophia; for by prudence, which they call phronesis, we understand something else, namely, the practical knowledge of things human and divine . . .

Corpus Juris Civilis
Institutes, Preface: In hos quattuor libros easdem institutiones partiri iussimus, ut sint totius legitimae scientiae prima elementa.

We ordain that these institutes be divided into four books, as being the first elements of the science of law.

I 1.1.1 (also D 1.1.10.2): Iurisprudentia est divinarum atque humanarum rerum notitia, iusti atque iniusti scientia.

Jurisprudence is the knowledge of things human and divine, and the science of what is just or unjust.

D 1.1.1 (Ulpian): Nam ut eleganter Celsus definit, ius est ars boni et aequi.

As Celsus elegantly puts it, law is the art of the good and the equitable.

For our purposes, perhaps the best account of the debate which deploys these topoi is that of Peter Gilkens, who records the arguments both for and against the scientific status of jurisprudence in his polemical work *Iurisprudentiam nedum constare ratione, sed esse scientiam proprie dictam*, published in 1605. His purpose is to refute those who think that they can apply the 'nuda philosophiae praecepta' (naked precepts of philosophy) to law; there may be a reference here to Ramist lawyers as well as to the two philosophers – Tio and Zabarella – he specifically names.[26] His allies are Jacques de Coras (1500–72) and Joachim Hopper (1523–76), who in fact argue that jurisprudence is both an art and a science; and Barthélemy de Chasseneuz (1480–1541), who devotes part of his *Catalogus gloriae mundi* of 1529, a major Renaissance source book on questions of precedence, to this question, and adduces eleven reasons for considering law to have the dignity of a science. Some of these are simple allegations of *auctoritates*, such as those set out above, or the many statements of the glossators: gl. ad C 11.91.1 asserts that 'iurisperiti et

[26] See Horst Dreizel, *Protestantischer Aristotelismus und absoluter Staat: die Politica des Henning Arnisaeus*, Wiesbaden, 1970, pp. 80–6, for an account of resistance to the infiltration of Ramism in Germany.

medici dicuntur esse philosophi veri profundioris scientiae et doctrinae' (jurists and doctors are said to be true philosophers possessing
deep knowledge and doctrine); and the gl. ad D 1.1.1 expands on
Ulpian's reference to the law as 'vera philosophia' and quotes
Porphyry's definition of art as 'de infinitis finita disciplina', (the finite
discipline of the indeterminate) describing it also as 'scientia finita'
(the knowledge of finite things); all of this is also alleged in answer to
the charge that jurisprudence is not 'in se versata'.[27] Some of
Chasseneuz's 'reasons' are simple assertions; e.g. justice is divine and
must therefore be the object of a science; or, as jurisprudence deals
with theoretical and practical knowledge it is thus doubly a science.
Some are exercises in inference from texts: the reference in D 1.1.1 to
'ars', for example, presupposes a 'praeexistens cognitio' which is the
science of jurisprudence; or, since laws are general (C 1.17.1), the
jurists must proceed by *ratio*, which is scientific in an Aristotelian
sense. Some are pure exercises in reasoning: as law deals with
definitions, causes and reasons, it must be higher than an art, for to
know causes is a recognized way of defining scientific knowledge (see
below, 2.4).[28]

Gilkens then records Zabarella's and Tio's objections to the status
of law as a science; some of these are in the form of simple
vituperation, others based on Aristotle's narrow definition of science
which cannot be of infinite things. This last point is conceded by a
number of jurists, among them Angelo Matteacci [Matthaeacius]
(1536–1600), Gilkens's tutor in Padua. He, like his pupil, records his
philosophical colleagues' insults, but chooses a less ambitious line of
defence: jurisprudence is part of practical philosophy, and is characterized by φρόνησις (prudence); this is indicated by the Roman
forebears of Renaissance jurists who were known as the *prudentes*; it is
an art in that it requires method and order. Hopper, and more
notably Coras, argue that the law is principally an art, but that it

---

[27] See Kelley, *History, law and the human sciences*, iv, vi; cf. Cicero, *De finibus*, iii.7.24, quoted
above, p.23. See also Alessandro Turamini, *Omnes iuris interpretationes habitae, dum in humanis
agebat, in titulos Digestorum de legibus, de legatis, de acquirenda possessione, et de iure fisci*. Venice,
1606, pp. 17off., on the contemporary debate about the self-sufficiency of the law.

[28] See also Quintilian, ii.18 and iii.6; Gilkens, *Jurisprudentiam*, p. 7, who cites Giovanni
Nevizzani (*Sylva nuptialis* (1521), v.76ff.) as well as Chasseneuz, Coras and Hopper; and
Ernst H. Kantorowicz, *The king's two bodies: a study in medieval political theology*, Princeton,
1957, pp. 139ff. The passage in Chasseneuz is to be found in his *Catalogus gloriae mundi* (1528),
Lyon, 1546, x.18, fols. 189–91.

contains the science of justice.[29] Other jurists do not allude to their institutional enemies – the 'scientiae nostrae oblatratores' – directly, but allude to the need of law for a general science, while conceding its enmeshment in particulars. Ideally the science of law is apodictic; but in reality, they concede, it is no more than 'probable' even though it is dignified by association with the science of causes.[30]

1.2.4

The case presented by Gilkens and his allies is a mixture of argument from authority, often in the form of quotations from the Corpus, and reasoning; when systematizers such as Bodin or Connan make the case for the scientific status of legal studies, they rely exclusively on the latter. Bodin's *Iuris universi distributio* of 1580 offers a threefold division of academic disciplines: theoretical (scientific), practical and aesthetic. It seems that at first sight the law should belong to the order of the practical where Aristotle's phronesis comes into play, and to which the distinctions evil/good, politic/impolitic (*utile/inutile*) pertain; but he argues with the Stoics that as all men carry in them the seeds of divine reason and justice, jurisprudence must be a science, for it

---

[29] *Tractatus de iuris arte duorum clarissimorum iurisconsultorum, Ioannis Corasii et Ioachimi Hopperi . . .*, Lyon, 1591, pp. 281, 570. These treatises were also printed in *Tractatus iuris universi*, Venice, 1584, i.59–103. See also Constantinus Rogerius, *De iuris interpretatione, ibid.*, i.393–5. The *leges* in the Corpus most referred to in this respect are D 1.1.7, D 1.2.2 and C 1.17.1.

[30] See also Pietro Andrea Gammaro, *De veritate ac excellentia legalis scientia*, in *Tractatus iuris universi*, i.132–47; Ludovicus Pelleus, *Confutatio eorum qui ius civile artis aut scientiae titulo non esse donandum asserere, ibid*, i.103–5. Among the *quaestiones* of Pelleus are found the following: an sint in iure civili antinomiae; an contraria praecepta in omni scientiarum genere; an leges iuris civilis certae, et constantiae sint; an universales; an ius civile naturae adversetur; an rerum distinctio sit iuri naturali conveniens, et a iure divino probata; an possit mutari ius naturale; an probet definitiones iurisprudentia; an facile possint omnia definiri; an sit scientia demonstrativa; an finitus, et certus legum numerus; an sit inepta, et confusa iuris civilis dispositio; an definitio constare possit pluribus differentiis; an sit bonum quid diversum ab aequo; an sit in iure quid non aequum. [whether there are antinomiae in civil law; whether there are contrary precepts in all kinds of disciplines; whether civil laws are certain, consistent and universal; whether civil law is in contradiction to nature; whether the division of things into classes is in accord with natural law and proven by divine law; whether natural law can change; whether jurisprudence can certify definitions; whether everything can be easily defined; whether jurisprudence is a demonstrative science; whether the number of laws is infinite or finite; whether the ordering of civil law is inept and confused; whether definition can consist in more than one differentia; whether the good is different from the equitable; whether there is anything inequitable in the law]. Many of these questions touch on interpretative issues discussed in chapter 3, below. There are further treatises on the question of legal science or art; e.g. Matthäus Wesenbeck, *De iuris arte et scientia comparanda consultatio* (reprinted in χειραγωγία *sive Cynosura iuris*, ed. Nicolaus Reusner, Speyer, 1588–9, i.41–53). See also Alciato, *Oratio in laudem iuris civilis*, in *Opera omnia*, Basle, 1582, iv.1022–31. On 'probable', see below 3.1.3.

permits men to distinguish the true from the false. To demonstrate the scientific nature of law, Bodin proceeds to build his universal system on Aristotle's four causes (see below 2.5; 3.4.1); and he logicizes the final cause of the law ('suum cuique tribuere' (D 1.1.10.1) (to give to every one his due)) by adding 'necesse est' to Ulpian's words. Although his brief *Iuris universi distributio* makes frequent allusions to the Corpus, he rejects its authority as a universal or systematic code on the ground that it relates to only one city and consists in the 'avulsa laceraque membra Romani Juris' (the torn and scattered limbs of Roman law).[31] Connan is as harsh in his judgement on the Corpus, which even *mos italicus* lawyers concede to be no more than a 'farrago' containing hypothetical examples and maxims from which the science of jurisprudence needs to be inferred. They admit, moreover, that even the sections on jurisprudence (principally the first five titles of book i of the Digest) are not comprehensive, and the presence of antinomiae is not denied.[32] The conclusion that the jurist must work on the text of the law to extract meaning and jurisprudential coherence has important consequences for the status of interpretation, as Donald Kelley has shown;[33] but there are other inferences which may be drawn from this debate which bear on the practice of textual analysis.

1.2.5

It is worth noting first how close the association of law with moral or practical philosophy is. Donald Kelley has already pointed to this in a number of articles, and has stressed the ambitious claims of jurists for their own trade. According to Ulpian, they are deservedly called the priests ('sacerdotes') of the legal art (D 1.1.1.1); a claim lawyers are fond of repeating.[34] Legal studies are opposed by them to mere speculative philosophy (which it encompasses) and allied both with

---

[31] Jean Bodin *Iuris universi distributio* (1580), trans. Lucien Jerphagnon, Paris, 1985, pp. 8–10; Bodin does not refer to the Stoic definition of the law given in D 1.3.2, but to Diogenes Laertius vii. 128 (τὸ δίκαιον οὐκ εἶναι θέσει, ἀλλὰ μονον φύσει). See also François de Connan, *Commentaria iuris civilis*, Paris, 1553, i.1–37.

[32] Connan's criticisms are cited by Turamini, *De legibus*, pp. 171–2; see also Hermann Vulteius, *Idea iuris logica*, Frankfurt, 1586, pp. 2–5, and Matthaeacius, *De via et ratione*, fols. 54–5.

[33] *History, law and the human sciences*, iv.

[34] Rogerius, *De legis potentia*, in *Tractatus iuris universi*, i.395 (where reference is made to canon law commentaries on this topos); Stanislaus Ilovius, *De laudibus iurisprudentiae oratio*, Bologna, 1565, pp. 10–11; François Hotman, *Iurisconsultus sive de optimo genere iuris interpretandi* in *Cynosura iuris*, i.110; Kantorowicz, *The king's two bodies*, pp. 118–24 (citing, among others, Budé).

ethics (though, as we shall see (below 3.6.1), not always felicitously) and the pursuit of wisdom; it is the 'vera philosophia'.[35] It is no coincidence that Cicero's definitions for philosophy and for wisdom and the Ulpian formulation in D 1.1.1 are so close. Even though it is not an apodictic science, jurisprudence is nonetheless a rational pursuit: we shall see below (2.4–5) how important the place of logic is. Moreover, a wide variety of rôles in the law is evoked in the discussion of its academic status: interpreter, teacher, drafter, judge, advocate, consultant. It is alleged that a complete jurist engages both in theory and in legal practice; great claims are made for the dignity and broad compass of the profession.[36] The debate about science and art also gives prominence to the rôle of legal interpreter. The law is as a text imperfect; it lacks complete and explicit expression of its norms and sense; it needs interpretation and the application of logic and ethics. As one commentator put it, 'si omnia scribi possent, nihil esset reliquendum arbitrio iudicantis' (if all things could be written down, nothing would be left for the judgement of the lawyer).[37] The space for interpretation is provided by the gap left between word and thing, universal and particular, past, present and future, one cultural norm and another. The words which are used in treaties, agreements, transactions, contracts, judgements, wills require definition and mediation. They are the 'words of the art' ('verba artis nostrae'):[38] an

---

[35] See Kelley, 'Vera philosophia' and 'Jurisconsultus perfectus'; also gl. ad D 1.1.10.2.

[36] See Quintilian, xii.3.10 ('posse oratorem non discendo tantum iuri vacare sed etiam docendo'); Hotman, *Iurisconsultus*, in *Cynosura*, i.110f.; Alberto Bolognetti, *De lege, jure et aequitate disputationes* (1570), Wittenberg, 1593, pp. 85–6, 179; Georgius Gallus, *Disputatio de legibus et longa consuetudine, deque iuris et facti ignorantia, . . . praeside Scipione Gentili*, Aldorf, 1591, thesis xlvi, p. 8; Johann Thomas Frey (Freigius), *Neüwe practica iuris*, Basle, 1574, fol., ii^v; Le Douaren, in *Methodica iuris utriusque traditio*, Lyon, 1562, p. 1012, cited by N.W. Gilbert, *Renaissance concepts of method*, New York, 1960, pp. 97–8, but cf. Eguinaire Baron, who distinguishes 'doctores legum' from 'pragmatici' (cited by Kelley, *History, law and the human sciences*, vii.266).

[37] Turamini, *De legibus*, p. 152.

[38] Alberigo Gentili, *In titulum Digestorum de verborum significatione commentarius*, Hanau, 1614, p. 2; for an English defence of law French, see Sir Edward Coke, *Institutes*, London, 1629, i.¢ 6^r:

> so many ancient Termes and words drawne from that legall French, are grown to be *Vocabula Artis*, Vocables of Art, so apt and significant to expresse the true sense of the Laws, and are so woven into the Laws themselves, as it is in a manner impossible to change them, neither ought legall termes to be changed. In Schoole Divinity, and amongst the Glossographers and Interpreters of the Civill and Canon Lawes, in Logick and other liberal sciences, you shall meet with a whole Army of words, which cannot defend themselves *in Bello Grammaticali*, in the Grammatical Warre, and yet are more significant, compendious and effectuall to express the true sense of the matter, than if they were expressed in pure Latine.

art which is controlled by university faculties or similar institutions in much of Europe that wish to preserve their monopolic hold. They are thus, like Gilkens, driven to argue that jurisprudence has a method of its own (in which case it is an art), *and* that it is a science (whose principles are ipso facto accessible to all, even to philosophers). Gilkens ends by arguing that the logic of law 'qui rei primordia caussas et omnes circumstantias explorat' (which explores the origins and causes of things and all attendant circumstances) – a clause which symptomatically reveals the unphilosophical mixture of the necessary and the contingent in jurisprudence[39] – is in fact superior to that of philosophy: one must, in order to grasp the generality of laws, know, as Hopper had said, their 'universalia principia', their 'genera' and their 'necessitas';[40] and one must pay special attention to the relationship between words and the intention of the legislator, which requires analytical skills equal if not superior to those required by simple logic (see below 2.4). Gilkens, furthermore, refers to imperial authority as immanent in the law, just as true faith is in theology.[41] By bringing together word, meaning, mediator and authority in this way, this debate about the status of legal studies has foreshadowed much of the coming discussion of interpretation. In it, writers unite abstract argument with concrete institutional issues, justification with special pleading, lofty claims to disinterested pursuit of wisdom with what Kelley calls 'guild sense'.[42] The same tensions are present in the more theoretical discussions of interpretative practice, but are less easy to detect.

---

[39] Gilkens, *Iurisprudentiam*, pp. 15–17. On the mixture of causes and circumstances, see below 2.4–5.

[40] Hopper, in *Tractatus de iuris arte*, pp. 311ff.; cf. Gilkens, *Iurisprudentiam*, p. 34.

[41] *Ibid.*, p. 37:
principia nostri iuris . . . non . . . subverti posse . . . cum ut Theologiae principia insigni ex parte fide nitantur quam cum sine vulnere conscientiae, et aeternae damnationis periculo in controversiam nemo vocaverit: ita etiam sine sacrilegii crimine negare non possumus legibus ab Imperatore, aut suoquoque principe promulgatis, esse parendum. [the principles of our law cannot be subverted . . . since just as the principles of theology rest on faith in large part and cannot be called into question by anyone without injuring their conscience and running the risk of eternal damnation, so also we cannot deny without committing the crime of sacrilege that laws promulgated by the Emperor or any sovereign whatsoever are to be obeyed. (Cf. C 9.29.2)

[42] Kelley, *History, law and the human sciences*, iv.181, xi, *passim*; see also Agrippa, *De incertitudine*, xciii–xciv; Coing, *Handbuch*, pp. 18–19.

LEGAL TEXTS: GENRES, PRODUCTION, PRESENTATION,
DISTRIBUTION

1.3.1

Another link between academic debate and the economic and
institutional conditions from which it arises is provided by the
printing, publishing and distribution of legal texts in the early
modern period. These fall into a number of more or less well defined
genres, many of which have their counterparts in the medieval
period.[43] *Consilia* (written consultations by prominent jurists on
precise points of law) and the decisions of courts such as the Rota
Romana are, of course, practical demonstrations of interpretation;
they were most often printed expensively in folio and advertised at
book fairs, presumably with a readership of practitioners in mind.
They are found alongside genres in which the issue of interpretation
and mediation is more theoretical and academic: theses, textbooks,
student introductions, commentaries on titles of the Digest or Code,
monographs, and editions of the Corpus. These publications are more
directly the concern of this study, and require further comment.[44]

Theses, or rather prospectuses for academic disputations, were
published at the author's own expense in short print runs from the
late sixteenth century onwards. They were produced either by the
candidate for a master's degree or doctorate or by his superior (the
praeses of the public disputation). They advertised the day and place
of the defence of the thesis on their title-page. They were usually
published in quarto by the local accredited university printer, and are
rarely longer than two or three gatherings (sixteen to twenty-four
pages): they were produced principally for examination in German
universities. Most address points at issue (*adnotationes*) in a law or a
title or explicate a given text (*repetitiones*); a few deal with broader

---

[43] For an account of medieval genres, see Robinson, Fergus and Gordon, *Introduction*, pp. 88–95;
such titles as *consilia, communes opiniones, summae, adnotationes, observationes* and *repetitiones* persist
into the Renaissance. There has been disagreement about the importance of publication to
the legal profession. Stinzing's history gives the impression that academic publication is the
lifeblood of the profession, whereas Rowan argues that juristic culture is predominantly
manuscript and concerned with the reproduction of established formulas. The focus of this
study is on the printed material, but Rowan's claim that the majority of lawyers were not
concerned with legal polemics also finds support here: cf. note 65 below.

[44] I have not included in the survey the genre of miscellany, which contained legal material and
commentary, but much else besides: two famous examples are Giovanni Nevizzani's *Sylva
nuptialis* (1521) and Antoine Tiraqueau's *De legibus connubialibus* (four editions between 1513
and 1554).

topics. In the period up to 1630, I could find only one (Georgius Gallus' *Disputatio de legibus et longa consuetudine . . . praeside Scipione Gentili*, delivered at Altdorf on 15 May 1591) which addressed directly the question of interpretation. As a genre, they lend themselves easily to parody: some very funny ones were produced.[45]

1.3.2
The publication of *libri scholastici* (books intended for use in a given school or university) may be equally local, and rarely advertised in book fairs; many of these were produced in octavo or duodecimo, and contained the outlines of lectures given by the local professor which a student transcribed (not always with his authorization).[46] Books which deal with propaedeutic disciplines (dialectics for legal students, topics for legal students, etc.) were designed for a broader readership: they were produced in folio, as well as in smaller formats, and distributed widely in Europe.[47] Plaintext student material, sometimes containing a few rudimentary explanations, sometimes designed as crib-books or basic introductions, seems also to have been aimed at a broad university readership. They have titles such as 'Enchiridion', 'Epitome', 'Paratitla' (that is, the paragraph-length summaries of Digest titles authorized by Justinian himself (see below 1.5.1)), 'Methodicus', 'Ars', 'Ratio'; that they were produced for 'adolescentes' or 'tyrones' was usually specified; they covered the preparations for legal training (reading techniques, logic, the first set texts) and were often designed for use by a number of academic institutions, being published for speculative profit by well-known humanist printers and businessmen such as Sebastian Gryphius, Jean Crespin and Guillaume Rouillé.[48] The adaptability of these texts (perhaps

---

[45] On these, see Wilhelm Erman and Ewald Horn, *Bibliographie der deutschen Universitäten*, Leipzig and Berlin, 1904–5, i, nos. 7405–576; and R.J.W. Evans, 'German universities after the Thirty Years War', *History of universities*, i (1981), 169–90, esp. 174–81.

[46] Rowan, 'Jurists', pp. 79–82; Gilissen, *Introduction historique*, pp. 314–33; Kisch, *Studien zur humanistischen Jurisprudenz*, pp. 65–104.

[47] On these see Troje, in Coing, *Handbuch*, pp. 718ff., who points to Erasmus' influence on the titles 'ars' and 'ratio'. The works by Claude Chansonnette (Cantiuncula), Hegendorf and Johannes Oldendorp are the most notable.

[48] E.g. Conradus Lagus, *Methodica iuris utriusque traditio*, Lyon, 1562, (printed with Cantiuncula, Le Douaren, Baron and Alciato); Petrus Corvesius, *Methodicus sive de ratione artis, in quo disseritur, an civilis scientia methodo tractari possit*, Lyon, 1547; *Paratitla*, Lyon, 1544; *Axiomata legum*, Lyon, 1547; *Institutiones . . .*, Geneva, 1574; *Tituli tractatusque iuris civilis studio in primis necessarii*, Geneva, 1574, 1589; *Enchiridion titulorum iuris*, Louvain, 1554; *Tituli . . . de verborum ac rerum significatione . . . de regulis iuris . . .*, Basle, 1590; *Enchiridion titulorum aliquot iuris*, Lyon, 1567; *Cynosura iuris; Clarissimorum et praestantissimorum iurisconsultorum tam veterum quam recentium varii utilissimi et diu multumque desiderati tractatus*, Cologne, 1585.

most notably Nicolaus Reusner's, which contains Ramist, traditional
and French approaches)[49] suggests that it would be unwise to draw
too sharp a distinction by the last decades of the sixteenth century
between *mos italicus* and *mos gallicus*; the introductory dialogues which
accompany this literature often do not make any distinction between
these modes of legal education, and the printing together of D 50.16,
D 50.17 and the Institutes suggests that regardless of the first text to be
studied – according to the recommendation of Lorenzo Valla, the
postglossators or Justinian respectively – all three eventually would
be read. Sometimes the table of affinity, D 45.1 (*De verborum
obligationibus*), some canon law, even D 1.2 (*De origine iuris*), are found
as well in these collections.[50] In pedagogical material, which is more
local in flavour, the methodological introductions by local professors
often quote the Senecan topos about trusting only one guide (the one
in your hands) in the confusing array of books about you.[51] These
were supplemented towards the end of the century by alphabetical
books of legal maxims (Axiomata) and comprehensive lexica,
produced expensively in folio; opinion was sharply divided about the
suitability of these last for beginners. Their size and scope suggest that

---

[49] See Troje, in Coing, *Handbuch*, p. 722. *Cynosura* contains twenty-nine items, mainly, but not
exclusively, by legal humanists, Ramists and eclectics; Petrus Horst's collection of treatises of
1585 (the *Clarissimorum et praestantissimum iurisconsultorum . . . tractatus*) contains works by such
disparate figures as Johannes Baptista de Caccialupis (*De modo studendi in utroque iure* (1472))
and Eguinaire Baron (see below note 93). See also the compendium attributed to Conrad
Lagus under the title *Methodica utriusque iuris traditio*, Lyon, 1562.

[50] See note 48. Paul Emile Viard, *André Alciat*, Paris, 1926, p. 122, attributes the vogue for D
50.16 to Maffeo Vegio rather than Valla. See also Troje in Coing, *Handbuch*, p. 719;
Robinson, Fergus and Gordon, *Introduction*, p. 295 (citing Le Douaren).

[51] See Troje, in Coing, *Handbuch*, p. 718, and most notably Rogerius' peroration to his *De iuris
interpretatione* (*Tractatus iuris universi*, i.394):
Ultimo, illud tibi persuadeo, quod non velis inniti multitudini librorum (ut inquit Seneca
lib. i Epistolarum ad Lucilium, Episto. 2). Distrahit librorum multitudo. Itaque cum
legere non possis quantum habemus, satis est habere quod legas. Idem Seneca de
tranquillitate animi: Onerat discentem turba librorum, non instruit, multoque satius est,
paucis te tradere auctoribus, quam errare per multos. Et sic expeditus sum de hoc singulari
Tractatu.
Finally, I would urge upon you that you should not set out to rely upon a multitude of
books (as Seneca says in *Epistulae morales*, ii). A multitude of books is a distraction. Thus it is
sufficient to own what you will read, since you cannot read as much as you possess. And as
Seneca says also in *De tranquillitate animi* [ix.5]: a host of books weighs down the student,
and does not instruct him; it is much more satisfactory to commit yourself to few authors
than to wander through many. On this note I shall deliver myself of this monograph.
There is a bibliography of such references in *Clarissimorum iurisconsultorum tractatus*, p. 265, and
two treatises (by Olradus de Ponte Laudensis and Giovanni Nevizzani) on the topic *utrum
expediat multos habere libros* (pp. 262–83).

they were produced more with practitioners than impecunious students in mind.[52]

Extensive commentaries on major titles, whether reprints of the work of fifteenth-century scholars or newly produced, appeared in octavo or quarto, but are also quite often published in folio: although commentary was a recognized form of teaching, these last were aimed not so much at students as at practitioners or scholars.[53] They sometimes contained several commentaries on the same title; and they were more often than not advertised at book fairs. D 50.16 (*De verborum significatione*) was very frequently expounded; it is to be supposed that this was particularly useful for draftsmen and those seeking legal formulas.[54]

Monographical material based on a section or sections of the Corpus Juris Civilis or on a given legal topic is not always easy to distinguish clearly from commentary; it can take the form of the *usus modernus Pandectarum*, in which customary law and recent imperial statutes are cited, or it can appear much more like historical studies or textual criticism: these last were common in France in the second half of the sixteenth century, as Donald Kelley has shown.[55] Monographs, like commentaries and *consilia*, were advertised and distributed at book fairs; but after the Index was instituted, some of the material was declared heterodox. By the turn of the century, German printers aspiring to a sale in Italy had to specialize in unimpeachable Catholic authors; and Italian publishers who used German printers (which they were tempted to do, as the costs of book production were about half those of Italy) were careful to disguise the fact that they were

---

[52] Jacobus Treterus, *Distributio titulorum juris de verborum significatione . . . et de regulis juris: ad Institutiones iustinianeas*, Frankfurt, 1625. A6ᵛ–8ʳ (against lexica); Vulteius. *De studio iuris*, in Michael Teuberus, *Tractatus tres de modo discendi, docendi et exercendi jura*, Lich, 1605, p. 91 (in favour of lexica). The earliest lexicon seems to be that by the postglossator Albericus de Rosate (d. 1354), which was published in Venice in 1573. Among the many sixteenth-century lexica the following are the better known: Petrus Praetorius, *Lexicon iuris civilis et canonica*, Lyon, 1567; Jacobus Spigelius (Spiegel) *Lexicon*, Strasbourg, 1538; Petrus Cornelius Brederodius, *Thesaurus dictionum et sententiarum iuris civilis*, Lyon, 1582; Barnabé Brisson, *Lexicon iuris*, Frankfurt, 1587; Johannes Calvinus (Kahl), *Lexicon iuridicum*, Frankfurt, 1600.

[53] On commentary as a form of teaching see *Der Kommentar in der Renaissance*, ed. August Beck and Otto Herding, Bonn, 1975, 'Introduction', pp. 8f. (referring in turn to B. Guarino, 'De ordine docendi et discendi', in *Il pensiero pedagogico dell' umanesimo*, ed. E. Garin, Florence, 1958, esp. p. 460).

[54] Alciato's dedicatory epistle to his treatise *De verborum significatione libri IIII* (1530), Frankfurt, 1582, pp. 3–8, and Turamini, *De legibus*, pp. 1–3, both stress the usefulness of their work for draftsmen.   [55] See Kelley, *Foundations*.

protestant.[56] These restrictions did not seem, however, to have much effect on the volume of publication, as Draudius' bibliography of books advertised at the Frankfurt Book Fair testifies. He lists over ten complete editions of the Corpus Juris Civilis published between 1569 and 1625; many of these were reprinted. They are produced in octavo, quarto and folio, to cater for the widest potential readership.[57]

1.4.1

This brief survey of the genera of law books – theses, pedagogical material, textbooks, commentaries, monographs, editions – has not yet touched on the degree of financial speculation involved in such publication. To appear in print is not straightforward: it requires money to finance labour and buy materials, commercial judgement about potential markets, connections to ensure distribution, protection of the product from illegal pirating by licence or privilege. For success in something beyond the local arena, it needs some of the outward signs of desirability: elegant presentation, a prestigious publisher known for his careful proof-reading, perhaps a dedicatee who might add lustre to the book by his name (although the great majority of law books seem to have been dedicated by their authors to colleagues),[58] even such additional touches as liminary verses or portraits. Where necessary, it needed to ensure its safe passage through the hands of a censor. But in scholarly books it is not usual to allow the signs of financial interestedness to become apparent. Some discreet signs of such interest emerge here and there: the naming on the title-page of the targeted readership ('tyrones', 'studiosi'; 'pragmatici', 'advocati', 'iudices'); the efforts made to publicize the book at book fairs; the purchase of expensive licences or monopolies for the production of a book in a given jurisdiction (licences which often refer to the 'magna impensa' of production and the 'speratum emolu-

---

[56] On the relative cost of books in Italy and Germany, see Rudolf Hirsch, *Printing, selling and reading 1450–1550*, Wiesbaden, 1967, p. 71, quoting Friedrich Kapp, *Geschichte des deutschen Buchhandels*, Leipzig, 1886, p. 312; Dennis E. Rhodes, 'Some neglected aspects of the career of Giovanni Battista Ciotti', *The Library*, vi.9 (1987), 225–39; also the catalogues of legal books of the publishers Johannes Gymnich (1588) and Zacharias Palthen (1595, 1598, 1608), discussed in Günter Richter, 'Bibliographische Beiträge zur Geschichte buchhändlerischer Kataloge im 16. und 17. Jahrhundert', in *Beiträge zur Geschichte des Buches und seine Funktion in der Gesellschaft: Festschrift für Hans Widmann*, ed. Alfred Swierk, Stuttgart, 1974, pp. 183–229.
[57] Georg Draut [Draudius], *Bibliotheca classica*, Frankfurt, 1625, s.v. Corpus iuris civilis (pp. 695–7).
[58] See Natalie Zemon Davis, 'Beyond the market: books as gifts in sixteenth-century France', *Transactions of the Royal Historical Society*, v.33 (1983), 69–88, esp. 77.

mentum' of the publisher);[59] the fact that in spite of such licences, books are pirated or reprinted outside the jurisdiction in question without permission. This last occurs frequently in late sixteenth-century Germany, where many Italian authors such as Jacopo Menochio (1532–1607) and Prospero Farinacci (1554–1618) were reprinted, and French and Swiss editions of the Corpus Juris Civilis were reproduced.[60] Further indications of financial interestedness have been charted by Guido Kisch, Steven Rowan and others, including the illicit printing of Ulrich Zazius and Konrad Hase [Lagus] (d. 1546) and the measures taken to protect both the quality of the editions and the sale of authorized versions of authors.[61] Finally, the insistence in licences and on title-pages that a given work is the 'latest' ('revised', 'improved', 'expanded', 'expurged') edition is significant in that it is precisely a condition of the legal protection of books to be 'new' in some sense: the apparent scrupulousness of authors demanding ever more accurate editions (or the institutional requirement that they show themselves to have surpassed previous generations of scholars) is a symptom also of the commercial interest which the book itself as an object occludes.[62] The legal and commercial constraints of the book trade thus encourage the interpretation boom which is detectable in all disciplines after 1550.[63]

[59] For examples of this see Bartholomaeus Caepolla, *In titulum de verborum et rerum significatione doctissima commentaria*, Lyon, 1551, Z.5ᵛ (the privilege which refers to the *labor* and *impensa* of the publisher); and in general, the imperial *Impressoria*, FZ 56 s.v. Palthen (25ʳ), Gymnich and others, preserved in the Haus-, Hof- und Staatsarchiv, Vienna. On privileges in general see Elizabeth Armstrong, *Before copyright: the French book-privilege system 1498–1526*, Cambridge, 1990.

[60] See Draut, *Bibliotheca classica*, s.v. Corpus iuris civilis (pp. 695–7) and on Farinacci and Menochio (published by Palthen and Gymnich respectively) p. 681 and p. 808. The entry for Alciato's *De verborum significatione* in the *Index aureliensis* testifies to this sort of pirating: see the editions recorded for 1546 and 1548 (a Giunta *Nachdruck* of the Gryphius edition); 1565 (simultaneous editions in Louvain and Lyon) and 1582 (editions in Frankfurt and Lyon); in the last two cases, the Gryphius presses protected their market share by reprinting.

[61] See Rowan, 'Jurists', and Kisch, *Studien zur humanistischen Jurisprudenz*, pp. 65–104. The 1562 edition of Lagus' *Methodica iuris utriusque traditio*, printed by Sebastian Gryphius at Lyon is 'ex ore Cor. Lagi annotata' by Justinus Goblerus.

[62] On this, see Ian Maclean, 'L'Economie du livre érudit: le cas Wechel (1572–1627)', in *Le Livre dans l'Europe de la Renaissance*, ed. Pierre Aquilon, Henri-Jean Martin and François Dupuigrenet-Desrousilles, Paris, 1985, pp. 230–9; and 'Philosophical books in European markets, 1570–1630: the case of Ramus', in *New perspectives on Renaissance thought*, ed. Henry and Hutton, pp. 253–63; cf. also the comment of Stanley Fish in *Is there a text in this class?*, Cambridge, Mass. and London, 1980, p. 350: 'the space in which a critic works has been marked out for him by his predecessors, even though he is obliged by the conventions of the institution to dislodge them'.

[63] On this see note 62 above, and Ian Maclean 'The market for scholarly books and conceptions of genre in northern Europe, 1570–1630', in *Die Renaissance im Licht der Nationen Europas*, ed. Georg Kauffmann, Wiesbaden, 1991, pp. 16–31.

A number of further points should here be made. The trade in legal books (indeed in all scholarly books) reflects the growing number of purchasers and consumers in the period 1570–1630, as has already been said: but it does not reveal the various uses to which these books were put. As has been pointed out by others, the purchase of expensive folio volumes of standard texts and *consilia* is, of course, necessary to someone in the legal profession if he wishes to establish a viable reference library; but his reference library consists as much in the outward, visible sign of his professional status as a corpus of texts to be read and studied. Sustained reading of such texts is rare; it is more common to leaf through them, or to use their indexes and tables as a means of access.[64] It may even have been common for no reference to have been made to them: they were there, as one contemporary put it, to impress the visitor, not to instruct the owner.[65] Certainly the apparent success of some enormous bibliographical undertakings – the twenty-nine volumes of the *Tractatus iuris universi*, the volumes of deliberations of the Rota Romana, even (in protestant Germany) the massive editions of canon law – can best be explained in this way. Moreover, some printing was commemorative or 'vanity publication', designed to celebrate the life and works of the author himself or a close relative rather than make a profit: the contents of these books may not bear as directly on the cultural nexus we are trying to describe, although at least one (that of Alessandro Turamini) is a remarkable piece of writing.[66]

1.4.2

It is worth pointing out also that the trade in scholarly books and, among these, in legal books, reflects certain confessional interests. I have already mentioned the Index; the Imperial Book Commission at the Frankfurt Book Fair was set up to keep an eye on legal as well as theological publication; the struggle between Calvinists and Luth-

---

[64] On this, see *Histoire de l'édition française*, ed. Henri-Jean Martin and Roger Chartier, Paris, 1983, i.77.

[65] See Gerhard Meuschen, preface to Thomas Bartolinus, *De libris legendis dissertationes*, 2nd ed., The Hague, 1711, *3ᵣff.

[66] On Turamini, see Luigi Rava, 'Alessandro Turamini Senense: giureconsulto filosofo del secolo XVI', *Studi senensi* v (supplement) (1888), 117–85. His *De legibus* was issued by his relative Virginio Turamini. For other examples of commemorative publication by a relative, see Alberigo Gentili, *In titulum Digestorum de verborum significatione commentarius*, Hanau, 1614, p. 1 (letter of Matthew Gentilis); Alciato, *Opera*, i.A2ᵛ (letter of Francisco Alciato); Joannes Borcholten, *Commentaria de verborum obligationibus*, Helmstedt, 1605 (dedication of Statius Borcholten).

erans, Ramists and followers of Melanchthon in northern and western Germany, in which a leading figure is the Basle lawyer Johann Thomas Frey [Freigius] (1543–83), spilt over into pedagogical issues (mainly philosophical, it is true, but also in part legal).[67] The publishers of legal material were clearly aware of these pressures on academe: they seemed to be aware also of a division between legal theory and pedagogy on the one hand, and legal practice on the other, which they reflected in their marketing of books by dividing their catalogues accordingly.[68] As has been noted, professional jurists claim themselves that there is no complete lawyer who is not both a practitioner and a theoretician: it seems that publishers knew otherwise.

1.4.3
The visual presentation of legal texts also impinges on this enquiry in so far as it has been alleged to support a celebrated thesis concerning the paradigm shift from the Middle Ages to the Renaissance. Early printed books reproduce the characteristic features of the manuscript tradition of law books: the lemma (the schematic reference to a text in the Corpus Juris Civilis or part of a gloss) and abbreviation are widely used; the gloss acts as a frame to the text; the academic forms of *quaestio, repetitio* and *disputatio*, and the internal ordering of the gloss itself – verbal analysis, parallel laws, antinomiae, notabilia – persist (fig. 1).[69] By the end of the sixteenth century, the *declamatio*, with its use of demonstrative rhetoric as well as dialectic, is found; some writers present their material in Ramist dichotomies (figs 2 and 3); commentaries appear in the old style (incorporating lemmas), or in a more humanist guise, with marginalia allowing for a less cluttered and disjointed text (fig. 4). Works in the *usus modernus Pandectarum* tradition incorporate vernacular quotation from imperial edicts into their texts as well (fig. 5). There is some evidence that, by the end of the sixteenth century, legal abbreviations were less well known, as handbooks of standard manuscript contractions are published for beginners; but there is also (especially in Italy), a strong conservative attachment to the old style. Legal theses in Germany either appear in

---

[67] On this see Dreizel, *Protestantischer Aristotelismus*, pp. 80–6, and Christian Jensen, 'Protestant rivalry, metaphysics and rhetoric in Germany 1590–1620', *Journal of ecclesiastical history*, xli (1990), 24–43. Cf. also, for an earlier period, James H. Overfield, *Humanism and scholasticism in late medieval Germany*, Princeton, 1984. [68] See note 56, above.

[69] See Robinson, Fergus and Gordon, *Introduction*, pp. 79–109.

the style of the Corpus Juris Civilis itself, that is, in aphorisms and paragraphs, or follow the practice of monographs, with citations of lemmas.

Alciato's essay on D 50.16 marks an important innovation, in that it separates a discursive essay on meaning addressed to legal drafts-men from a commentary on the text: later writers imitate him in this (rather repetitive) disposition of material which none the less allows the introduction of material outside the strict ambit of legal studies (such as ancient poets and writers of miscellanies, who themselves have their imitators among Renaissance jurists).[70] But the readers of the first edition of his *De verborum significatione* would have been very much at home with the first page of his commentary (fig. 6), even if the title-page announced a humanist challenge to the insularity of legal studies (fig. 7). It is only in later editions that the commentary itself appears in humanist guise (fig. 4). Even the discursive essay is not as innovative as it might seem, as there is much unacknowledged semi-quotation from the Corpus Juris Civilis; if the lemmas were restored to the text, it would take on again the look of an earlier age of legal writing.[71] Equally, the revolutionary use of Ramist dichotomies can be shown to be but a typographical variation on a technique of logical disposition found in the Digest itself, and commonly employed by the postglossators (fig. 1) (see below 3.3.4).

This last point is of course highly contentious, in view of the Ong thesis about Ramism in particular and the visuality of early modern culture in general.[72] The humanist desire to liberate the text is, after all, literally achieved: the host text is no longer visually encapsulated in its parasite gloss. But the control of the interpreter remains, if in more discreet forms. In nearly all cases of monographical material from the fifteenth century onwards, individual chapters are divided up into points which are listed at the beginning (fig. 8); this is both authoritative and logical in its implication. Authoritative, because each point is supported by its lemma; logical because the sequence of

---

[70] See note 44, above. The practice of including quotations from Horace and other ancient poets seems to have begun in the fifteenth century: Caepolla, Rogerius and de Federicis all contain such references.

[71] This would even be the case with Alciato's *De verborum significatione*; in the first few pages, I noted the unacknowledged quotation of D 2.1.3 and D 50.17.144; a more instructed eye would no doubt note many other instances.

[72] See Walter J. Ong, S.J., *Ramus, method, and the decay of dialogue* (1958), New York 1974, pp. 104–12 (this thesis has since been considerably developed by the author); *Histoire de l'édition française*, ed. Martin and Chartier, i.77.

points (which very often includes refutation of contrary argument) represents a claim to rationality and necessity; the attractiveness of such secure argumentation is found also in Ramist dichotomies, which appear to be necessary and exhaustive. This form of present- ation is well suited to the law. As I have suggested elsewhere, Renaissance jurisprudence is to be distinguished from medicine by its predilection for the *species contraria immediata* of opposition:[73] persons are masculine or feminine, guilty or not guilty, persons, things and actions are in a given category or are not, words are used literally or figuratively; there is no third term or coexistence of possibilities. The authoritative and logical summaries of points in commentary and monograph encourage this decisiveness, which lawyers see as a distinguishing mark of their art.

1.4.4

A point should be made here about the threat of infinite rearrange- ment and interpretation which the Corpus Juris Civilis apparently offers. It is divided into books, titles, rubrics, laws (*leges*) or rules (*regulae*), paragraphs; these can be cited in any sequence or selection. The gloss which surrounds the text contains argument, inference and exposition which can be separately cited (as 'arg[umentum] [of the paragraph, law or rule, title, book]' or 'ded[uctio] in . . .'). This would seem to constitute a sort of syntax and to open up an infinity of possible combinations.[74] Yet, the more one reads of the interpretative and exegetical material, the more one is struck by the relatively small range of reference, especially where general points are at issue. There are several reasons for this. First, the material adduced and the way it is adduced are very derivative; a given corpus of rules and glosses seems tacitly to be accepted as applicable to a given issue. Second, the rules for combining points into arguments are themselves included in the text of the Corpus Juris Civilis, and these inhibit certain sorts of combinations[75] (see below 2.4). Third, the corpus of references is *de facto* restricted, so that even when lexica are produced which generate apparently new configurations of Roman law based on words rather than the gloss, these do not in fact open up new areas of enquiry.

---

[73] See *The Renaissance notion of woman*, Cambridge, 1980, pp. 67–81.
[74] Cf. the comments of Michel Foucault on 'le savoir pléthorique' of the Renaissance in *Les Mots et les choses*, Paris, 1966, pp. 45–9.
[75] These rules are not grouped together, although the majority of them are to be found in D 1.3, D 50.16 and D 50.17.

Hidden in the glosses, commentaries and lexica is a tacitly agreed agenda of analysis, a pre-interpretative set of constraints on 'open' or 'productive' interpretation; they act in a similar way to the *quaestiones* which Edward Grant sees as constraining medieval scholasticism to a well-delimited area of enquiry.[76] This does not, of course, mean that there are not conflicting accounts, or that writers do not claim to be original or never disagree with predecessors, or that the results of *consilia* could be known in advance: only that institutional closure was in fact possible; that conservative forces were at work to preserve technical vocabulary and the terms of debate from change; and that the realm of law and legal interpretation operated as a coherent and recognizable practice.[77]

1.4.5

A final, and crucial, point needs to be made about the distribution of law books and the 'universe of discourse' they constitute. From the citation lists published at the beginning of monographs and academic

---

[76] 'Aristotelianism and the longevity of the medieval world view', *History of science*, xvi (1978), 93–106; see also the comments of Hastings Rashdall, *The universities of Europe in the Middle Ages*, ed. F.M. Powicke and A.B. Emden, Oxford, 1936, i.256ff.

[77] See Coke, *Institutes*, i.¢ 6ʳ, quoted above, note 38. It does not seem that two different styles of commentary develop in legal studies as they do in humanism, according to Anthony Grafton and Lisa Jardine, *From humanism to the humanities: education and the liberal arts in fifteenth- and sixteenth-century Europe*, Cambridge, Mass., 1986, pp. 58ff.

Fig. 1 *Digestum novum cum commentariis*, Lyon, 1569, fol., p. 627. The text (of the Florentine Digest) shown here is D 43.1.1, encapsulated by the gloss of Accursius and succeeded by the commentary of Bartolus (in italics). D 43.1.1 is an example of a discursive four-term *divisio* (as opposed to a Ramist dichotomy): it may be transcribed as follows:

Interdicta competunt	1. de divinis rebus
	2. de humanis rebus
Divinae res sunt	1.1 loci sacri
	1.2 loci religiosi
Humanae res sunt	2.1 quae sunt alicuius
	2.2 quae sunt nullius
quae sunt alicuius sunt	2.1.1 publica
	2.1.2 singulorum
publica competunt	2.1.1.1 de locis publicis
	2.1.1.2 de viis
	2.1.1.3 de fluminibus publicis
quae sunt singulorum	2.1.2.1 aut ad universitatem pertinent
	2.1.2.2 aut ad singulas res
quae sunt nullius competunt	2.2.1 de liberis personis

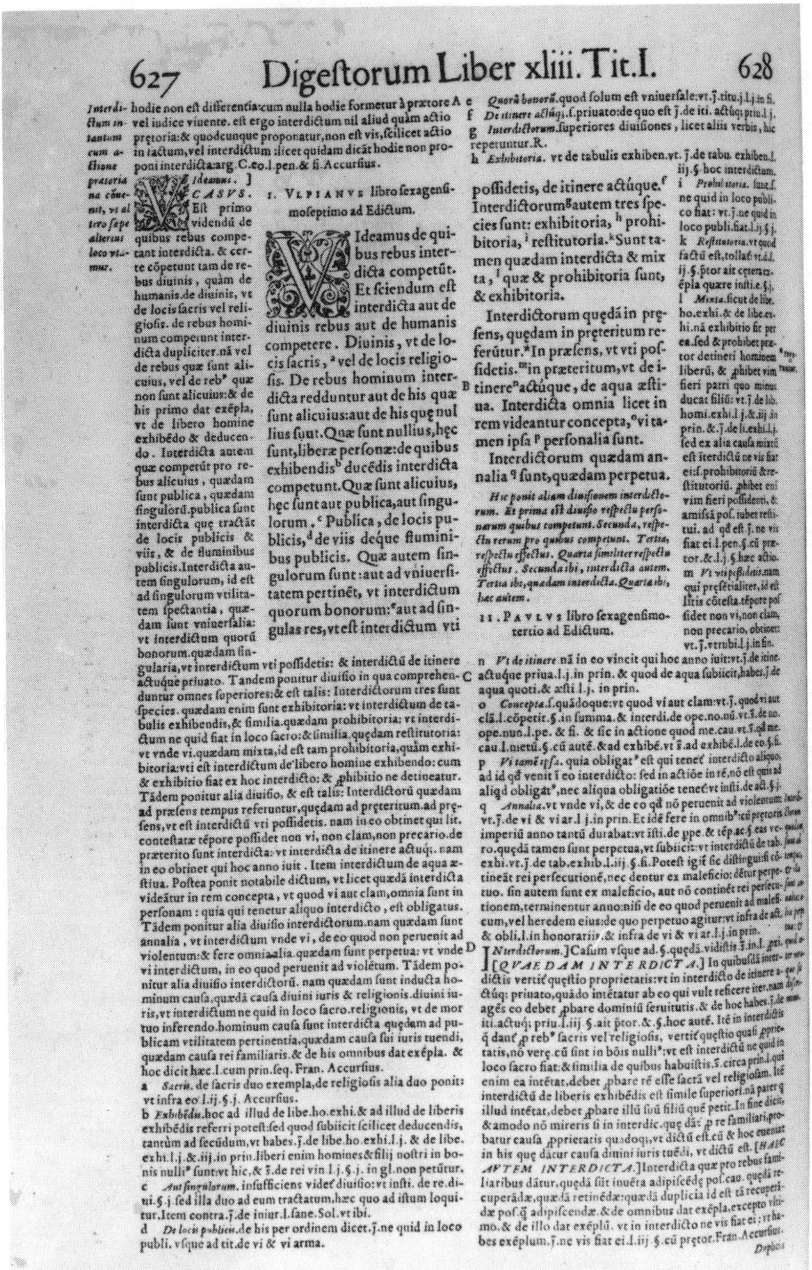

627 Digeſtorum Liber xliii. Tit. I. 628

Interdiſtum intantum cum actione prætoria conuenit, vt alterò ſæpe alterius loco vtamur.

hodie non eſt differentia: cum nulla hodie formetur à prætore A vel iudice viuente. eſt ergo interdictum nil aliud quàm actio prętoria: & quodcunque proponatur, non eſt vis, ſcilicet actio in factum, vel interdictum: licet quidam dicãt hodie non proponi interdicta: arg. C. eo. l. pen. & fi. Accurſius.

V *idemus.*] *CASVS.* Eſt primo videndũ de quibus rebus competant interdicta. & certe cõpetunt tam de rebus diuinis, quàm de humanis. de diuinis, vt de locis ſacris vel religioſis. de rebus hominum competunt interdicta dupliciter. nã vel de rebus quæ ſunt alicuius, vel de reb[9] quæ non ſunt alicuius: & de his primo dat exẽpla, vt de libero homine exhibẽdo & deducendo. Interdicta autem quæ competũt pro rebus alicuius, quædam ſunt publica, quædam ſingulorũ. publica ſunt interdicta quę tractãt de locis publicis & viis, & de fluminibus publicis. Interdicta autem ſingulorum, id eſt ad ſingulorum vtilitatem ſpectantia, quædam ſunt vniuerſalia: vt interdictum quorũ bonorum. quædam ſingularia, vt interdictum vti poſſidetis: & interdictũ de itinere actuque priuato. Tandem ponitur diuiſio in qua comprehen- C duntur omnes ſuperiores: & eſt talis: Interdictorum tres ſunt ſpecies. quædam enim ſunt exhibitoria: vt interdictum de tabulis exhibendis, & ſimilia. quædam prohibitoria: vt interdictum ne quid fiat in loco ſacro: & ſimilia. quędam reſtitutoria: vt vnde vi. quædam mixta, id eſt tam prohibitoria, quàm exhibitoria: vti eſt interdictum de libero homine exhibendo: cum & exhibitio fiat ex hoc interdicto: & ꝓhibitio ne detineatur. Tãdem ponitur alia diuiſio, & eſt talis: Interdictorũ quædam ad præſens tempus referuntur, quędam ad pręteritum. ad pręſens, vt eſt interdictũ vti poſſidetis. nam in eo obtinet qui lit. conteſtatæ tẽpore poſſidet non vi, non clam, non precario. de præterito ſunt interdicta: vt interdicta de itinere actuq;. nam in eo obtinet qui hoc anno iuit. Item interdictum de aqua æſtiua. Poſtea ponit notabile dictum, vt licet quędã interdicta videãtur in rem concepta, vt quod vi aut clam, omnia ſunt in perſonam: quia qui tenetur aliquo interdicto, eſt obligatus. Tãdem ponitur alia diuiſio interdictorum. nam quædam ſunt annalia, vt interdictum vnde vi, de eo quod non peruenit ad violentum: & fere omnia alia. quædam ſunt perpetua: vt vnde vi interdictum, in eo quod peruenit ad violẽtum. Tãdem ponitur alia diuiſio interdictorũ. nam quædam ſunt inducta hominum cauſa, quędã cauſa diuini iuris & religionis. diuini iuris, vt interdictum ne quid in loco ſacro. religionis, vt de mortuo inferendo. hominum cauſa ſunt interdicta quędam ad publicam vtilitatem pertinentia, quædam cauſa ſui iuris tuendi, quædam cauſa rei familiaris. & de his omnibus dat exẽpla. & hoc dicit hæc. l. cum prin. ſeq. Fran. Accurſius.

a *Sacris.* de ſacris duo exempla, de religioſis alia duo ponit: vt infra eo l. ij. §. j. Accurſius.

b *Exhibẽdis.* hoc ad illud de libe. ho. exhi. & ad illud de liberis exhibẽdis referri poteſt: ſed quod ſubiicit ſcilicet deducendis, tantùm ad ſecũdum, vt habes. ȷ̃. de libe. ho. exhi. l. j. & de libe. exhi. l. j. & iij. in prin. liberi enim homines & filij noſtri in bonis nulli[9] ſunt: vt hic, & ſ̃. de rei vin. l. j. §. j. in gl. non petũtur.

c *Aut ſingulorum.* inſufficiens videt' diuiſio: vt inſti. de re. diui. §. j. ſed illa duo ad eum tractatum, hæc quo ad iſtum loquitur. Item contra. ȷ̃. de iniur. l. ſane. Sol. vt ibi.

d *De locis publicis.* de his per ordinem dicet. ȷ̃. ne quid in loco publi. vſque ad tit. de vi & vi arma.

I. VLPIANVS libro ſexageſimoſeptimo ad Edictum.

V Ideamus de quibus rebus interdicta competũt. Et ſciendum eſt interdicta aut de diuinis rebus aut de humanis competere. Diuinis, vt de locis ſacris,[a] vel de locis religioſis. De rebus hominum interdicta redduntur aut de his quæ ſunt alicuius: aut de his quę nullius ſunt. Quæ ſunt nullius, hęc ſunt, liberæ perſonæ: de quibus exhibendis[b] ducẽdis interdicta competunt. Quæ ſunt alicuius, hęc ſunt aut publica, aut ſingulorum.[c] Publica, de locis publicis,[d] de viis deque fluminibus publicis. Quæ autem ſingulorum ſunt: aut ad vniuerſitatem pertinẽt, vt interdictum quorum bonorum:[e] aut ad ſingulas res, vt eſt interdictum vti poſſidetis, de itinere actúque.[f] Interdictorum[g] autem tres ſpecies ſunt: exhibitoria,[h] prohibitoria,[i] reſtitutoria.[k] Sunt tamen quædam interdicta & mixta,[l] quæ & prohibitoria ſunt, & exhibitoria.

Interdictorum quędã in pręſens, quędam in pręteritum referũtur.[*] In præſens, vt vti poſſidetis.[m] in præteritum, vt de i- B tinere[n] actúque, de aqua æſtiua. Interdicta omnia licet in rem videantur concepta,[o] vi tamen ipſa[p] perſonalia ſunt.

Interdictorum quædam annalia[q] ſunt, quædam perpetua.

Hic ponit aliam diuiſionem interdictorum. Et prima eſt diuiſio reſpectu perſonarum quibus competunt. Secunda, reſpectu rerum pro quibus competunt. Tertia, reſpectu effectus. Quarta ſimiliter reſpectu effectus. Secunda ibi, interdicta autem. Tertia ibi, quædam interdicta. Quarta ibi, hæc autem.

II. PAVLVS libro ſexageſimotertio ad Edictum.

e *Quorũ bonorũ.* quod ſolum eſt vniuerſale: vt. ȷ̃. titu. j. l. j. in fi.

f *De itinere actúq;.* ſ. priuato: de quo eſt ȷ̃. de iti. actúq; priu. l. j.

g *Interdictorum.* ſuperiores diuiſiones, licet aliis verbis, hic repetuntur. R.

h *Exhibitoria.* vt de tabulis exhiben. vt. ȷ̃. de tabu. exhiben. l. iij. §. hoc interdictum.

i *Prohibitoria.* ſunt. ſ. ne quid in loco publico fiat: vt. ȷ̃. ne quid in loco publi. fiat. l. ij. §. j.

k *Reſtitutoria.* vt quod factũ eſt, tollat: vt. d. l. ij. §. ꝑtor ait cęteraq. exẽpla quære inſti. e. §. j.

l *Mixta.* ſicut de libe. ho. exhi. & de libe. exhi. nã exhibitio fit per ea. ſed & prohibet prætor detineri hominem liberũ, & ꝓhibet vim fieri patri quo minus ducat filiũ: vt. ȷ̃. de lib. homi. exhi. l. j. & iij. in prin. & ȷ̃. de li. exhi. l. j. ſed ex alia cauſa mixtũ eſt interdictũ ne vis fiat ei: ſ. prohibitoriũ & reſtitutoriũ. ꝓhibet enĩ vim fieri poſſidenti, & amiſſã poſ. iubet reſtitui. ad qđ eſt ȷ̃. ne vis fiat ei. l. pen. §. cũ prætor. & l. j. §. hæc actio.

m *Vt vti poſſidetis.* nam qui pręſẽtialiter, id eſt litis cõteſta. tẽpore poſſidet non vi, non clam, non precario, obtinet: vt. ȷ̃. vtrubi. l. j. in fin.

n *Vt de itinere.* nã in eo vincit qui hoc anno iuit: vt. ȷ̃. de itine. C actuque priua. l. j. in prin. & quod de aqua ſubiicit, habes. ȷ̃. de aqua quoti. & æſti. l. j. in prin.

o *Concepta.* ſ. quãdoque: vt quod vi aut clam: vt. ȷ̃. quod vi aut clã. l. cõpetit. §. in ſumma. & interdi. de ope. no. nũ. vt. ſ̃. de no. ope. nun. l. pe. & fi. & ſic in actione quod me. cau. vt. ſ̃. qđ me. cau. l. metũ. §. cũ autẽ. & ad exhibẽ. vt ſ̃. ad exhibẽ. l. de eo. §. fi.

p *Vi tamẽ ipſa.* quia obligat[9] eſt qui tenet' interdicto aliquo. ad id qđ venit ĩ eo interdicto: ſed in actiõe in rẽ, nõ eſt quis ad aliqd obligat[9], nec aliqua obligatiõe tenet': vt inſti. de act. §. j.

q *Annalia.* vt vnde vi, & de eo qđ nõ peruenit ad violentum: vt. ȷ̃. de vi & vi ar. l. j. in prin. Et idẽ fere in omnib[9]: cũ prętoris imperiũ anno tantũ durabat: vt iſti. de ꝑpe. & tẽp. ac. §. eas vero. quędã tamen ſunt perpetua, vt ſubiicit: vt interdictũ de tab. exhi. vt. ȷ̃. de tab. exhib. l. iij. §. fi. Poteſt igit' ſic diſtingui: ſi cõtineãt rei perſecutionẽ, nec dentur ex maleficio: dẽtur perpetuo. ſin autem ſunt ex maleficio, aut nõ continẽt rei perſecutionem, terminentur anno: niſi de eo quod peruenit ad maleficum, vel heredem eius: de quo perpetuo agitur: vt infra de act. & obli. l. in honorariis. & infra de vi & vi ar. l. j. in prin.

D I *Nterdictorum.*] Caſum vſque ad. §. quędã. vidiſtis ſ̃. in. l. pri. [*QVAEDAM INTERDICTA.*] In quibuſdã interdictis vertit' quęſtio proprietatis: vt in interdicto de itinere actúq; priuato, quãdo intẽtatur ab eo qui vult reficere iter. nam agẽs eo debet ꝓbare dominiũ ſeruitutis. & de hoc habes. ȷ̃. de iti. actuq; priu. l. iij. §. ait ꝑtor. & §. hoc autẽ. Itẽ in interdictis q̃ dant' ꝓ reb[9] ſacris vel religioſis, vertit' quęſtio quaſi ꝓprietatis, nõ verę, cũ ſint in bõis nulli[9]: vt eſt interdictũ ne quid in loco ſacro fiat: & ſimilia de quibus habuiſtis. ſ̃. circa prin. l. qui enim ea intẽtat, debet ꝓbare rẽ eſſe ſacrã vel religioſam. Itẽ interdictũ de liberis exhibẽdis eſt ſimile ſuperiori. nã pater q illud intẽtat, debet ꝓbare illũ ſuũ filiũ quẽ petit. In fine dicit, & amodo nõ mireris ſi in interdic. quę dãt' ꝓ re familiari, probatur cauſa ꝓprietatis quãdoq;, vt dictũ eſt. cũ & hoc eueniat in his quę dãtur cauſa diuini iuris tuẽdi, vt dictũ eſt. [*HAEC AVTEM INTERDICTA.*] Interdicta quæ pro rebus familiaribus dãtur, quędã ſũt inuẽta adipiſcẽdę poſ. cau. quędã recuperãdæ, quædã retinẽdæ: quædã duplicia id eſt tã recuperãdæ poſ. q̃ adipiſcendæ. & de omnibus dat exẽpla, excepto vltimo. & de illo dat exẽplũ. vt in interdicto ne vis fiat ei: vt habes exẽplum. ȷ̃. ne vis fiat ei. l. iij. §. cũ prętor. Fran. Accurſius.

Duplicia

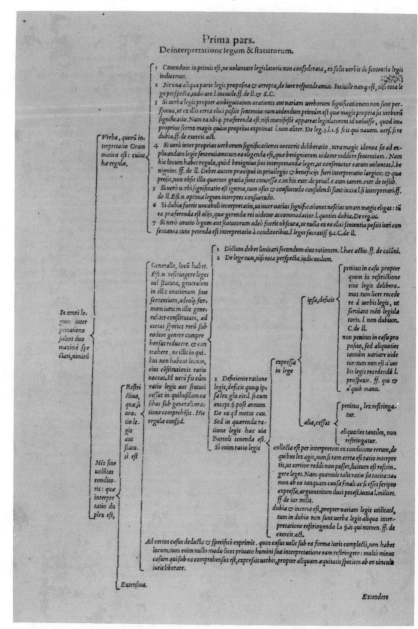

Figs. 2–3 Frey, *Partitiones iuris utriusque*, Basle, 1571, fol., ff. 4ᵛ–5ʳ. Frey links his Ramist dichotomies specifically to *divisio* or *partitio* in the title. The dichotomies set out represent the schema of interpretative modes: for Caepolla's earlier discursive version of this, see below pp. 117–19

Prima pars. 5

1. *Expediti iuris est, quòd lex ultra id quod eius dispositio exprimit, non sit extendenda. l. si uerò. §. de iure. ff. solut. matr.*

2. *Quæ sunt stricti iuris, in illis casus non expressus, habetur pro omisso. l. quicquid astr. ngendæ. ff. de uerb. oblig. Statuta autem sunt stricti iuris. §. actionum Instit. de action.*

3. *Casus omissus in lege aut statuto, relinquitur regulariter dispositioni iuris communi, & lex siue forma iuris in lege constituta ad eum non extenditur. l. si cum dotem. ff. solut. matr.*

Extédere legem aut statutã, est iura constituta ad casus orationé legis aut statuti nõ expressos propter rationis similitudinem deducere & transferre. Est autem huius extensionis, non leuit aut contemnenda causa. Nam cùm nõ omnium casuum formæ sigillatim aut legibus aut statutis comprehendi possint, hoc remedio utimur, ut cùm inaliqua simili causa, sententia & forma iuris manifesta sit, inde exemplum, quod sequamur in dicendo iure, i alijs casibus sumamus. l. non possint. De ll & S.C. At talem legum & statutorum extensionem non indiscriminatim nobis quærere ubiq in legibus & statutis licet. Nam

4. *Bartol. ad hæc iura, quæ extensioné legum & statutorum prohibere uidétur, in 4. quæst. ult. princip. circa l.omnes populi. De iust. & iur. ita respõdet, quòd extensionum alia sit*

Actiua, quæ leges & statuta per cõmodã accõmodatione similitudinit ad casus in illis expresé nõ cõprehensos trãsferútur. Sed ut hac extensione circã spectè utamur, ob seruandum dicit, quòd si isti casus ad quos cupimus trãsferre uel extédere legé aut statutum, antea iure cõmuni decisi & definiti

Non ius, &

Sint, tum non est quærẽda alia eorum decisio per legum aut statuto rum extensionem: sed relinquendi sunt in dispositione iuris commu nit, ut in l. quod constitutum ff. de mil. test. Atq ita accipiẽda sunt ea iura quæ prohibent extendere leges l. si uerò §. de uiro ff. solut. matr. l. constitutionibus in si. Ad municip.

ratio eorũ cõueniat rationi legis, tum licet formã iuris in eam constitutã ad illos casus extendere. Atq ita accipienda est gl. in l. non possint. ff. de ll. quæ plæraq recenset exempla huius extensionis, quæ propter similitudinem rationis leges ad casus in ea non expressos, transfert.

non possint confici, quod l. uel statuto permissum est, nisi alia quædam, licet lege non sint comprehensa aut expressa, concedantur, idem accidit, ut in l. non distinguemus. §. de offic. ff. de recept. arb. Sic Bartol de statutis quoq; respõdet, quòd quamuis ea sint stricti iuris tamen si ea quæ à statuto inducta sunt, non pos sunt fortiri commodè effectum, nisi ad ea quoq; quæ in illis non sunt expresé promissa, extendantur, licitum esse ea extendere.

exemplo & autoritate maiorum.

Pauli l. C. l. 1. §. lex Falcidia. ff. Ad l. Falcid.

Hermogeniani. l. 1. §. personarũ in si. De mun. & hon.

Passiua, quæ leges aut statuta, non ad casus in illis expresé non comprehensos, sed ad alias leges aliaq; statuta, quæ de eodem schemate iuris agunt, extendútur, ut inde modum exercendi sui iuris accipiant, & ab illis tanquam gubernatore experto pro necessitate conferuãdi iuris mo derentur. Quòd autem leges & statuta ita possint aut debeant extendi ad alias leges cõmunes Reip. liquet

regula, quæ dicitur: Quòd si quod ius à commu ni iure discrepet, illud ad ius commune redu cédum eo, à quo cum legibus eiusdẽ Reip. concordeat. l. unica. C. de inoff. dot. & in gl. eum dilectus. in uerb nec iuri communi. ex. do consuetudine. Nam cum per extensionem hãc statuta ordinatione ciuili longius ab æquitae & naturali progressa remouentur, & ll naturã libus tanquam suis natalibus restituútur: cum munis omnium legum ratio & autoritas hanc nobis ministrat potestaté, ut statuta iure com muni interpretemur. Et hæc regula simul ad omnes speciei interpretationis legum pertinet. Nam quæq; interpretatio sic facienda est, ut quanti fieri possit, nulli sit onerosa. Id sit com modissimè si ad ius commune reducãtur leges & statuta. c. causam quæ. ex. de rescrip.

5. *Huc pertinet quæstio. An statuto caueri possit, ne aliqua interpretatio statutorum huius uel illius ciui tatis aut collegij admittatur uel recipiatur.*

De fictione Iuris.

In hac parte consyder.

1. *Fictionem iuris esse iustissimam. Sæpe n conditores atque interpretes legum aliqua æquitate moti, nimirum ne quis inno cens seueritate iuris læderetur, factum pro non facto, & non factum pro tanquam facto haberi uolunt. Nam cum in omni bus rebus potior debeat esse iustitiæ æquitatisq; ratio, stricto iure l. placuit. C. de iudic. non sunt ueritii ipsæ leges accom modare casibus: etsi regulariter alioqui contrarium fieri oporteat. Nam cum ita lege scribi non possint, ut omnes casus comprehendant, l.neque leges. De ll. consultò factum est à sapientibus, ut nonnumquam etiam leges sua fictione cogerent reb. incidentibus seruire, ac pati aliquam obliquitatem in facto, ut uoluntas earum, quæ omnibus ex æquo ac bono prodesse cupiunt, conseruaretur.*

2. *Vtrum liceat per interpretationem extensiuam tales fictiones iuris ad casus in legibus non comprehensos extendere, sicut cæteræ leges extenduntur, in quibus non est talis fictio. Dd. negant: arg. l. ait Prætor. §. hæc uerba. ff. negot gest. Vt tamen licitum non sit cuiuis, hoc tamen iudicibus uidetur concessum, ut negotij circumstantijs exigentibus ueterum exemplo statu tum fictione extendant ac mitigent.*

ANDREAE ALCIATI IVRECONSVLTI ME-MEDIOLANENSIS,

De Verborum & Rerum significa-tione, Rubrica.

SVMMAE.

2   Verborum acceptio multiplex.
4   Proprietas causæ res, persona, negotium & figura.
5   Limitationum causæ.
7   Figurarum genera & vsus.
15   Verba potentialiter plerunque accipi.
16   Subaudienda, reijcienda & quandoque verba.
19   Verba peritorum vsu in quauis actu accipi.
21   Abusus non, nisi ex causa locum esse.
24   Interpretamur ex mente leges, hominum actus non item, nisi ex causa.
26   Argumenta ad interpretationem referri.
28   Res signaq; plerunque significant.
30   Verbi, dictionis, rei q; discrimen.
32   Verba voce, dictione sensu intelligi.
33   Significationes pro persona etiam sumendæ.

E VERBORVM. Cum inuenta sint verba * vt dicentis intentio-nem exprimant, merito eius vo-luntas in primis spectada est. Co-gnoscitur autem ex eo quod ver-bis ipsa indicant. Ex quatuor tñ mo-dis accipiuntur: ex proprietate, ex vsu, ex abusio-ne, & per interpretationem. Prima species ita in-telligitur vt in quacunque materia, etiam poena-li, verba * extenus capiantur, quatenus proprie-tas sermonis ferre potest, nisi non ita voluisse autorem; præsumamus: tunc enim ex coniectu-

rarefringuntur. Ea varijs † ex causis assumuntur Exre. Quid enim fideret am modica vel leuia-gatur, vt operæpretium non sit dispofitionem legis generaliter in ea seruari ? Ex persona, vt cum lex imponit certam pœnam delicto, & ini-quum esset, si amplissimi gradus homines ca-cecerentur, nam † ex amicitia, adffinitate, oddio, paupertate, maxima excellentia, multa constitu-ta sunt quibus a generalibus regulis recessum est. Ex negotij qualitate, vt si necessitas suadeat, vel periculum sit in mora, vel absurdum aliquid cõsequatur, res ve ad eum casum deueniat, quem maxime autor abominetur, & si qua similia. In hac parte etiam continentur, quæ figuratè dicun-tur: quoniam figuræ ad ornatum orationis per-tinent & * propriecati cohærent: possentq; ferè omnium tam quæ à Grammaticis, quam quæ ab oratoribus traduntur exempla, apud Iuriscon-fultos reperiri, sed satis sit, pauca admonendi cau-sa in medium attulisse. Et † in primis latissima ea est species, quæ † per translationem sit: vt cum domus pro familia, ciuitas pro ciuibus, venter pro qui adhuc in vtero est, ponitur. Parricida non qui patrem * solum occidere, sed & qui ca-teros coniunctos, quorum lex Pompeia memi-nit, intelligitur. Custodia pro ipsis custoditis, seu carcere inclusis b accipitur. Sic cum lex no-xium ære puniri mandat, in bonis patrimo-niove exercendam vltronem interpretamur. Sic & si is qui apud se fugitiuum * receperit, plecti mandetur, non de eo qui iuxta se tenuerit, sim-pliciter accipimus, sed qui refugium præstiterit in domo sua, vel aliena, idq; occultandi causa.

Ad hanc cognitionem etiam pertinent alia fi-gurarum genera, vt quod affectionem * voca-mus, velut cum in lege quandoque, adulter, fur, aleator dicitur, qui hæc crimin. affectat, quam-uis non perfecerit. Et fugitiuus, qui conf.lium fugiendi habuit d, licet adhuc fugam non arri-puerit.

Fig. 4 Alciato, *De verborum significatione*, Frankfurt, 1582, 8vo, pp. 204–5. In this late, inexpensive, edition, the text appears uncluttered and lemmas are banished to the margin

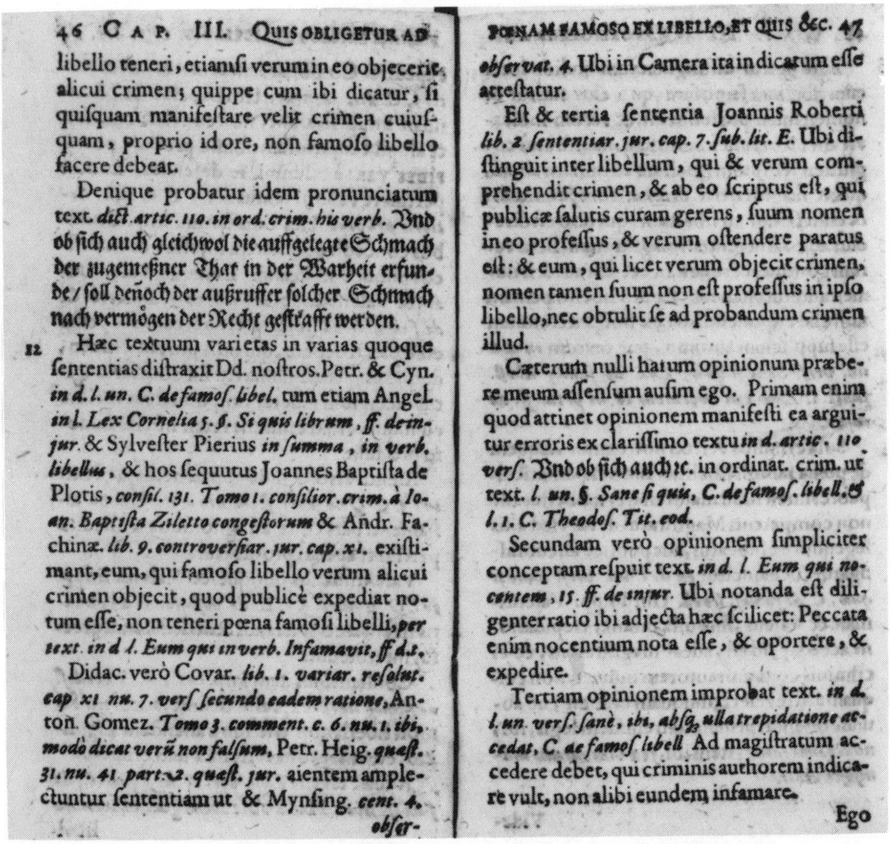

46 CAP. III. QUIS OBLIGETUR AD

libello teneri, etiamsi verum in eo objecerit alicui crimen; quippe cum ibi dicatur, si quisquam manifestare velit crimen cuiusquam, proprio id ore, non famoso libello facere debeat.

Denique probatur idem pronunciatum text. dict. artic. 110. in ord. crim. his verb. Vnd ob sich auch gleichwol die außgelegte Schmach der zugemeßner That in der Warheit erfunde / soll deñoch der außruffer solcher Schmach nach vermögen der Recht gestrafft werden.

12 Hæc textuum varietas in varias quoque sententias distraxit Dd. nostros. Petr. & Cyn. in d. l. un. C. de famos. libel. tum etiam Angel. in l. Lex Cornelia 5. §. Si quis librum, ff. de injur. & Sylvester Pierius in summa, in verb. libellus, & hos sequutus Joannes Baptista de Plotis, consil. 131. Tomo 1. consilior. crim. à Ioan. Baptista Ziletto congestorum & Andr. Fachinæ. lib. 9. controversiar. jur. cap. xi. existimant, eum, qui famoso libello verum alicui crimen objecit, quod publicè expediat notum esse, non teneri pœna famosi libelli, per text. in d. l. Eum qui in verb. Infamavit, ff d. t.

Didac. verò Covar. lib. 1. variar. resolut. cap xi nu. 7. vers. secundo eadem ratione, Anton. Gomez. Tomo 3. comment. c. 6. nu. 1. ibi, modò dicat verũ non falsum, Petr. Heig. quæst. 31. nu. 41 part. 2. quæst. jur. aientem amplectuntur sententiam ut & Mynsing. cent. 4. obser-

PŒNAM FAMOSO EX LIBELLO, ET QUIS &c. 47

observat. 4. Ubi in Camera ita indicatum esse attestatur.

Est & tertia sententia Joannis Roberti lib. 2 sententiar. jur. cap. 7. sub. lit. E. Ubi distinguit inter libellum, qui & verum comprehendit crimen, & ab eo scriptus est, qui publicæ salutis curam gerens, suum nomen in eo professus, & verum ostendere paratus est: & eum, qui licet verum objecit crimen, nomen tamen suum non est professus in ipso libello, nec obtulit se ad probandum crimen illud.

Cæterum nulli harum opinionum præbere meum assensum ausim ego. Primam enim quod attinet opinionem manifesti ea arguitur erroris ex clarissimo textu in d. artic. 110. vers. Vnd ob sich auch rc. in ordinat. crim. ut text. l. un. §. Sane si quis, C. de famos. libell. & l. 1. C. Theodos. Tit. eod.

Secundam verò opinionem simpliciter conceptam respuit text. in d. l. Eum qui nocentem, 15. ff. de injur. Ubi notanda est diligenter ratio ibi adjecta hæc scilicet: Peccata enim nocentium nota esse, & oportere, & expedire.

Tertiam opinionem improbat text. in d. l. un. vers. sanè, ibi, absq; ulla trepidatione accedat. C. de famos. libell. Ad magistratum accedere debet, qui criminis authorem indicare vult, non alibi eundem infamare.

Ego

Fig. 5 Bocerus, *Commentarius . . . de famosis libellis*, Tübingen, 1611, 8vo, pp. 46–7. An example of a text in the *usus modernus Pandectarum* tradition, with its reference to sixteenth-century edicts as well as the Corpus Juris Civilis. The lemmas are incorporated in the text, but distinguished by the use of italics

102   D. ANDREAE ALCIATI .

autoritatem proprie dici. Alioquin Tyrannus improprie de malo principe diceretur, cū
olim sui natura qualēctq; significaret. quod
& de Religiofo & Deuoto dicendum estet,
cum olim hæ uoces in malam partem solum
acciperentur, at hodie so
lum in bonam. Is usus
uarie accipitur. In testa   *De uerborum & rerum*
mentis patriffam, consue   *significatione* [b]
tudo spectanda: in cōtractibus, ipsorum contrahē
tium: in priuslegijs, eius qui concedit. .Præfu
mitur q; secundum eum usum qui communi
ter in ciuitate obseruetur quēlibet agere, nisi
de contraria obseruatione probatum sit, uel
ille usus nuper & citra decēnium inualuerit:
nec em uerisimile est, tam cito omnes in eius
obseruantiam confensiffe. Per abusum uer
k *l. cum filio.* ba regulariter non accipiunt, nisi aliter actus
s. de leg. iij. uel periret[k], uel elusorius redderetur. Idem
& si eadem ratio nos inducat, ut quod ex pro
prio sensu dictum est, ad improprium trahamus : nam ex præsumpta mente disponentis
huiusmodi interpretatio etiam in statutis &
correctorijs positiōibus admittet. Hocq;
casu nihil nos deterrebit, quominus personā
de uniuerfitate dicamus, testamentum de co
l Alex. l. ij. s. dicillis, curatorem pro tutore[l]. Idem & tūc
de leg. j. dicendum erit, cum aliter uerba legis captarentur frausũ; illi fieret. Quapropter si lege
m e. si ciuitas. municipali triticum extra territoriũ abspor
de sent. exc. tare nemini liceat[m], nec farinam deferri con
in 6. ceffum erit. Ex interpretatione quæ admittuntur, si extra uim uerborum ueniāt, soliq;
n l. quidā cũ menti innitantur, nec in contractibus nec in
filium. s. de testamentis obseruantur[n]. Quoniam in eis li
bered. inst. cet primum locum mens obtineat, attamen
eam oportet aliquo modo uerbis salte impro
prijs exprimi. Non ita est in legibus, qm uel
o c. certii. de sola mens legis obligat[o]. Quapropter in eis
reg. iur. argumentũ de similibus ad similia pasfim serua
in 6. tur, & si eadem ratio subsit, una lex ad aliā tra
hitur, nisi correctiones uel pœnalia odiosaue
aliqua inducerent. Quæ nō ita generaliter in
cōtractibus & testamentis locũ habent, si uer
ba aliquo modo nō patiantur, nisi uel natura
rei, uel cōsuetudo adiuuet. Idem si aliqua alia
ratione suadeat. Et ad hanc speciē pertinent
plura argumentorņ genera, ut quod à cōtra
rio sensu dicitur, & quod à connexis, sitq; per
interpretatiōe, ut quod cōmune est dicatur
meũ, ut uerbũ maioris summæ significatiuī
minorē cōtineat, ut quod per me nō possum.
per alios facere prohibear, ut in uno capite di
cta in sequens repetita uideant, ut in simplici

bus mixtũ cōtineat. Aliaq; q; plurima argu
menta quotœ exēpla in topicis Cicero refert.
R ERVM. Verba significant, res significantur. Tametsi & res quandocq; etiam
significent, ut hieroglyphica apud Horum
& Chæremonem, cuius
argumenti & nos carmine libellũ compofuimus,
cui titulus est Emblemata. Sed & ex certis signis
præsumptiones oriũtur,
uerum hæc minime ad hunc tractatum perti
nent, capitur hic ergo significatio & in actionis & in pasfionis sensu, sicut & testamenti factio[p]. Potest & hic locus ex dialecticorņ tra *p l. filius sam*
ditionibus interpretationem assumere, qui *s. de tesla.*
ut Fortunatianus tradit, hanc differētiam inter uerbum, dictionem, & rem, cōstituunt, ut
uerbum sit quod ex se & materialiter (ut uul
go loquimur) prolatũ est, dictio uerbi ipsius
sensum habet, qui in proferentis animo cum
latuiffet per uerbi expreffionem exijt, sic uer
bum cum sensu dictio est, res est quæ exprimi
tur & ex uerbo dictioneq; declaratur: ut si in
terrogem, uerbum si quis, quid comprendit:
si quis, quatenus nudã pronũtiationem propter se respicit, uerbum est, quatenus sensum
habet quem ego ante animo concæpi, dictio
est, masculi uero & fœminæ ex eo uerbo signi
ficatæ, res sunt. Quã rem sic Virg. explicuit:
Littera rem gestam loquif res ipsa medullam
Verbi, quã uiuax mens uidet, intus habet.
Sané in antiquis codicibus aliqui negāt uerbum rerum reperiri, simpliciterq; scriptam
rubricam, De uerborum significatione.
b ¶ SIGNIFICATIONE. Sumitur hæc significatio uarijs modis, nunc habito respectu
ad ipsum proferentem, ut si uir imperitus sit
craffã Minerua accipiantur uerba, nunc con
sideratã eius persona ad quem uerba dirigun
tur, plerumq; & secundum naturam eius rei
de qua sermo habetur, uel quæ in cōtractum
deducitur, accipiantur q; huiusmodi declaratio
etiã si præcisa indefinita generalia uerba sint,
Quoniam nihil impedit quin ad habsem uerisimilemq; casum retrahantur, & boni uiri
arbitratu intelligantur, qui consuetudini loquentis multum tribuet, ex proximis claufu
lis mentem coniectabit, quandocq; & distan
tium rationem ducet, interpretabimurq; ut
cum effectu prolata sint, ut secundum debitũ
ordinem, ut actus potius sustineatur quàm
pereat, ne superuacua sint, sed aliquid operen
tur, ut in potiorē sensum disponant, ut ad am
pliationem inducta nō diminuant, ad liberationem

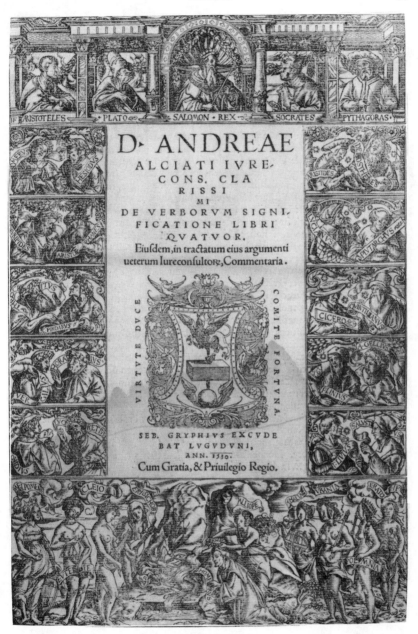

Fig. 7 Alciato, *De verborum significatione*, Lyon, 1530, fol., title-page. The humanist propaganda is unmistakable

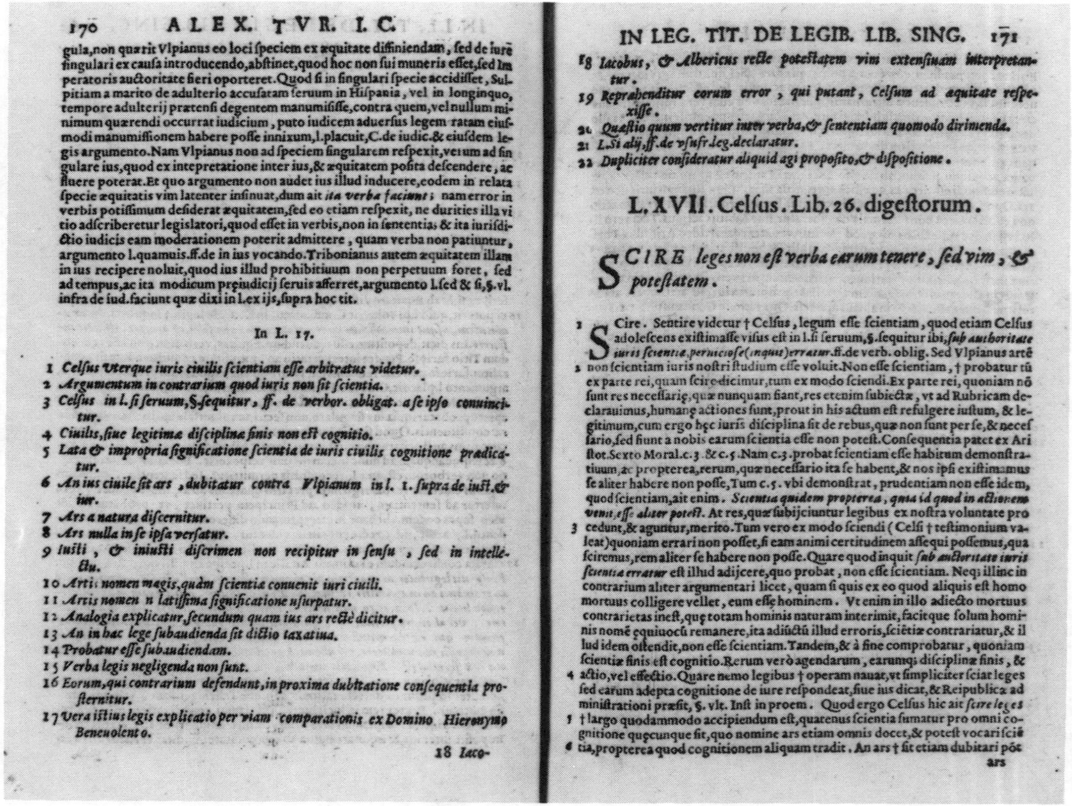

Fig. 8 Turamini, *De legibus*, Venice, 1606, 4to, pp. 170–1. The numbering of points contributes to the appearance of a sustained consecutive argument, although the text is far from constituting a seamless piece of logic (see below, pp. 168–9 (on point 17))

theses it is possible to constitute (as others have done) a sort of ideal-typical bibliography of texts to which a significant number of lawyers make reference; this bibliography would be both temporally and geographically extensive, including books published throughout the Continent, and would cover nearly all the genres of law books both *in more gallico* and *in more italico*.[78] It is also possible to show that many authors envisaged an international audience.[79] National differences would, of course, emerge: German jurists would be found on the whole to refer to a broader range of sources, both geographically and temporally, not only than their French colleagues, whose historical studies after 1550 form a genre on their own, but also their Italian colleagues, who refer copiously to medieval material but much more rarely to near-contemporary studies produced in northern Europe. But one important omission from such a bibliography should be noted: that of the *De legibus* of the famous Jesuit philosopher Francisco Suarez (1548–1617), published apparently for international con-sumption in Coimbra in 1612, Antwerp in 1613, Lyons in 1613 and 1618, and Mainz in 1619 and 1621. He has been singled out by one modern historian of legal interpretation (Charles Lefebvre) as the most rigorous and sophisticated thinker on issues of textual interpret-ation and meaning of his time;[80] but he is not cited by contemporaries, although there is some evidence that his book was sought after later in the century, even in protestant circles.[81] The probable explanation for this is illuminating. Suarez was published expensively in folio, whereas many monographs appeared in smaller, cheaper, formats; and his work was not included under the rubric 'libri juridici' in the book fair catalogues. Instead, his volume, financed initially by the Bishop of Egitania and not, apparently, by a speculative publisher, was produced with the needs of conventual houses and Jesuit colleges in mind, and was addressed to canon, not civil, lawyers.[82] Lefebvre's study points persuasively to the qualities of Suarez's work in

---

[78] The most compendious citation index (above 400 works) is to be found in Valentin Förster. *Interpres sive de interpretatione iuris libri duo*, Wittenberg, 1613.
[79] See Rowan, 'Jurists', p. 79.
[80] See Charles Lefebvre, *Les Pouvoirs du juge en droit canonique*, Paris, 1938, esp. pp. 61–6.
[81] From Thomas James's printed catalogue, it emerges that the Bodleian Library acquired a copy of Suarez's work before 1620; and Professor Germaine Warkentin has kindly let me know that there is a copy recorded in the library catalogue of the Sydney family at Penshurst Place, which was produced no later than 1665.
[82] *Tractatus de legibus, ac deo legislatore*, Coimbra, 1612, ¶4ʳ (dedicatory letter to Alfonso Furtado de Mendoça, Bishop of Egitania): 'tuus est hic liber, quia tuo iussu ac ductu in lucem prodiit'.

comparison with that of his contemporaries, but it did not form part of the common stock of ideas and theories in the first third of the seventeenth century, even if it necessarily falls within the conceptual paradigms of that time. I shall refer to Suarez's work in this regard (below 4.1); my own focus is, however, not on qualitative judgements, but on the interplay of academic, institutional and economic interests, and on the theory and practice of interpretation as evinced by a whole discipline over a long period. In this context, Suarez's text, for all its merits, belongs to a different configuration of forces; and its celebration by Lefebvre belongs to a different (perhaps more Whiggish and positivist) conception of intellectual history.[83]

JUSTINIAN'S PROHIBITION OF COMMENTARY AND ITS INTERPRETATION

1.5.1

Issues of meaning and interpretation arise, as has been said, in all genera of law books to a greater or lesser degree; they are most prominent in direct forms of textual explanation. Commentary is, however, a vexed issue in legal studies. As is well known, Justinian's text itself is a selection from a vast corpus of legal writings which, according to the Emperor himself, had swamped the law itself and needed to be drastically culled and made coherent. As Justinian says in his various prefaces, the Corpus authorized by him and produced by Tribonian and others was designed to be self-sufficient. Although consisting largely of the writing of jurists, it was produced to prevent such writing proliferating further. In the introduction to the Digest (*De confirmatione Digestorum* (*Tanta*) §21) which repeats in part the letters reproduced in the Code (C 1.17.2.18), the Emperor concedes that human law can never be of its nature eternal:

Humani vero iuris conditio semper in infinitum decurrit, et nihil est in ea quod stare perpetuo possit, multas etenim formas edere natura novas deproperat, non desperamus quaedam postea emergi negotia quae adhuc legum laqueis non sunt innodata.

---

[83] Cf. also the allegation of evidence from publishing by legal historians such as the following: Ernst Andersen, *The Renaissance of legal science after the Middle Ages: the German historical school no bird phoenix*, Copenhagen 1974, p. 10: 'The fact that Bartolus's works . . . were reedited in 1588–9 in an expensive edition proves [!] that Bartolus's influence on the study of Roman Law at the University had not come to an end in the last half of the sixteenth century'; Troje, in Coing, *Handbuch*, p. 719: 'Hegendorphinus' *Libri dialecticae legalis V* (1531), eines der bedeutendsten Werke seiner Art, ist relativ selten gedruckt.'

It is the condition of human law always to decline endlessly, no part of it can ever stand unchanged for ever, and nature makes haste to bring forth many new forms; we expect therefore that subsequent [to our endeavours] some situations will arise which thus far have not been captured in the web of the law.

In order to meet this challenge to his law, he ordains that the authority of the Emperor should be sought when such problems rise ('si quid igitur tale contigerit, augustum imploretur remedium'); this is more forcefully stated in *De confirmatione Digestorum* (*Tanta*) §21): 'Si quid vero . . . ambiguum fuerit visum, hoc ad imperiale culmen per iudices referatur et ex auctoritate Augusta manifestetur, cui soli concessum est leges et condere et interpretari' (if anything were to appear obscure, this is to be referred by judges to the very summit of the empire and be made clear by imperial authority, to which alone is granted the right both to make and to interpret laws).

But all interpretation of the Corpus beyond that which is authorized (word-for-word translation into Greek, particular points of difficulty in given passages, paratitla (brief explanatory notes or summaries)) is forbidden on pain of deportation and confiscation of all property (the poena falsi: see D 48.10.1.13), so as to prevent 'verbosi' from generating further 'discordia':

Hoc autem . . . nobis videtur et in praesenti sancire, ut nemo neque eorum, qui in praesenti iuris peritiam habent, nec qui postea fuerint audeat commentarios isdem legibus adnectere: nisi tantum si velit eas in Graecam vocem transformare sub eodem ordine eadem consequentia, sub qua voces Romanae positae sunt (hoc quod Graeci κατὰ πόδα dicunt) et si qui fortisan per titulorum subtilitatem adnotare maluerint et ea quae παράτιτλα nuncupantur componere. Alias autem legum interpretationes, immo magis perversiones eos iactare non concedimus: ne verbositas eorum aliquid legibus nostris adferat ex confusione dedecus, quod et in antiquis edicti perpetui commentatoribus factum est, qui opus moderate confectum huc atque illuc in diversas sententias producentes, in infinitum detraxerunt, ut paene omnis Romana sanctio esset confusio.[84]

---

[84] The Krüger/Mommsen edition has 'ut paene omnem Romanam sanctionem esse confusam' for the last clause. Cf. D deo auctore [De conceptione Digestorum] §12:

. . . nullis iuris peritis in posterum audentibus commentarios illi applicare et verbositate sua supra dicti codicis compendium confundere: quemadmodum et in antiquioribus temporibus factum est, cum per contrarias interpretantium sententias totum ius paene conturbatum est [no jurist (may) presume to compose commentaries [on this Digest] and confuse this brief work with his own verbosity, as was done in past times when almost all of the law was thrown into confusion by the differing opinions of interpreters].

On the connection between the poena falsi, counterfeiting and illicit interpretation, see the suggestive remarks of Waswo, *Language and meaning*, p. 15.

It seems now appropriate for us to decree that no one – neither those who presently practise jurisprudence, nor those who will practise it in future – may presume to compose commentaries on these laws, except only in the case of those who wish to translate them into Greek by the method known to the Greeks as 'foot by foot' (that is in the same order and form as the Latin words), and those who might wish to annotate the titles to explain any fine points, or compose what are called paratitla (summaries).

We hereby prohibit [jurists] from producing any other interpretations, or rather perversions, of our laws: lest their verbosity should bring dishonour to our laws by its confusion, as was done by the commentators on the Perpetual Edict, who by extracting new senses from one or another part of this well-made edict, reduced it to a multitude of meanings, causing confusion to arise in nearly all Roman decrees.

1.5.2

This prohibition is well enough known to be cited in several satires of the law:[85] it was an embarrassment to jurists from the beginnings of the revival of Roman law studies in the twelfth century. This embarrassment can clearly be detected in the early propaedeutic dialogue between student and teacher entitled *Questiones de iuris subtilitatibus*, once attributed to Irnerius himself.[86] The student disingenuously asks how to reconcile three *leges*: C 1.14.1 ('inter aequitatem iusque interpositam interpretationem nobis solis et oportet et licet inspicere' (Emperors alone may investigate the relationship between equity and justice): cf. D *De confirmatione Digestorum* (*Tanta*) §21; C 1.14.12); D 1.3.12 ('Non possunt omnes articuli singillatim aut legibus aut senatus consultis compraehendi: sed cum in aliqua causa sententia eorum manifesta est, is qui iurisdictione praeest ad similia procedere atque ita ius dicere debet' (it is not possible for every point individually to be covered by laws or in senatus consulta; but if in any case their meaning is clear, the president of the court shall apply them to similar cases and declare what the law is)) and D 1.3.37 ('optima enim est legis interpres consuetudo' (the best interpreter of laws is custom)). Which, asks the student, of the Emperor, the judge and custom may interpret the law? The teacher is characteristically analytical in his reply:

Est interpretatio quae, quamvis recte se habeat, nichil [tamen] in se necessitatis habet: disputantium forte seu precipientium. alia est quae

---

[85] Agrippa, *De incertitudine*, xciv; Noël du Fail, *Les Contes et discours d'Eutrapel* (1585), Rennes, 1603, fol. 24ᵛ; Montaigne, *Essais*, iii.13, p. 1042.

[86] By Hermann Fitting, in his edition of the *Questiones*, Berlin, 1894.

necessitatem quidem habet, sed in specie dumtaxat: iudicis enim interpretatio tenet in eo negotio quod ipse decidit, se[d] non est aliis iudicibus hoc
exemplo iudicandum. que autem generaliter optinet, principi competit soli.
eiusmodi est et illa quae consuetudine inducta est, ne tamen illis relinquatur
ullus locus que prosiliunt ex errore.

There is a form of interpretation which, although it is rightly called
interpretation, has no necessary force, e.g. an interpretation by disputants or
teachers. There is a form of interpretation with necessary force, but which
applies only to individual cases; this is the form practised by a judge in
reaching judgments, but it cannot be invoked as precedent by other judges.
The form of interpretation which has general force may be exercised by the
Emperor alone. Interpretation with general force is also by custom, except
where custom is based on error.[87]

We shall return to the terms of this answer below (3.1.3); it is sufficient
to note here that the last clause ('except where custom is based on
error') lets the 'disputant and teacher' back in at the highest level, for
if they can establish the error, they become effectively general
interpreters of the law. This circular path from modest to grandiose
claims by mediators of meaning or truth is characteristic of other
aspects of legal interpretation, as we shall see.

1.5.3

As well as being an embarrassment to jurists themselves, Justinian's
prohibition has been an embarrassment to historians. More than one
attempt has been made to find a convenient medieval imperial edict
releasing jurists from the interdict. Such an edict might explain the
sudden expansion in Roman law studies better than developments in
scholastic practices or the rediscovery of the text of the Digest and of
its relevance to the Code. Among the significant moments in this
process, there has been cited an exchange between the Emperor
Henry IV, Lotharius and Azo, the tacit approval of the Emperor
Lotharius II, and, most recently, the 'double privilege' granted by
Frederick I Barbarossa to academics which he caused to be inserted in
the Code (4.13.5) in 1159.[88] This was referred to in a polemical work

---

[87] *Ibid.*, p. 57.
[88] See Myron Piper Gilmore, *Argument from Roman law in political thought 1200–1600*, Cambridge,
Mass., 1941, pp. 15ff.; Kisch, *Gestalten und Probleme*, pp. 67–8; Kelley, 'Civil science in the
Renaissance: the problem of interpretation', in *The languages of political thought in Early Modern
Europe*, ed. Anthony Pagden, Cambridge, 1987, pp. 57–78; and 'Jurisconsultus perfectus', p.
94; Rashdall, *Universities*, i.113ff., 143f., contains a more sceptical view. There is a
considerable literature on the precise meaning and scope of Justinian's prohibition: see F.

by the jurist Joannes Oldendorp (?1480–1567) in 1543; but it is not the statute which would provide the hoped-for, neat historical explanation. Barbarossa's 'privilegium duplex' is not granted just to jurists (although they are named), but to all academics; it is 'duplex' because it grants them both protection where they teach and on journeys, and the right to be tried in the local court of their election. Oldendorp invokes the edict to point to the allegedly shameful treatment of a priest-academic of Lutheran sympathies called Joannes Meynertzhagen, who was hounded out of Cologne by pettifogging lawyers (*legulei*) of the Catholic party for having given communion in the two kinds. He had not been granted the right (accorded under C 4.13.5) to appeal to the Archbishop's Court, where he would have been assured of a favourable hearing by the then Archbishop, who was sympathetic to Reformers.[89] It is true that Oldendorp invokes the Justinian prohibition in C 1.17.2 to condemn Meynertzhagen's enemies for the casual allegation of the 'Commentators' (see above 1.1.2); but there is no connection made in the text between this and the issue of privilege.[90]

1.5.4

It seems much more likely that the growth of commentary was simply tolerated by Emperors who may not even have been aware of their

Pringsheim, 'Justinian's prohibition of commentaries to the Digest', *Revue internationale des droits de l'antiquité*, v (Mélanges Fernand de Visscher iv) (1950), 383–415; Georg S. Mandarikis, 'Justinians Verbot der Gesetzeskommentierung', *Zeitschrift der Savigny-Stiftung für Rechtsgeschichte: Romanische Abetilung*, lxxiii (1956), 369–75; Manfred Fuhrmann, 'Interpretatio. Notizen zur Wortgeschichte', in *Sympotica Franz Wieacker*, Göttingen, 1970, pp. 80–110, esp. 98ff.

[89] See R. Ennen, *Geschichte der Stadt Köln*, Cologne, 1863–80, iv.448f.; Erik Wolf, 'Oldendorp', in *Grosse Rechtsdenker der deutschen Geistesgeschichte*, 2nd ed., Tübingen, 1951, pp. 171f.; Joannes Oldendorp, *Responsio ad impiam delationem parochorum coloniensium, de communicatione sacramenti corporis et sanguinis Christi sub utraque specie; Confutatio iudicii abominabilis quorundam secundariorum (ut sese vocant) atque leguleorum Coloniae Agrippinae, dictati haud ita pridem adversus Dn. Ioannem Meynerzhagium; Interpretatio privilegii duplicis, quod Friderichus primus, omnium imperii ordinum consensu, summa aequitatis ratione motus, concessit bonarum literarum studiosis . . . ex constitutione habita C. ne fili pro patria* [Marburg], 1548, pp. 5–11. On Meynerzhagen, there is a contemporary broadsheet preserved in the Herzog-August-Bibliothek, Wolfenbüttel (press-mark 79 Jur 2⁰(4)), and a refutation of his ideas by Johannes Stammel.

[90] Nor is there any mention of C 4.13.5 by those who list either the privileges of doctors of laws or by those who record the privileges of the university of Bologna: see Petrus Lenauderius, *De privilegiis doctorum*, in *Tractatus iuris universi*, xviii.3–21; Ludovicus Bologninus, *Commentaria in privilegium Theodosii imperatoris pro universitate Bononensium* (1388), Bologna, 1491 (on which, see Rashdall, *Universities*, i.142). On citation of C 4.13.5, see Robinson, Gordon and Fergus, *Introduction*, p. 95; Alciato, *De verborum significatione*, p. 146; and Rashdall, *Universities*, i.143f. The most comprehensive treatment of privilege is that by Pierre Rebuffi, *De privilegiis universitatum collegiorum et bibliopolarum . . .*, Frankfurt, 1585.

powers of confiscation and banishment for infringement of Justinian's decree. Such is the impression given by Budé's scornful account of Accursius' reaction to the prohibition, the force of which Accursius acknowledged and confessed to be an unequivocal condemnation of his gloss. Budé, like Oldendorp, was using the prohibition for polemical purposes, to devalue the work of all *mos italicus* jurists, and especially to inveigh against their misappropriation of the Greek passages of the Digest and Code and the abuse of the permitted forms of paratitla and brief annotation.[91] Equally polemical is the use made of the prohibition by Johannes Fichard (1512–81), who, in his introduction to the 1535 edition of the *De legis interpretatione* of Stephanus de Federicis (see below 3.4.1), asks the then powerful imperial prochancellor Mathias Held to take on the rôle of a new Tribonian and to eliminate much of the existing corpus of legal interpretation by the authority of C 1.17.2.21, which is quoted in full (somewhat ironically, in view of the text of de Federicis which follows). Fichard's concern is directly political; he sees the proliferation of secondary legal materials as a contributory factor to the political and religious unrest of his age, and envisages the production of a clear, unambiguous code of law as a bulwark against it. The *Constitutio criminalis carolina* is singled out for praise in this respect, especially as it specifies that ignorance of the law is no excuse in its preface and first paragraph: a lucid, generally recognized set of statutes is clearly preferred to any amount of jurisprudential interpretation.[92]

---

[91] Budé, *Annotationes in Pandectas* in *Opera omnia*, Basle, 1557, ii.ii. p. 106, quoted by Kisch, *Gestalten und Probleme*, p. 46n; see also Kelley, *History, law and the human sciences*, vii.268.

[92] Stephanus de Federicis, *De interpretatione iuris commentarii IIII*, ed. Ioannes Fichardus, Frankfurt, [1535], preface, a iv[r]:

atque utinam quod ille caetera quidem summus Imperator obtinere non potuit, neque satis cavere, saltem hoc saeculo aliquando contingat, ut et immensa illa infinitaque voluminum copia, diligenti iudicio repurgaretur, adque necessarium numerum redigeretur, et posteris suis etiam modus statueretur . . . In qua quidem re, clarissime Mathia, quum alter ipse huius aetatis apud Opt[imum] Max[imum] Imperatorem [Carolum] Tribonianus existas, et pro summa eruditione prudentiaque tua, et excellenti magistratus tui authoritate, tantum praestare possis, quantum alius fere nemo . . .

But I only hope that what that otherwise excellent emperor [*scilicet* Justinian] did not manage to bring about or stipulate, at least would come to pass at some time in this age, so that the almost boundless production of volumes might be reduced by diligence and good judgement to the smallest possible number, and moderation be imposed on his successors . . . in which matter, honoured Mathias, as the Tribonian of this age in the service of our present emperor [Charles V], because of your learning, prudence and high authority in the exercise of your office, you would be able to stand out better than almost anyone else . . . See also D 22.6 and *Constitutio criminalis carolina* §1 on the question of the ignorance of the law.

1.5.5

Other reactions to the prohibition are also found. The commentator Jacobus de Ravanis had used legal topics (see below 2.5) ingeniously to provide lawyers with a line of defence: by translating C 1.14.12 'si enim in praesenti leges condere soli imperatori concessum est, et leges interpretari solum dignum imperio esse oportet' into the form 'cuius est legem condere, eius est et interpretari' (to whomsoever it falls to make laws, to him also it falls to interpret them), he establishes that by the locus *a maiore et minore* (see below 2.5) that interpretation is less than legislation, and that it can therefore be engaged in by jurists without fear of the poena falsi. A similar defence is found in the writings of the fifteenth-century jurist Bartolomeo Cipolla [Caepolla] (d. 1477), who claims that to determine the sense of a law *ex mente legis* is not to interpret transgressively in the sense of the interdict; this line of argument is that enshrined in the distinction *interpretatio necessaria/probabilis* (see below 3.1.3), as Pietro Andrea Gammaro (d. 1528) makes clear in his *De extensionibus* (*c.* 1510). The *mos gallicus* writer François de Connan, in claiming that judges do not interpret the law in the sense of the Justinian interdict, adopts a similar defence, but his colleague Eguinaire Baron (1495–1555), in a famous lecture delivered at the University of Bourges in the mid-1540s, argues by implication that all *mos italicus* jurisprudence was made invalid by C 1.17.2.21.[93]

---

[93] See Kelley, *Foundations*, p. 100, and Du Fail, *Les Contes et discours d'Eutrapel*, fols. 24–5:
Eguinaire Baron . . . auec son compagnon Duarenus, tous deux Bretons, auoit tiré des vniuersitez et nations tant en deçà que de là des monts, tous ceux qui vouloient apprendre le Droit en sa netteté et splendeur. Il se courrouçoit asprement contre ceux qui auoient obscurez la beauté des loix, par vne infinie multitude et amas de commentaires: et entre autres vn iour que monsieur l'hospital, lors conseiller au parlement de Paris, et depuis Chancelier de France allant aux Grands-Ours de Rion le vint escouter . . . le bonhomme estant dans sa chaire, accoustré d'vne robe de taphetas auec sa barbe grise longe et epoisse, voyant qu'en son eschole y auoit des auditeurs non accoustumez, commence à plaindre les deffences que l'Empereur Iustinien auoit fait de non escrire et faire commentaires sur le Droit Ciuil, disant à ce propos, comme il estoit facetieux, et riche en tous ses discours, que si vn chien a pissé en quelque lieu que ce soit, il n'y aura mastin, leurier, ne briquet, d'vne lieuë à la ronde, qui là ne vienne leuer la iambe, et pisser comme ses compagnons. Ainsi Bartole, Balde ou autre Protenotaire du Droit, ait en quelque passage, voire tout esloigné et hors bord qu'il soit, traité vn point et disputé, toute la tribale et suite des autres Docteurs viendront illec compisser l'œuvre et mesme passage, y escrire par conclusions, limitations, notables raisons de douter et decider, ampliations, intellectes repetitions et autres aparats du mestier, et feroient grand' conscience traiter les contrats, testamens, et successions, sinon en autre titre à trauers pays, et tout au rebours.
See also Jacques de Révigny, gl. ad C 1.14.12.3, cited by Otte, *Dialektik und Jurisprudenz*, p. 205; Caepolla, *De verborum et rerum significatione doctissima commentaria*, Lyon, 1551, col. 134

There are replies to such a position, which include a few spirited defences of the Accursian gloss. Boniface Amerbach (1495–1562), in his *Defensio interpretum iuris civilis* (1524–5) argues that interpretation is necessary since laws are general and cannot encompass the infinite diversity of human actions and events without the intervention of the jurist (this is very much the case made for equity over justice by Aristotle in *Nicomachean Ethics*, v.10, quoted above 1.2.3); and Johannes Saxonius (d. 1561) in his *Assertio de glossis Accursiani et Bartoli* of 1548 claims that C 1.17.2.21, D *De conceptione Digestorum* (*Deo auctore*) §12 and D *De confirmatione Digestorum* (*Tanta*) §21 are obsolete as law, not only because circumstances have changed (as Justinian himself envisaged could happen) but also because the Emperor and his team of jurists left behind many antinomiae in the Corpus Juris Civilis which glossators and postglossators have had to struggle manfully to resolve; their activity could not thus be described as otiose.[94]

1.5.6

A more qualified defence is found in the work of Alessandro Turamini (?1556–1605) and Valentin Forster (or Förster) (1539–1608). It is noted in these texts that Ulpian refers in one text to jurists as 'iuris conditores', i.e. legislators (C 2.12.23), which would seem to give them the authority to interpret laws; but this was thought no more than 'honoris caussa', and to be superseded by the more assertive imperial constitutions C 1.14.1. and C 1.14.12, according to which Emperors alone may interpret the law. The solution adopted to this apparent antinomy is that of Azo and Accursius: in interpreting, 'ratio legis debet attendi in sua generalitate, id est in generis singulorum, non in singulis generum' (the purpose of the law should be considered in its generality, that is, in the way general laws apply to individual cases, not in the way individual cases should give rise to general laws). The laws which the Emperor alone may interpret are

---

('illud quod fit ex mente legis, non dicitur esse interpretatio, sed ipsa lex'); Gammaro, *De extensionibus*, x, in *Tractatus iuris universi*, xviii.248; Connan, *Commentarii iuris civilis*, i.11, fols. 45–8.

94 See Kisch, *Gestalten und Probleme*, pp. 67ff., 152f. Saxonius' point has been made elegantly by André Tournon in a recent article ('Self-interpretation in Montaigne's *Essais*', *Yale French Studies*, lxiv (1983), 63: 'if two assertions are logically incompatible and cannot be related, a third voice has only to intervene indicating the difficulty, and coherence is restored, and meaning explicit or implicit becomes possible. A system constructed in such a fashion requires exegesis, makes it legitimate and guides it . . .').

'singula generum, non genera singulorum' (individual laws applying to general cases, not general laws in their particular application).[95] There is a hint here of the Aristotelian distinction between equity and justice, and between the generality of laws and the particularity of cases, which is very frequently invoked, even when the prohibition itself is not quoted.

1.5.7

Some jurists pass over the embarrassing interdict in silence, or merely refer to it without producing an apology;[96] Matthaeacius adopts a more complex position. In a chapter dealing with the authority of jurisprudential opinion, he reviews several well-known versions of legal authority, including the view that the most authoritative opinion is that held by the majority of jurists expressing an opinion on a given case. This is explicit in the Theodosian Code (1.4.1); there a solution is even provided for cases in which an equal number of opinions is expressed for both sides ('let the opinion of Papinianus prevail'). Matthaeacius refers to 'recent' jurists whose opinions had been given particular weight (Filippo de Dexia [Decius] (1454–1536), Jason de Mayno (1435–1519), Alciato, Zazius), but concludes that 'communis opinio' is still most to be revered. He cites Justinian's prohibition, and the assertion of imperial authority as a solution to questions of interpretation, and then addresses the following scathing aside to his presumed readership of legal students:

Verum post Iustiniani imperium supra mille ab hinc annis coepit communis haec iurisprudentium opinio regiam sibi arrogare auctoritatem, ac potestatem, et principium, seu legislatorum vires in omnibus exercere. Haec una Imperatoribus ad maiora intentis et occupatis, terrarum orbi consulere, iura legesque dare, et iuris responsa, haud secus, ac antiquorum oracula consulentibus ferre et praescribere ausa est. Quanto igitur in honore habendi sunt iurisconsulti, vos hinc facile coniicere potestis.[97]

---

[95] Turamini, *De legibus*, pp. 145–60; Förster, *Interpres*, pp. 6–11 (who refers back to de Federicis, Rogerius, Caepolla, Mathesilanus, Hotman, Mercier, Doneau and Everaerts). Reference is also made to Azo's gl. 7 ad C 1.14.5 (*ibid.*, p. 3: and Horn, *Aequitas*, pp. 31–3) and Aquinas, *Summa theologiae*, 2a 2ae 120 1 ad 1. See also below 3.1.3.

[96] E.g. Alciato, *Lucubrationes in ius civile*, Basle, 1557, pp. 86ff.; Jacques Cujas, *Paratitla*, Paris, 1569, introduction, both cited by Kelley, *History, law and the human sciences*, vi.778, v.179; see also Joannes Dhumbert, *In omnes titulos novem primorum librorum Codicis Justiniani . . . explicationes*, Lyon, 1558, p. 13; Rebuffi, *In titulum Digestorum de verborum et rerum significatione* (1557), Lyon, 1586, pp. 1–2.

[97] *De via et ratione*, fol. 125. Matthaeacius is one of the few jurists to refer to the Theodosian Code's rule about Papinianus (*ibid.* fol. 123).

Legal opinion began indeed some thousand years after Justinian's reign as Emperor to arrogate to itself authority and influence and to exercise the powers of princes and legislators in all domains. Such opinion has dared, while Emperors have been preoccupied by and intent on higher things, to give legal advice to the world, to lay down laws and statutes, to make, no less than the oracles of old, authoritative replies and to prescribe courses of action to those seeking legal advice. You may easily infer from this in what great esteem therefore jurists are to be held.

THE DEFENCE OF LEGAL PEDAGOGY

1.6.1

There is more than a hint in the texts quoted above that jurists have usurped a rôle which was not theirs. A similar sense may be drawn from the defences made of the use of D 50.16 *De verborum significatione* as a text for introducing students to the law. This title supplanted the Institutes and D 50.17 (*De regulis iuris antiqui*) by the 1530s, even in quite traditional universities; its use needed justification, not only because it is a treatise on terms rather than a pedagogical tool, but also because it contains at least one text which seems to doubt the value of approaching the law through terms (D 50.16.6.1; see below 3.6.1). Why then begin with it? Pierre Rebuffi (1487–1557) of Toulouse gives an ingenious answer:

Iste titulus in fine Digestorum, et non in principio locatus fuerit, quia non potest elici verborum significatio, nisi prius verbis positis. Et sic necesse fuit leges praescribere, et ex illis postea vocabula colligere, ut Iurisconsulti fecerunt, qui post quinquaginta libros Digestorum haec vocabula ex illis extraxerunt. Nempe ex nihilo nihil colligi potest, arg. 1. decem ff. de verb. oblig. Sic dicit Iuriscons. de tit. de regulis iuris 1.1 in tit. proximo ibi *sed ex iure quod est regula fiat*. Ergo oportuit prius ius scribere et postea ex iure verborum significationes, et regulas elicere, ut factum exstitit. Et sic non est absurdum, sed necessarium eum, qui iura civilia profiteri cupit, ab initio hunc titul. audire et memoriae mandare, quamvis Iurisconsulti in fine locaverint.[98]

This title was placed at the end of the Digest and not at the beginning, because the signification of words cannot be elicited from them until the words themselves are set down. Thus it was necessary to write the laws first, and afterwards to collect together words from them; as was indeed done by the jurists who after finishing the fifty books of the Digest extracted these

---

[98] *In titulum Digestorum de verborum et rerum significatione*, p. 3. The maxim 'nihil ex nihilo colligi potest' is Hippocratic (see *On regimen*, i.4). On the relationship of *lex* to *regula* referred to here, see below chapter 3, note 263.

words from them. For nothing can be extracted from nothing (arg. in D 45.1.116) . . . And the jurist says in the first rule of the title after the *De verborum significatione* that rules (*regulae*) are made from existing law. Therefore the law had first to be written and afterwards the meaning of the words of the law and the rules (*regulae*) elicited from it, as indeed has been done in this case. Thus for any who wish to profess civil law, it is not absurd but necessary to listen to and to commit to memory this title (the *De verborum significatione*) from the very beginning, although the jurists placed it at the end of the *Digest*.

According to this account, the title *De verborum significatione*, although situated nearly at the end of the Digest and explicitly parasitic on its text, none the less comes to precede the study of the laws themselves and in a sense to dominate them by authorizing the understanding of the words of which they are composed. 'Et sic non est absurdum', declares Rebuffi, referring here both directly to the logic of interpretation,[99] and indirectly to the apparent illogicality of asserting that the instruments of sense – words – are logically prior to sense. An art – the art of understanding and construing words – which is dependent on and posterior to a set of legal rules or norms (which they are used to embody) comes to precede these rules or norms and act as their origin; and as the *De verborum significatione* is to the Digest, so is the interpreter to the law itself. From an apparently subordinate and humble position, he emerges through the structures of pedagogy and the practice of linguistic analysis as the master, not the servant, of the text. One is here irresistibly reminded of Nietzsche's aphorism: 'In Wahrheit ist Interpretation ein Mittel selbst, Herr über etwas zu werden.'[100]

In different ways, the dominant position of the interpreter emerges in the practice of both *mos italicus* and *mos gallicus*. Among practitioners of the latter, systematizers of the law and those who insist that it be understood historically are less bound to the text of the law than to jurisprudence itself; their authority is vested in *recta ratio*, that which Cicero saw as the principle of all law and justice ('est enim lex nihil aliud nisi recta ratio, imperans honesta, prohibens contraria'[101]

---

[99] Rebuffi also uses the catachrestic phrase 'nec erit *omnino* absurdum' (my italics: p. 4). See also Otte, *Dialektik und Jurisprudenz*, p. 81.

[100] *Der Wille zur Macht*, 643, in *Werke*, ed. Karl Schlechta (1969), Stuttgart, 1980, iii.489; cf. also his reference to the 'ungöttliche' or 'unendliche Möglichkeiten' of interpretation (*Also sprach Zarathustra*, ibid., ii.250).

[101] Cf. above 1.2.4; Cicero, *Philippics*, xi.28; *De legibus*, i.6.18; Gammaro, *De extensionibus*, cl, in *Tractatus iuris universi*, xviii.257: 'licet lex mutetur tamen ratio legis est aeterna et immutabilis'; this quotation is attributed to Panormitanus (alias *abbas siculus*, alias Nicholaus de Tudeschis (Tedeschi] (1389–1445)).

(the law is nothing other than right reason, prescribing those things which are honourable and prohibiting those which are not)). Practitioners of the *mos italicus*, who accept the authority of texts, subordinate themselves to the *ratio legis* or to the *mens legislatoris*: 'interpretari est sensum latentem et verbis non expressum ex ratione legis depromere' (to interpret is to derive the latent sense not explicit in the text from the *ratio legis*), declare some; others assert that 'veras legum interpretationes, non in cumulandas doctorum opiniones, sed in explorandam mentem legislatoris consistere' (true interpretation of the law consists not in the accumulation of the opinions of good authorities, but in the exploration of the intention of the legislator); yet others adduce right reason, as do practitioners of the *mos gallicus*, describing interpretation as 'ex ratione, sententia et regulis cum rectaque ratione id quod in legibus obscurum est explanare' (the explanation of that which is obscure in the text of the law by appeal to the *ratio legis*, the intention of the legislator and rules, through the application of right reason).[102] In all these question-begging descriptions, which will be examined in depth in the following chapters, the priority of the text and its producer is acknowledged, but the fact remains that it is the interpreter who determines the sense or 'makes it visible' (quite literally in some cases, as in that of Detlev Langenbeck who turns Alciato's *De verborum significatione* into a wall chart).[103] Moreover, through strategies which will be examined in detail below (3.4.4), the jurist, already the acknowledged guardian of the specialist language of the law, turns himself into the arbiter of general language usage.[104] Even grammar is said to fall in a special way in the domain of the legal interpreter, who ends up by making extensive claims to intellectual territory; Cujas, for example, states quite

---

[102] Turamini, *De legibus*, p. 46; Matthaeus Gribaldus alias Mopha, *De methodo ac ratione studendi libri III*, Cologne, 1553, p. 64; Helfrich-Ulrich Hunnius, *De authoritate*, Marburg, 1630, p. 229.

[103] *D. Andreae Alciati . . . libri de verb [orum] sig[nificatione] in gratiam studiosorum in perutilem et iucundam tabulam contracti*, Cologne, 1555.

[104] See Hunnius, *De authoritate*, p. 264:

Quod si accidat ut alius sit communis usus loquendi apud omnes vulgares, alius vero apud doctos et literatos, tunc ille attendi debet qui est hominum doctorum et literatorum cum praesumatur legislatorem cum doctis potius quam cum indoctis et illiteratis loqui voluisse.

If it should happen that the general manner of speech diverges from that of learned and literate men, then attention should be paid to the latter, as it is to be presumed that the legislator would have wished to communicate with learned men rather than the illiterate and uninstructed.

bluntly that 'iurisconsulti sunt peritiores verborum quam grammatici' (jurists are more expert in words than grammarians).[105] Historians who date the existence of a pluridisciplinary hermeneutics from the writing of Johann Conrad Dannhauer's *Idea boni interpretis* of 1630 seem to have overlooked the grandiose pretensions of interpreters of law.[106]

Also explicit (but not systematized) in sixteenth-century commentaries is the distinction between *subtilitas intelligendi*, *subtilitas explicandi* and *subtilitas applicandi* attributed to Rambach.[107] Here the most important division for the Renaissance is between the pedagogical function (*intelligere, explicare*) and the legal practice of magistrates.[108] But both pedagogues and judges, for all their differences, come to supplant the law in a similar way. The rôle of the teacher in a discipline based upon texts, like that of the *mos italicus*, is to act as mediator; he must 'make visible' the text and its sense and yet remain transparent or invisible himself; but in the nature of things, it is his words, not those of the text that he transmits, which impose themselves on his pupil. Equally, judges are enjoined not to make, but only to apply the law; but in their application of law to particular cases, they threaten to become superior to the law as, in Aristotle's terms, equity becomes superior to justice by 'rectifying' it (see above 1.2.3). This danger was to become the particular preoccupation of the nineteenth-century British legal thinker John Austin;[109] but it is

---

[105] *Ad titulum de verborum significationibus* [sic] *commentarius*, Frankfurt, 1959, p. 273. Kelley, in *History, law and the human sciences*, v.785, quotes Rebuffi as saying 'grammarians will not fight with jurists if they understand them aright, for justice must have the priority'. Rebuffi's text in fact reads 'Grammaticus forte non pugnare cum iuriscons[ulto] si utrique recte intelligantur' (i.e. 'there would be no disagreement between the grammarian [Isidore] and the jurist [Alciato] if each is understood correctly'): *Explicatio ad quatuor primos Pandectarum libros*, Lyon, 1589, p. 1; Kelley seems to have derived 'for justice must have the priority' from Rebuffi's record of the debate about the relative antiquity of the words 'iustitia' and 'ius' ('iustitia prius tempore fuit': see also gl. ad D 1.1.1: 'auctor iuris est homo, iustitiae deus'). But the sentiment Kelley records is expressed elsewhere by Rebuffi (*In titulum Digestorum de verborum et rerum significatione*, p. 4). See also Alciato's attack on Valla in *De verborum significatione*, pp. 186–203, and in *Parerga*, ii.7 (*Opera*, Basle, 1582, iv.323), quoted by Viard, *Alciat*, pp. 212–13. Rebuffi refers in fact to another chapter of the *Parerga* (i.29, *Opera*, iv.304) in the passage cited by Kelley.
[106] See Henry-Evrard Hasso-Jaeger, 'Studien zur Frühgeschichte der Hermeneutik', *Archiv für Begriffsgeschichte*, xviii (1974), 35–84. Dannhauer's book declares on its title-page that it is 'omnium facultatum studiosis perquam utilis'.
[107] See Hans-Georg Gadamer, *Wahrheit und Methode* (1960), 3rd ed., Tübingen, 1972, pp. 290–1.
[108] See Caepolla, *De verborum et rerum significatione doctissima commentaria*, p. 35; and below 3.4.1.
[109] *Lectures on jurisprudence* (1828–32), 4th ed., London, 1873, pp. 642ff.

found in sixteenth-century texts, where the Platonic topos 'non leges magistratibus sed magistratus legibus dominentur' is frequently quoted.[110] Legal practitioners who interpret or apply the law on behalf of clients – advocates on behalf of defendants, notaries on behalf of testators, and legal draftsmen on behalf of legislators – threaten to become dominant in the same way, and for the same reason: the interpreter, the magistrate, the notary, the draftsman are 'interpositae personae' who embody the meaning of the legislator, the voice of equity, the intention of the client or the science of law by their act of mediation.[111] The humble, subservient, neutral transmitter of the law desired by Justinian seems in practice to be something altogether more substantial and assertive. In such uncontroversial definitions of the work of interpretation as the following (by Förster), one can detect the confident declaration of institutional functions and exclusive access to texts, in which the interests of the legal profession are delicately clothed in innocuous-sounding, abstract procedures:

Textum iuris qua verbum aut integram orationem obscurum et ambiguum, aut difficilem et perplexum, non recte lectum vel intellectum, congrue exponere et planum, facilem, iustum atque genuinum reddere, causas etiam sive rationes ipsarum constitutionum et notanda subiicere, verba legum et scripta cum mente sententiaque conferre, verumque sensum earum elicere, quae adversari videbuntur amoliri, et alia huc pertinentia expedire.[112]

To explain in appropriate terms the text of the law *qua* word or sentence where it is obscure or ambiguous, difficult or puzzling, wrongly read or understood; to convey the text in full, simply, correctly and authentically; to set down the purpose or cause of laws and to draw attention to salient points; to compare the words of the law or of documents with the thought and intention they embody; to elicit the true sense of laws; to refute that which appears to be inconsistent with this sense, and set forth other pertinent points.

Other indications may be found of this reversal of authority between text and interpreter. In Alciato's commentary on D 50.16, the first sentence (to both the introductory essay and the commentary proper) reads 'cum inventa sint verba, ut dicentis sententiam

---

[110] *Laws*, iv.715D; Turamini, *De legibus*, p. 154.
[111] See Agrippa, *De incertitudine*, xciii–xciv; and on the 'interposita persona' who bears a message or mediates a meaning, Jerome Sapcote, *Ad primas leges Digestorum de verborum et rerum significatione*, Venice, 1579, p. 5. [112] *Interpres*, pp. 12–13.

exprimant, merito eius voluntas in primis spectanda est'[113] (as words
are chosen to express the meaning of their speaker, it is right to look
first at his intention); but within a few pages he considers both the
topic of definition (i.e. the 'objective' meaning of words determined
by the legal interpreter) and the authority of 'prudent men' (who are
none other than jurists themselves) in deciding word usage.[114] This
authority mirrors that – in itself equally surprising – of words over
facts: a much-quoted maxim of Modestinus is 'interdum plus valet
scriptura quam quod actum est' (the written record is sometimes
worth more than the facts of the case) (D 33.2.19).[115] Words are
'instrumenta docendi discernendique' (instruments for teaching and
perceiving),[116] and as instruments seem subordinate to their function;
but they take on pedagogical and epistemological priority once they
come to supplant the object, event or fact to which they refer. It is
perhaps for this reason that jurists from the school of Bologna onwards
appropriate for themselves so eagerly the developments in the
analysis of language of their day, whether this be the 'logica nova' (by
the postglossators), Agricola's revision of dialectics (by Hegendorf),
Quintilian's analysis of figures (by Alciato), Hermagoras' version of
topics (by Hotman) or Ramus' dichotomies (by Frey and Fraunce)
(see below 2.5). Clearly, lawyers had to react to developments in
grammar, dialectic and rhetoric, as their trade was so closely related
to linguistic and logical issues; but they also appropriated these
developments to maintain the integrity of their discipline and to
strengthen its claim to independence and superiority. The extent to
which these appropriations constitute a break with past analytical
practice will be examined in greater detail below; one may merely

---

[113] *De verborum significationes*, pp. 10, 104; the topos in the Digest is D 33.10.7.2 (Celsus)
quorsum nomina . . . nisi ut demonstraverit voluntatem dicentis? . . . nam . . . prior atque
potentior est, quam vox, mens dicentis . . . (what is the use of words except to indicate the
wishes of the speaker? . . . for the intention of the speaker is prior to and more powerful than
the spoken word). The topos, or Alciato's formulation of it, is frequently cited: see Jean
Breche, *Ad titulum Pandectarum de verborum et rerum significatione commentarii*, Lyon, 1556, p. 19;
Rebuffi, *In titulum de verborum et rerum significatione*, p. 3; and *A discourse upon the exposicion and
understanding of statutes* (c. 1567), ed. Samuel E. Thorne, San Marino, 1942, p. 140: 'for synce
that wordes were but invented to declare the meaning of men, we muste rather frame the
wordes to the meanynge then the meanynge to the wordes'.

[114] See above, note 104, and below 3.4.4.

[115] Quoted by, e.g., Guillaume Fournier, *In titulum de verborum significatione commentarii*, Orléans,
1584, p. 22; Turamini, *De legibus*, p. 174: Doneau, *Ad titulum Digestorum de rebus dubiis
commentarius*, Bourges, 1571, p. 10. Mommsen gives this text as 'plus valet scriptura quam
peractum sit', but records the version given here as a variant. I have found it in that form in
most Renaissance texts, although not in Doneau's.

[116] Rebuffi, *In titulum de verborum et rerum significatione*, p. 3; and below 3.6.3.

note here in passing that the discipline which in ancient times was thought most appropriate to the law – namely topics, in which rhetoric and dialectics, the pragmatic and the semantic, the contingent and the necessary meet – has been very recently asserted to be the characteristic science of the law; and that the problems which most preoccupy Renaissance jurists can have a remarkably modern ring to them.[117]

1.7.1

It would thus be misleading to conclude this chapter with too great an emphasis on the distinction between *mos gallicus* and *mos italicus*. Certainly, humanist propaganda against the medieval gloss and scholastic logic is strident: Budé, Muret and Hotman provide powerful examples of such vituperation. But there are humanists, or humanistic jurists at the very least, who defend the logical and analytical procedures of the glossators and postglossators: Alberigo Gentili (1552–1608), Alberto Bolognetti (1539–85), Turamini, Saxonius, Amerbach. Among the unimpeachably humanist lawyers there are those, moreover, who continue both to recommend and to practise the traditional *mos italicus*: Alciato (whose couplet of acceptable juristic models includes the names of Jason de Mayno, Bartolus and Baldus),[118] Coras, Rebuffi, Jean Breche (d. ?1560) and Fournier (d. ?1611). Even systematizers may at times be suspected of an interest in their work (Bodin and Connan). Differences in approach incontestably exist: but so does a corporate sense of professional continuity, which manifests itself in a number of discreet ways. Just as in the Middle Ages, jurists vie for precedence with other disciplines, annexe their techniques and procedures, and set out to dignify their profession with the status of science as well as art. The advent of the printing press allows, it is true, for a wider circulation of interpretative works to be achieved, and a greater volume published; and one can argue that the commercial organization of the book trade encourages scholars to supplant existing texts with new exegeses and revised editions; but it causes also the hallowed texts of the *mos*

---

[117] This has been argued most forcefully by Theodor Viehweg, *Topik und Jurisprudenz*, Munich, 1953; cf. also Helmut Coing, *Die juristischen Auslegungsmethoden und die Lehren der allgemeinen Hermeneutik*, Cologne, 1959, pp. 22–3.

[118] See *Parerga*, ii.42, *Opera*, iv.346, cited in Hegendorf, *Epitome tyrocinii iuris civilis*, Basle, 1540, p. 32; *Clarissimorum et praestantissimorum iurisconsultorum tractatus*, pp. 146–7; in the appendix of Lagus, *Methodica iuris utriusque traditio*, p. 1022; and by Hieronymus Elenus in his *De optima facilimaque iuris civilis perdiscendi ratione*, reprinted in *Cynosura iuris*, i.87.

gallicus – glossators and postglossators – to be perpetuated, because the eclectic nature of the *mos italicus* can happily accommodate the accumulation of opinions in this way.[119] Furthermore, the genres of legal writing remain much the same, and for all their differences in visual presentation, medieval and Renaissance legal texts reflect similar principles of organization. From the earliest days of Bologna to the end of the Renaissance, jurists were keenly aware that they had to come to terms with Justinian's prohibition of commentary, and they set about the task of justifying their analysis of texts in much the same way. Many of theses features do not emerge as explicit statements in juristic texts; but I believe them to be a factor in their production. As one turns one's attention to the subtle distinctions and lofty abstractions of Renaissance legal theory and methodology, these signs of economic and institutional interests will tend to disappear; but some at least are embodied in a discreet way in the physical object – the book itself – which one looks through, or rather overlooks, as one seeks to make sense of such subtle distinctions and lofty abstractions.

---

[119] See above, notes 63 and 74, and Wilhelm Schmidt-Biggemann, *Topica universalis: eine Modellgeschichte humanistischer und barocker Wissenschaft*, Hamburg, 1983, for a general survey of the encyclopedic aspirations of scholars at the end of the Renaissance and their eventual collapse.

CHAPTER 2

Interpretation and the arts course

Triplicem omnino iuris interpretandi rationem invenio: quarum prima Grammaticorum, altera Dialectorum, tertia Iurisconsultorum propria est.

> (François Hotman, *Iurisconsultus sive de optimo genere iuris interpretandi*, 5th ed., Geneva, 1589, p. 39)

I have found a tripartite comprehensive method of interpreting the law: the first element in this method is that peculiar to Grammarians, the second that peculiar to Logicians, and the third that peculiar to Jurists.

2.1

Interpretation is a process of decoding; it begins with a sign taken to be meaningful – script, gesture, speech – and derives meaning from it. The arts course of the medieval period is structured in the reverse way; it teaches pupils how to encode; it is concerned principally with the production of argument and meaning, not with their testing or interpretation. The trivium of grammar, dialectics and rhetoric have first to be learnt before its products in the form of speeches and texts can be interpreted. The first two of these disciplines, and to a more limited degree the third, provide the analytical tools necessary to the jurist before he can begin his operation on the text of the law. In this sense it is not presumptuous for jurists at this time to describe grammar and logic as the handmaids of jurisprudence (see above 1.6.1); nor is it misplaced for Alciato and others to turn to Quintilian's rhetoric as an interpretative technique. But this deployment of the language arts has its limits. Jurisprudence both in the medieval and the Renaissance periods is taken to be a practical pursuit, not a speculative or purely analytical enterprise; as we have seen, its attitude to language and to logic is functional. Words are 'instrumenta docendi discernendique' (instruments for teaching and perceiving); or as Helfrich-Ulrich Hunnius (1583–1636) puts it on the authority of the Digest, 'sunt enim verba tantum instrumenta voluntatis ut quae sint ad hoc adinventa, ut mentem animique sensum exprimant'[1] (words are instruments of the will to the degree that they are devised for the purpose of expressing intentions and thoughts). This stress on the functionality of words does not extinguish all abstract speculation about them, but it severely curtails it, as some jurists point out;[2] in a similar way, speculative discussion of issues in what now might be called the philosophy of law, such as rights, legal norms, or distinctions such as public/private, self/other, nature/culture, is rarely encountered, except in the most cursory form.[3]

2.2

The Corpus Juris Civilis itself, although containing a general introduction to the law (the Institutes), is not methodologically self-sufficient: a solid grounding in grammar, logic and legal argument is presupposed. There are, it is true, a number of logical rules enshrined in the Corpus which are expressed in technical terminology (genus, species; disjunctives, subdisjunctives; definition, and so on); there is also a great deal of material which touches on the distinction between sense and intention.[4] But this is not sufficient to serve as a complete guide to a novice interpreter. As Quintilian's *Institutes* and Cicero's *Orator*, both written before the composition of the Corpus Juris Civilis, make clear, and as is widely recognized in the Middle Ages and Renaissance, the educational requirements for a specialist in forensic practice are wideranging, and encompass all the elements of the trivium.[5] It is often said that the third element, rhetoric, was neglected in the medieval period, although this is less true of that part of it (*inventio*) which is most relevant to legal studies: but even *inventio* benefited from the discoveries of humanists in the early fifteenth

---

[1] Hunnius, *De authoritate*, p. 233; D 33.10.7; see also Rebuffi, *In titulum de verborum et rerum significatione*, p. 3.   [2] See Turamini, *De legibus*, pp. 70ff.
[3] See Turamini, *De legibus*, pp. 70ff.
[4] These issues arise principally in discussions of D 1.1 (*De iustitia et iure*) and D 1.5 (*De statu hominis*), and take the form of recital of other laws and rules in the Corpus Juris Civilis which show the application of the principles recorded there.
[4] These rules are recorded systematically in such works as Jacobus Treterus' *Distributio titulorum juris de verborum significatione et de regulis juris ad institutiones iustineaneas*, Frankfurt, 1625 and *Axiomata legum*, Lyon, 1547. The rules dealing with sense and intention are found principally in D 31, D 32 and D 33; D 1.3 and D 34.5 contain guidance on ambiguity and obscurity; D 34.5.13.3, D 50.16.124, 237 and D 50.17.80, 113, 147 cover other logical rules.
[5] On the trivium, see Rashdall, *Universities*, 1.33ff., 233ff.; on Cicero's *Orator*, see Grafton and Jardine, *From humanism to the humanities*, pp. 210ff.

century, when the complete text of Quintilian and the later Ciceronian texts on topics were recovered in St Gall and Lodi respectively. These, together with the rediscovery of less well known rhetoricians, writers of compendia, and grammarians such as Varro, give new impetus to rhetorical studies, just as the restitution of the *Posterior Analytics*, *Topics* and the *De sophisticis elenchis* which together make up the 'logica nova', had lent new life to logic in the thirteenth century.[6] Both extensions to the canon leave their mark on legal studies, first in the work of the postglossators, and later in that of Alciato, Hegendorf and others; but the general context remains recognizably Aristotelian. Underlying Renaissance teaching, just as it underlies the medieval trivium, is the Organon, consisting in the *De interpretatione* which deals with grammatical categories and propositions; the *Categories* which deal with terms; the books of syllogistic logic (the *Prior* and *Posterior Analytics*); the *Topics*, which treats of dialectics (that is, argument from plausible premises) and the *De sophisticis elenchis*, which investigates fallacy in argument. In the medieval period the Organon was known also through the *Isagoge* of Porphyry, and the schematic account given in the first two books of Isidore of Seville's *Etymologiae*, as well as through such popular textbooks as Peter of Spain's *Summulae logicales*. Boethius' *De divisione* and Victorinus' *De definitione* (usually attributed to Boethius), which draws on different ancient texts, as does Boethius' *De topicis differentiis*, are also widely used. In grammatical study, the *Doctrinale* of Alexandre de Villedieu and Donatus are most commonly encountered, although in legal texts these are rarely adduced, whereas after 1500 it is not uncommon to come across references to Priscian.[7] It is

---

6 On the rediscovery of Quintilian and Cicero, see James J. Murphy, *Rhetoric in the Middle Ages*, Berkeley and London, 1974, pp. 358–60; George A. Kennedy, *Classical rhetoric and its Christian and secular tradition from ancient to modern times*, London, 1980, pp. 195–219; on that of Varro, see W. Keith Percival in *The Cambridge history of later medieval philosophy*, ed. Norman Kretzmann, Anthony Kenny and Jan Pinborg, Cambridge, 1982, p. 812; on the developments in logic see *ibid.*, *passim*, and Otte, *Dialektik und Jurisprudenz*. Not all the discoveries of the humanists were incorporated into university syllabuses: it is still common in the mid-sixteenth century to find references to the Aquinan rather than the Aldine text of Aristotle.

7 See *The Cambridge history of later medieval philosophy*; Terrence Heath, 'Logical grammar, grammatical logic, and humanism in three German universities', *Studies in the Renaissance*, vi (1971), 9–64, esp. 12ff., 42–3 (it is of interest to note that there is no reference in any of the legal texts I have read to Niccolò Perrotti's humanist *Rudimenta grammatica*, nor to Valla's *Elegantiae*, except to refute them on points about legal terminology). On Priscian, see *ibid.*, pp. 35–40; on Boethius, see Henry Chadwick, *Boethius*, Oxford, 1981; *Boethius: his life, thought and influence*, ed. Margaret Gibson, Oxford, 1981, esp. Osmund Lewry O.P., 'Boethian logic in the medieval West', pp. 90–134, and Anthony Grafton, 'Boethius in the Renaissance', pp. 410–15.

beyond the scope of this study to set out to give a full account of all
these works, but a short review is necessary as an introduction to the
following chapter. Grammar, logic and rhetoric (topics) will be
examined in turn; some parallels with other senior disciplines
(theology and medicine) will then be drawn, and the last sections of
this chapter will be devoted to a survey of the changes which may be
detected in Renaissance pedagogical approaches, and the genres of
pedagogy itself.

GRAMMAR

2.3

Several Renaissance *artes legales* and several commentaries on D 50.16
begin with notes on grammar.[8] These are usually surrounded by
humanist trappings (references to Plato's *Cratylus* and to the first book
of Quintilian's *Institutes*), but in fact follow fairly closely the more
traditional texts: the *De Interpretatione*, chs. 1–4 (in which are discussed
the relationship of language to thought, and of language to the
true/false distinction, and in which definitions of noun, verb and
sentence are given), and Priscian, from whom are drawn the
distinctions between 'dictio' (the word as a meaningful linguistic
unit) and 'pars orationis' (a part of speech, having a grammatical
function within the sentence), between noun and verb, proper and
common nouns, abstract and concrete nouns, categorematic and
syncategorematic words, signification and consignification, 'vox
inarticulata' (expression without meaning) and 'vox articulata'
(expression with speaker's meaning).[9] Several jurists who give an
account of grammatical issues show that they are aware that
traditional grammar is conceived in terms not ideal for their
purposes: the pragmatic function of language (the relationship
between language and its user) tends to be overlooked, and a

---

[8] E.g. Aurelius David Savius, *In Pandectarum titulum de verborum et rerum significatione tractatus isagogicus*, Lyon, 1546; Jerome Sapcote, *Ad primas leges*, pp. 3ff.; Rebuffi, *In titulum de verborum et rerum significatione*, pp. 3f.; Johannes Goeddaeus, *Commentarius repetitae praelectionis in titulum XIV libri. 1. Pandectarum* (1591), Herborn, 1594, pp. 3ff. .

[9] On Priscian see Padley, *Grammatical theory*, pp. 12–13, pp. 264–7; the list of words pertaining to grammar given by Waswo, *Language and meaning*, p. 86 is not reliable. See also Paul Vincent Spade, Gabriel Nuchelmans and Norman Kretzmann in the *Cambridge history of later medieval philosophy*, pp. 190ff. On the awareness of the humanist use of Greek rather than Latin to designate grammatical features, see Jean Breche, *Ad titulum Pandectarum de verborum et rerum significatione commentarii*, Lyon, 1556, p. 5, cited by Maclean, 'Montaigne and humanist jurists', p. 270n.

description given which, as in the *De interpretatione*, is slanted towards logical usage. Aurelius David Savius points out in 1546 that words are not only the correlates of things, but also of intentions: and that intention is a thing to be signified as much as the significate itself. This insight seems to have been gained also by the 'modistae', or medieval speculative grammarians, but their work was not influential, and seems hardly to have been noticed at all in this domain.[10] Later in the century, Johannes Goeddaeus retrieves from Varro a distinction between subjective and objective language usage ('voluntaris' vs. 'naturalis') which makes the same point:[11] as in the case of Alciato's use of Fortunatianus (see below 3.2.1), he develops a part of the text for his own purposes, in a way which says more about the need for jurists to find ancient authority for their own ideas than the importance of the idea or hypothesis in question in the original text. Rebuffi goes yet further, and argues that for lawyers, words are not just vehicles for signification but have other functions ('effectum et utilitatem') which hint at their performative aspect (see below 3.6.5).[12]

As is well known, prominent humanists declared themselves in favour of the minimum amount of grammar learning and advocated that access should be given to the texts themselves as early as possible;[13] this is not easily achieved in law in which the very words used to describe legal activities – *vox, verbum, nomen, appellatio, libellus* – have a multiplicity of meanings which need constantly to be monitored. Pierre Rebuffi's digression into grammar at the beginning of his commentary on D 50.16 is occasioned, for example, by the word *verbum* in the title itself (*De verborum significatione*), in which he distinguishes no less than six senses.[14] The same difficulty arises in respect of such terms as *intellectus, sensus, mens, ratio, sententia, voluntas, intentio*; as well as carrying other meanings, they designate various

---

[10] See Heath, 'Logical grammar', pp. 52–3, R.H. Robins, *Ancient and medieval grammatical theory in Europe*, London, 1951, pp. 81–90; Jan Pinborg, *Die Entwicklung der Sprachtheorie im Mittelalter*, Munich and Copenhagen, 1967, pp. 30ff. and below 3.4.1 and 3.6.3. One sign of the influence of the 'modistae' is found in de Federicis, *De iuris interpretatione*, i.1, in *Tractatus iuris universi*, Venice, 1584, i.210: his *modi interpretandi* recall their *modi significandi*.

[11] Varro, *De lingua latina*, viii.9.21–5, on the forms of declension which are either 'a communi consensu' ('naturalis declinatio') or 'a singulorum voluntate' ('declinatio voluntaris'): Goeddaeus, *Commentarius*, pp. 10–11.

[12] Rebuffi, *In titulum de verborum et rerum significatione*, p. 4.

[13] See W. Keith Percival, in the *Cambridge history of later medieval philosophy*, p. 809; Padley, *Grammatical theory*, pp. 15–16; Health, 'Logical grammar', pp. 39–40.

[14] Rebuffi, *In titulum de verborum et rerum significatione*, pp. 3f.

semasiological aspects of words. But this group of terms does not belong to grammar as such in this period, as modern scholarly accounts have conceded, although they exercise greatly the minds of jurists. Their claim to surpass grammarians and rightfully to treat their discipline as merely propaedeutic to legal studies is based to a large degree on the attention which they pay to semantic and pragmatic issues. But for all formal description of language, they rely heavily on traditional grammar, and do not call into question the explicit mentalism of Aristotelian linguistic analysis.[15]

LOGIC AND DIALECTICS

2.4

The second element of the trivium, logic, is concerned with correct inferences and deductions from premises (ἀρχαί) which may vary in status: 'scientific' premises are apodictic, and constitute the highest level of knowledge ('scire est rem per causas cognoscere': (to have certain knowledge is to know the causes of something: *Metaphysics*, ii.1.5 (993b20); see above 1.2.3); fully satisfactory knowledge of the truth through demonstration can only be obtained at this level.[16] Those who claim scientific status for jurisprudence, from the postglossators to Bodin, stress the need to know its *principia* (ἀρχαί) in order to be able to apply logic satisfactorily to the understanding and application of the law.[17] For this reason, legal propositions are

---

[15] *Ibid.*, p. 4: 'adde quod jurisconsultus nonnihil ultra grammaticos et rhetores tractare voluerunt: voluerunt, inquam, et verborum significationes describere, et rerum, id est sententiarum, quaestionum, et materiarum effectus' (to which should be added that jurists have wished to go beyond the work of grammarians and rhetoricians, by which I mean that they have set out to describe the meanings of both words and things, that is the effects of opinions, questions, and matters under discussion). See also above, 1.6.1, and chapter 1, note 105. For a clear definition of mentalism, see L. Bloomfield, *Language*, New York, 1933, p. 142: adherents of mentalistic psychology . . . believe that prior to the utterance of a linguistic form, there occurs within the speaker a non-physical process, a *thought, concept, image, feeling, act of will* or the like . . . The mentalist therefore can define the meaning of a linguistic form as the characteristic mental event which occurs in every speaker and hearer in connection with the utterance or hearing of the linguistic form . . . For the mentalist, language is the expression of *ideas, feelings* or *volitions*.

[16] The phrase 'scire est rem per causas cognoscere' is a topos: see Oldendorp, *De iure et aequitate disputatio*, Cologne, 1573, p. 13; also Virgil, *Georgics*, ii.490.

[17] Rebuffi, *Explicatio*, p. 1: 'Nam necesse est enim, qui iura scire cupit, ut prius cognoscat principia iuris, alioqui corruet eius studium deficiente principio et fundamento' (for it is necessary that anyone wishing to know the law should first know the principles of the law; otherwise his studies will collapse for want of foundations and sound beginnings). Rebuffi refers to the glosses of Accursius and Baldus on D 1.1.1, and to D 44.2.26, which makes the same point in a much more concrete way.

depragmatized by writers such as Baldus, and the infinite or indefinite nature of many legal situations (that is, their enmeshment with particulars) is repressed in the process of textual explanation and interpretation.[18] This is done by treating indefinites as universals, ignoring the existential features of particulars, and claiming the internal consistency of jurisprudence as a science satisfying the condition καθ'αὑτό (*Posterior Analytics*), i.4 (73b25).[19] By these means, Porphyry's definition of an art ('de infinitis scientia finita') can be applied to law, and syllogistic procedures can be used to determine its sense. These procedures are most evident in determining the sense of copulas and disjunctives,[20] in questions concerning excluded middles, and in those concerning contraries.[21] Such maxims as 'quae nominatim lex non prohibet, ea permitti intelliguntur' (those things not expressly forbidden by the law are taken to be permitted by it) clearly indicate the applicability of logical tables of contraries and subcontraries to the law, and to the problems of validity of inference which can arise from legal formulas.[22] The accounts given in legal pedagogical texts of the Aristotelian taxonymy of opposition (correlatives, contraries with or without middle terms, privatives, contradictories: *Categories*, x (11b15) indicate the importance placed on a sound knowledge of this aspect of logic.[23] Another frequently encountered device is *divisio*, usually called *distinctio* by jurists; this is Plato's διαίρεσις, which, as both Coras and Bodin point out, he describes as a divine instrument of thought. Also well known to both medieval and Renaissance scholars was Porphyry's 'tree' by which he sets out to

[18] Baldus, gl. ad. D 1.1.1, cited by Otte, *Dialektik und Jurisprudenz*, p. 7: cf. I.M. Bocheński's account of the development of scholastic logic, *A history of formal logic*, Notre Dame, 1961, pp. 148ff.

[19] The same point is made by Heath, 'Logical grammar'. See Goeddaeus, *Commentarius*, pp. 8–10 ('nulla ars inquit lex καθ'αὑτό, quidquam alienum usurpato, nec quidquam alterius generis immisceto' (let no art usurp material extraneous to it or be mixed with anything of another genus)): see also Alciato, *De verborum significatione*, p. 116, gl. ad D 31.44: 'nota quod indefinita [lex] aequipollet universali' (note that an indefinite counts for a universal [law]). See also Rogerius, *De iuris interpretatione*, ii, in *Tractatus iuris universi* i.387. On the non-referential status of the subjects of particular premises, see Otte, *Dialektik und Jurispurdenz*, pp. 122–4. Cf. also Cicero, *De finibus*, iii.7.24, quoted above 1.2.3.

[20] See D 50.16.124, 237; Otte, *Dialektik und Jurisprudenz*, pp. 134ff.

[21] See *ibid.*, pp. 67ff., citing Boethius, *In categorias*, iv.264D–265A. Cf. also Plato, *Republic*, iv.436B.

[22] See Bocheński, *A history of formal logic*, pp. 234–6; Otte, *Dialektik und Jurisprudenz*, p. 127; D 22.3.5, D 3.3.43.1.

[23] The various legal treatises on dialectics and topics give accounts of opposition: e.g. Hegendorf, *Dialectica legalis*, Lyon, 1536, pp. 50ff.; Cantiuncula, *Topica legalis*, Basle, 1545, i.60ff.; Gammaro, *Legis dialectica*, in *ibid.*, ii.205; Oldendorp, *Topica legalia*, in *Opera*, Basle, 1559, i.129ff.

demonstrate how one can pass from the *genus generalissimum* (substance) to the *species specialissima* or *infima*.[24] *Divisio* is more than just the heuristic enumeration of subject matter for the convenience of the orator, since it deals the necessary distinction between genera and species, wholes and parts, various meanings of words, and accidents and subjects[25] (see below 3.3.4). All of these distinctions pertain to definition, which is looked upon as a crucial part of legal interpretation, although it is not without its problems, as we shall see (below 3.3.2).

But the status of formal logic in legal studies is fragile – more fragile than in theology, for example – and is recognized as such. It emerges from the attempts made to give logical notation to the maxim that the exception proves the rule (regula); Otte has elegantly catalogued the various attempts at dealing logically with D 50.17.1, which fail not only because of the intrinsic difficulty of the exercise, but also because 'regula' is inadequately defined.[26] The notion of truth is also problematic: Aquinas' formula 'adaequatio intellectus et rei' refers to logical meaning and logical objects, but is difficult to apply to subjective understanding and contingent things. Lawyers are much closer to Scaliger's concept of truth as 'orationis adaequatio cum ipsis speciebus' (see below 3.6.3), which admits both of real discourse and particulars, but which fails as a formula to satisfy the truth conditions required by formal logic.[27] Jurists also practise inductive reasoning (rules, it will be remembered, are the product of reasoning from

---

[24] Bodin, *Iuris universi distributio*, p. 8: 'Plato dicere solebat nihil divinibus sibi videri quam apte dividere'; cf. *Phaedrus* 266B, and *Sophist*, 218ff.; Coras, in *Tractatus de iuris arte*, pp. 40ff. The principal source is Boethius' *De divisione*, on which see Otte, *Dialektik und Jurisprudenz*, pp. 73ff. On Porphyry's tree, see his *Isagoge*, and especially Boethius *In Isagogem Porphyrii*, iii.4; also Otte, pp. 87–9. It is reproduced in Peter of Spain's *Tractatus* (see *The Cambridge translations of medieval philosophical texts*, vol. i: Logic and philosophy, ed. Norman Kretzmann and Eleanor Stump, Cambridge, 1988, p. 83; also pp. 11–38 (a translation of Boethius' *De divisione*), and see below 3.3.4. *Distinctio* is of course a technical term (for a division of the text) in canon law. See also *Posterior Analytics*, ii.13 (96b16) and ii.14(98a1).

[25] On this distinction see Cicero, *Topica*, v.28.

[26] *Dialektik und Jurisprudenz*, pp. 215f.; gl. ad D 50.17.1 and D 50.17.202 provide the sources for Otte's record of conflicting views on the relationship of *regula* and truth.

[27] *Categories*, v (4a22); *Metaphysics*, i.2 (993a30); Aquinas, *Quaestiones disputatae de veritate*, i.1; *Summa theologiae*, 1a 16 and 1; 1a 21 ad 2; Scaliger, *Exotericae exercitationes de subtilitate contra Cardanum* (1557), Frankfurt, 1592, p. 8; Irena Backus, 'La Survie des *Artes* de Raymond Lull au 16ᵉ siècle: le traitement des "prédicats absolus" dans les commentaires d'Agrippa (ca. 1510) et de Valerius (1589)', *Archiv für Geschichte der Philosophie*, lxvi (1984), 281–93, esp. 291. According to Pinborg (cited by Heath, 'Logical grammar', p. 53) the prevalent attitude by the late fourteenth century to the pragmatic aspect of language is nominalist, in so far as the *propositio mentalis* is defined as having both *connotationes* and *suppositiones*, but neither connotation nor supposition (reference) entails real existence or reference to the world external to the utterance.

particular instances) and couple this with *regressus* from 'probable' conclusions:[28] both of these procedures are inappropriate in formal logic, but are important features of practical reasoning; a reasoning which 'ad particularia descendit', and which determines that individual cases are true in order to begin its logical processing of them, whereas formal logic works from the general to the particular: 'ad veritatem universalis requiritur omnes singulares esse veras' (to establish the truth of a universal, all particulars are required to be true: cf. D 34.5.13.3 and Bartolus' gloss on D 12.1: 'ad cognitionem specierum debet praecedere cognitio generis' (the knowledge of genera must precede the knowledge of species)).[29] With such maxims, we have passed from the sphere of analytics to that of dialectics, the science of reasoning from plausible premises. In other words, we have left the domain of the apodictic, and entered that of the 'probable' (ἔνδοξον), in which even the *opinio communis doctorum* can be given the status of a premise. The relevant Aristotelian treatise is the *Topics*; as the method of drawing conclusions from probable premises, this is sometimes classed with the logical works, sometimes seen as a repository of argumentative procedures (loci or topoi) and regarded as a treatise on the part of rhetoric known as *inventio*. The logical aspect of topics was much discussed in the medieval period, especially with reference to conditional inferences (*consequentiae*) which are relevant to law, in that many of the *regulae* of the Corpus Juris Civilis are in the form of hypothetical statements;[30] but it is convenient here to treat topics as part of rhetoric, and to use it as the focus of a discussion of the third element of the trivium.

TOPICS AND RHETORIC

2.5
Modern commentators have claimed that in topics and in rhetoric, the criterion of truth may be abandoned altogether in favour of

---

[28] Otte, *Dialektik und Jurisprudenz*, pp. 191ff., 212ff.; Kelley, 'Jurisconsultus perfectus', p. 99; Coras in *Tractatus de iuris arte*, pp. 21ff. 'Probable' here (ἔνδοξον) may appear in the Corpus Juris Civilis as 'verisimile' (Cf. D 50.16.142), and is opposed to 'certum' or 'apodictic' (Boethius, *De differentiis topicis*, i.1180c–2B.) As Otte points out, topics deal with plausible or generally accepted propositions which may or may not be true, whereas apodictic logic deals with true premises which may or may not be generally accepted (*Dialektik und Jurisprudenz*, pp. 188f.).

[29] *Ibid.*, pp. 128, 190–1, *Axiomata legum*, p. 274. See also Fonseca and others cited by Screech, *Montaigne and melancholy*, p. 148. Ramus also declares that teaching is a movement from the generic to the specific: see Ong, *Ramus, method and the decay of dialogue*, p. 204, and below 3.3.4.

[30] On *consequentiae*, see Eleonore Stump in the *Cambridge history of later medieval philosophy*, pp. 273ff.; Heath, 'Logical grammar', p. 45.

plausibility and successful (i.e. persuasive) argument or counter-argument:[31] this would not have been conceded by medieval or Renaissance jurists. What regulates not only the legislator in the production of law, but also the judge in its application and the interpreter in its exegesis may not be the apodictic criteria of science, but it must have the same authority as truth: D 1.5.25 (also D 50.17.207) (Ulpian): 'res iudicata pro veritate accipitur'[32] (legal judgements have the status of truth). Dialectical techniques are employed to this end: *divisio* or *distinctio* helps to provide the decisiveness and the exclusion of middle terms which lends force to the law;[33] the *regulae* of the Corpus Juris Civilis may be treated as axioms, which are the product of inductive reasoning;[34] the *communis opinio doctorum* is given the respectability of truth,[35] as is that which is 'probabilis' (i.e. acceptable to the wisest: see below 3.1.3) 'credibilis' and 'verisimilis'.[36] Jean Breche, for example, points out that a dialectician takes a 'terminum' to be 'eum in quem resolvitur oratio' (that which can be reduced to a proposition); but a jurist on the other hand takes it to be a 'limitem vicinum agrum disterminantem' (a limit which determines the meaning of adjacent terms), a more decisive and more solidly referential category.[37] It is useful to stress this commitment to truth, even in topical argument. This could be studied in a number of widely accessible texts; of these the most influential are the *Topics* of Aristotle, the relevant treatises of Boethius (the *De topicis differentiis* and the commentary on Cicero's *Topica*), the rhetorical treatise known as the *Ad Herennium*, once attributed to Cicero, Cicero's other, authentic, treatises – the *De inventione, De*

---

[31] See Gerard A. Press, 'The subject and structure of Augustine's *De doctrina christiana*', *Augustinian studies*, xi (1980), 120.

[32] Kelley, 'Jurisconsultus perfectus', p. 95. Agrippa, *De incertitudine*, xci, satirically amplifies D.1.5.25 with D 1.3.32 ('ipsae leges nulla alia ex causa nos tene[nt], quam quod iudicio populi receptae sunt': statutes themselves bind us for no other reason than that they are accepted by the judgement of the people), and produces the conclusion 'communis error facit ius, et res iudicata veritatem' (common error makes law and legal judgements make truth). Cf. Montaigne, *Essais*, iii.13, p. 1049: 'or les loix se maintiennent en credit, non par ce qu'elles sont justes, mais par ce qu'elles sont loix. C'est le fondement mystique de leur authorité; elles n'en ont poinct d'autre.'

[33] Cf. D 1.5.10; Coras in *Tractatus Corasii et Hopperi*, pp. 40ff.

[34] See Otte, *Dialektik und Jurisprudenz*, pp. 114–15.

[35] See Robinson, Fergus and Gordon, *Introduction*, pp. 114–15.

[36] See D 50.16.45; Otte, *Dialektik und Jurisprudenz*, pp. 187ff.; and Goeddaeus, *Commentarius*, p. 18, for similar use of *verior* (vs. *falsior*) to qualify a 'probable' conclusion.

[37] Breche, *Ad titulum de verborum et rerum significatione*, p. 4: cf. Coke, *Institutes*, ¢ 6ʳ, quoted above, chapter 1, note 38.

Oratore, Brutus, Topica, Orator – and the *Institutes* of Quintilian; the rediscovery of the latter two authors in the fifteenth century helped revive an interest in the application of rhetoric to the law.

The field of forensic rhetoric (one of the three divisions of rhetoric, with the deliberative and demonstrative, and, according to the author of the *Ad Herennium*, the most difficult and important),[38] is split up in a number of ways. One division is attributed by Cicero to the Hellenistic rhetorician Hermagoras, and concerns the types of proposition (theses and hypotheses: very approximately, general propositions or questions about ethics and politics as opposed to specifically legal issues) which occur in forensic discourse. This distinction is developed in the Renaissance by François Hotman, but by few other writers, and seems not to have preoccupied the postglossators.[39] More influential is the division into *causae* or *status* ('issues'): this is sometimes bipartite (*causae rationales/causae legales*), and sometimes tripartite (*causae coniecturales/causae legales/causae iuridicales*). There is no clear agreement about the relationship between these two divisions: the *causae iuridicales* are subsumed in the twofold division under *causae rationales* and given another name ('status qualitatis'); definition is ascribed by some writers to the category *causae rationales*, and by others to the *causae legales*.[40] For the sake of clarity, it is most convenient to adopt the tripartite division. The *causae* or *status iuridicales* concern the rightness or wrongness of an action, and involve arguments about expediency and necessity; they do not contribute much to the science of interpretation.[41] The *causae* or *status coniecturales* concern questions of fact: in this category falls the consideration of evidence, both in the form of *inartificiales probationes* (brute signs of all kinds – circumstantial evidence, rumours, the depositions of witnesses, the results of torture and interrogation) and *artificiales probationes* (approximately, what the art of the advocate can

---

[38] *Ad Herennium*, ii.1.1: 'causarum tria genera sunt: demonstrativum, deliberativum, iudiciale. Multo difficillimum iudiciale est.'

[39] *Iurisconsultus*, in *Cynosura iuris*, ii.117ff.; Quintilian, ii.21.12; iii.5.12; Cicero, *De inventione*, i.6.8, i.8.12; *De oratore*, iii.107; Josef Martin, *Antike Rhetorik*, Munich, 1974, pp. 15ff.

[40] *Questiones de iuris subtilitatibus*, exordium; Kantorowicz, 'The *quaestiones disputatae* of the glossators', *Tijdschrift voor Rechtsgeschiednis*, xvi (1939), 1–67; Quintilian, vii; *Ad Herennium*, i.11.19ff; Cicero, *De inventione*, ii.40.116–51.154; *Topica*, xxiv.92ff.; Martin, *Antike Rhetorik*, pp. 29ff., 36–7, 44f.

[41] Quintilian, vii.8; *Ad Herennium*, ii.12.19–13.20; Cicero, *De inventione*, ii.21.62–39.115.

make of these for the benefit of his client).[42] Interpretation arises here in its modern sense in the construal of evidence, which is discussed in legal tracts under the headings 'praesumptio' and 'coniectura' (see below 3.2.1). The *causae legales* concern questions of law: the commonly encountered headings which fall under this category are 'scriptum et voluntas' (debates about the spirit as against the letter of the law), conflicting laws, ambiguity, definition, 'ratiocinatio' (argument from similar laws) and 'translatio' (arguments about process, jurisdiction and the appropriateness of a given law for a given case).[43] The issue of interpretation comes to the fore here in questions of language (*scriptum et voluntas*, ambiguity, definition: see below 3.3.2, 3.4.3, 3.6.1) and it arises in ratiocination, translation and conflicting laws in the determination of the *ratio legis* (see below 3.6.1). In so far as there are ancient sources for the textual exegesis of the law, it is to be found in the extensive sections devoted to the *causae legales* in Quintilian, in the *Ad Herennium*, and in Cicero's *De inventione*. But even in these sections, the material is presented in the form of practical legal argument *in foro*, both on behalf of clients and against the case made by the opposing advocate; no codification of interpretative rules is provided beyond the broad taxonomy given above.

The major part of *Topics* (from which the book gets its name) is devoted to the discovery (*inventio*) and classification of 'topoi', or 'loci' or 'sedes argumentorum': the places from which dialectical arguments (that is, arguments from 'probable' premises) may be derived. In his *De topicis differentiis*, Boethius gives two ancient lists of topical arguments – those of Themistius and Cicero – which he combines with material from Aristotle's *Topics*. Boethius was very well known in the later Middle Ages; he is also much published in the early years of the sixteenth century,[44] much more so, in fact, than the humanist Rudolph Agricola, whose place logic borrows very heavily from him, and to whom (rather than to Boethius) is attributed an important contribution to the development of thought and intellectual

---

[42] Quintilian, v.1–14; *Ad Herennium*, i.14.24–15.25; Cicero, *De inventione*, ii.4.14–16.51. It would, of course, be argued by many today that there is no such thing as a *probatio inartificialis* or unmediated, brute fact.

[43] Quintilian, vii.6–8, *Ad Herennium*, ii.1.3–8.12; Cicero, *De inventione*, ii.40.116–51.154. Direct citation of these passages is not uncommon: see, e.g. Alberto Bolognetti, *De lege, iure et aequitate*, i.34, in *Tractatus iuris universi*, i.321.

[44] For a list of editions of the *Topica* and the *De differentiis topicis* in the sixteenth century (nineteen in all), see Lewry, in *Boethius* ed. Gibson, pp. 120–1; see also Stump in the *Cambridge history of later medieval philosophy*, pp. 273ff.

method.[45] This attribution was made in the early years of the sixteenth century by a number of figures involved in legal pedagogy: notably Claude Chansonnette [Cantiuncula] (d. *c.* 1555) and Christoph Hegendorf (1500–40), both of whom produced propae-deutic handbooks for students of law. The list of topical arguments produced by Cantiuncula is long – loci *a praeiudiciis, a definitione, ab etymologia, a conjugatis, a toto, a partibus, a genere, a specie, a forma, ab ordine, a simili, a differentia, a contrariis, ab adiunctis, a connexis, ab antecedentibus, a consequentibus, a repugnantibus, a correlativis, a causa, ab effectis (eventis), a comparatione (maiorum, parium, minorum), a scripto, a sententia contra scriptum,* and finally *a verisimili,* which is subject to a further subdivision: *a more, ab opinione, a natura, a qualitate, re vel persona, a tempore praeterito, instanti vel consequenti, a loco, a signis vel circumstantiis.*[46] It would be possible to give examples of all of these, and to point to their relationship to other logical and dialectical procedures (such as definition, etymology, *divisio,* the *causae legales,* and so on). Much of this has already been excellently done by Otte and others.[47] It is a characteristic of topical arguments that the same argument can be used to support contradictory propositions, and that the list of loci itself contains contradictories ('a scripto': 'a sententia contra scrip-tum'). The implications of this for the law – that it can be seen, for example, as little else than a corpus of ex post facto justifications for particular decisions – have already been mentioned (see above, pp. 6–7). For the purposes of this book, only a few points need to be made about the most common of these topical arguments: *a simili, a correlativis, a causa, a signis et circumstantiis.*

The locus *a simili* is perhaps the most commonly encountered form of argument. Like the locus *a comparatione,* it rests on a significant element of identity, while conceding difference. Nearly all examples of analogical reasoning fall under this heading; the most important

---

45 On Agricola see Ong, *Ramus,* pp. 92ff.; Troje, in *Festschrift Hempel,* ii.158ff.; Heath, 'Logical grammar', p. 62; Schmidt-Biggemann, *Topica universalis,* pp. 3ff. It is worth noting that de Federicis refers in 1493 to 'topica mea' (*De iuris interpretatione,* in *Tractatus iuris universi,* i.210); no trace of this work survives except in this reference, but it indicates that teachers of law were producing their own version of topics already by that date, i.e. before Agricola's work was widely known. Cf. also Nicolaus Everardus, *Topica seu loci legales,* Louvain, 1516.

46 See above, note 23: the 1545 edition of Cantiuncula contains commentaries by Joannes Appellus and Pietro Andrea Gammaro, which, like book iv of Boethius' *De differentiis topicis,* attempt to provide a concordance and reconciliation of topical arguments.

47 *Dialektik und Jurisprudenz,* pp. 186ff.; see also the works of Aldo Mazzacane, *Scienza, logica e ideologia nella giurisprudentza tedesca del secolo XVI,* Milan, 1971, and Piano Mortari, referred to above, chapter 1 note 3.

issue is the establishment of an identical *ratio legis* which will allow the application of the law to a *casus omissus* or *non expressus* (a case not specifically named in the statute in question). But as the scholastic tag has it, *omnis similitudo claudicat* (all comparisons are invalid in some way); analogy is a very vulnerable procedure. The formulas 'ad similia procedere' (D 1.3.12; cf. D 27.1.10.6), 'procedendum est de similibus a similia' (gl. ad D 3.5.29) or 'a pari materia' are question-begging and fraught with difficulty, as is Cicero's injunction 'valeat aequitas, quae paribus in causis paria iura desiderat' (that form of equity which desires the same law to be applied to the same cases is to be commended) (*Topica*, iv.23: see below 3.9.1).[48]

The locus *a correlativis* is quite frequently encountered in legal argument, especially in the form of comparatives: *benignior–durior, latior–augustior, improbabilior–probabilior*, even *verior–falsior*. The advantage of this category of opposition is that it permits an empirical and particular account of reality and of the referents of the law to be given: no claim to absolute knowledge is being made. Human affairs and the objects of the real world are infinitely variable and diverse; to make a correlative statement is to avoid enmeshment with insuperable problems of definition, and to allow the law to be decisive: if the sex of a hermaphrodite has to be determined for legal purposes, says Ulpian, 'magis puto eius sexus aestimandum, qui in eo praevalet' (D 1.5.10: I rather think that he or she should be considered to be of that sex to which he or she is more alike). The need for cumbersome definition of gender has been obviated.[49]

The locus *a causa* recalls the Aristotelian doctrine of the four causes (material, formal, efficient, final: see above 1.2.3); but these are sometimes reduced to two (*causa impulsiva* and *causa finalis*). This locus plays a significant part in legal studies. It is used by postglossators such as Bartolus and Baldus (see below 3.7.1), but also by humanists such as Bodin and Turamini, and by eclectics such as Jean de Coras

---

[48] See Piano Mortari, *Diritto, logica, metodo*, pp. 334ff.; Otte, *Dialektik und Jurisprudenz*, pp. 200ff.; cf. the *in pari materia* rule adduced in English jurisprudence (Sir Rupert Cross, *Statutory interpretation*, London, 1976, pp. 18, 127–9). On the scholastic adage 'omnis similitudo claudicat' see Carol Clark, 'Montaigne and the imagery of political discourse in sixteenth-century France', *French studies*, xxiv (1970), 338. The most extensive discussion of non-identity of similia is found in Gammaro, *De extensionibus*, xc, in *Tractatus iuris universi*, xviii.253.

[49] This seems not to have been a prominent feature of medieval legal reasoning; Otte does not mention it. It appears in Cantiuncula's and Hegendorf's lists; Alciato, *De verborum significatione*, p. 87, makes use of it, but in referring to it suggests that it is not widely known as a procedure ('quod in correlativis (ut vocant) . . .'). On the decisiveness of the law, see 3.4.2.

(see below 3.4.1). It is a powerful and much invoked analytical method.[50]

The locus *a signis et circumstantiis* is in some ways yet more significant. The *circumstantiae* – encapsulated in the mnemonic questions quis? quid? ubi? quando? quomodo? quibus adminiculis? – not only admit particulars into the realm of argument but also the pragmatic considerations which arise from the contingency of agent, event and meaning.[51] The *circumstantiae* are closely related to the logical predicaments (those things which may be predicated of a subject: *Categories*, iv, 1b25); they belong properly in rhetoric to *narratio* rather than *inventio*; their intrusion into place logic represents the reaffirmation of *res* in their most irreducible forms: not only persons, things, events, actions, but also intentions. This reaffirmation is connected both to humanism and to their revival of rhetoric. It is a commonplace that humanists welcomed the reassertion of things over (mere) words; in this, jurists had always been their allies, for words are for them only instruments: 'res magis quam verba intuenda sunt' (attention must be paid to things more than words) (D 23.3.41.1). Laws are imposed on things, not words: as Justinian points out (C 6.43.2) 'nos enim non verbis sed ipsis rebus imponimus'. Words must have 'effect' and 'utility' to be significant in jurisprudence; truth is said to reside in things, not words, even if propositions alone can be attributed with the epithet true or false.[52] This somewhat unlogical way of looking upon things has its correlate in an equally unlogical way of looking at words. Aristotle had made clear early on in the *De interpretatione* (17a5) that the force of words in so far as this represented itself as the expression of mental states or their persuasive effect on the hearer belonged not to logic, but to rhetoric;[53] jurists had, however, to contend with the full ranges of intentions and effects which words embody (D 1.3.7 (Ulpian): 'legis

---

[50] See Otte, *Dialektik und Jurisprudenz*, pp. 193f.; Cortese, *La norma giuridica*, i.213 ff.

[51] See Quintilian, v.10.104; Boethius, *De differentiis topicis*, i.4; Irnerius, gl. ad D 20.1; Martin, *Antike Rhetorik*, p. 111. Cantiuncula makes the contingent nature of *circumstantia* clear: 'circumstantia vero est accidens in concreto' (*Topica legalis*, p. 159): cf. Aquinas, *In ethica Aristotelis*, iii.13.37. The *circumstantiae* are to be found also in the Digest (24.35; cf. D 48.19.16.1).

[52] *Categories*, v (4b8); xii (14b21); cf. also Rebuffi, *In titulum de verborum et rerum significatione*, p. 4; Wesenbeck, *Prolegomena iurisprudentiae*, Leipzig, 1584, pp. 115–16; Connan, *Commentaria*, i.669.

[53] See also *Rhetoric*, i II.12, 1356a1; i II.22.3, 1358a25; and Quintilian, viii.pr.15: 'eloqui enim est omnia, quae mentis conceperis, promere atque ad audientes perferre' (to be an orator means to produce and communicate to your audience all that you have conceived in your mind).

virtus haec est imperare, vetare, permittere, punire'; D 1.3.17
(Celsus): 'scire leges non hoc est verba earum tenere, sed vim ac
potestatem': see below 3.6.5). It is for this, among other reasons, that
Renaissance lawyers of Alciato's generation, and even those who
preceded him in a less humanistic mode, such as Caepolla, were so
keen to appropriate the discoveries of humanists in rhetoric and topics
to their own discipline. The work of Rudolph Agricola is taken up by
Chansonnette [Cantiuncula], Apel, Gammaro, Oldendorp, Hegendorf and others; Alciato himself extended the use of Quintilian in legal
studies to include the analysis of figures and tropes, thus introducing
elocutio to jurisprudence as an analytical tool; and he also makes
reference to less well-known rhetoricians such as Fortunatianus to
whom he attributes (on somewhat slender evidence) a theory of the
articulation of *dictio, sensus* and *res* (see below 3.2.2); later in the
century, Johann Thomas Frey and Johannes Althaus (Althusius)
(1556?–1637?) employ their near-contemporary Ramus' dichotomies
and logic for jurisprudential purposes.[54] These appropriations were
all claimed to be innovative, and were in tune with the humanistic
age in which they were made; whether they in fact marked an
advance on medieval exegetical methods is another question.[55]

INTERPRETATION IN THEOLOGY AND MEDICINE

2.6

From this brief account of the trivium, it is appropriate to pass to
other contemporary practices of interpretation which are related to
jurisprudence but distinct from it (at least in the minds of jurists). A
full account of these is beyond the scope of this study. Theological

---

[54] Alciato, *De verborum significatione*, iv, pp. 164–86; Quintilian, viii.2–ix.1. Not everyone
approved of Alciato's initiative: see Franciscus Floridus, *In M. Actii Planti aliorumque latinae
linguae scriptorum calumniatores apologia et De iuris civilis interpretibus liber*, 2nd ed., Basle 1540, pp.
144ff.; Savius, *In titulum de verborum et rerum significatione*, p. 55; Goeddaeus, *Commentarius* p. 8.
Hegendorf also introduced into pedagogical literature intended for law students forensic
rhetoric (i.e. the practice of advocates in foro), but without much impact, it would seem, if
the number of surviving copies and the fact that the books were not reprinted or reissued can
be taken as indicative of only modest success. See esp. his *Rhetoricae libri duo*, Frankfurt, 1541,
his commentaries on Cicero's *Partitiones oratoriae*, letters and selected speeches (*In
Philippicas quatuor scholia* (1535); *Adnotatiunculae in Verrinas* (1529)). On the analysis of figures
and tropes, see Mazzacane, *Scienza*; Kelley, *History, law and the human sciences*, xi.31 (but cf.
'Jurisconsultus perfectus', pp. 96–7 where Fraunce is wrongly said to be an anti-Ramist);
Johannes Althaus, *Iurisprudentiae romanae methodice digestae libri duo*, 2nd ed., Herborn, 1592.
[55] Cf. above 1.4.3 and figs. 2 and 3, which cast 3.4.1 below in the form of Ramist dichotomies.

interpretation in its various guises, from orthodox Catholic (the doctrine of the four senses of scripture) to Lutheran is the most elaborate of such practices.[56] The other senior university faculty, medicine, also has its mode of interpretation of natural signs (signatures), and its theories of sense-making procedures (intellection) to which we shall allude below (3.6.3). Jurists recognize these as separate and autonomous domains, and are at pains to distinguish their own activity from them.[57] In a few instances, theological writing is of such authority that it is cited in jurisprudence: this is notably the case with Aquinas whose discussion of law in the *Summa theologiae* (1a 2ae 90–7) is quoted with respect, especially by writers such as Gammaro and de Federicis who deal with both canon and civil law;[58] but for the most part Renaissance texts treat interpretation as a secular issue. This is made clearest when the relationship of civil law to natural law, divine law and eternal law is invoked, usually in order to mark off the territory of the civilian and to ensure that he is not accused of *verba indisciplinata*.[59]

THE DEVELOPMENT OF LEGAL PEDAGOGY

2.7
A final word needs to be said about the chronological development of the theory of interpretation in juristic writing itself. Such inveterate commentators as the glossators and postglossators could not have failed to have a great deal to say about interpretation, although it

---

[56] On theological interpretation in the Middle Ages, see Beryl Smalley, *The study of the Bible in the Middle Ages*, Oxford, 1952, esp. pp. 247ff.; Henri de Lubac, *Exégèse médiévale, les quatre sens de l'Ecriture*, Paris, 1959–64; Hennig Brinkmann, *Mittelalterliche Hermeneutik*, Tübingen, 1980; G. Ebeling, *Evangelische Evangelienauslegung: eine Untersuchung zu Luthers Hermeneutik*, Darmstadt, 1962. Friedrich Beisser, *Claritas scripturae bei Martin Luther*, Göttingen, 1966; Johannes Müller, *Martin Bucers Hermeneutik*, Gütersloh, 1965.

[57] See Foucault, *Les Mots et les choses*, pp. 40ff.; E. Ruth Harvey, *The inward wits: psychological theory in the Middle Ages and the Renaissance*, London, 1975; Jean Starobinski, *Montaigne en mouvement*, Paris, 1982, pp. 168ff. For juristic awareness of the limits of their enquiries, see Rebuffi, *In titulum Digestorum de verborum et rerum significatione*, p. 3 ('ne misceam sacra profanis, cum quaelibet scientia suos habeat terminos, theologis et medicis sua relinquam, et mea sorte contentus, iurisconsultorum verba interpretabor' (lest I mix the sacred with the profane, and as every discipline has its frontiers, I shall abandon to theologians and to doctors their own particular concerns and, happy with my fate, interpret the texts of jurists)). Cf. also Alberigo Gentili, *In titulum de verborum significatione commentarius*, Hanau, 1614, p. 2.

[58] See Gammaro, *De extensionibus, passim*; de Federicis, *De iuris interpretatione, passim*; Piano Mortari, *Diritto, logica, metodo*, pp. 197ff.

[59] See gl. ad D 1.1.1; Turamini, *De legibus*, pp. 1–12.

seems that no monographs devoted exclusively to the subject were written before the fifteenth century. Before that, the issue was treated in the various parts of the gloss which deal with the relevant titles of the Corpus Juris Civilis: D 1–3 _De iustitia et iure, De origine iuris, De legibus_, D 34.5 _De rebus dubiis_, D 50.16 _De verborum significatione_, D 50.17 _De regulis iuris antiqui_, C 1.14 _De legibus_. As well as these titles, there are individual _regulae_ in the form of maxims or hypothetical cases scattered throughout the Digest which attract commentary about the theory or practice of interpretation.[60] The first monographs to appear on the subject are difficult to date with precision: Matthaeus Mathesilanus' short _Tractatus extensionis ex utroque iure elucubratus_, probably produced around 1435, is presented as a series of notes and practical examples: the _De interpretatione legis extensiva_ of Bartolomaeus Caepolla, who was writing in the 1460s, is longer and divided into chapters, prefaced by a general account of extensive interpretation. Constantinus Rogerius' _Tractatus de iuris interpretatione_, dated 1463, is more comprehensive still, and obviously designed to fulfil a pedagogical purpose: it begins with definitions of law and interpretation, before considering the relative authority of the interpreter and the application of interpretation to different kinds of written law. Stephanus de Federicis's _De interpretatione legum_ (_c._ 1495), which, together with the text of Rogerius, was selected for inclusion in the first edition of the _Tractatus iuris universi_ of 1549, follows more or less the Ciceronian list of _causae legales_ ('Quando plus aut minus intellectum est quam scriptum'; 'Quando leges invicem videntur esse contrariae'; 'Quando verba legis sunt ambigua'; 'Quando controversia diffinita esse non reperitur, tamen a similitudine alicuius legis diffiniri posse videtur': cf. _De inventione_, ii.40.116).[61] Alciato's famous essay on the meaning of words, which precedes his commentary on D 50.16, appeared first in 1530; it is divided into four books which radically reorder the traditional materials for discussion, and which end with an account of _elocutio_ taken from Quintilian books viii

---

[60] See above, note 4.
[61] The Ciceronian text reads: 'in scripto versatur controversia cum ex scriptionis ratione aliquid dubii nascitur. Id fit ex ambiguo, ex scripto et sententia, ex contrariis legibus, ex ratiocinatione, ex definitione' (a controversy turns upon the written word when some doubt arises from the text. This comes about from ambiguity, from a clash between the letter of the law and the intention of the legislator, from conflict of laws, from reasoning by analogy, and from definition); cf. _Ad Herennium_, i.11.19. The stemma of texts suggested here is more or less that produced by Förster, _Interpres_, p. 10.

and ix, and with an attack on Valla's philology.[62] All of these Italian works enjoy republication in the course of the sixteenth century, and influence strongly most later monographs.

Other sources of interpretation theory are the commentaries on D 50.16, and, to a lesser degree, on D 1.3, D 34.5 and D 50.17. Caepolla's clear exposition of D 50.16 was produced in 1460, according to its colophon; it is cited together with Alciato's by Pierre Rebuffi in 1534; he, in turn, is referred to by Jean Breche; by the end of the century, Johannes Goeddaeus includes mention not only of Breche, Rebuffi and Alciato but also Cujas, Doneau, Le Douaren and others in his compendious *De verborum et rerum significatione* which enjoyed six editions between 1591 and 1622. Mention should also be made here of Alessandro Turamini's posthumous *De legibus* of 1606, which is a general essay on problems of legal drafting followed by a commentary on D 1.3, calqued on the design of Alciato's *De verborum significatione*. His essay addresses general questions of extensive interpretation and equity which appear in the mid-century writings of French systematizers (especially Doneau and Connan) and the Italian Alberto Bolognetti, whose *De lege iure et aequitate* appeared in 1570, and was reprinted in the 1585 edition of the *Tractatus iuris universi*. It goes without saying that by the middle of the century, most pedagogical material also devotes space to the topic.

2.8

Can one say that by the end of the sixteenth century, a new approach has been developed? What was the effect of the input of humanist material in the course of the fifteenth and sixteenth centuries? I would venture to reply: not very great. Cantiuncula's list of loci is almost identical to that of Boethius' *De topicis differentiis* (a text which enjoyed far more frequent republication in the first half of the century than his own); Alciato's essay on meaning, for all of its novelty in its ordering of material and inclusion of Quintilian's figures, is very close to the approach of the postglossators who are extensively cited by him with respect; the *divisio* technique of logical analysis is effectively as dichotomic as is the method of Ramus, even if it does not present itself in the same visual form (see above 1.4.3). To conclude from this that *nihil novi sub sole* would be clearly wrong; but it would equally be a mistake to underestimate the continuity provided by, on the one

---

[62] For an account of Alciato's *De verborum significatione*, see Viard, *Alciat*, pp. 149–51.

hand, the Aristotelian tradition and its characteristic modes of thought, and, on the other, the concerns proper to the legal profession itself which predispose it to a certain set of assumptions about the relationship of words and things. To investigate this further will be the concern of the next chapter.

CHAPTER 3

Theories of interpretation and meaning

Quid enim in rerum natura explicari, quid investigari, quid demonstrari potest, sine sermonis verborumque rem significant-ium beneficio? Sine interpretationis ministerio?

(Johannes Goeddaeus, *Commentarius repetitae praelectionis in tit. XVI libri L. Pandectarum de verborum et rerum significatione*, 5th ed., Herborn, 1614, p. 2)

For what can be explained, investigated or demonstrated about the nature of things without the assistance of speech and words which signify things? Or without the ministry of interpretation?

3.1.1

The need for interpretation arises from a fundamental asymmetry in the law itself. The written law is, on the one hand, not the law; rather it embodies more or less directly and successfully the norms and force of the law; as a long series of jurisprudential texts have warned the student, to know the words of the law is not to know the law.[1] The law,

---

[1] D 1.3.17 (Celsus) 'Scire leges non hoc est verba earum tenere, sed vim ac potestatem' (To know the law is not to know the text of the law but its force and power); cf. D 50.16.6.1, quoted below 3.6.1, and D 44.7.38 (Paulus) 'Non figura litterarum sed oratione quam exprimunt litterae obligamur . . .' (We are bound not by the form of written words but by the proposition they express); see also Alciato, *De verborum significatione*, p. 14 ('leges non tam in verborum forma quam in ratione consistunt'); Doneau, *Commentaria de iure civili*, 1595, i.13, in *Opera omnia*, Lucca, 1762, i.87–106, who writes at length on the dual proposition 'neque omne quod scriptum ius est; neque omne quod scriptum non est, ius non est' (not everything that is written is law; nor is everything not written not law); Sapcote, *Ad primas leges*, p. 56: 'nam certe hoc verum est, quod legis verba tantum perdiscere, legis ipsius cognitio non est' (for it is certain that only to learn the words of the law by heart is not to know the law); and Muret, *Commentarius in quattuor titulos*, pp. 114–15: 'si omnes qui tenent legum verba, leges scirent, omnes pueri Romae olim fuissent iurisconsulti: ita enim ediscebant legem XII tabularum ut carmen necessarium ait Cicero [*De legibus* ii.5.11–6.14]' (If all those who knew the words of laws knew the law, then all Roman boys were once jurists: for they used to learn by heart the law of the twelve tables as a compulsory poem, according to Cicero). Muret relates this both to the ignorance of the law not being an excuse (see C 1.14.9) and with the 'guild sense' of the legal profession '[scire leges] praeterea requiritur ut vis ac

87

on the other hand, *is* the spoken or written law; no matter how much jurists might wish to invoke non-verbal controls on the law such as legal norms or equity or custom, in the end, the *ius non scriptum* is only known because it can be translated into the medium of speech or writing. This is arguably true even of systems based on precedent; it is certainly the case with statutory systems such as the Corpus Juris Civilis, in which 'judgement is made by statute and not by precedent' and in which the function of the words of the law is to 'make the sense of the law and the intention of the legislator visible'.[2]

This sense and intention become visible when the judge applies the law, and the interpreter communicates it to his pupil or client.[3] In a perfect world, the act of application or communication would involve no more than verbatim restatement; but as we have seen, even absolutist legislators such as Justinian recognize that this is not a perfect world.[4]

Given the multifaceted nature of interpretation, it is neither easy to treat it in a rigorous order nor possible to avoid a certain amount of reiteration; nor is it convenient simply to follow the disposition of Ciceronian topics, as questions arise which are not addressed there. The *degré zéro* of interpretation and the relative authority of interpreters are two such questions with which this investigation begins, after which the following issues will be treated in turn: the distinction between interpretation on the one hand and signification, conjecture and presumption on the other; the procedure or method of interpretation; the various modes of interpretation *in more italico* and *in more gallico*; verbal propriety, ambiguity and usage; the excess of interpretation (cavillation); legal fictions; literal, subjective and objective meanings; performative aspects of language use; and finally non-verbal interpretative modes (custom and equity).

---

potestas earum intelligatur: quod sine magno et diuturno studio fieri not potest. Et hoc modo soli iurisconsulti dicuntur scire leges' (besides, in order to know the law it is necessary to grasp its force and power, which cannot be done without long and deep study. Hence only jurists are said to know the law).

[2] C 7.45.13: 'non exemplis sed legibus iudicandum est'; Turamini, *De legibus*, p. 202: 'nec verba legis existimanda sunt lex, nisi quatenus sensum legis et legislatoris voluntatem manifestant'. See also *ibid.*, p. 63. The relationship of *exemplum* to *casus* raises again the question of the rhetorical or topical status of legal argument: see Schmidt-Biggemann, *Topica universalis*, p. 13.

[3] See Rebuffi, *In titulum de verborum et rerum significatione*, pp. 1–2.

[4] See above 1.5.1; and C 1.14.12, C 1.17.2, and Hunnius, *De authoritate*, p. 109.

THE SELF-EVIDENT TEXT

3.1.2

Modern proponents of philosophical hermeneutics would, of course, claim that there is no *degré zéro* of interpretation:[5] but Renaissance jurists and their medieval predecessors do not agree. Bartolus, following D 1.3.12 and D 1.3.23, claims that judges may interpret the law 'nisi verba essent plana, quia tunc non potest aliter interpretari quam verba loquuntur' (except in cases when the words are clear: in these cases it is not possible to interpret in any other way than according to the literal meaning); or as Bolognetti has it, the words of the law cannot be attenuated 'cum verba legis illud ipsum aperte decidunt, de quo disceptatio est, ut sine vitio scripturae inflecti non possunt, tunc nulla interpretatione, nullaque aequitate evitari potuerunt, aut ad eum sensum contorqueri, qui prorsus a verbis alienus sit' (in cases where the words of the law clearly settle the issue so that they cannot be twisted in any way without violating the text; then they cannot be set aside by any act of interpretation or appeal to equity, nor can they be forced to bear a sense alien to the words themselves).[6]

This injunction is implicit in the κατὰ πόδα rule of translation imposed by Justinian in C 1.17.2.21 (see above 1.5.1), and in Neratius' claim in D 22.6.2 that the law can and must be certain (finitum).[7] Now this *degré zéro* may not be as uncontroversial as it sounds, since what is 'planus' or 'tam apertus' has to be established as such, and if some further guarantee of clarity is not adduced (such as common sense, undeniable consensus, rationality) then the epithets 'manifestus', 'clarus', 'planus', 'apertus' merely become rhetorical devices for warding off fundamental questions. The frequent occurrence of such phrases as 'res clara et dilucida', 'clarae rationes', 'manifestissimus sensus' (C 6.28.3) 'evidentissima ratio' and the invocation of 'nuda verba' (brute words) are indicative of the outer

---

[5] On this view, see Gadamer, *Wahrheit und Methode*, ii.2.5, pp. 299ff.

[6] *De lege, iure et aequitate*, i.34, in *Tractatus iuris universi*, i.321. See also Alciato, *De verborum significatione*, pp. 204, 222; de Federicis, *De iuris interpretatione*, lxi, in *Tractatus iuris universi*, i.221 ('absurdum est a verbis certis propter dubiam mentem recedere'); D 40.9.12; D 32.25 (Paulus): 'Cum in verbis nulla ambiguitas est non debet admitti voluntatis quaestio' (where there is no ambiguity in the words, questions about intention are not admissible).

[7] Neratius' claim ('ius finitum et [potest] esse et [debet]' is alluded to by Turamini, *De legibus*, p. 152.

limits, the *nec plus ultra* of legal discourse; they occur at points in a
discussion where fundamental issues or principles come into question,
but where the jurist does not wish to embark on the laborious task of
establishing them.[8] Turamini, commenting on the words 'quae certa
sunt' in D 1.3.21 makes this point explicitly: 'In iis, quae certa sunt,
non oportet inquiri rationem, cum enim certa sese nobis offert
voluntas legislatoris, studiosa rationis investigatio temeritatem demonstrat inquirentis' (one should not investigate the rationale of
those things which are self-evident, for where the legislator's intention
offers itself to us unambiguously, curiosity about it merely reveals the
temerity of the inquirer).[9] But he offers no rules by which 'certain' can
be identified; indeed there is only one offered by the gloss and that is
not particularly helpful.[10] The practitioners of the *mos italicus* such as
Turamini and Bolognetti are willing to devote lengthy discussion to
the meaning of the law, the *ratio legis*, but while they are able to
express the proposition that such discussion might be wholly
redundant for political reasons or even ill-founded logically, they are
unable to analyse it. They chose instead to 'make visible' the sense,
that is, to restate it in different words,[11] and in doing so to set in
motion the endless process of interpretation which has come to be
known as 'the logic of the supplement' (see below 3.6.2).

[8] Rebuffi, *In titulum de verborum et rerum significatione*, pp. 54–5; Turamini, *De legibus*, p. 154; 194;
cf. Max Weber, 'Die Objektivität socialwissenschaftlicher und sozialpolitischer Erkenntnis',
1904, in *Gesammelte Aufsätze zur Wissenschaftslehre*, ed. J. Winckelmann, Tübingen, 1968, pp.
152ff. (on that which is 'als selbstverständlich gegeben').

[9] Turamini, *De legibus*, p. 193, cf. Savius, *In Pandectarum titulum de verborum et rerum significatione*,
p. 106: 'ubi verbum de se planum est atque apertum nulli interpretationi locus relinquitur'
(where words are clear and manifest in sense there is no room for interpretation) – Savius
refers here to D 32.25; see Rebuffi, *In titulum de verborum et rerum significatione*, p. 55: 'unde dicit
Bartolus in 1.ab. executore col. pen. ff. de appellat quod licet iudex . . . possit interpretari
iura, tamen hoc intelligitur, nisi verba essent plana, quia tunc non potest aliter interpretari
quam verba loquuntur' (where Bartolus (gl. ad D 49.1.4) says that a judge may interpret the
law, it must be understood to imply that the judge may not interpret the law when the words
are clear, because in such circumstances he may only take them in their literal sense). See also
de Federicis, *De iuris interpretatione*, lxi, in *Tractatus iuris universi*, i.221, quoted above, note 6. A
slightly different slant is given to the issue of interpretation by opposing 'simple' to 'complex'
modes: see Conal Condren, 'Rhetoric, historiography and political theory: some aspects of
the poverty controversy reconsidered', *Journal of religious history*, ii (1984), 15–34, esp. 23.

[10] Gl. ad D 9.2.51 (Julianus) Multa autem iure civili contra rationem disputandi pro utilitate
communi recepta esse, innumerabilibus rebus probare potest (for it can be proved by
countless examples that many things have been accepted in civil law for the common good
against the logic of the argument), cited by Hunnius, *De authoritate*, p. 3. This is, of course, a
tacit acceptance of inductive arguments in law (see above 2.4).

[11] 'Nonnullis argumentis hanc ipsam veritatem non tum probare quam aperire' (by argument
to show truth rather than prove it): Turamini, *De legibus*, p. 50. This sounds deceptively
Wittgensteinian; but is most appropriately read in the context of 3.2.1.

AUTHORITY AND INTERPRETATION

3.1.3

The command 'do not interpret that which is clear' is, of course, implicit in Justinian's prohibition of interpretation by jurists and his reservation of interpretation for the Emperor-legislator alone; we have already encountered one ingenious answer to this interdict (above 1.5.3). Nearly all medieval and Renaissance commentators record the fact that Emperors alone have authority to interpret the law (C 1.14.1, 12). Indeed, the Emperor is above positive law although not above the law of God or nature[12] (D 1.3.31: 'Princeps legibus solutus est'): and his decisions constitute the law (D 1.4.1 'Quod principi placuit, legis habet vigorem' (the wishes of the prince have the force of law).[13] As faith is to theology, so is the Emperor to the law, which he in a certain sense embodies, as does the Pope in his domain: 'papa imperator leges animatae in terra vocantur'.[14] He also embodies equity, and alone has authority to adjudicate its relationship to written law (C 1.14.1). Some Renaissance commentators (notably those belonging to beleaguered minorities) argue from this that the different legal systems prevalent in Germany at the end of the sixteenth century are justified politically because different princes embody different notions of equity.[15]

What is at issue here is the relationship of authority to interpretation. That authority with respect to the power of magistrates is a vexed issue has long been known: the commentaries on D 2.1.3 (Ulpian's distinction between *merum imperium* and *mixtum imperium*) have been subjected to close scrutiny, most recently by Myron Piper Gilmore; the questions of delegation of powers and of jurisdiction are

---

[12] Turamini, *De legibus*, p. 36; see also Hunnius, *De authoritate*, pp. 44–64.

[13] On this law and its fortunes, see Kantorowicz, *The king's two bodies*, pp.146–59.

[14] Savius, *In Pandectarum titulum de verborum et rerum significatione*, p. 115; see also Kantorowicz, *The king's two bodies*, pp. 127–38; Condren, 'Rhetoric, historiography and political theory', p. 21 (on John XXII's bull *Ad Conditorum*); Lefebvre, *Les Pouvoirs du juge*, p. 16 (quoting canon law sources). Marquard Freher, *Sulpitius sive de aequitate commentarius ad 1.1 C. de legibus*, Frankfurt, 1608, p. 17, refers the topos 'lex semper loquitur' to Aristotle, *Politics*, ii.8, although I cannot find the phrase anywhere in book ii. For an aggressive satire on this topic, see Agrippa, *De incertitudine*, xci: 'iuris scientiae facultatis hodie principes sunt Papa et Imperator, qui gloriantur, se habere iura omnia in scrinio pectoris sui recondita' (the rulers of the faculty of jurisprudence these days are the Pope and the Emperor, who boast that they have all laws written in the cabinets of their breasts . . .).

[15] See Freher, *Sulpitius*, p. 23. On this issue in general, see *International Calvinism*, ed. Menna Prestwich, Oxford, 1985.

clearly very closely related to the question of authority in interpretation, but this is rarely pointed out by medieval and Renaissance
commentators.[16] Bartolus invokes authority as the prime means of
determining sense (before recourse is had to definition and etymology): in doing this he subordinates the truth of the text or
utterance to the truth of its allegation: that is, he asks the question 'is it
true that the emperor said this?' before asking the question 'is what is
said here true?' This hierarchy is implicit in the commonplace that
princes interpret 'by the law of majesty', and judges and jurists 'by the
authority of the prince'.[17] The distinction in those modes of
interpretation is enshrined in the opposed epithets *necessarius* and
probabilis. The prince interprets in a necessary, i.e. binding mode;
others (who certainly include the 'doctores aetatis nostrae')[18] in a
'persuasive' mode. The use of the term *probabilis* is not easy to
evaluate: it has up to now been argued that it means '[what] appears
to many, and especially to wise men, to be true' and characterizes the
plausible but not apodictic premises on which topical argument is
based; but Cicero's use of the adjective in *De inventione*, i.30.47–9, and
the use of such terms as *verisimilis, credibilis* and even reference to
'gradus certitudinis' suggest more modern connotations of plausibility.[19] Both *necessarius* and *probabilis* carry with them connotations of
proof, or entailment (both modes can produce *consequentiae*), in
contradistinction to *possibilis* or *causalis*, from which no consequences
can be drawn.[20] The 'probable' (ἔνδοξον) mode may only be applied,

---

[16] See Gilmore, *Argument from Roman law*, pp. 15ff.; gl. ad D 1.21.1; Alciato, *Opera*, i.150.

[17] Förster, *Interpres*, pp. 4–5, citing Bartolus, gl. ad D 1.1.10; cf. Hegendorf, *Epitome*, p. 34 citing Panormitanus, *De postulatione prelatorum*, i, in *Super prima pars primi libri Decretalium Commentarii*, Lyon, 1524, fols. 106–9. On the question of authority in general, see Hunnius, *De authoritate*, who considers the relative claims of reason, the legislator (*princeps*), conscience, the texts of the Corpus Juris Civilis and subsequent legal texts and principles, ending with the authority of the *communes doctorum opiniones*.   [18] Hegendorf, *Epitome*, p. 34.

[19] This is a problematic domain, in which the major point of difficulty arises over the nature of certainty: is this a psychological phenomenon in the perceiver or an objective feature of a given class of knowledge? The Aristotelian loci are *Metaphysics*, i.2 (982a20) and *Nicomachean Ethics* i.3 (1094b12); see also *Ad Herennium*, ii.2·3; Aquinas, *Summa Theologiae*, 2a 2ae 9.1 ad 1; 1a 2ae 96.6 ad 4; 97.3; D 50.17.114 (Paulus) 'in obscuris inspici solere quod verisimilius est aut quod plerumque fieri solet' (in obscure cases one must look at what is more plausible or what is more usually done) and D 34.5.24, which speaks of 'id quod credibile est'; see also Alciato, *De verborum significatione*, pp. 209, 223; Doneau, *Opera*, i.96; Martin, *Antike Rhetorik*, pp. 84, 126–7, 252; Ong, *Ramus*, p. 32n; Th. Deman O.P., 'Probabilis', in *Revue des sciences philosophiques et théologiques*, xxiii (1933), 260–90.

[20] De Federicis, *De iuris interpretatione*, i.77, in *Tractatus iuris universi*, i.212. The 'proofs' in question are, of course, 'probationes artificiales': see above 2.4, and Martin, *Antike Rhetorik*, pp. 95–119.

however, to arguments about particulars or species.[21] The distinction between necessary and probable is at play also in the problematic notion of extensive interpretation (see below 3.4.1) by which judges and jurists extend existing law to meet particular circumstances and embrace *casus omissi*; only legislators can, by 'necessary' interpretation, extend the scope of the law. The major disagreements between texts on equity and interpretation (for example, those between Turamini, Bolognetti and Connan) arise from discussion of the question of extensive interpretation; the liberal view allows for some exercise of equity by jurists, while the more conservative opinion favours restricting this to princes alone. As might be expected, Aristotelian strictures about the generality of law in *Nicomachean Ethics*, v.10 [v.14] (see above 1.2.3) are frequently invoked in the debate by both sides.[22]

The probable mode is represented by *communis opinio* (the consensus of the best available legal opinion, not, as in humanistic writing, a prejudiced or unfounded belief;[23] but rather the product of premises which are not apodictic, as in Aristotle). In the probable mode of interpretation, a choice may arise if the *communis opinio* is not unanimous, but rather contains equally balanced contrary views: in this case, historically, the Theodosian Code provided for a solution, as has been noted above (1.5.7). Such an argument from the relative authority of jurists is not, however, found either in the Middle Ages or in the Renaissance; it seems that the profession was unwilling to allow its luminaries to be ranked in a binding hierarchy.[24]

All this fits neatly together: but it has to be reconciled to two further claimants to authority. One is the text of the law; the other is the end or final cause of the law, namely *bonum commune* or *commodum reipublicae*, or *utilitas*. These two authorities are represented in the opposition *directus/utilis*, usually applied to actions but also applied to orders of interpretation: *directus* refers to the literal sense of the law which concurs with its intention or purpose; *utilis* refers only to the

---

[21] On the coming together of particulars and species in legal argument, see above 2.4.

[22] Cf. the discussion of *aequitas generalis* and *aequitas specialis*, below 3.8.1; Agrippa, *De incertitudine*, xci; Turamini, *De legibus*, pp. 95ff. (discussing Connan and Bolognetti).

[23] See above 2.4, and Rogerius, *De iuris interpretatione*, iii, in *Tractatus iuris universi*, i.387–8.

[24] On Papinianus, see Cujas, *Opera*, Lyon, 1606, iv.1–1343 and Antoine Favre, *De iurisprudentiae Papinianae scientia*, Lyon, 1607; on jurists' awareness of relative authority in other domains (in this case theology), see Rogerius, *De iuris interpretatione*, ii, in *Tractatus iuris universi*, i.387 (on Jerome, Augustine and Gregory as authoritative in matters of translation, doctrine and moral theology respectively).

intention of the legislator, whose aim is always conceived to be the 'utilitas reipublicae'.[25] It is by invoking the common good that the legislator can change the law, and that the 'probable' interpreter can justify his interpretation of it.[26] But both the text of the law and the authority of the principle of common good pose problems for the interpreter. It would seem uncontroversial in an age of humanist philology to claim that the Corpus Juris Civilis in its pristine form and with its historical sense restored to it would be more authoritative than first the gloss, second the postglossators' additions to the gloss, and finally the elucubrations of subsequent generations of jurists on the postglossators' additions. It would also seem self-evident that the authority of any juristic text declines as it departs from the text itself and chooses to comment on commentaries on commentaries.[27] But as Hotman, Cujas and those who follow them point out, the text cannot be authoritative if it contains interpretations and mistranscriptions: and as Cujas declares of the transmission of any textual tradition in the form of writing, 'nulla res est quae facilius depravari potest' (there is nothing which is more easily corrupted).[28] As for the principle of the common good, which is placed above rationality by some commentators, it is never correlated with the figure of the prince, although it is assumed to be his concern.[29] Aquinas describes it as the final cause of the law (1a 2ae 90.4), but it is not much adduced by glossators and postglossators, who refer more frequently to the authority of 'prudentes', 'legislator' and 'communis et rationabilis intellectus'.[30] The delimitation of the zone of hermeneutic activity in which jurists *qua* interpreters of texts may operate is therefore precarious: their activity

---

[25] See D 3.5.46; D 48.23.3; C 2.18.17; Alciato, *De verborum significatione*, p. 223; Fournier, *In titulum de verborum significatione*, p. 22; Rebuffi, *In titulum Digestorum de verborum et rerum significatione*, p. 56; Kelley, 'Civil science in the Renaissance', in *The languages of political thought*, pp. 74–5; Cortese, *La norma giuridica*, i.266, 309ff.

[26] Rebuffi, *In titulum Digestorum de verborum et rerum significatione*, p. 56; Turamini, *De legibus*, pp. 52f.; cf. also Cicero, *De inventione*, i.38.69, and Condren, 'Rhetoric, historiography and political theory'.

[27] See Montaigne, *Essais*, iii.13, pp. 1045–6; and Nicolaus Vigelius, *Examen iurisconsultorum*, n.p., 1593, p. 9, on the accumulation of legal argument.

[28] Cujas, *Observationes* (1577) i.1, in *Opera*, iv.1345; Hotman, *Tractatus . . . de distractione pignorum et hypothecarum* [D 20.5], in *Opera omnia*, Geneva, 1599, ii.337–40; Goeddaeus, *Commentarius*, p. 18; Hunnius, *De authoritate*, pp. 96–8. The same question arises with respect to the *Basilica*. Kelley attributes this view also to Alciato and Doneau (see *History, law and the human sciences*, iv.273).   [29] See Turamini, *De legibus*, pp. 47ff.

[30] Caepolla, *In titulum de verborum et rerum significatione doctissima commentaria*, p. 26; Rebuffi, *In titulum Digestorum de verborum et rerum significatione*, p. 3, citing Baldus, gl. in rub. D 38.1. In England, the common good is more frequently alluded to, because of the tensions between the common law and the monarch: see below 4.2.

can be extinguished by the prince from whom their authority derives, or by textual revision, which may undermine the authority of the text on which they depend, and is subject to a principle of general utility which has no clear relation to the 'communis et rationabilis intellectus' by which they operate. To support them in their activity they have, of course, that which can broadly be described as general legal norms: custom and equity; but the practice of the latter of these is claimed exclusively by the prince (C 1.14.1) and the former poses problems as soon as it takes on written form (see below 3.7.1).

SIGNIFICATION, REFERENCE, EVIDENCE AND ITS INTERPRETATION

3.2.1

Interpretation is the act of making meaning certain ('sententiam incertam reddere certam');[31] it must 'declare' or 'represent' the law. It is distinguished from other operations on language or signs, namely signification, conjecture or presumption. Signification is the process of giving sense, the act of representing something, usually by a word, external to the thing signified: 'verba significant, et res significantur', as the Accursian gloss has it: 'Et est significare, demonstrare rem de qua quaeritur, proprio nomine ei attributo (gl. ad D 50.16: 'words signify, things are signified. And to signify is to demonstrate the object in question, having attributed to it its proper name').[32] *Res* in this sentence is not easy to translate; but in nearly all contexts, it refers to a prior, existent object, matter, action or mental state, and thus is implicitly referential (or, in medieval logical terms, suppositional). For most purposes, jurists are happy to accept a grammatical sense of signification, namely the process by which speech is imposed on the extralinguistic world; but in respect of legal fictions, they come closer to accepting a philosophical or logical sense, as the act which provides

---

[31] Turamini, *De legibus*, p. 152: see also Förster, *Interpres*, pp. 12–13, quoted above 1.5.1.

[32] Azo also has this formula (gl. ad C 6.28 n. 2): 'Significatio autem proprie nihil aliud est quam demonstratio facta proprio nomine rei, de qua quaeritur, attributo . . . sed illud sciendum est, quia illud verbum "significatione" active ponitur quantum ad verba: passive autem quantum ad res, ut ait M. Fabius. Nam verba habent significare: res autem habent significari.' See Otte, *Dialektik und Jurisprudenz*, p. 38; and Caepolla, *In titulum de verborum et rerum significatione doctissima commentaria*, p. 24 ('significare est . . . proprie et vere exprimere, notificare vel designare'). I have been unable to locate the locus in [Fabius] Quintilian, unless it is loosely derived from i.4.18 (on the distinction of nouns and verbs 'quia alterum est quod loquimur, alterum de quo loquimur'). Cf. also iii.6.37, which deals with *voces* and *res*; and viii.pr.32 (on *verba* and *res*).

significant terms for analysis. There is also uncertainty as to whether 'res' can refer to an intention incorporated in speech, or only an intention which is not invoked in the given act of signification.[33] The boundary between interpretation and signification is clearly set by Caepolla: 'significatio est, quando non receditur a vero et proprio intellectu vocabuli, sed quando dilatatur, seu extenditur, vel coarctatur seu restringitur intellectus vocabuli, tunc ista non dicitur significatio, sed interpretatio'[34] (we are dealing with signification when we stick to the true and proper sense of a word, but when we expand or extend, limit or restrict the sense, we are dealing with interpretation, not signification). The purpose of signification is, therefore, to express and to demonstrate the 'true', 'proper' meaning: the 'strict signification' of words is their definition.[35] We find ourselves again in the realm of the 'manifest': Caepolla's authority for his definition is D 32.69 (Marcellus) 'non aliter a significatione verborum recedi oportet, quam cum manifestum est aliud sensisse testatorem' (one should only depart from the sense of words when it is clear that the testator meant something else). Signification, like interpretation, is an act of 'representing' or 'making visible', ('rei ipsam essentiam veluti picta quadam in tabella exprimere'); Jerome Sapcote quotes a Socratic injunction to an interlocutor: 'Speak so that I may see you', to indicate that signification is ideally as unproblematic as is visual representation. It is conceded, however, that there can be signification of an invisible and indeed non-existent object: the goat-horse, the hippocentaur (I 1.3.19.1), the chimera, the 'res incorporales' of the law (obligations and so on: see below 3.6.3).[36]

3.2.2

Difficulties soon arise, however. Rebuffi, after Baldus, defines 'represent' (*demonstrare*) as 'vere et proprie exprimere, notificare, designare':

---

[33] On supposition, see L.M. de Rijk, in the *Cambridge history of later medieval philosophy*, pp. 164–6; Spade, in *ibid.*, pp. 188–9; E.J. Ashworth, *Studies in post-medieval semantics*, London, 1985, iii, 'Chimeras and imaginary objects: a study in the post-medieval theory of signification' (1977). See also Heath, 'Logical grammar', p. 48; Otte, *Dialektik und Jurisprudenz*, pp. 38ff., 59ff. (on legal fictions); Savius, *In Pandectarum titulum de verborum et rerum significatione*, pp. 8, 21 ('voluntas hominis etiam res est').

[34] Caepolla, *In titulum de verborum et rerum significatione doctissima commentaria*, p. 25.

[35] *Ibid.*; cf. Savius, *In Pandectarum titulum de verborum et rerum significatione*, p. 99.

[36] Sapcote, *Ad primas leges*, p. 3; Breche, *De verborum et rerum significatione commentarii*, p. 5; Savius, *In Pandectarum titulum de verborum et rerum significatione*, pp. 19–21; Förster, *Interpres*, p. 346; Goeddaeus, *Commentarius*, pp. 7ff. On fictional objects, see above, note 33. See also John Magee, *Boethius on signification and words*, Leiden, 1988, pp. 61ff.

'vere et proprie' are difficult to make sense of in relation to words which, being conventional and not natural signs, cannot easily be assigned a 'proprium', and still less a truth-value (see *De interpretatione*, ii (16a20)) and 'exprimere', as we shall see (below 3.2.5), contaminates signification with the question of subjective sense.[37] In other descriptions, such representation is said to be narrow or broad, proper or improper;[38] if improper, it will precisely require the very interpretative activity from which it is so carefully distinguished by Caepolla (see below 3.4.2). The passage from the pure representation of a 'clear' signification to an authoritative act of interpretation is best exemplified in Goeddaeus' account of the word in his commentary on D 50.16. He begins by stressing its objective and manifest nature: 'significatio est proprius et verus verborum rerumque intellectus, quo quaelibet res tanquam in picta tabella oculis quasi subjicitur et declaratur' (signification is the proper and true meaning of words and things by which a certain thing is as it were laid before, and made manifest to our eyes as in a painting): but he soon switches course, insisting that the sense obtained is complex: not just from single words but from sentences which express both the thing and the *animi intentio* (which can itself be a *res*, as we have seen). As there are more things than words in the world (a maxim culled from the *De sophisticis elenchis*, 165a14–16), true and proper expression is not always sufficient to designate a given object: we sometimes must have recourse to tropes and figures. Goeddaeus digresses here to attack Alciato's account of these (see above 2.5): but his real point is not Alciato's failings as a rhetorician, but rather his introduction of rhetoric into the domain of law. Jurisprudence, he avers, is a separate science: it understands words in ways different from natural philosophers, grammarians, moralists and historians (here Breche's attack on Valla is invoked). The law has two vocabularies: its own, the 'significatio iuris', and that of the community of all men, the 'significatio facti'. The former is immutable, the latter variable;[39] the former essential, the latter accidental. To give correct signification to the words of men, you must know their intentions, which may entail that it is necessary to abandon correct usage. But this may also be necessary in the case of the words of the law itself: 'in legis latore et

---

[37] Rogerius, *De iuris interpretatione*, ii, in *Tractatus iuris universi*, i.387.
[38] Breche, *De verborum et rerum significatione commentarii*, p. 5; Gentilis, *In titulum de verborum significatione*, p. 3.   [39] See D 30.4. and Coke, *Institutes*, ¢ 6ʳ.

publice quid statuente primum attenditur, quid dixerit; deinde, qua occasione, quo intuitu, qua mente' (we must pay attention, in considering the words of legislators and those who lay down the law in public first to what they say; then to the occasion on which they said it, their meaning and intention). It seems that the great distinction between legal and common signification has to be abandoned very fast; for the introduction of features of linguistic context (*occasio, intuitio, mens*) turns the act of legislation into a pragmatic event. Furthermore one can abandon usage (*vocum proprietas*) if the intention can be gleaned 'per legitimas conjecturas' (on which, see below 3.2.5). Goeddaeus is now able to quote the jurist Julianus' description of 'strictam verborum significationem' as 'subtilitatem';[40] 'sub qua', Goeddaeus adds, 'saepe perniciose erratur' (logic-chopping, by which we are often led to err perniciously), reversing thereby the initial characterization of signification as 'proper, true and adequate representation'. He is thus able triumphantly to offer his own signification of signification: 'verborum iuris et de iure quid facientium vero sensu, et proprio, ex vera cuiusque verbi vel rei attributione emergente, intellectus, declaratio, demonstratio sive expositio' (the meaning, declaration, demonstration and exposition of words of the law and of those who go to law, through the emergence of the true and proper sense from the correct attribution of any word or thing). Signification is identified explicitly by him with the practice of interpretation (*expositio*): Caepolla's careful distinction collapses.[41]

3.2.3

Signification is also controversial with respect to *res*. We have already noted the commonplace of scholarship that humanists value *res* above *verba*: it is therefore ironic that they should be faced with a philological dilemma over this by the Florentine text of the Corpus Juris Civilis, which gives the title of D 50.16 as *De verborum significatione*, omitting the *et rerum* which had up to then been accepted.[42] It was, as has been seen, generally accepted that a non-*res* can be signified; what is at issue here is whether *res* can signify. It is universally agreed that they

---

[40] D 12.1.20.
[41] Goeddaeus, *Commentarius*, pp. 7–14; the same identification of signification and interpretation is found in Albericus de Rosate, *De statutis*, i.9.36, in *Tractatus iuris universi*, ii.4, cited by Savius, *In Pandectarum titulum de verborum et rerum significatione*, p. 99 ('interpretatio quandoque nihil aliud est quam aperta verbi significatio').
[42] See Goeddaeus, *Commentarius*, pp. 14–20.

are signified by words: but can they signify themselves? No doubts had been cast by humanist jurists on the authenticity of the title of C 6.38, *De verborum et rerum significatione*: some cite this as evidence that *res* are able to convey meaning actively. Alciato dismisses this as a misunderstanding of *significatio*, which as a noun can designate both active and passive meanings (as can, for example, *factio*). He confesses that in his *Emblemata*, he argued that *res* could signify actively in the form of hieroglyphics: but bases his rejection in law of the active signification of *res* on the division he attributes to the ancient rhetorician Fortunatianus between *verbum, dictio* and *res*. In this system (which Alciato elaborates ingeniously from a short subordinate clause) *verbum* designates the material support of the word, or its *nuda pronuntiatio*; *dictio* the combination of this with a meaning; and *res* the referent. Thus, 'si quis' for a lawyer consists of a sound, a sense ('quem ego ante animo concepi': roughly equivalent to a concept) and a referent (which for lawyers means in this case 'designating either a male or a female person'). He supports this analysis with a couplet which he attributes to Virgil, although it appears not to be by any poet of that name:

> Littera, rem gestam loquitur, res ipsa medullam
> Verbi quam vivax mens videt, intus habet.[43]

The letters express the event; the event itself contains intrinsically the marrow of the word which the human mind perceives.

The slippage here from *vox* (*nuda pronuntiatio*) to *littera* is symptomatic of a difficulty about *viva vox* to which we shall return below (3.7.1).

Alciato dismisses as irrelevant to D 50.16 the fact that *res* can be signs in the *causae coniecturales*; others develop this point. André Tiraqueau, Rebuffi and Goeddaeus all mention examples of this (bloodstains, nodding as sign of consent to a will or contract, acts as signs of intent, even 'signa ignobilia', that is tradesmen's marks or shop signs).[44] One reason for making this claim is to stress that laws

---

[43] *De verborum significatione*, pp. 200–2: D 50.16.1 (si quis); the quotation from Virgil also appears in Goeddaeus, *Commentarius*, p. 16. Fortunatianus, who is cited by Isidore of Seville, was edited in the Renaissance by Theodorus Gaza (1400–78): his *Rhetoricorum libri tres* was first published in Venice *c.* 1500, by Christophorus de Pensis. The relevant clause appears in iii.20 ('ut res ex sensibus constat, ita et sensus verbis explicantur': see *Rhetores latini minores*, ed. Karl von Halm, Leipzig, 1863, p. 132).

[44] Rebuffi, *In titulum Digestorum de verborum et rerum significatione*, p. 4; Tiraqueau, *De legibus connubialibus*, vii.81, cited by Didacus Rodericus Alvaradus, *De coniecturata mente defuncti ad methodum redigenda*, Frankfurt, 1599, p. 11; Goeddaeus, *Commentarius*, pp. 14ff.

are about *res* (as well as *personae* and *actiones*: D 1.5.1) and not words: words are no more than 'rerum notae', as Cujas says, recalling *De interpretatione*, i and Cicero, *Topica*, iii.35 (where they are called 'symbola mentis').[45] Cujas goes on to argue that Alciato is wrong to attribute to *significatio* a passive sense: Gentilis in turn, quoting various ancient authorities attacks Cujas's view.[46] Behind this debate there lurks the far more complex question of words as signs which had such importance in medieval theology, in which the distinction between human discourse and Holy Writ (drawn from Augustine) rested on the claim that in the latter things signified directly, whereas the former possessed only the *significatio vocum*. This is evoked by at least one Renaissance jurist (Sapcote).[47] In the debate over the title D 50.16, there was no clear outcome: Cujas presses the case for the Pandecta florentina, but Goeddaeus who gives a clear and comprehensive account of both views argues from doubts about the correctness of the Florentine text, from the presumptive sign (e.g. nodding for assent), and from examples drawn from D 50.16 itself that the traditional version of the title is 'probabilior, perfectior et verior'.[48]

3.2.4

Significatio is used in connection with both subjective and objective meaning: rather like *intellectus*, which can designate either the faculty of the mind or the objective sense of a word or proposition, the contexts in which it is used require careful consideration. When Baldus defines it as 'proprius et verus sensus adtributus dictioni ab intellectu' the faculty of mind is in question; an objective meaning is implied by *sensus*, and a subjective one by *ab intellectu*.[49] This tension is made clearer in Rebuffi's paraphrase: 'ratio sermonis est natura verborum, id est virtus attributa dictioni ab intellectu ad propositum

---

[45] *Ad titulum de verborum significationibus [sic] commentarius*, Frankfurt, 1595, p. 2: 'verba sola significationes conficiunt, id est voces quae proferuntur, et pronuntiuntur vel litteris consignantur: res dicuntur, non proferuntur' (only words produce meanings, that is, utterances which are brought forth and said, or signified by letters; things are mentioned, but not brought forth); see also Brinkmann, *Mittelalterliche Hermeneutik*, p. 40, and Piano Mortari, *Dogmatica e interpretazione*, pp. 177ff.

[46] Gentili, *In titulum Digestorum de verborum significatione*, pp. 2–3. Gentili refers to Quintilian vi.4 (although i.4.18 and iv.2.36 seem more relevant) and Seneca, *Epistulae morales*, xc.15.

[47] Sapcote, *Ad primas leges*, p. 5; Brinkmann, *Mittelalterliche Hermeneutik*, pp. 23ff.

[48] Goeddaeus, *Commentarius*, pp. 14–20.

[49] See Piano Mortari, *Dogmatica e interpretazione*, p. 178; Baldus is here cited from gl. ad rub. C 6.38. It is a frequently cited locus: see e.g. Rogerius, *De iuris interpretatione*, ii.1, in *Tractatus iuris universi*, i.387.

mentis significandum, quia verba debent aptari menti et significationi'[50] (the sense of speech is the nature of words, that is, the property
attributed to speech by the mind to the end of signifying a mental
content, because words should be chosen in virtue of both intention
and signification). Once a distinction is drawn between *sensus* and
mens, between objective and subjective meaning, pragmatics enters
the arena. We must, according to Goeddaeus, determine *significatio*
with our 'mind's eyes' (*mentis oculi*), by asking not only what is
designated, but why, in what way and by whom; for among the *res*
which words can signify is the 'animi intentio'.[51] Alciato is very
explicit about this: 'sumitur significatio [verborum] variis modis:
nunc habito respectu ad ipsum preferentem, ut si vir imperitus sit,
crassa Minerva accipiuntur verba: nunc considerata eius persona, ad
quem verba diriguntur; plerumque et secundam naturam eius rei de
qua sermo habetur, vel quae in contractum deducitur'[52] (the
signification of words is obtained in various ways: sometimes with
respect to the verbal habits of the speaker, so that if he is not erudite,
the words will be taken to be used loosely; sometimes with respect to
the addressee; sometimes with respect to the subject matter of the
discourse or the nature of the contract). The awareness of the
distinction between speaker's meaning and hearer's meaning is, as
has been noted (2.5), a feature of ancient rhetoric; in Renaissance
jurisprudence, it arises in the determination of *naturalis sensus* as
opposed to *civilis sensus*, the words of the community as a whole as
opposed to the specialist vocabulary of the law. This distinction
requires, as we have seen, an interpreter to determine it: again,
linguistic issues lead us back to the authority of the jurists.[53]

3.2.5
Coniectura or *praesumptio* have different boundaries with interpretation: they fall into the category of *causae coniecturales* rather than

---

50 *In titulum Digestorum de verborum et rerum significatione*, p. 4.
51 Goeddaeus, *Commentarius*, p. 8; cf. Savius, *In Pandectarum titulum de verborum et rerum
significatione*, p. 21: 'cum ipsa hominum voluntas sive intentio res sit, citia controversiam
fatendum est, si verba inventa fuerunt ad demonstrandum exprimendumve res ipsas,
instituta consimiliter sunt, ut loquentium mentem, sive intentionem insinuent' (as human
will or intention is itself a thing, it must be acknowledged without dispute that if words are
chosen to designate and express things, they are similarly instituted to express the meaning or
intention of speakers).
52 *De verborum significatione*, p. 209; cf. the perception of the 'modistae' on this point, referred to
below, note 131.   53 See above, chapter 1, note 38, and 1.6.3.

legales (see above 2.5), and are, like interpretation, 'probable'. They are linked with *significatio* in so far as they process signs, although these are not verbal, but rather facts and omens. *Praesumptio* is defined by Hopper as a 'probabilis suspicio, iuris vel iudicis, qua creditur id alicui adesse vel abesse quod naturaliter vel ut plurimum adesse vel abesse solet'[54] (a plausible guess, in law or by a judge, by which something is believed to be present or absent which either is usually present or absent, or is present or absent in most cases). Its 'probability' is not only based on what is accepted by the majority of jurists; there are also degrees of certainty associated with presumptive proof.[55] *Praesumptio* is an 'artificial' method of proof, as opposed to 'inartificial', i.e. as opposed to an event or clue such as witnesses' depositions, rumour, oaths, the result of interrogation, or circumstantial evidence:[56] these are subject to interpretation, whereas 'praesumptio' is a reasonable assumption which 'se quasi insinuat in animas hominum et solerter indagat, quid factum sit, quid non sit'[57] (insinuates itself as it were into men's minds and ingeniously indicates what was or was not done). Interpretation and conjecture are linked by Hopper to the specific context of determining the meaning of evidence (silence, blushing, trembling); Coras defines *praesumptio* as that which 'ex naturali causa, circumstantiis negotiorum aut personarum proficiscitur' (arises from natural causes, or the circumstances attendant on events or persons), linking it to the pragmatics of a legal event (see above 2.5).[58] It is formally defined as 'res dubiae coniectura verisimilis': evidently no clear distinction was made between presumption and conjecture, both referring to plausible construction on the basis of empirical facts. In certain contexts, legal fictions take on the nature of *praesumptiones* or *coniecturae*.[59] Where these operations seem to differ from interpretation proper is in the fact that they do not necessarily relate to that which is obscure or difficult in some way, and do not relate to words *qua* semantic units (although

[54] Hopper, in *Tractatus de iuris arte*, p. 444. On the predictive element in presumption see Breche, *Ad titulum Pandectarum de verborum et rerum significatione*, p. 5: 'Est enim significare, aliquando iudicare et praedicere aliquid venturum, ut cum dicimus de signis pluviam vel ventos vel quid aliud significantibus' (it is a case of signification when there is judgement about or prediction of a future event, as when we speak of signs indicating rain or wind or the like).

[55] See *Ad Herennium*, ii.5.8.

[56] For a full account of this, set out according to the element of time in presumption (before, during, after the event), see *Ad Herennium*, ii.5.8. See also above 2.4, on the distinction artificial/inartificial.　　　[57] Hopper, in *Tractatus de iuris arte*, p. 440.

[58] Coras, *ibid.*, pp. 175ff.

[59] See *Axiomata legum*, p. 114, referring to D 19.2.14, C 4.65; cited below 3.5.2.

oaths, performatives, replies to interrogation can give rise to presumption and conjecture). In modern terms, they would, of course, be linked directly to interpretation in so far as they deal with evidence and determine its meaning.[60]

THE METHOD

3.3.1

It is pertinent next briefly to mention the series of procedures or method associated with interpretation. These have been exhaustively studied by others, and are not particularly controversial. They are, of course, very closely linked to pedagogical practice: a precise sequence of exercises is prescribed and demonstrated for students which is intended to guide their future activity as interpreters. It operates as a sort of algorithm for the performance of a difficult operation: Erasmus illustrates the need for method in such circumstances by evoking the physical problem involved in moving a heavy weight; many hands can attempt the task, but success will only come through a methodical approach. This insight is sometimes said to be novel, and to have a marked effect on legal pedagogy; but it has many echoes in the earliest texts of the school of Bologna.[61] The glossator Odofredus, for example, sets down such a procedure, advising students to begin with the whole context of the Corpus Juris Civilis, then to proceed through the title to the given text. First grammatical, syntactical and lexical problems would be addressed. Next, parallel passages (*similia*) would be referred to, together with any antinomiae (*contraria*), which would be resolved by recourse to *distinctio* (see above 2.4). *Brocard(ic)a* or antithetical pairs of arguments would then be related to the specific text; after which its use as an argument would be demonstrated, before *notabilia* (especially notable points) were extracted. Not all these steps would, of course, be necessary in every

---

[60] For important Renaissance works on presumption and conjecture, see Alciato, *Tractatus de praesumptionibus*, ed. Joannes Nicolaus Arelatanus, Lyon, 1551; Francisco Mantica, *Tractatus de coniecturis ultimatum voluntatum*, Venice, 1580; Jacopo Menochio, *De praesumptionibus, coniecturis, signis et indiciis commentarii*, Cologne, 1615; Didacus Rodericus Alvaradus. *De coniecturata mente defuncti ad methodum redigenda libri iv*, Frankfurt, 1599.

[61] Erasmus, *De ratione studii epistola*, ed. Craig R. Thompson, in *Collected works*, Toronto, Buffalo and London, 1978, p. 665. For earlier echoes, see Robinson, Fergus and Gordon, *Introduction*, pp. 78f., and Kelley, *History, law and the human sciences*, vi.781 (on Cyno di Pistoia (1270–1336)). On Renaissance method in general, see Gilbert, *Renaissance concepts of method*; pp. 92–8 deal summarily with legal methodology.

case, but the general structure is broadly adhered to, and can be traced in much of the *glossa ordinaria* itself. The approach is very much in harmony with scholastic techniques used in theology and philosophy; the greater rôle given to rhetoric and topics by Renaissance jurists modifies it, without changing it radically. Wesenbeck, for example, suggests the amended sequence *definitio, divisio, causae, actiones, cognata, contraria.*[62] By the 1550s, Matthaeus Gribaldus alias Mopha is able to produce a couplet which sets out the eight things especially to bear in mind when elucidating the law ('in cuiusque legis elucidatione octo maxime observanda'):

> Praemitto, scindo, summo, casumque figuro,
> Perlego, do causas, connoto et obiicio.[63]

Stinzing's account of this method (which follows that of Förster, who used Gribaldus' couplet to structure his *Interpres* of 1613)[64] exposes it as a rejuggling of earlier techniques: terms are defined ('praemitto'), a partitio or distinction is made, ('scindo'); a summary follows ('summo'); the details of the case are set out ('casum figuro'); a formal reading ensues ('perlego'), before the rational bases for judgement (including the purpose of the law in question) are investigated ('do causas'). *Similia, contraria* and *brocardica* complete the process ('connoto et obiicio'). The Ramist Johann Thomas Frey subjected this to a withering satire: but he could have chosen as his target yet more involved procedures.[65] If the terminology and precise sequence are set aside, however, it is difficult to see in what ways elucidation in general (of which interpretation is a part or a species) could consist in different elements.

DEFINITION, ETYMOLOGY, DIVISION

3.3.2

In both the medieval and Renaissance systems of textual analysis, the first element is definition: it is pertinent to discuss this next. Although highly recommended as an initial strategy by Cicero, not all humanists embrace the practice with the same degree of ardour:

---

[62] See Alfred Söllner, in Coing, *Handbuch*, pp. 501–65, esp. p. 530.
[63] Gribaldus, *De methodo ac ratione studendi libri III*, Cologne, 1553, pp. 94–8.
[64] Förster, *Interpres*; see also Stinzing, *Geschichte der deutschen Rechtswissenschaft*, i.105–9, 395–424.
[65] *Ibid.*, i.105–9; Frey, *Neüwe practica juris*, p. 3f.; a Dassel, *Idea boni iurisconsulti*, C 2ᵛff. Similar techniques were employed in customary law: see *Le Style de la chambre des enquêtes*, ed. P. Guilhiermoz, in *Enquêtes et procès*, Paris, 1892.

Montaigne particularly was scathing about it, and clearly associated it (somewhat unfairly, as it happens) more with scholastic than with ancient writing.[66] It also has a bad press in the Digest:

D 50.17.202 (Javolenus) omnis definitio in iure civili periculosa est: rarum est enim ut non subverti posset[67]

every definition in civil law is precarious: for it is rare to find one which could not be subverted.

This might well be a quotation from Aristotle's *Topica* (vii.5 (155a19) 'definition is the easiest of all things to destroy but the most difficult to confirm');[68] there a whole book (vi) is dedicated to the subversion of definition, description and composition. In the *Posterior Analytics* (ii.7–10, esp. 92a26–7) an important distinction is made between definition of objects and of names: 'in defining one exhibits either what the object is or what its name means'. The first of these is analytic, that is, it confirms the essence of an object; the second is synthetic, that is, it determines *de dicto* the sense to be attributed to a word. Cicero places definition in his *Topica* and *De inventione* in the category of *causae legales* (although later rhetoricians were to place some sorts of definition among the *causae coniecturales*, as they deal solely with brute facts (*res*));[69] he, too, distinguishes the definition of objects from the definition of concepts, but in a different way from Aristotle. Whereas the Stagirite claims that nominal definition alone is possible of non-existents such as goathorses (τραγέλαφοι), the chimera, the sphinx and so on, and distinguishes this from the real definition of existent entities, Cicero opposes definition of concrete things to definition of abstractions, including legal norms and categories; this is the distinction between *res corporales* and *incorporales* adopted by the Corpus (I 2.2.1–2; D 1.8.1).[70] He furthermore

---

[66] See Montaigne, *Essais*, ii.10, p. 393.

[67] There is a debate as to whether the text should read 'rarum est' (as argued by Budé) or 'parum est' (i.e. 'there is too little to prevent it being subverted'), following the Florentine text, recommended by Joannes Ferrarius. See *Commentarii ad titulum Digestorum de regulis iuris antiqui . . . Decii Ferrarii, Cagnoli, Franci et Raevardi*, Lyon, 1593, p. 772.

[68] Boethius' translation of this reads 'manifestum autem qua de causa omnium facilimum est terminum distruere'.

[69] *Topica*, v.26–viii.37; *De inventione*, i.13.17, ii.17. 52–6, ii.51.154–6; *Ad Herennium*, i.12.21; Quintilian, vii.8; Martin, *Antike Rhetorik*, pp. 32–3, 45.

[70] See above 3.2.1, and note 36; the Aristotelian loci are *De interpretatione*, i, 16a14; *Prior Analytics*, i.38, 49a23; *Posterior Analytics*, ii.7, 92b4 Because all non-existents are postulated to be combinations of features of realia, they do not breach the maxim 'nil in intellectu quod non prius in sensu'. The legal norms and categories cited by Cicero in *Topica*, v.26–7 include obligation, heredity and usufruct.

distinguishes between definition by *partitio* (the listing of parts of a whole) and definition by *divisio* (analysis of genera into species (see above 2.4)); we shall return to this procedure below (3.3.4). Cicero's influential discussion of definition, moreover, distinguishes it from etymology (below 3.3.3) although in medieval logic this came to be known as 'diffinitio vocabuli'.[71]

Boethius' various works and translations concerning topics take these discussions a stage further. Definition is distinguished from description (roughly nominal definition), and is said to 'rei substantiam monstrare' (or as the postglossators record it, 'diffinitio rei essentiam demonstrat').[72] Its logical status is determined partly by its convertible relationship to the thing it defines ('diffinitio convertitur cum suo definito');[73] partly by its components. Quintilian, following Aristotle, had suggested that definition is made through the four predicables *genus, species, proprium* and *differentia*; Porphyry's *Isagoge* adds *accidens* to this list.[74] In topical argument, only two predicables (*genus* and *differentia*) are said to be necessary; this view is attributed by Alciato to Hegendorf, but it is implicit already in Aristotle and Boethius,[75] and explicit in the jurist Philippus Decius (1454–1535), whose lucid commentary on D 50.17.202 (which first appeared in 1525) represents the *communis opinio doctorum*:

Glos intelligit omnis definitio, dicendum est, ut not[at] Bart[olus]. quod definitio debet ponere substantialia rei definitae, et per hoc debet continere genus sub quo res est definita . . . Item debet continere differentias, ut appareat quod res definita differt ab illis speciebus contentis sub illo genere . . . Et illa est bona definitio quae convertitur cum definito . . . Et non est bona definitio si causa definitur per effectum. Et propter hoc dicitur hic, quod definitio est periculosa in iure: quia difficile est explicare quiditatem et essentiam rei definitae, secundum quod Philosophi veram definitionem perscrutantur, considerando quiditatem et essentiam rei definitae. Sed secundum Legistas videtur quod definitio non sit ita

---

[71] Cicero, *Topica*, v.26–viii.37; Otte, *Dialektik und Jurisprudenz*, p. 103.

[72] See *ibid.*, pp. 98ff.; also *Questiones de juris subtilitate*, i.8.

[73] This Boethian locus is quoted by Peter of Spain in his *Summulae logicales* (see Stump in the *Cambridge history of later medieval philosophy*, p. 282).

[74] *Categories*, i–ii; Quintilian, vii.3; Baldus cites Porphyry's five predicables (see de Federicis, *De iuris interpretatione*, i.15–16, in *Tractatus iuris universi*, i.210).

[75] Alciato, *De verborum significatione*, pp. 13–14; Aristotle, *Topics*, vi, *Metaphysics*, vii.12 (1037b26); Boethius, *De topicis differentiis*, discussed by Stump, in the *Cambridge history of later medieval philosophy*, pp. 274f. Joannes Appellus cites five sorts of definition following the *quinque voces* of Porphyry: see his commentary on cantiuncula, *Topica legalis*, Basle, 1545, p. 138. See also Coras, in *Tractatus de iuris arte*, pp. 47ff. (using Priscian's example of *homo*) and Alciato, *Parerga*, ix.21, in *Opera*, iv. 524–7 (who gives a taxonomy of twelve kinds of definition).

periculosa: quia dato quod quiditas et essentia rei non exprimatur, satis est definitionem constare ex genere et differentiis, ideo quandoque res definitur considerando rem prout est in fieri.[76]

The Gloss understands all definitions to be referred to here; as Bartolus notes, we must point out that a definition should state the substance of the definiendum, and thus should state the genus in which the definiendum is included . . . it should also state the differentiae, so that it will become clear how the definiendum differs from other species contained in the same genus . . . A sufficient ('bona') definition is one which is convertible with its definiendum: it is not sufficient if a cause is defined by its effect. This is why legal definition is said here to be precarious; because it is difficult to state the quiddity and essence of the definiendum; and philosophers search for a true definition precisely by considering quiddity and essence. But it seems that for jurists definition is not as precarious as all that: because even given the fact that quiddity and essence are not stated, it is sufficient for their purposes that a definition consist in an account of the genus and differentiae of the definiendum; thus, whenever something is defined, it is sufficient to do this by considering the thing in question in so far as it is in its coming about ('in fieri').

The *regula* of Javolenus (D 49.17. 202) acts here as a grain of sand in the juristic oyster, much as do D 1.3.17 and D 50.16.6.1 (see below 3.6.1); it is an irritant, because it threatens to invalidate the very practice of textual exposition and commentary which is essential to the activity of jurists. The most extensive defence of this juristic practice is that of Girolamo Cagnoli (1493?–1551) in his commentary on D 50.17, published posthumously in 1576. He begins symptomatically (and transgressively, with respect to his host text and his own conclusion) with a definition of definition, which is also an attack on the *communis opinio* set out by Decius above; we are reminded here both of the parasitic nature of interpretation (here a commentary on a comment on a legal practice which is itself an exposition), and of the general economy of professional exegesis, by which succeeding generations of scholars seek to justify their own activity by modifying and displacing the work of their forebears (see above 1.6.3). These features emerge particularly clearly from the 1593 edition of Cagnoli's commentary, which was printed with the text of D 50.17 itself and the commentaries of Decius and three other scholars.[77]

---

[76] Decius in *Commentarii de regulis iuris*, pp. 771–2: 'definiendum' is used here for convenience to render 'definitum' (the object defined), not to imply any prescriptive sense.

[77] The first printing of Cagnoli's commentary was in 1576; that of Francus appeared first in 1499, of Decius in 1525, of Ferrarius in 1541, and of Raevardus in 1568.

Cagnoli makes considerable use of Aquinas' exposition of the Organon and *Metaphysics*, and preserves its terminology. In his discussion, echoes of the medieval debate between nominalism and realism can clearly be heard. He distinguishes 'definitio quid rei' which is analytic, convertible, proper and scientific in the Aristotelian sense (i.e. providing certain knowledge of causes and demonstrating essence or 'quidditas') from the 'definitio quid nominis', which is the 'ratio interpretativa significationis nominis', and is improper, 'abusive', non-convertible, synthetic, and pertinent to indefinite or infinite things.[78] Like Boethius, he attributes the designation 'descriptio' to the latter category. He wishes to make the heterodox claim that description, and not definition by genus and differentiae, is the form of definition appropriate to civil law; but he does not wish to accept the corollary, namely that as the objects of law are indefinite, there can be no knowledge of them, and that jurisprudence is thus not a science (see above 1.2.3–4). He avoids this problem by claiming that law belongs to the lowest level of certainty (below the ascending trio of physics, mathematics and metaphysics), and is characterized by a weakness peculiar to human reason, namely its tendency to move 'a confusis ad distincta, a potentia ad actum, ab universalibus ad species specialissimas' (from mixed categories to distinct ones, from potency to act, from universals to infimae species).[79] This is perfectly consistent with the position of the postglossators: Bartolus had written that 'ad cognitionem specierum debet praecedere cognitio generis':[80] but Cagnoli ingeniously links this with the Aristotelian argument of the imperfect nature of written law (*Nicomachean Ethics*, v.10, quoted above 1.2.3) which cannot legislate for all cases. It is in the nature of a rule to permit exceptions: such words as 'si', 'nisi', 'aut' and 'praeter' do not appear in scientific 'definitiones quid rei', as Cagnoli points out; nor do homonyms and synonyms which are, however, found in legal language.[81] In the words of another commentator on the same

---

[78] As has already been noted, there is no knowledge of infinites in Aristotelian philosophy: see *Metaphysics*, ii.2.13, 994b28. The distinction between *res* and *nomen* here is, of course, related to the medieval debate between realism and nominalism: on this see Cicero, *Topica*, vii.31, and the *Cambridge history of later medieval philosophy*, pp. 192, 418ff.

[79] On 'mixed' (*confusus*) in its technical sense see *ibid.*, pp. 167, 232n, 418ff.

[80] Cf. above 2.4; *Posterior Analytics*, ii.13, 97b28–30 ('it is easier to define the particular than the universal: and therefore we should proceed from particulars to universals') seems to contradict this, but in one case knowledge (*cognitio*) is in question, in the other definition.

[81] See also Hunnius, *De authoritate*, p. 306, Cagnoli, in *Commentarii de regulis iuris*, p. 781; (on 'praesertim', 'etiam' and 'maxime'); Montaigne, *Essais*, iii.11, p. 1007; and references to the problem of polysemy (e.g. that of Rogerius, *De iuris interpretatione*, ii.19, in *Tractatus iuris*

passage (Johannes Ferrarius, d. 1558), 'Iureconsultus plerunque descriptionibus *quibusdam* et *non absolutis* omni numero definitionibus uti *videtur*' (jurists seem to use most of the time sorts of descriptions and not altogether perfect definitions) (my italics). All definitions in law are normative: for a lawyer, men have one head, but the exception (that someone may be born with two) cannot be ruled out, and lawyers need rules of thumb to allow them to distinguish between men and monsters (see D 1.5.11). Cagnoli concludes that it is for this reason Javolenus declares definition (i.e. 'diffinitio quid rei') to be dangerous: it is suitable for philosophers, but not for jurists, for whom description is sufficient, since it is appropriate to the nature of the rule (i.e. that which occurs 'regulariter', as opposed to that which has the authority of *communis opinio* ('communiter')), to the designation of entities in law (which need not be scientific, but should be normative), and to the speculative nature of human law itself, 'quia proprium legis est dare formam futuris negotiis . . . quae sunt infinita; ut diximus: ideo non est reprehensibile si omnes casus non fuerunt in lege comprehensi, imo hoc est impossibile propter fragilitatem intellectus humani'[82] (because it is the distinguishing feature of the law to give form to future transactions . . . which are, as we have said, indefinite; thus it is not a bad thing, if all cases are not covered by the law; indeed this is an impossible aim, given the fragility of the human intellect). From Cagnoli's discussion, it emerges that he considers lawyers to be nominalist in their attitude to linguistic definition, and realist *qua* users of language.

3.3.3
Descriptions are thus indispensable to jurists; so are names, which are essential to man's communication with other men and his grasp on the world of objects: 'nisi enim homines convenirent in significatione nominum non posset de rebus inter eos esse disputatio'[83] (unless men agreed about what names designate, there could be no discussion between them about things). The jurists whose writings are preserved in the Corpus Juris Civilis themselves often begin with a definition of terms: and in this process they may engage in etymology (called

---

universi, i.387). On the impossibility of defining *regula*, see Otte, *Dialektik und Jurisprudenz*, pp. 215ff. The topical arguments *a simili*, *a correlativis* and *a maiore aut minore* are also not applicable in scientific demonstration *quid rei*.

[82] Cagnoli in *Commentarii de regulis iuris*, p. 783.

[83] *Ibid.*, 773. Cagnoli's long commentary runs from p. 773 to p. 784.

'notatio' in Cicero's *Topica*, (viii.35)) and nomination. The former of these activities, which is, as Breche implies, quite rarely used in law,[84] involves the determination of sense by breaking the word into its component parts and, in some cases, associating it with a derivation. Some of these are frequently quoted in law (*donatio* from *doni datio*, *mutuum* from *meo tuum*, *testamentum* from *testatio mentis*, *verbum* from *verberatus aeris* or *veritas*, even *definitio* from *dis* and *finito*);[85] but the practice is not without its problems. As Aquinas points out, *lapis* may well be derived from *laesio pedis*, but that does not entail that a piece of iron on which one stubs one's foot is a stone.[86] Another simple interpretative process which resembles definition is replacement of a term by a better known word (which Cagnoli, after Boethius, calls *definitio impropria*): that is, a description of the *proprietas verbi* which makes 'clearer' ('apertior') what the sense of a term is. The Boethian example given by Cagnoli is 'conticescere' explained as 'tacere'. This resembles a dictionary definition; we have already noted the use and proliferation of lexica in the late sixteenth century. Some contemporaries are scornful of their value; but they may well have influenced legal language by fixing the actual synonyms used and thus acting as a conservative force on linguistic change.[87]

Names are also pedagogical instruments: Rebuffi and Savius describe them as 'instrumenta rerum substantias docendi' (instruments for teaching the essence of things), after a passage in Plato's *Cratylus* which compares words to the instruments of a weaver.[88] The essentialist doctrine of words, that is, the claim that they contain in some sense the essence of what they designate, which Cagnoli was so eager to banish from legal terms has crept back in this definition of words as instruments and in Cagnoli's own admission that words

---

[84] *Ad titulum Pandectarum de verborum et rerum significatione*, p. 4 ('sed ad etymologiae auxilium confugimus, quandocunque significandi modus non erit a iure traditus': we seek the help of etymology whenever the mode of signifying is not given by the law'). See also Bartolus, gl. ad D 1.1.9.

[85] Alciato's attack on Valla (see Chapter 1, note 105, above) was provoked by Valla's scorning of 'testatio mentis' as etymology. See also Rebuffi, *In titulum de verborum et rerum significatione*, p. 3; Cagnoli, in *Commentarii de regulis iuris*, pp. 773, 776–7; Quintilian i.6.39.

[86] *Summa theologiae*, 1a 13.2 ad 2; 2a 2ae 92 2 ad 1; Brinkmann, *Mittelalterliche Hermeneutik*, p. 45.

[87] Boethius, *In topica Ciceronis commentarii*, iii ('nomen exponitur per aliud nomen notius'); Cagnoli, in *Commentarii de regulis iuris*, p. 773; on the relationship between dictionary definition and the designation of corporate bodies, see below 4.3. Montaigne is, as one would expect, scathing about nominal definition of this kind: *Essais*, iii.13, p. 1046.

[88] *Cratylus*, 378A, 433; Quintilian, i.5; Rebuffi, *In titulum de verborum et rerum significatione*, p. 3; Savius, *In Pandectarum titulum de verborum et rerum significatione*, pp. 8–9. See also Gérard Genette, *Mimologiques: voyages en Cratylie*, Paris, 1976.

possess a communicative function, which causes men to attribute *substantiae* to them. But to insist on the wholly conventional nature of terms, as Aristotle does in the first chapter of the *De interpretatione*, poses no less of a problem for lawyers, since to insist on the conventionality of terms threatens to unhitch them from their attachments to the real world, and puts in jeopardy, moreover, the possibility of acceding to the *proprietas verborum* (see above 3.2.4). De Federicis links nomination to the Aristotelian four causes and ten predicaments, but admits that this is in the final analysis an arbitrary procedure, since men can choose to change the names given to objects at any time.[89] There is no hint here of the essentialist doctrine of the *impositio nominum* derived in part from the Cratylus, and found in mystical and theological writing at this time;[90] but rather a prosaic account of an awkward feature of human language. Through the evocation of this Neoplatonist and Aristotelian debate, we find ourselves again in the complex labyrinth of arguments surrounding the scientific nature of the law, the rôle of language and signification in legal studies, and the priority of things over words, of substantial discourse over chop-logic, of objects over their designations, perhaps also of humanist quasi-realism over scholastic nominalism. Nor will it be the last time that these issues arise in this study.

3.3.4

It is pertinent to return briefly to the question of *divisio* or *distinctio* evoked above. It is explicitly linked to Platonic διαίρεσις both by ancient writers and their medieval and Renaissance successors.[91] It has already been noted that Cicero distinguishes *divisio* from *partitio*; Boethius goes further, and breaks division down into four classes: genus into species (e.g. animals into irrational and rational animals); whole into parts (e.g. house into roof, walls and foundations); polysemic words or propositions into words or propositions with single senses (e.g. 'dog' into four-legged animal and constellation); and finally *divisio secundum accidens*, which itself is subdivided into three classes: subjects divided by accidents (e.g. some men are black, some

---

[89] De Federicis, *De iuris interpretatione*, i.64, in *Tractatus iuris universi*, i.221: 'sicut ex voluntate hominum rebus nomina imposita sunt, ita eorum contraria voluntate mutari et alterari possunt' (just as names are imposed upon things by the will of men, so also they can be changed by a contrary movement of their will).

[90] See M.A. Screech, *Montaigne and melancholy*, London, 1983, p. 82; Claude-Gilbert Dubois, *Mythe et langage au XVIe siècle*, Paris, 1969.

[91] Boethius, *De divisione*, §1; Coras, in *Tractatus de iuris arte*, pp. 40ff.

white); accidents divided by subject (things desired are either desired by the body or the soul); accidents divided by accidents (some white things are solid (pearls), some liquid (milk)). What preoccupied Boethius most in his treatise *De divisione* is the relationship of these classes to syllogistic logic and predication; he investigates the status of differentia and the modes of opposition applicable to *divisio*, sets down rules for distribution (i.e. the distinction to be made between division and subdivision), and deals with problems arising from conversion, inference and indefinites. It is important to note that he banishes open sets (there can be no infinite or indefinite number of species or parts).

Renaissance jurists adopt much of his analysis, but apply it in topical as opposed to logical ways. Thus Coras divides *divisio* into three modes: the Ciceronian *divisio* and *partitio*, and a third category, *enumeratio* ('multorum quae uni alicui insunt distinctio et recensio': the distinction and evaluation of many things which are contained in any one thing), which precisely allows for a sort of division disqualified by Boethius. Coras gives as an example of this last 'Ulpian', who is a *prudens*, a jurist and a persecutor of the Christians (and no doubt many other things besides). This is a sort of *divisio secundum accidens* without the logical exhaustiveness of Boethius' category. Like Boethius, Coras examines differentia in respect to *divisio* proper, and subdivides this into differentiae *ab efficiente, a materia et forma, ab effectu, ab accidentibus*, giving examples of each from Roman law.[92]

Much of this work had already been done by the glossators and postglossators, who both stress the fact that *divisio* is indispensable to pedagogy, and crucial to any cognition whatsoever.[93] But several problems arise from this insistence on the heuristic value of *divisio*. Is it possible to distinguish between necessary distinctions and those which are employed simply to secure a rough and ready grasp of undifferentiated material?[94] What constitutes a *species infima* or *specialissima* (is

---

[92] *Ibid.* Cf. Aristotle, *Rhetoric*, i.13 (1374b), cited above, 1.2.3.

[93] *Ibid.*; Azo, *Summa Institutionum*, cited by Otte, *Dialektik und Jurisprudenz*, p. 95: 'facilior per divisiones trad[i]tur doctrina. Partitio enim sive divisio animum legentis incitat, mentem intelligentiae praeparat, memoriam artificiose reformat' (doctrine is transmitted more easily by division . . . for partition or division stimulates the mind of the reader, provides sense to the intellect and cleverly moulds the memory). See also Placentinus, *Summa Institutionum*, ii.1, cited by Otte, and Aristotle, *Metaphysics* i.2.15 (983a11).

[94] Cf. Irnerius, gl. ad I 1.3, quoted by Otte, *Dialektik und Jurisprudenz*, p. 81; 'non enim est absurdum aliquid extra regulam inveniri' (for it is not absurd for something to be found to be not covered by the rule). On the deficiencies of the category 'regula', see above 2.4.

there, for example, such a thing as a *nudum verbum*)?[95] How does *divisio* relate to the drafting of laws? This last problem appears most clearly in the choice which draftsmen face between first citing general terms (e.g. 'dwelling') and leaving the judge or jurist to interpret them; secondly, providing comprehensive lists of all species of a general term (e.g. castle, manor, house, boat, tent); and thirdly, supplying an illustrative but not exhaustive list, leaving to future interpreters the resolution of marginal or unforeseen cases (is a shed a dwelling?). These problems are cited in the discussion of the more general issue concerning the value of *divisio*: does it promote clarity, as some claim (e.g. Placentinus, who declares 'quanto magis res omnis distinguitur, tanto melius aperitur' (the more you submit anything to *divisio*, the more clearly it appears));[96] or does it result in incoherence, as the sceptical Montaigne affirms:

Les princes de cet art [i.e. jurisprudence], s'appliquans d'une peculiere attention à trier des mots solemnes et former des clauses artistes ont tant poisé chaque sillabe, espluché si primement chaque espece de cousture, que les voilà enfrasquez et embrouillez en l'infinité des figures et si menuës partitions, qu'elles ne peuvent plus tomber sous aucun réglement et prescription ny aucune certaine intelligence . . . en divisant ces subtilitez, ou apprend aux hommes d'accroistre les doubtes.[97]

The commonplace accusation directed at scholasticism by humanists, that of hairsplitting, is here directed at jurists; but it is not the number of angels on a pinhead, but rather the relationship of legal words to the real world that is at issue. As has been noted elsewhere, this problem (that of applying division to an infinite object, namely the infinite particulars of human life and of its as yet unrealized, future, forms) may be simply resolved by the same peremptory mechanism which can always be relied upon to operate in the law: *res iudicata pro veritate accipitur*. *Divisio* is thus assimilated into a topical and pedagogical context as a heuristic tool: its function is to provide a grasp of 'probable' data. It is that which, in Porphyry's definition of an art

---

[95] The loci classici of the question of *species infima* are *Posterior analytics*, ii.13 (97b28) and *Metaphysics* x.7–9 (1057a18). On 'nudum verbum', see Sapcote, *Ad primas leges*, p. 57, and Du Moulin, *De eo quod interest*, in *Tractatus iuris universi*, v.240. The category 'nudum' is used quite extensively in law: one finds references to 'pactum nudum' (D 2.14.45), 'factum nudum' (D 45.1.52), 'nuda voluntas' (Turamini, *De legibus*, p. 48), 'nuda interpretatio verborum' (*ibid.*, p. 160), 'nudum vocabulum' (Goeddaeus, *Commentarius*, pp. 7–8), 'nudum praeceptum' (see Cortese, *La norma giuridica*, ii.242ff.), even 'nudus equus' (Petrus Salazar, *De usu et consuetudine tractatus*, Frankfurt, 1600, p. 220, referring to D 13.6.5.9).

[96] Quoted by Otte, *Dialektik und Jurisprudenz*, p. 95.   [97] *Essais*, iii.13, p. 1043.

('de infinitis finita scientia') makes jurisprudence an art. In this sense it is an interpretative instrument. Examples in Renaissance jurisprudence are found in Rogerius (the species of 'potentia verbi', see 3.6.5), Cagnoli (the species of definition, see above), Ludovicus Gilhausen (the species of slander, see 4.3), and Frey, who uses Ramist typography to represent division (see above, pp. 42–3).

MODES OF INTERPRETATION: DECLARATIVE, EXTENSIVE, RESTRICTIVE

3.4.1

We now come to the taxonomy of interpretation: its division into modes. This is implicit in the earliest *mos italicus* writings: it burgeons in the writings of Azo, Bartolus and Baldus; it generates over time (as one would expect) a great clatter of technical vocabulary and late terminist epithets: (*interpretatio*) *expositiva, correctiva, taxativa, ampliativa, inductiva, fictiva, translativa, intensiva, extensiva, restrictiva, naturalis, genuina, collectiva, paraphrastica, metaphrastica.*[98] It would be unwise to assume that these epithets always carry the same sense throughout the two centuries of their use, but the shifts in usage are not great, and the continuity more noteworthy than any peripheral evolution. For the sake of clarity, I have chosen to give first Caepolla's account, written in 1460; I shall then survey those of Rogerius (1463), de Federicis (*c.* 1495) and Gammaro (*c.* 1510), although not in chronological order; the views of *mos gallicus* writers and systematizers follow, together with the innovatory *mos italicus* writers Matthaeacius and Turamini, writing at the end of the sixteenth century.

Caepolla begins by distinguishing between the following senses of interpretation:

(i) *expositio vocabuli* By this he means the scholastic practice of definition and grammatical and etymological analysis (see above 3.3.2). It is of interest to note that Bartolus in his much quoted gloss on D 1.1.9 says that the *proprietas* of a word can be determined 'ab auctoritate, a diffinitione, ab etymologia':[99] the first of these methods is much in evidence in all legal texts which abound in references to

---

[98] These epithets are taken from Albericus de Rosate, *De statutis*, i.9, in *Tractatus iuris universi*, ii.3–5 (an important source for later writers), a Dassel, Caepolla, Althusius, Rogerius, Gammaro and de Federicis.

[99] See above 3.1.3, and Coras, in *Tractatus de iuris arte*, p. 206.

grammatical authorities: Aristotle, Boethius, Priscian, Varro and others.[100]

(ii) Translation As will be remembered, Justinian prescribed only one form of translation:

[C 1.17.2.21] Leges ... in Graecam vocem transformare sub eodem ordine, eaque consequentia, sub qua voces Romanae positae sunt (hoc quod Graeci κατὰ πόδα dicunt)

to translate laws into Greek by the method known to the Greeks as 'foot by foot' (that is, in the same order and grammatical form as the Latin words)

But Baldus in his glosses on C 6.28.4.8 and C 6.28.3 recommends that 'ista interpretatio non debet fieri ad literam, sed ad sensum verborum, quia sensus verborum praevalet' (translation should not be done literally, but according to the sense, which is more important than the letter), and Caepolla follows him in this. The authority quoted for translation according to the sense (spirit) rather than the letter (which often provokes also a quotation of St Paul (2 Cor. 3:6: 'the letter killeth, but the spirit giveth life')) is Jerome, whose strictures on interpretation in his letter to Pammachus and in his commentary on Galatians are well known.[101] As *probabilis interpretatio* – the mode attributed to jurists (see above 3.1.3) – is justified precisely because it looks to the *mens* of the legislator, it is difficult to see how the word-for-word style of translation could be sanctioned, even in Justinian's own terms (see above 1.5.1); Caepolla does not attempt a justification. The practice of non-literal translation itself is sometimes cited by other writers but without elaborate argument.[102]

(iii) 'interpretatio per quam verba exponuntur ad verum intellectum ponderata ratione potius quam cortice et superficie vocabulorum' (interpretation by which words are expounded according to their true meaning by considering their objective sense (*ratio*) rather than the words themselves') *Ratio* here can only refer to the semantic autonomy of words: this is said, in a common image which we will

---

[100] See above 2.2 and 3.1.3.
[101] See Jerome, *Epistolae*, lvii, ad Pammachum, *PL*, xxii.568; *Commentarius in Epistolam ad Galatas*, i.11–12 [vii.386], *PL*, xxvi.322 (also 473). On literal translation in antiquity, see Fuhrmann, 'Interpretatio'; on loss of meaning in translation, see Anthony Grafton, 'Casaubon on Hermes', *Journal of the Warburg and Courtauld Institutes*, xlvi (1983), 85.
[102] E.g. by Sapcote, *Ad primas leges*, p. 3, quoting Decretal.5.40.8 ('rogo non verbum ex verbo sed sensum ex sensu transferre').

meet again (below 3.6.1), to be behind or below the phonetic or graphic exterior; the cortex/superficies image is that favoured by Jerome also.[103]

(iv) *adhaesio intellectus* (sticking to the sense)   It is not immediately clear what Caepolla designates by this term, especially as *intellectus* could mean here either 'intellect' or 'sense': the example he quotes is from C 6.28.3, which purports to show 'cum enim manifestissimus est sensus testatoris, verborum interpretatio nusquam tantum valeat ut melior sensus existat' (when the meaning of a testator is patently clear, no better sense can be established in any way by any construction placed upon the words). *Adhaesio intellectus* obviously involves the preference of intended subjective meaning, perceived intuitively, over literal sense: Alciato also uses the verb *adhaerere* in this sense.[104]

(v) 'modus significandi attributus dictioni ab intellectu' (a signification attributed by the mind to discourse). This formula recalls Baldus' much quoted definitions of *significatio* and *proprietas* (see above 3.2.4 and below 3.4.2).[105] It will be remembered that Caepolla distinguishes interpretation from signification in the same work; in this context, he apparently subordinates signification to interpretation. Here, as elsewhere, the initial divisions by which categorizations of linguistic practices are made appear to collapse into tautology.

(vi) *disputandi subtilitas*   This phrase recalls Rambach's more celebrated division of interpretation into *subtilitas intelligendi, subtilitas explicandi* and *subtilitas applicandi* (see above 1.6.3)). It may be related also (as it is in de Federicis's work) to the *modi significandi* of medieval grammarians, in which the parallel categories are the *modus essendi*

---

[103] See above, note 101.

[104] *De verborum significatione*, p. 15 'si una [ratio] tantum probabilis sit, potius credendum est illi adhaesisse legislatorem' (if only one [purpose in making the law] is plausible, it is rather to be believed that the legislator adopted that one) cf. Cagnoli, in *Commentarii de regulis iuris*, p. 783; and John Locke, *An essay concerning human understanding*, iii.1.5 (on 'adhere').

[105] The distinction between *significatio, interpretatio* and *proprietas* (defined respectively as the attribution to words by the intellect of 'proprii et veri sensus', 'modi significandi' and 'viris cuiusdam') is, of course, inadequate; it fails to express the difference between *significatio* and *interpretatio* as that between genus and species of mental operation on words, and between both of these and *proprietas* as an accident of signification.

(the level of being), the *modus intelligendi*, and the *modus significandi* (divided by de Federicis into *modus loquendi* and *modus scribendi*: that is, the process by which words are brought to signify things).[106] In Caepolla's work, the 'disputandi subtilitas' designates the four (sometimes five) modes of interpretation which are derived from the postglossators' commentary on D 1.1.9.[107] They are as follows:

(a) *interpretatio declarativa*   This is understood by all commentators to designate the removal of obscurity 'per congruam verbi obscuri expositionem'. The postglossators are equivocal about this as a mode of interpretation proper, but their successors do not harbour doubts about it. It is the practice which underlies all commentary: namely, the provision of explanation to enable obscure passages to become clear.[108]

(b) *interpretatio expositiva*   Caepolla does not think this is a separate mode, since it involves only the practice of definition, etymology or signification which he attributes to modes (i), (iv) and (v) above.

(c) *interpretatio correctiva*   This refers to the transference of a legal action, issue or case from one context to another: D 39.1.1.1, for example, indicates that a given set of circumstances falls under a different rubric, in spite of the apparent applicability of D 39.1.

(d) *interpretatio restrictiva*   By this, the scope of a law is reduced by appeal to the intention of the legislator or the true purpose (*ratio*) of the statute.

(e) *interpretatio extensiva*   This is the most controversial form of

---

[106] See above, chapter 2, note 10, and below, note 131.

[107] The early history of these terms is obscure, but gl. ad D 49.1.4, gl. ad C 6.28.3, Albericus de Rosate and Paulus Castrensis all rehearse them: see the references in Rogerius, *De iuris interpretatione*, ii.4, in *Tractatus iuris universi*, i.387 and Savius, *In Pandectarum titulum de verborum et rerum significatione*, pp. 89ff., who provides a simplified guide (*interpretatio declarativa* is 'congrua expositio verbi obscuri'; *correctiva* is 'modificatio'; *ampliativa* (usually *extensiva*) is 'augmentum per expositionem' and *restrictiva* is 'diminutio per expositionem'. De Federicis distinguishes between 'ampliativa' (where more is understood than the literal meaning) and 'extensiva' (i.e. extension by analogy): *De iuris interpretatione*, i.6, i.11, in *Tractatus iuris universi*, i.210. Cf. also Rogerius (*De iuris interpretatione*, i.29, *ibid.*, i.386) who distinguishes between 'active' interpretation and 'passive' interpretation, the latter being extension 'per identitatem rationis', i.e. analogy; see also Cortese, *La norma giuridica*, ii.328f.. Kelley, *History, law and the human sciences*, vi.787–8, offers a different and, in my view, erroneous account of the distinction between *restrictiva* and *extensiva*. The phrase 'interpretandi subtilitas' occurs in the Codex (12.15.1), and in C.Theod. 6.21.1; see Pringsheim, 'Justinians Verbot', pp. 387–8.

[108] See Turamini, *De legibus*, p. 46 quoted above 1.6.1. This is the sense in which Freud, for example, understands interpretation ('Deuten heisst einen verborgenen Sinn finden': *Studienausgabe in 10 Bänden*, Frankfurt, 1969, i.104). The formula does not resolve the major predicament of modern hermeneutics, since it is not clear whether the hidden or obscure sense is recovered or is instituted by the interpreter.

interpretation. Kelley claims that the commentators Jacques de Révigny and Pierre de Belleperche are the first to have recourse to extensive interpretation; but all commentary is extensive in Justinian's sense (see above 1.5.1), because it passes beyond verbatim restatement: and, as Hopper points out, 'eius est proprie quid deest supplere cuius est ab initio condere'[109] (it is appropriate (only) for the legislator to supply anything which is missing from the law). Others, however, argue that 'addere ex mente non est extendere' (to add by appeal to the intention is not to extend), especially if this is done only by reference to the immediate legal context (the rubric of the title, adjacent laws).[110] Extensive interpretation, by which the law is supplemented to encompass *casus omissi*, exemplifies elegantly the 'logic of the supplement' which Derrida has recently made famous: either the law is a complete expression of the will of the legislator, in which case it needs no supplement, or the law is incomplete when laid down, in which case it is not an adequate expression of the will of the legislator.[111] The same logic works in reverse in the case of *interpretatio restrictiva*. Caepolla wrote a monograph on extensive interpretation, the *De extensione interpretativa*, which transposes noun and epithet, and stresses the connection between extension and intension, that is, aspects of meaning attributable to the general context of the law and meaning derived from inherent semantic features. He gives there a close scholastic definition of the term which indicates some of the difficulties to which it gives rise:

Extensio interpretativa est progressio iusta de dispositivo expresso ad non expressum . . . Extensio . . . est extra tensio, ad denotandum quod extensio habet duo extrema, unum a quo sit, aliud ad quod sit, sicuti habet fictio translativa sive extensiva.[112]

---

[109]   Kelley, 'Civil science in the Renaissance', in *The languages of political theory*, p. 60; Hopper, in *Tractatus de iuris arte*, p. 363.
[110]   Rogerius, *De iuris interpretatione* i.24, in *Tractatus iuris universi*, i.386 (referring to Albericus de Rosate and Jacobus de Arena; cf. Turamini, *De legibus*, pp. 97ff.; D 1.3.11–12; and M. Sbriccoli, *L'interpretazione dello statuto*, Milan, 1939, pp. 149ff., cited by Jean-Louis Thireau, *Charles du Moulin (1500–1566)*, Geneva, 1980, p. 176.
[111]   See Derrida, *De la grammatologie*, Paris, 1967, pp. 203ff. also *L'Ecriture et la différence*, Paris, 1967, p. 423; Hopper, in *Tractatus de iuris arte*, p. 263.
[112]   *De interpretatione legis extensiva*, Venice, 1557, fol. 7ᵛ. Caepolla distinguishes between thirteen types of extensive interpretation: 'interpretatio respectu praesentis'; 'interpretatio largo modo'; 'progressio'; 'transgressio'; 'productio'; 'tractio'; 'porrectio'; 'ampliatio'; 'suppletio'; 'repletio'; 'prorogatio'; 'adaptio'; and 'serptio'. They are all forms of extension by inference, entailment, presupposition (of intention) and analogy. He does not allow 'translatio', 'stipulatio' and 'fictio', on which see below 3.5.2. Caepolla's division of interpretation as set out above is to be found in his *De verborum et rerum significatione doctissima commentaria*, cols. 35ff.

Interpretative extension is the correct progression from what is expressed to what is not; extension is 'extra tension', which indicates that it has two *termini*, one *a quo* and the other *ad quem*, just as translative or extensive (legal) fiction has.

After this schematic account of Caepolla's system, it is convenient first to consider Gammaro's *De extensionibus*, which fits *extensio* into a different scheme, and employs a slightly different spatial metaphor. There are two *genera interpretandi* for him, one *circa verba* and one *circa mentem* (roughly, interpretation of objective and subjective aspects of meaning): both are subjected to close analysis. The *genus circa mentem* is divided into *intensio* and *extensio*, the latter term is here given a technical legal sense, designating the practice of deciding a legal case by appeal to a *convenientia rationis* (an identical cause, purpose or logical content) which is identified in another case explicitly covered by positive law (cf. D 1.3.12). For him, the practice of determining the sense of specialized legal language in a broader way than would be sanctioned by the determination of the literal sense (i.e. construing the phrase 'si quis' to apply to women as well as men), is not *extensio* by *interpretatio ampliativa*.[113]

This is also a distinction made by Stephanus de Federicis, whose *De interpretatione iuris commentarii* is disposed according to the Ciceronian partition of the *causae legales* (see above 2.5). He divides interpretation into four categories:

(i) 'quando ampliamus vel restringimus verba propter mentem' (when we extend or restrict the sense of words by appeal to the intention of the legislator);

(ii) 'quando leges quae invicem videntur oppositae concordantur' (when apparent antinomiae are resolved). This category of interpretation develops into the *Conciliator* literature of which the most celebrated example is the book of Joannes Mercerius (Mercier) of 1587. He proposes a four-step procedure for this: textual criticism (is the text itself correct?); resolution of ambiguity; resolution of problems concerning *ratio* and logic; and if all these steps fail to resolve the issue, recourse to the best available authority. This last step is problematic, however, as there was no agreed hierarchy of authorities in law as there was in theology (see above 3.1.3), and the rule of the Theodosian Code ('when in doubt, prefer the opinion of Papinianus') is of limited efficacy;

---

113 Gammaro, *De extensionibus*, in *Tractatus iuris universi*, xviii.247–60; also above, note 107.

(iii) 'quando verba sunt ita ambigua quod possunt trahi in duplicem intellectum, tamen unus intellectus solus verus esse potest' (when words are ambiguous in such a way that they can be taken to have two meanings, only one of which can be true);

(iv) 'quando volumus extendere legem a simili vel a pari vel per subauditionem, vel ab argumento non necessario' (when we wish to extend a law to similar or identical cases either by implication or by 'probable' argument). *Subauditio* (sometimes *subintellectio*) will be encountered again in other contexts: it means drawing inferences from the linguistic context and arises in the question of *proprietas verborum* (3.4.2), and the power of words (3.6.3). The locus classicus is I 1.2.2 ('cum poetam dicimus nec addimus nomen, subauditur apud Graecos egregius Homerus, apud nos Vergilius' (when we mention 'the poet' without giving a name, Homer is implied in a Greek context and Virgil in a Latin one)). Sapcote says that *subauditio* 'completes' *oratio*; it is, therefore, in his eyes a sort of supplement, a contextual element necessary to the sense, but absent in the text, linked to the original utterance of the *oratio*. Others claim that *subauditio* only limits the sense, and never can be said to extend it.[114]

De Federicis's notion of verbal extension and restriction uses the relationship between meaning and sense, *mens* and *verba* to define the rôle of the interpreter; he is not alone to do this. When *mens* exceeds *verba*, extensive interpretation is justified; when *verba* exceeds *mens* (although not all jurists accept that this is possible), it is a case for restrictive interpretation; interpretation *praeter verba* or *contra verba* is either corrective or arises when a higher instance – the common good, absurdity arising from the text of the law, desuetude, for instance – is invoked (see above 3.1.3).[115] In the case of an equivalence of *mens* and *verba*, expository interpretation arises; when obscurity or ambiguity are encountered (see below 3.4.3), declarative interpretation applies.[116]

There is a third monograph on interpretation selected for inclusion in the *Tractatus iuris universi* which is worthy of mention: like those of

---

[114] De Federicis, *De iuris interpretatione*, in *Tractatus iuris universi*, i.208–25; Sapcote, *In primas leges*, p. 56; Turamini, *De legibus*, pp. 172–3. Valla, *Dialectica*, 124.17–25 (cited by Monfasani, 'Was Valla an ordinary language philosopher?', p. 318) distinguishes *subaudire* and *subintelligere* thus: 'hac appellatione "homo" subauditur "animal" sive subintelligitur significatio animalis'. Derrida, *Marges de la philosophie*, Paris, 1972, pp. 365–93 discusses this issue. The terms 'subdeclarare' (to imply) and 'subinterrogare' (to ask consequentially) also occur: see e.g. Salazar, *De usu*, pp. 219–20.

[115] On *verba* never exceeding *mens*, see Gallus, *Disputatio de legibus*, xxvii, p. 5; on interpretation *praeter* or *contra verba*, see Turamini, *De legibus*, pp. 159–60.

[116] De Federicis, *De iuris interpretatione*, i.6ff., in *Tractatus iuris universi*, i.210.

Gammaro and de Federicis, it is written by an Italian. Constantinus Rogerius' *Tractatus de iuris interpretatione* adopts a different distribution of material. He records the traditional fourfold division into modes (ii.2), but cross-references this with the genera of interpretation appropriate to legislators (*principes*), judges and jurists: these mediate respectively the force, the norms and the text of the law. He next considers the question of custom as a means of interpretation (see below 3.7.1), and then shows how the various modes apply to different categories of laws (*correctivae, exorbitantes, poenales*, and so on). Gammaro also supplies an ordered application of intensive and extensive interpretation to different categories of laws, although his taxonomy is more refined (*primaria, limitativa, correctoria, correcta, exorbitans* (including treatment of *privilegia*), *poenalis*). Rogerius and Gammaro make explicit in this way what is assumed in all these treatises on interpretation: namely that interpretation applies differently to different categories of law both with respect to their context (penal, contractual, and so on) and with respect to the form of the law itself, which might command or permit, punish or prohibit, and might be expressed negatively or positively: thus, for example, penal statutes expressed negatively are subject to different rules of explication than permissive laws.[117] But, as they point out, the duty of the interpreter in every case is to make sense of the law, for 'res . . . magis valeat quam pereat' (D 34.5.12; legal instruments should rather be validated than allowed to lapse). This well-known maxim is in legal terms the equivalent of the philosopher Donald Davidson's 'principle of charity': it is a prerequisite of all interpretation that sense is assumed to inhere in the text or speech to be interpreted.[118]

---

[117] On penal laws being interpreted differently see D 49.19.42 (Hermogenianus): 'Interpretatione legum poenae mollicendae sunt potius quam asperandae' (punishment is to be made more lenient by the interpretation of laws rather than harsher). Cf. also the distinction made between beneficial interpretation for the testator (D 50.17.12) (Paulus): 'In testamentis plenius voluntates testantium interpretamur' (in wills we interpret in the fullest possible way the wishes of the testators), and disbeneficial interpretation for those entering into contract (D 2.14.39 (Papinianus): 'Veteribus placet pactionem obscuram vel ambiguam venditori et qui locavit nocere, in quorum fuit potestate legem apertius conscribere' (it was decided by old jurists that an obscure or ambiguous contract should damage the sellor or lessor in whose power it was that the terms of the legal contract were more clearly set out). The general rule is given by D 50.17.9 (Ulpian): 'Semper in obscuris quod minimum est sequimur' (we always interpret as little as possible in cases of obscurity). For a historical and philosophical account of the origin, nature, parts and modes of laws, see Antonio Agustín, *De legibus et senatusconsultis liber*, Rome, 1583, pp. 1–45.

[118] See Davidson, 'Radical interpretation', *Dialectica*, xxvii (1974), pp. 313–28; cf. D 1.3.7, 22, 25, 30; D 50.17.20, 41, 43, 85. Cf. also Cross, *Statutory interpretation*, pp. 19–20. This principle does not, of course, exclude the possibility that absurdity in the law will need correction; cf. D 1.3.19.

These various treatises between them contain most of the strategies adopted to expound interpretative modes throughout the period of the late Renaissance: variations occur, but within the broad framework provided by Caepolla, de Federicis, Rogerius and Gammaro, which is itself largely derivative from the glossators and postglossators, and tends to exploit a narrow range of metaphors: *extensio, ampliatio; restrictio, arctatio, angustius (strictius)/latius, durius/benignius.* Such metaphors are almost inevitable; they occur also in *mos gallicus* writings, both of the pedagogical type (Hegendorf's *Dialectica legalis,* Cantiuncula, Apel, Oldendorp, Alciato) and in those who attempt to systematize legal studies. These latter writers can appear to be radically innovative in approach. Hotman, for example, sees jurisprudential interpretation as distinct from the grammatical or logical modes: he divides it into three areas of *controversia: ex iure* (conflict of law and equity, and of unwritten and written law (see below 3.7.1); *ex scripto* (ambiguity, *contrarietas* (antinomiae) and *dissidentia sententiarum*) and *ex verbo* (ambiguity again, and obscurity arising from definition). One can see here, redistributed in the last two categories, the Ciceronian *causae legales,* whereas the first category confirms Hotman's commitment to the Hermagorean theses (general propositions about moral and political issues which Cicero argued were not part of forensic argument). Because Hotman is close to the Ciceronian text, his approach has much in common with late scholastic writers who use Boethius, although the terminology and disposition may appear very different; the innovative aspect of his treatise is, in fact, quite limited.[119]

Stronger claims for originality may be made for other *mos gallicus* writers. In the works of systematizers such as Connan, Doneau and Bodin, interpretation derives not from traditional scholastic logic and grammar but from the rational system of law itself; in this, great importance is given to the notions of equity and custom as aids to the identification of legal norms.[120] Historians of law also reconfigure the

---

[119] Hotman, *Iurisconsultus*; cf. Althusius, *Iurisprudentiae Romanae methodice digestae libri duo,* Herborn, 1592, pp. 3–5, who organizes the traditional categories of interpretation around the categories *interpretatio naturalis* or *genuina* ('ubi recta ratio praesidet': that is, interpretation by appeal to equity against *strictum ius*) and *interpretatio collectiva* ('in qua coniectura magis quam ratio dominatur': this is either *ex verbis* or *ex mente,* the latter category subsuming *interpretatio restrictiva* and *extensiva*). Cf. also Thireau, *Du Moulin,* pp. 128–209, for another account of an eclectic approach. See also Frey, *Partitiones iuris utriusque,* Basle, 1571, fols. 4–5 (figs 2 and 3) for a derivative approach in the Ramist mode.

[120] Connan, *Commentaria iuris civilis,* Paris, i.9ff.; Doneau, *Commentaria de iure civili,* i.13, in *Opera,* i.87ff. (who relates the postglossators' categories of *interpretatio* 'quae vulgo restrictiva appellatur', 'quae vulgo extensiva dicitur' to his own); Bodin, *Iuris universi distributio.*

issue of interpretation: of these, Baudouin is perhaps the most noteworthy example. In his *Justinianus* of 1560, he argues either for palingenesis or for total modernization of the Digest to fit sixteenth-century circumstances. These alternatives form his 'interpretatio duplex', which has few echoes outside France, as the Corpus Juris Civilis constituted positive law and hence overrode the distinction which Baudouin wished to make. There, 'interpretatio duplex' had a rather different sense.[121] Writers in the *mos gallicus* tradition are quoted by those of the other persuasion, in Germany at least; but as has been noted before, the *mos italicus* has the property of being able to absorb even that which is inimical to it, and is able to embrace eclectically all approaches. There are cases of resistance to new approaches, especially directed against Alciato,[122] but assimilation is much more common. Hotman and Doneau are pressed into service alongside Caepolla and his successors by Hunnius, a Dassel, Förster and Althaus;[123] Breche, Rebuffi and Fournier show acquaintance with both *mores*, as does Coras, who commends to his readers Le Douaren, Wesenbeck, Pacius and Vulteius, and who is used in turn by Hunnius and Matthaeacius.[124] By the 1580s, as Reusner's *Cynosura iuris* shows, one could read in the same volume a number of competing accounts of interpretative methods without apparently passing out of one conceptual paradigm and into another.[125]

Novel descriptions or dispositions of material do occur even in the increasingly agglutinative development of the *mos italicus*: some are relatively trivial, some more ambitious. Two are worthy of brief description. That of Matthaeacius, without introducing new material, offers an extensive rearrangement of existing materials in a compendious systematic account of jurisprudence *in more italico*:[126]

---

[121] Troje, 'Peccatum Triboniani: zur Dialektik der "Interpretatio duplex" bei François Baudouin', *Studia et documenta historiae et iuris*, xxxvi (1979), 341–58, who refers in turn to R. Feensha, *Interpretatio duplex: een beschouwing over de zgn crisis von het Romeinse recht*, Zwolle, 1952; cf. also Olinger's attack on Lagus for having subjected jurisprudence to a division between *cognitio philosophica* and *cognitio historica*: *Iuris artis totius atque methodi absolutissimae verae et principalissimae divisionis, quae hactenus plaerosque iurisconsultos excellentissimos latuit singularis et brevissima quaedam elucidatio*, Strasbourg, 1555, pp. 3–4. For the *mos italicus* sense of *interpretatio duplex*, see Hopper, in *Tractatus de iuris arte*, p. 363 ('interpretatio iuris est duplex: una, ad intelligendum; altera ad supplendum').   [122] See above, chapter 2, note 54.

[123] Hunnius, *De authoritate*, pp. 2ff. a Dassel, *Idea boni iurisconsulti*, A3ʳff.; Förster, *Interpres*, p. 224; Althaus, *Iurisprudentia romana*, pp. 1ff.

[124] Coras, in *Tractatus de iuris arte*, p. 18; Hunnius, *De authoritate*, pp. 2ff.; Matthaeacius, *De via et ratione*, fols. 54ff. On Rebuffi, Breche and Fournier, see Maclean, 'The place of interpretation'.

[125] Troje would not agree with this view: see 'Alciats Methode'; but Kelley has argued in favour of it: see *History, law and the human sciences*, vi, vii.   [126] *De via et ratione*, fols. 73–125.

that of Turamini uses the locus *a causa* (in this case, the Aristotelian four causes: see above 2.5) to analyse the law and to strengthen the claim of jurisprudence to the status of a science (see above 1.2.3). In this he opposes Cagnoli who, as we have seen, argues that legal definition cannot aspire to an account of causes (above 3.3.2); what makes this conflict of views particularly interesting is the fact that Turamini, like Cagnoli, claims to be a minimalist in interpretation, and writes against those who argue that jurists may practise its extensive mode.[127] Turamini acknowledges two predecessors – Connan and Bolognetti – on the question of the relationship of statute to equity, but believes his approach to laws themselves to be original: he adapts the fourfold causal model to his subject as follows. The efficient cause of laws is the legislator himself (or in the case of divine law, God); their material cause is the will of the legislator; their formal cause is their *ratio* – both their principle of coherence, and the purpose for which they were enacted; and their final cause is the common good. In this configuration, the issues of authority (3.1.3), sense as opposed to intention (3.6.1) and logic in relation to interpretation (2.4) are ingeniously redistributed; it may be possible for this reason that Turamini (with the help of his tutor) has much that is interesting to say about the intentional and performative functions of language, as we shall see (below 3.6.4).[128]

But the separation of *mens* (*causa materialis*) and *ratio* (*causa formalis*) is not without problems, as we shall see (below 3.6.1): *ratio* in different senses is present in both the formal and final causes; and there is no clear place accorded in this analysis to the *causa impulsiva* of the law (i.e. the mischief which gives rise to the law, as opposed to its remedy (the *causa finalis*). The two-cause analysis in this way shows up the four-cause mode's deficiency.[129] The four-cause model of analysis is, however, much more frequently encountered in jurisprudence: Baldus, for example, analyses *consuetudo*, by this method, and Coras, Bodin, Mundius, Papponius and Cagnoli all make use of it.[130]

---

[127] *Videlicet*, Connan, Coras and Bolognetti; see above 3.1.3, and esp. note 22.

[128] *De legibus*, pp. 25–118; see also below 3.4.2 and note 131, on the question of causal analysis of language and meaning.

[129] The relationship of mischief to remedy in the English system is implicitly a two-cause analysis: see below 3.9.1; cf. also Otte, *Dialektik und Jurisprudenz*, pp. 195f.

[130] Papponius, *Interpretatio tituli Digestorum de verborum obligationibus*, Venice, 1604, pp. 8–10 (on obligation); on Coras and the analysis of the four causes of law in general, see Kelley, 'Civil science in the Renaissance', in *The languages of political theory*, p. 69; Bodin's *Juris universi distributio* is organized according to the four-cause model; see also Cagnoli, in *Commentarii de regulis iuris*, p. 775 (on definition).

Turamini, as far as I know, is the first jurist to apply it to language, although the Aristotelian scholar Julius Caesar Scaliger had done something similar in his *De causis linguae Latinae* of 1540. There, language is said to have a *causa materialis* (the sound), *causa formalis* (the sense), *causa efficiens* (the speaker) and *causa finalis* (the expressive dimension: the *inclinatio animi* or 'what is felt or thought').[131] Whereas Turamini makes intention the *causa materialis*, Scaliger assigns this to the *causa finalis* and possibly the *causa formalis* (if subjective sense can be included in this cause). While an influence is not impossible, Turamini's different focus (written law, not human speech) and the fact that the four-cause model, being a locus cited in most Topics, was frequently used by jurists, makes it plausible that when he claims to be original, he is justified in so doing. The account Turamini produces is impressively coherent and persuasive. He also, interestingly, addresses his treatise specifically to drafters of legislation, as Alciato had done;[132] this is no commonplace pedagogical text.

WORDS AND THINGS: PROPRIETY, AMBIGUITY, USAGE

3.4.2
The question of modes of interpretation arises also in strict reference to *verba*. *Verbum* denotes both term (*nomen, terminum*) and proposition (*integra oratio*); the correctness of the interpretation of a proposition can be judged in respect of the truth-value of the proposition itself; the correctness of the interpretation of a term relates to its referential value, since in this sense of truth 'veritas rebus inest, et verbis non mutatur' (is in things, and is not changed by words);[133] and as 'leges

---

[131] On Scaliger, see Padley, *Grammatical theory*, pp. 58–77. He may have medieval precursors; for as Heath ('Logical grammar', pp. 52–3) points out, the medieval grammarians known as the 'modistae' set out to define a more or less perfect construction as that which satisfies the mind of the hearer more or less well, according to the following definition of construction (produced by Thomas of Erfurt. *Grammatica speculativa*, ch. 54): 'Constructio est constructi-bilium unio ex modis significandi ab intellectu causata ad exprimendum mentis conceptum compositum finaliter adinventa' (a construction is a coming together of constructible elements from the modes of signifying, caused by the intellect and chosen to express purposively the composite mental conception). In this definition, the *constructibilia* are said to be the material cause, the *unio* the formal cause, *ex modis significandi* the intrinsic efficient cause and *ad exprimendum mentis conceptum* the final cause. Of interest here is the distinction between the *causa efficiens intrinseca* (*ex modis significandi*: i.e. the objective sense of the words or proposition according to the conventions of language) and the *causa efficiens extrinseca* (*ab intellectu causata*, i.e. the intention, or more precisely, the link between the *verbum cordis* and the *cogitatio*: see below 3.6.3). See also above, chapter 2, note 10.

[132] See Alciato, *De verborum significatione*, pp. 5–8; Turamini, *De legibus*, pp. 78–9.

[133] *Categories*, 4b8; 14b21; Connan, *Commentaria iuris civilis*, p. 669; de Federicis, *De iuris interpretatione*, i.5, in *Tractatus iuris universi*, i.210.

magis rebus quam verbis impositae sunt' (laws are imposed more on things than on words: except, that is, where the *verbum* is a *res*, as in an oath, the utterance of a contract, an insult, etc.), the *rei proprietas* is of greatest importance.[134] Two *regulae* make this explicit:

D 23.3.41.1 (Paulus) Res magis quam verba intuenda sunt

more attention is to be paid to things than to words

C 6.43.2 (Justinian) Nos enim non verbis sed ipsis rebus leges imponimus

we impose our laws on things themselves, not on words.

The determination of the *res*, however, must be done through the medium of *verba*. It is pertinent here to recall the grammatical foundation for this process (above 2.2). Some commentators take *verba* to be primarily the expression of subjective meaning: this is Alciato's contention in his essay on the meaning of words. Others begin with the Aristotelian designation of words as *mentis notiones* or *animi passiones*, in which their objective sense and conceptual nature is stressed; some consider subjective and objective sense equally.[135] All are agreed that words consist in a phonic and a semantic element (*vox* and *sensus*), which together constitute a *dictio*, and that as *partes orationis* they can have a grammatical function also (the word is sometimes defined as 'minima pars orationis significativa').[136] All are agreed also that the purpose of words is to signify things, which are perceived or thought of before the words which represent them are uttered, and that what can be predicated of things is encompassed by the ten predicaments or categories of Aristotle.[137] But *dictiones* can be meaningful even without reference: in law, legal fictions are examples of such *dictiones*.[138]

---

[134] *Ibid.* i.14; Wesenbeck, *Prolegomena iurisprudentiae*, pp. 115–16; such *res* may of course be *incorporales* (see above 3.3.2).

[135] See above 2.4 and 3.2.1ff. in relation to the work of Alciato, Sapcote and Goeddaeus.

[136] Rebuffi, *In titulum Digestorum de verborum et rerum significatione*, p. 3, refers to three further senses of *verbum* not treated here, *videlicet* verb (as opposed to noun), promise and adage.

[137] See Alciato, *De verborum significatione*, pp. 204ff.; Sapcote, *Ad primas leges*, pp. 3ff.; Savius, *In Pandectarum titulum de verborum et rerum significatione*, pp. 8ff.; Goeddaeus, *Commentarius*, pp. 4ff.

[138] Savius, *In Pandectarum titulum de verborum et rerum significatione*, p. 9; Coras, in *Tractatus de iuris arte*, pp. 165ff. But non-existents can also invalidate the law: see e.g. I 3.19.1: 'at si quis rem, quae in rerum natura non est aut esse non potest, dari stipulatus fuerit, veluti Stichum, qui mortuus sit, quem vivere credebat, aut hippocentaurum, qui esse non possit, inutilis erit stipulatio' (but if anyone is stipulated to be given something which either does not or could not exist in the realm of nature, such as the late Stichus, who was yet thought to be alive, or a hippocentaur which cannot exist, the stipulation is void). Cf. also Otte, *Dialektik und Jurisprudenz*, p. 39.

Words can be technical (as the 'terms of the art') or in general use; they may be properly or improperly employed. The function of the interpreter is to determine their use in a given context and to resolve any ambiguity or obscurity arising from their use. Baldus offers four distinguishing categories: *natura* 'quando certa et praecisa est vocabulis significatio'; *aptitudo* (the choice of the most apt sense when ambiguity is in question); *consuetudo loquendi* (principally applied to words in general use rather than legal terms); and figurative usage.[139] All of these categories are treated in traditional forensic rhetoric and topics; it is, therefore, not surprising that when Alciato comes to produce a fourfold treatment of the same question in his *De verborum significatione*, his categories are uncannily similar to those of Baldus (viz. *proprietas, improprietas, usus, interpretatio*). By this last Alciato means extensive interpretation in de Federicis's sense.[140] No acknowledgement is made, however, to his juristic forebear, whose schema he has enriched with a discussion of ambiguity and a reiteration of figures of speech. It is worthwhile examining some of these categories – *proprietas*, ambiguity, *usus* – in some detail.

The first, *proprietas*, resembles *significatio* closely: it is, according to Baldus in a now very familiar formula, a 'vis quaedam attributa dictioni ab intellectu, ad exprimendum apte et proprie conceptum mentis'.[141] It is accessible through authority (an existing determination of sense from a good source e.g. the *auctoritas prudentium*), through definition and through etymology.[142] According to Alciato, the *verborum proprietas* can include figurative usage.[143] A problem, however, arises in the case of names: as has already been noted, Aristotle declares in the *De sophisticis elenchis*, 165a14–16 that there is an infinity of things, and a finite number of words, and that as a result human language has had to have recourse to polysemy and homonymy.[144] Moreover, as one thing can have several names,

---

[139] Rebuffi, *In Digestorum titulum de verborum et rerum significatione*, p. 4 (referring to Baldus, gl. ad rubr. D 12.1); Caepolla, *De verborum et rerum significatione doctissima commentaria*, col. 6.
[140] Alciato, *De verborum significatione*, pp. 10, 115, 204–5; he refers to Bartolus, gl. ad D 33.10.7. On his respect for, and debt towards, the postglossators, see Viard, *Alciato*, pp. 139–64. See also Kelley, 'Civil science in the Renaissance', in *The languages of political theory*, pp. 61–2; Piano Mortari, *Diritto, logica, metodo*, pp. 361–2.
[141] Gl. ad C 6.38; Caepolla, *De verborum et rerum significatione doctissima commentaria*, p. 24.
[142] *Ibid.*, p. 26; cf. Quintilian, xii.3.7 (on the authority of legal experts).
[143] *De verborum significatione*, p. 205.
[144] Cf. Savius, *In Pandectarum titulum de verborum et rerum significatione*, p. 10; also Cicero, *Pro Caecina*, xvii.51:
  an hoc dubium est quin neque verborum tanta copia sit non modo in nostra lingua, quae dicitur esse inops, sed in alia quidem ulla, res ut omnes suis certis ac propriis vocabulis

synonymy also can pose a problem for *proprietas*.[145] In these cases, questions of ambiguity and obscurity arise (see below 3.4.3); indeed, the very word *verbum* is a case in point, having a range of meanings, each meaning being able to be represented by a number of other words.[146] There are even occasions when words must be understood in their improper sense; these are determined by the context (*circumstantiae*), and occur also in legal fictions, and failed or bungled rituals (where one must understand an act to have been accomplished): Alciato cites the example of a baptism at which the formula 'Baptizo te in nomine patria, filia et spirita sancta' is uttered, but which still constitutes a baptism. A further justification for accepting improper sense is the need to avoid iniquity or absurdity in the law, resulting from literal interpretation; what in England came to be known as the 'golden rule'.[147]

3.4.3

As well as questions of *proprietas* and *improprietas*, the issue of ambiguity and obscurity arises; this is, as we have already noted, one of the *causae legales* (see above 2.5). In the first case (ambiguity) the choice of a number of clear meanings is in question: in the second (obscurity), no

nominentur, neque vero quicquam opus sit verbis, cum ea res cuius causa verba quaesita sint intelligatur? Quae lex, quod senatusconsultum, quod magistratus edictum, quod foedus aut pactio, quod – ut ad privatas res redeam – testamentum, quae iudicia aut stipulationes aut pacti et conventi formula non infirmari ac convelli potest, si ad verba rem deflectare velimus, consilium autem eorum qui scripserunt et rationem et auctoritatem relinquamus?

Is it to be doubted that there are words in sufficient quantity, either in Latin – which is said to be poor in words – or in any other language, to name all things by their certain and proper names; or indeed that there is any need for words, since the thing for which the words were sought is understood. What law, senatusconsult, magistrate's edict, treaty, pact or (to come back to the private sphere) will, judgement, stipulation, or form of words relating to contract or agreement, is there which cannot be weakened and subverted, if we decide to concentrate on the words themselves and neglect the opinion, reasons and authority of those who wrote them?

(Cited by Fournier, *In titulum de verborum significatione*, p. 21)
See also Blaise de Vigenère, *Traité des chiffres*, Paris, 1587, fol. 42ᵛ, who points out that this problem does not arise at the level of letters, which are more or less infinitely combinable and therefore can generate a near-infinite number of words (Vigenère computes the number to be 112,400,254,082,719,680,000) to designate the infinite particulars of nature (see also fols. 51ff.). But such an infinite lexicon could not answer the need to communicate for which general terms are indispensable: see Foucault, *Les Mots et les choses*, p. 112.

145 Rogerius, *De iuris interpretatione*, iii.19, in *Tractatus iuris universi*, i.387; Savius, *In Pandectarum titulum de verborum et rerum significatione*, p. 10; Cagnoli, in *Commentarii de regulis iuris*, p. 783.
146 See Rebuffi, *In titulum Digestorum de verborum et rerum significatione*, p. 3.
147 *De verborum significatione*, p. 72; also p. 169 ('ex absurdo ut evitetur impropria significatio accepi poterit': the improper sense [of a word] can be taken to avoid absurdity); Cross, *Statutory interpretation*, p. 14, and below 4.2.

clear meaning is available to the interpreter. As Cujas elegantly puts it, 'ambiguum est, si dubitetur utrum dictum sit: obscurum est si dubitetur quod dictum sit'[148] (with ambiguity we wonder which of two things has been said; with obscurity, we wonder what has been said). Ambiguity arises as *aequivocatio* (a term with several meanings or a proper name with several referents)[149] and as *amphibologia* (ambiguity arising from a combination of words or a sentence): it can therefore be associated with both figures (metaphor, synecdoche, catachresis, etc.) and tropes (irony); but it inhabits only words, never things. It is the subject of a number of *regulae* which are frequently cited by jurists:

D 34.5.3 (Paulus) In ambiguo sermo non utrumque dicimus, sed id dumtaxat quod volumus: itaque qui aliud dicit quam vult, neque id dicit quod vox significat, quia non vult, neque id quod vult, quia id non loquitur.

In speaking ambiguously we do not say both things which might be understood, but only that which we mean; thus whoever says something different from what he intends to say neither says what the words mean, because he does not intend them, nor what he intends, because that is not what he says.

D 34.5.21 (Paulus) Ubi est verborum ambiguitas, valet quod act[um] est, veluti cum Stichum stipuler et sint plures Stichi, [hominemve] Carthagini, cum sint duae Carthagines . . .

Where there is verbal ambiguity, the facts of the matter are decisive, as in the cases where I stipulate Stichus and there are several persons of that name, or a man at Carthage, and there are several Carthages.

D 34.5.12 (Julianus) Quotiens in actionibus aut in exceptionibus ambigua oratio est, commodissimum est id accipi, quo res de qua agitur magis valeat quam pereat.

Where there is ambiguity in the formulation of an action or a defence, it is most appropriate to accept the sense which validates the legal instrument rather than causing it to lapse.

D 26.2.30 (Paulus) Duo sunt Titii, pater et filius, datus est tutor Titus: nec apparet de quo sensit testator: quaero, quid sit iuris? Respondit, is datus est, quem dare se testator sensit. Si id non apparet, non ius deficit, sed probatio igitur neuter est tutor.

---

148 *De verborum significationibus*, p. 273; cf. Quintilian, vii.9–10. See also Henry Swinburne, *A brief treatise of testaments and last wills* (1590–1), London, 1635, iv.26, pp. 343–4, who refers to other discussions of this point; and above, note 117.

149 See Brinkmann, *Mittelalterliche Hermeneutik*, p. 27; I 2.2 (on *poeta*, cited below 3.4.4).

There are two men called Titus, father and son. Titus is appointed tutor and it is not clear which one was meant by the testator. What is the law on this point I ask? The reply was: the man who is appointed is the one intended by the testator. If that cannot be known, the law is not at fault, but proof is lacking; therefore neither is tutor.

In these cases, as in others (see below 3.6.1), the law is decisive, even if illogical: for if the only access to the intention of the speaker is the written word, then that intention can never be established with certainty. D 26.2.30 is saved from absurdity by its last clause, which offers a practical rule, as does D 34.5.12; the issue is settled because 'res iudicata pro veritate accipitur' (D 1.5.25). Ambiguity can simply be determined by a court not to exist; by adjudicating what the meaning is (even if the form of words could not possibly warrant such a decision on linguistic grounds alone), the law effectively avoids the pitfalls of relativism or scepticism. Perhaps the best example of this is a modern one. When in 1962 the House of Lords determined that a clause in the Income Tax Act of 1952 was unambiguous, they did so by a decision which went against the conclusions reached by a lower court. This apparently embodies an absurdity, for the text which is declared to be unambiguous had given rise to two contradictory readings. This represents a reversal of the normal priority of a constitutive rule over a regulative rule; that is to say, the determination *sine qua non* of ambiguity is that there be radical disagreement as to meaning; and this determination in this case has been made subservient to the rule that an appeal court should settle matters of meaning one way or the other. A Renaissance parallel might be the story of judge Bridoye in Rabelais's *Tiers livre*, who is arraigned for having reached a wrong judgement; however, Bridoye reached judgements by throwing dice, and admitted only to having misread the dice, not to having employed the wrong means of adjudication.[150]

Most commentators refer to classical debates about ambiguity: not only the sections dealing with ambiguity in forensic rhetoric, such as that of Quintilian, whose 'statuam hastam auram tenentem' (either 'a statute holding a golden spear' or 'a golden statute holding a spear') is frequently cited, but also the argument between Chrysippus and Diodorus recorded in Aulus Gellius' *Noctes atticae* (xi.12):

---

[150] See G.S.A. Wheatcroft, 'The Hinchy case', *Modern law review*, xxiii (1960), 425–8; G. Marshall, 'Natural, alternative and reasonable meanings'; *Public Law*, cxxxii (1960), 132–4; on constitutive and regulative rules, see John Searle, *Speech acts*, Cambridge, 1969, pp. 33ff.; on Bridoye, see Rabelais, *Tiers livre*, chs. 39–43.

Quod Chrysippus philosophus omne verbum ambiguum dubiumque esse dicit, Diodorus contra nullum verbum ambiguum esse putet. Chrysippus ait omne verbum ambiguum natura esse, quoniam ex eodem duo vel plura accipi possunt. Diodorus autem, cui Crono cognomentum fuit, 'nullum', inquit, 'verbum est ambiguum, nec quisquam ambiguum dicit aut sentit, nec aliud dici videri debet, quam quod se dicere sentit is, qui dicit. At cum ego', inquit, 'aliud sensi, tu aliud accepisti, obscure magis dictum videri potest quam ambigue; ambigui enim verbi natura illa esse debuit ut, qui id diceret, duo vel plura diceret. Nemo autem duo vel plura dicit, qui se sensit unum dicere.'

Where the philosopher Chrysippus claims that every word is ambiguous and obscure, Diodorus on the contrary thinks that no word is ambiguous. Chrysippus avers that it is in the nature of all words to be ambiguous, because from any word two or more senses may be derived. On the other hand, Diodorus (whose other name was Crono) says: 'No word is ambiguous, for nobody says or thinks something ambiguous, nor does it seem that anything can be said but what the person who said it meant. But if, says Diodorus, I mean one thing and you take it to mean another, it seems that something obscure rather than ambiguous has been said: for the nature of ambiguous speech should be that who utters it should mean two or more things. But no one says two or more things who means to say only one.

There are adherents of both views: Matthaeacius agrees with Chrysippus that all words are polysemic and that meaning can only be determined from the objective facts of speech; Corvinus supports Diodorus' view based on the subjective sense of words that no person can mean two things at the time of utterance. The issue is of course academic, in so far as there can be no knowledge of that which is ambiguous; even formulas which are in principle undecidable (e.g. 'statuam auream hastam tenentem') must in the end be determined *de jure* to mean one thing or the other, but not both.[151]

---

[151] Quintilian vii.9, esp. vii.9.8; Matthaeacius, *De via et ratione*, fol. 76ᵛ: 'neque enim semper, qui audit, qui legit, qui respondet unum tantum audit. Nam aliquando dubitat, quid sibi iussum dictumque fuerit, tum vel maxime cum vox ipsa per se plures habuerit significationes, possitque multifariam intelligi, vel ab interrogante vel a respondente, vel ab utroque vel a tertio' (hearers, readers and interlocutors do not always comprehend one thing only. For they doubt on occasions what was ordered or said, principally because the words themselves have several meanings and can be understood in a variety of ways, either by the questioner or by his respondent, or by both, or by a third party). This development of Chrysippus' point amounts to a radical pragmatization of meaning. Cf. Arnoldus Corvinus, *Ad titulum Digestorum de verborum significatione commentarius*, Amsterdam, 1646, p. 184. See also Breche, *Ad titulum Pandectarum de verborum et rerum significatione*, p. 4; Turamini, *De legibus*, pp. 64ff., 175 ff.; Doneau, *Ad titulum Digestorum de rebus dubiis commentarius*, Bourges, 1571, pp. 9–13, 94–9 (a highly intelligent discussion).

3.4.4

We shall return to the issue of ambiguity in connection with intention below (3.6.3); it is pertinent here to complete our survey of Baldus' and Alciato's four categories of interpreting words by investigating further the category *usus* or *consuetudo loquendi*. This has been the subject of a heated debate (in the context of Valla's *Elegantiae*) between Waswo and Monfasani; the former claiming that for Valla, language structures our knowledge of reality and that language usage is a function of meaning; the latter suggesting that Valla's conception of usage is very close if not identical to a traditional scholastic understanding of the term by which *usus* does not imply any priority of language use over mental perception.[152] This debate is closely connected to the debate about mentalism in Renaissance philosophy which will be examined below (3.6.3); here it should be pointed out that the *usus communis loquendi* is a perennial concern of lawyers, and applies both to legal and non-legal language.[153] In both cases, the sense of terms is subject to both context and history. Meaning may be dependent on the context by *subauditio* as we have seen (I 1.2.2; D 1.8.1): thus, *poeta* means Homer if uttered by a Greek, Virgil if uttered by a Roman. Other cases of context which are adduced include regional variations in meanings and usus defined by class: *docti* and *literati* speak in one way; *vulgares* and *rustici* in another.[154] But they also vary according to historical context. D 33.10.7 is the locus classicus of this point; in this *regula*, two imaginary interlocutors, Tubero and Servius, squabble over the household effects (*suppellex*) of a testator whose meaning is not clear, as the word used to refer to one sort of object that now refers to another. The *regula* determines that the (historical) sense of the testator should apply. According to D.33.7.18.3 (also frequently adduced), meanings which are determined according to historical and geographical variation do not represent *propriae verborum significationes*; but some commentators claim that 'verba propriam significationem accipiunt a vulgari et communi loquendi usu' (words receive their proper meaning from vulgar and common language use), and that words can change in sense.[155]

---

[152] See 'Introduction', note 3.

[153] Breche, however, argues that usage is a matter of fact, not of law (*Ad titulum Pandectarum de verborum et rerum significatione*, p. 2); cf. above 3.2.1–4.

[154] Hunnius, *De authoritate*, p. 264. Savius, *In Pandectarum titulum de verborum et rerum significatione*, p. 70.

[155] Breche, *Ad titulum Pandectarum de verborum et rerum significatione*, p. 2; Rebuffi, *In titulum Digestorum de verborum et rerum significatione*, p. 4; Coras, in *Tractatus de iuris arte*, pp. 204f.; D 32.54.4; gl. ad D 1.1.9.

Horace's *Ars poetica* (60–2, 70–2) is frequently cited in support of this:

Ut silvae foliis pronos mutantur in annos,
Prima cadunt, ita verborum vetus viterit aetas,
Et iuvenum ritu florent modo nata vigentque . . .
Multa renascentur quae iam cecidere cadentque
Quae nunc sunt honore vocabula, si volet usus
Quem penes arbitrium est et ius et norma loquendi[156]

As forests lose their leaves with each year's decline and the oldest drop off; so also the old order of words dies and the new order flourishes and grows strong, like the young of humankind . . . Many terms that have fallen out of use shall be born again, and those shall fall which are now held in esteem, if usage which regulates the laws and norms of speech so wills it.

Aulus Gellius (*Noctes atticae*, xii.13.1) is cited also in this regard by Alciato: 'Non enim verborum tantum communium verae atque propriae significationes longiore usu mutantur, sed legum quoque ipsarum consensu tacito oblitterantur.'[157] (The true and proper meanings of common words change with long usage, but also the meanings of laws themselves come to be forgotten by tacit consensus.)

We touch here upon another modern debate about the history of language. It is generally assumed that until the writing of German eighteenth-century philosophers, ideas or concepts were not thought themselves to have a history, but only words: and it was asserted that the prevalent attitude to words in the Middle Ages and Renaissance was that they began their life as full of meaning, and gradually declined or degenerated in this respect.[158] Such a view does not seem to me to characterize at all well the attitude to language and concepts held by jurists. The idea that the semantic content of words changes over time does not seem on the one hand to be associated with decline, but to be regarded as a permanent process: 'consuetudo enim et usus loquendi potest vocabuli significationem immutare et novam dare'[159] (custom and word usage can change the meanings of words and confer new ones on them). On the other hand, the idea that concepts do not have a history, i.e. that they do not function in different ways in

---

[156] These lines are cited by Caepolla, de Federicis, Rogerius, Alciato, Breche, Rebuffi and others.
[157] Alciato, *De verborum significatione*, pp. 78–9; Aulus Gellius attributes these words to Sulpitius Appolinaris. See also Quintilian, i.5–6.
[158] See Robert A. Hall jun., *The Italian Questione della lingua*, Chapel Hill, 1942, p. 36, cited by Waswo, *Language and meaning*, p. 84.
[159] Rebuffi, *In titulum Digestorum de verborum et rerum significatione*, p. 4; Bolognetti, *De lege iure et aequitate disputationes*, Wittenberg, 1594, pp. 314ff.; de Federicis, *De iuris interpretatione*, i.64, in *Tractatus iuris universi*, i.221.

different cultural settings, is clearly refuted both by the notion of extensive interpretation, itself comprehensively described by Caepolla,[160] and by the specific *regulae* dealing with such change, cited above. Furthermore, in a simple example involving a version of what we now might call the sense/reference distinction, Turamini shows how over time the *tyro* and *veteranus* can both denote *miles*. The *nuda voluntas* of the person making the reference is not here linked to the use of a given common noun: and if legislation is in question, the *voluntas imperandi* inherent in the law citing a soldier is prior to and more important than the legislator's *cogitatio*. To preserve the law, one must preserve the *voluntas imperandi*, not the *cogitatio*, which is subject to change (see below 3.6.3).

There is another modern debate which is also relevant to the category *usus*. Donald Kelley's *Foundations of historical scholarship: language, law and history in the French Renaissance* elegantly developed the theory that historical sense or historicity arises from humanist-inspired philological investigators into the history of the Corpus Juris Civilis. In later studies ('Clio and the lawyers: forms of historical consciousness in medieval jurisprudence' (1974) and 'Civil science in the Renaissance: jurisprudence Italian style' (1979)), he examines the medieval prefiguration of such historicity, especially with respect to commentaries on D 33.10.7, discussed above. The historical consciousness to which he refers is, of course, implicit also in the topical and rhetorical category of *circumstantiae* (see above 2.5), which makes explicit the pragmatic aspects of an event, and hence its historical context; such analysis can extend to a full enquiry into the interests involved in an act, as proposed in Fortunatianus' *Ars rhetorica*, which Alciato cites.[161] Historical sense is also built into law in D 1.2, C 1.17, and the prefaces to the Digest which give a history of the evolution of the Corpus. Thus *consuetudo* or *usus communis loquendi* is not in itself remarkable in showing historicist features, but rather symptomatic of a feature of legal studies which until recently had been associated only with more modern developments in jurisprudence.

It is pertinent finally to note that even though the interpretation of meaning in extra-legal contexts is described as a matter of fact and not of law, in effect lawyers themselves decide on such interpretation as

---

[160] See above 3.4.1.
[161] Cited also above, p. 12. Cf. also D 1.3.32.1; Otte, *Dialektik und Jurisprudenz*, p. 216.

well as on matters pertaining to the technical language of the law. Quintilian had made this clear in his *Institutes* (i.6–7; xii.3.7), where after conceding at one point that 'auctoritatem sermonis consuetudo superat' (usage prevails over authoritative designations of meaning), he goes on immediately to state that 'consuetudinem sermonis vocabo consensum eruditorum' (I call proper usage the consensus of learned men). What appears to be a separate and objective yardstick, a matter of fact, turns out to be an affirmation of the peremptory powers of the profession. This point has been made both by legal historians and modern judges.[162]

CAVILLATION: INTERPRETATION IN BAD FAITH

We may note in passing one curious omission from interpretative rules. Given the nature of the modes *expositiva* and *declarativa*, both of which involve restatement, one would have imagined that verbal redundancy would have emerged as a preoccupation. Not only is this a feature of earlier and subsequent legal drafting (the deployment of formulas to cover as many eventualities as possible, no matter whether the terminology overlapped or not)[163] but it is also a feature of standard rhetoric, where it is known usually as *amplificatio*. But whenever the question of redundancy – *otiosa operositas, verbositas, clausulae supervacuae* – arises, it is dismissed as dangerous, misleading, or in bad style, as in Quintilian (viii.3.50–58).[164] Although it does not appear to be stated anywhere, one might speculate this rejection of verbal redundancy has something to do with the desire to emulate the aphoristic quality of much of the Corpus Juris Civilis, whose terseness and sharp focus were seen as characteristic of legal style and juristic decisiveness in general. Yet there is one feature of legal drafting which somewhat resembles redundancy: namely the tendency to make compendious lists of all possible applications of the law, or all possible persons or objects affected by it. It arises from the need felt by

---

[162] Coing, *Die juristischen Auslegungsmethoden und die Lehren der allgemeinen Hermeneutik*, p. 20; O.W. Holmes, *Collected legal papers*, New York, 1920, p. 204.

[163] See Thorne, introduction to *A discourse upon the exposicion of statutes*, p. 25; and above 3.3.4.

[164] See Justinian, C 1.17.2.21, cited above 1.5.1; Caepolla, *De verborum et rerum significatione doctissima commentaria*, p. 15; Alciato, *De verborum significatione* p. 204; Cagnoli, in *Commentarii de regulis iuris*, p. 776; Turamini, *De legibus*, p. 78 (referring to Quintilian, viii.8, which he summarizes as 'superfluum est verbum omne, quod neque intellectum neque ornatum adiuverat' (all words which do not contribute to sense or style are superfluous); see also Martin, *Antike Rhetorik*, p. 252.

legislators and legal draftsmen to legislate for the future as comprehensively as possible, and is connected also with the problems of
division which have been already discussed (3.3.4). This tendency is
clearly connected with avoidance or attempted avoidance of the law
by categories not specifically named in the law. This is another form
of transgression or excess which attracts universal condemnation and
which is a hallowed vice of the legal procession. It is sometimes called
subtilitas (although that term has positive connotations in some
contexts),[165] sometimes *sophisticatio*, most often however 'cavillatio';
and it is described in two near-identical loci classici (D 50.16.177: cf.
D 50.17.65):

Natura cavillationis, quam Graeci σωρίτης appellaverunt, haec est, ut ab
evidenter vera per brevissimas mutationes disputatio ad ea quae evidenter
falsa sunt, perducatur.

It is the nature of cavillation (called *sorites* by the Greeks) to construct an
argument by the shortest route from that which is manifestly true to that
which is manifestly false.

Cavillation is not taken lightly, being associated with fraud:
'Contra legem facit, qui id facit quod lex prohibet, in fraudem vero,
qui salvis verbis legis sententiam eius circumvenit' (D 1.3.29: whoever
does what the law prohibits by fraudulently circumventing the spirit
of the law but sticking to its letter contravenes the law). Other similar
formulations are found: they all associate cavillation or avoidance of
the law with the poena falsi, which entails confiscation of property
and banishment, as in the case of Justinian's prohibition (above
1.5.1).[166] It is sometimes also associated with vexatious litigation
(*calumnia*: D 3.6 *De calumniatoribus*); satirists of the law associate this
practice particularly with advocates and notaries.[167]

Hunnius derives the practice of cavillation from a 'naturalis

---

[165] See above, note 107. Cf. also D 1.3.30 (Ulpianus) 'Fraus enim legi fit, ubi quod fieri noluit,
fieri autem non vetuit, id fit' (fraud on the law is committed when something is done which
the law does not wish to be done, but which it does not expressly prohibit).

[166] Rebuffi, *In titulum Digestorum de verborum et rerum significatione*, p. 1, explicitly links cavillation
with Justinian's prohibition of commentary. Coras associates this issue with the common
claim (see above, note 1) that the words of the law are not the law ('non in verbis sed in sensu
leges consistunt'): *Tractatus de iuris arte*, p. 204: cf. also de Federicis, *De iuris interpretatione*, i.4,
in *Tractatus iuris universi*, i.219: 'leges enim intelligere secundum corticem verborum non
secundum mentem est legum calumniatio, et eas circumvenire' (to understand laws literally
and not according to their intent is egregious misreading and evasion of the law): he refers
here to D 10.4.19. Curiously, no parallels seem to be drawn with the ninth commandment
(concerning false witness).   [167] Agrippa, *De incertitudine*, xciii–xciv.

hominum ad discutiendum facilitas'; Brisson, by describing it as a 'captiosa ratiocinatio', suggests more that it arises from a perverse delight in twisted reasoning; Oldendorp refers similarly to man's deceitful (*mendax*) nature, which creates the need for written law, but at the same time immediately subverts it; perhaps significantly, the obvious motive (to serve one's own or one's client's interest by misconstruing the law) is not stated, but everywhere understood.[168] Cavillation resides in a misuse of language and logic; Aristotle's *De sophisticis elenchis*, 165b23 provides a codification of it into arguments false in their premises (*materia*), or in their logic (*forma*), or in both; this is widely quoted.[169] Some of his examples include an analysis of the figures which Alciato recommends for use in the interpretation of the law; the Italian jurist in fact includes *cavillatio* among the figures of speech he analyses in the fourth book of his essay on verbal meaning.[170] As Turamini points out, cavillation can arise from defects (*vitia*) in drafting laws; but he also concedes that it can arise in legal argument.[171] According to Ferrarius, there is no legal definition which cavillation cannot undermine.[172] But cavillation is not a vice confined to the law; it is much cited in theology, where it is often linked to scholastic hairsplitting and unevangelical adherence to the letter and not the spirit.[173]

Moreover, the issue of cavillation is connected to that difficult area of self-evidence in law which we have already touched upon above (3.1.2): 'ea quae sunt *evidenter* falsa'. In this case, what is 'evident' or 'obvious' (*apertus*) is associated with good faith in the reader of the law, or the maker of a contract. To talk, as Rebuffi does, of twisting the words of the law into a different sense from that which is to be accepted ('verba legum torquere in alienum sensum') is to presuppose that there is a certain (i.e. apodictic) sense which can be stated; to talk about *consensus ad idem* in contracts is to assume with Doneau that 'id quod aperte contrahentes dixerunt' can be in some objective

---

[168] Hunnius, *De authoritate*, p. 4; Brisson, *Lexicon iuris*, Frankfurt, 1587, s.v. cavillatio; Oldendorp, *De iure et aequitate forensis disputatio*, Cologne, 1573, pp. 80–1. 'Ratiocinatio' may, in Brisson's usage, have the technical sense of reasoning by analogy (see Cicero, *De inventione*, ii.50.148). See also Cortese, *La norma giuridica*, ii.305f.

[169] See Turamini, *De legibus*, p. 74; Alciato, *De verborum significatione*, p. 518.

[170] *Ibid.*, p. 177.   [171] Turamini, *De legibus*, p. 178.

[172] *Commentarii de regulis iuris*, p. 772; cf. also D 15.1.6.

[173] On this, see Augustine's treatise *De littera et spiritu*, *PL*, xliv.199–246, and Kathy Eden, 'The rhetorical tradition and Augustinian hermeneutics in *De doctrina christiana*', *Rhetorica*, viii (1990), 45–63.

sense established, as is implicit in C 8.4.4: 'Qui dicit malam fidem debet eam probari' (whoever claims bad faith [in another] must prove it). In the first case, Rebuffi bravely states that his commentary on the title *De verborum significatione* will provide the certainty required; in the second, Doneau more cautiously suggests that such determination can only be 'more likely than not' (*verisimilius*).[174] Clearly, an infinite regress threatens to come about here, as more and more words are used to define or determine an initial verbal message: this is even indicated in the Digest (D 49.14.40) which refers to someone who 'seeks to circumvent not only the law but also the construction put on the law' ('qui non tantum legem circumvenire voluit, sed etiam interpretationem legis').[175]

LEGAL FICTIONS

3.5.2

Cavillation is also dangerously close to the approved method of reconciling laws and avoiding absurdity in the application of the law known as legal fiction, which in the Middle Ages and Renaissance is defined variously as 'falsi pro vero, aequitate suadente, facta assumptio' (the assumption made that something false is true, in the name of equity) and 'commentum iuris civilis ad visum vitae communis contra natura rerum contraque veritatem accommodatum'[176] (a falsehood in civil law made against the nature of things and truth in the interest of the common weal). As Kantorowicz has shown, fictions giving access to truth in figurative or allegorical manner are a common feature of medieval writing; this has its parallel in the Renaissance in the arguments adduced (often from Neoplatonist sources) in favour of fables and myths which are said to contain veiled truth, while being literally untrue.[177] Fictional legal arguments

---

[174] See Rebuffi, *In titulum Digestorum de verborum et rerum significatione*, p. 1; *Axiomata legum*, p. 172; Doneau, *Ad titulum Digestorum de rebus dubiis*, p. 96, alluding to D 50.17.114: (Paulus) 'in obscuris inspici solere, quod verisimilius est aut quod plerumque fiere solet' (it is usual when obscurity arises to look to what is more likely or what is done in most cases).

[175] Cited by Rebuffi, *In titulum Digestorum de verborum et rerum significatione*, p. 55.

[176] Coras in *Tractatus de iuris arte*, p. 165; Althusius, *Iurisprudentia Romana methodice digesta*, p. 5; Otte, *Dialektik und Jurisprudenz*, p. 59; see also Caepolla, *De interpretatione extensiva*, fol. 5ᵛ, who disqualifies fiction as a form of extension.

[177] *The king's two bodies*, pp. 291–313: cf. also types of narration as described in rhetoric (*Ad Herennium*, i.8.13: Cicero, *De inventione*, i.19.27; Martin, *Antike Rhetorik*, pp. 76ff.). On the argument from veiled truths, see Grahame Castor, *Pleiade poetics*, Cambridge, 1964, pp.

can take various forms – inductive, privative and translative – which Coras illustrates; they are distinguished from cavillation not in their formal or material elements (i.e. their argument or premises) but in their purpose. Legal fictions are inspired by equity and are designed to further the common good; cavillation is motivated by self-interest and the good of the individual, and seeks to evade the force of law. The problem of providing adequate notation to distinguish these two contrary motives will be investigated further below (3.6.2); it is similar in kind to the problem of distinguishing dialectical argument from declamation which arises in polemical literature at this time.[178] An echo of this may be heard in Neideccerus' warning that his legal dialectics should not be put to sophistical use.[179] When, to describe cavillation, the phrase *inutiles subtilitates* is encountered, the epithet *inutiles* may well mean more than just vapid, and may denote that which is against the public good; this is made explicit in Langenbeck's introduction to his tabular version of Alciato's commentary on D 50.16, which, like Rebuffi's, aspires to unequivocal representation of true sense.[180]

The insistence on the need for secure communication in good faith is often linked to the issue of cavillation and is a common theme: it is also a perennial one. The most recent attempts at codification of interpretative practice by jurisprudential writers make reference to it; the German philosopher of law Robert Alexy, for example, sets down the following as the first four rules governing legal discourse:

(i) No speaker may contradict himself;

117ff. Cf. also Hopper, in *Tractatus de iuris arte*, p. 430, who defines a legal fiction as a 'constitutio iuris qua id quod non est nec esse potest in specie licet in genere possit habetur pro eo, ac si esset, idque alicuius maioris absurdi vitandi vel boni constituendi cause' (a legal enactment by which that which does not exist not can exist *in specie* although it could exist *in genere* is taken to exist, in order to avoid some greater absurdity or to bring about good legislation).

178 See Ian Maclean, 'The interpretation of natural signs: Cardano's *De subtilitate* versus Scaliger's *Exercitationes*', in *Occult and scientific mentalities in the Renaissance*, ed. Brian Vickers, Cambridge, 1984, pp. 231–52, esp. 240–1; Siraisi, 'Medicine, physiology and anatomy', in *New perspectives on Renaissance thought*, p. 215.

179 *Dialectica iuris civilis*, Mainz, 1601, titlepage.

180 Turamini, *De legibus*, pp. 70ff.; Matthaeacius, *De via et ratione*, fols, 88ff.; Langenbeck, *D. Andreae Alciati . . . libri de verborum significatione in gratiam studiosorum in perutilem et iucundam tabulam contracti*, Cologne, 1555, A2ᵛ: 'Lex tam circumspecte vel scripta est vel scribi potest, quam non sit facile cavillando (quod in iudiciis quotidie usu venire videmus) in alienum atque iniustum sensum detorquere' (the law is, or can be, couched so carefully in words that it is not easy to twist it into a different and inequitable sense by cavillation (which we see, however, being practised daily in the courts). See also Ian Maclean, 'Montaigne, Cardano: the reading of subtlety / the subtlety of reading', *French Studies*, xxxvii (1983), 143–56.

(ii) Speakers may only affirm that which they themselves believe to be the case;

(iii) Speakers who apply a predicate *F* to an object a must be prepared to apply *F* to any other object which is in relevant ways the same as a;

(iv) Different speakers may not use the same expression with different meanings.[181]

Alexy's source for some of this is the analytical philosopher H.P. Grice, who set down a number of 'principles of conversation', including a co-operative principle ('make your contribution such as is required at the stage at which it occurs, by the accepted purpose or direction of the talk exchange in which you are engaged') and a maxim of quality ('do not say what you believe to be false; do not say that for which you lack adequate evidence').[182] These modern texts have a long and impressive genealogy in legal writing, beginning with Cicero's *Pro Caecina*, from which the following passage (xviii.52) is much quoted by Renaissance jurists:

Sermo hercule et familiaris et quotidianus non cohaerebit, si verba inter nos aucuparabimur. Denique imperium domesticum nullum erit, si servulis hoc concesserimus ut ad verba nobis obediant, non ad id quod ex verbis intelligi possit, obtemperent.[183]

Why, everyday familiar speech will not remain coherent, if we chase after words between ourselves: there can be no authority in the home if we concede to our most junior servants that they may obey us in the letter of our words, and not comply with that which can be properly inferred from our words.

We shall return below (3.6.1) to the question of bona fides and its connection with the law inscribed in the hearts of men (Rom. 2:15; 2 Cor. 3:3); it is pertinent in the context of cavillation to make a further point. In the gloss on D 50.17.65, it is argued that cavillation is for the

---

[181] *Theorie der juristischen Argumentation*, Frankfurt, 1983, pp. 234–8. The translation is my own.

[182] H.P. Grice, 'Logic and conversation', in *Syntax and semantics 3: speech acts*, ed. P. Cole and J.L. Morgan, New York, 1975, pp. 44–58; 'Further notes on logic and conversation', in *Syntax and semantics 9: pragmatics*, ed. Cole and Morgan, New York, 1978, pp. 113–28; also Donald Davidson, 'A coherence theory of truth and knowledge', in *Truth and interpretation: perspectives on the philosophy of Donald Davidson*, ed. Ernest LePore, Oxford, 1986, pp. 307–19, esp. 314ff.

[183] Cited by Alciato, Fournier, Goeddaeus, Gentili, Bolognetti: cf. also D 10.4.19: (Paulus) ' . . . non oportere ius civile calumniari neque verba captari, sed qua mente quid diceretur, animadvertere convenire' (the civil law should not be egregiously misread or interpreted by cavillation, but rather it is appropriate to consider the intention behind utterances). Other relevant *regulae* are D 33.10.7, D 27.1.13, C 4.18.10 and C 5.3.7.

jurist what *fallacia* is for the logician;[184] thus the proper use of logical procedures which prevent *fallacia* should, in the case of cavillation in law, have the same effect. This ingenious apology for the use of legal dialectics is made by Oldendorp and others;[185] it provides a link with the distinction *mendax/fallax* on which scholastics and humanists alike rely. For human discourse to operate properly, it is crucial to separate utterances by which the speaker deceives others from those by which he deceives himself; in law, there could be no application of *mens rea* unless such a distinction were alleged to be possible.[186] There is, however, a problem here with formalism in law (that is, the doctrine that human actions may be judged without reference to their motives). Strict liability, which is an enduring form of formalism, takes no account of *mens rea*, and by punishing unintentional and intentional deeds alike, acts like a sort of cavillation in reverse; the bona fides of the agent does not come into question. This issue is discussed in the Renaissance with reference to such phrases as *stricti juris, rigor juris, dura lex*, and arises also when the question of ignorance of the law (D 1.3.1; D 2.2.6) is investigated; in most cases, the issue is linked to that of equity as a corrective to what is seen as a potential vice of the law: its inflexibility.[187] But it must be admitted that discussion of strict liability is rare. What makes this noteworthy is

---

[184] Otte, *Dialektik und Jurisprudenz*, pp. 166ff.; see also gl. ad D 45.1.80; gl. ad D 50.16.177; gl. ad D 50.17.65 ('apud nos cavillatio, apud dialecticos fallacia').

[185] Oldendorp, *Topica legalis* in *Opera*, Basle, 1559, p. 82, cited by Piano Mortari, *Diritto logica metodo*, pp. 134ff.

[186] See Quintilian, ii.17–19; Valla, *Elegantiae*, I.ii.649, cited by Waswo, *Language and meaning*, p. 96; Johannes Schneidewinus, *In quatuor Institutionum Imperialium libri commentarii* (1573), Strasbourg and Frankfurt, 1677, col. 1056 (on the grave implications of lying in oral cultures); also Mundius, *De diffamationibus*, p. 39, on the necessity of *mens rea* to the law ('contra naturalem aequitatem est ignoranter peccantes punire': it is against natural justice to punish those who break the law unknowingly). On the relationship of *fallax* to *mendax* in theology, see Johann P. Sommaville, 'The new art of lying: equivocation, mental reservation, and casuistry', in *Conscience and casuistry in Early Modern Europe*, ed. Edmund Leites, 1988, pp. 159–84; also Sissela Bok, *Lying: moral choice in public and private life*, Hassocks, 1978. As well as quoting the loci in Augustine and Aquinas, Sommaville quotes Franciscus Toletus, S.J., *Instructio sacerdotum summam casuum conscientiae complectens*, Lyons, 1601, p. 922: 'Mendacium potest sic describi: verbum falsum cum intentione fallendi. Non est mendacium dicere, quod non ita est, sed dicere aliter quam homo putat, sive sit, sive non sit ita in re: ob id dicitur mentiri, quasi contra mentem ire' (a lie can be described thus: a false utterance accompanied by the intention to deceive. It is not lying to say something that is not so, but it is lying to say something other than what you believe, whether it is in fact so or not; for 'mentiri' is derived as it were from 'going against your inner thought'.).

[185] Papponius, *Interpretatio tituli Digestorum de verborum obligationibus*. Venice, 1604, p. 141 (referring to D 1.2.6 and D 28.2.29); Horn, *Aequitas*, pp. 23–4.

the fact that in theological writing of this time, especially in the doctrine of double predestination derived from Augustine, it is very much at issue; whether man's voluntary acts are relevant or irrelevant to his salvation is fiercely debated. But in law little is said about it, and even *verba solemna* (that is, utterances necessary for the performance of rituals and certain legals acts) are accorded only historical interest.[188]

LITERAL, SUBJECTIVE AND OBJECTIVE MEANING 'VERBA', 'MENS LEGISLATORIS' AND 'RATIO LEGIS'

3.6.1

In the interpretative methods and modes which have been surveyed here, a number of common preoccupations emerge which cluster around Cicero's categories of textual controversy (see above 2.5). For our purposes (that is, for the study of semantics rather than the history of positive law), conflict of laws and arguments from *ratiocinatio* (similarity) – both *causae legales* – can be subsumed under the category 'scriptum et sententia'.[189] This category consists in fact of three elements: *verba, ratio* and *mens* (or *sententia*, or *voluntas*). *Verba* are taken in a narrower sense than that which we encountered above (3.4.1) and usually indicate the 'literal meaning', to which is opposed both the evaluation of the logical or causal analysis of a legal text (the *ratio legis*) and the intention of its maker, the 'mens legislatoris seu testatoris'. The literal determination of meaning is sometimes referred to, on patristic authority, as 'Jewish': 'illi qui intelligunt textum ad literam secundum corticem et non secundum mentem dicuntur Iudaice intelligere, sicut Iudaei intelligunt testamentum vetus . . . Nam Iudaei nunquam volunt a verbis recedere'[190] (those who read texts literally and not according to their [true] meaning are said to understand in a Jewish manner, as the Jews understand the Old Testament . . . for the Jews refuse to depart from the literal meaning). Recovering the intention, however, is specifically as-

---

[188] See Brisson, *De formulis et solemnibus patriae Romanae verbis*, Paris, 1583.

[189] See Martin, *Antike Rhetorik*, pp. 46–8, 51–2.

[190] Caepolla, *De verborum et rerum significatione doctissima commentaria*, pp. 9, 134 (on the authority of gl. ad. C 1.14.5); cf. also Du Moulin, *In consuetudinem Parisiensem*, i.33.1.3, 89; ii.78.3.21, cited by Thireau, *Charles Du Moulin*, pp. 168–9. The patristic authority seems to be Jerome, *PL*, xxxv.42, 322–3. See also D 32.69, quoted above, p. 96.

sociated with jurisprudence.[191] The pursuit of these 'rational' and 'intentional' principles of interpretation betrays a similar structure which is worthy of close analysis. Both *ratio legis* and *mens legislatoris* belong to the order of *res incorporales* (see above 3.3.2), about which, none the less, the jurist must obtain 'vera et certa scientia' (D 50.17.76).[192] In a sense, it is trivial to claim that all attempts to define or classify non-linguistic entities (intentions, states of mind, etc.), being necessarily mediated by words, can only inform us about the articulations of words with other words and cannot give us access to true knowledge.[193] This is a late nominalist and academic view, often expressed to refute the 'sophistical cavillations' of scholastic theologians, but expressed also by lawyers such as Montaigne whose formulation of it is very well known:

Nostre contestation est verbale. Je demande que c'est que nature, volupté, cercle et substitution. La question est de parolles, et se paye de mesme. Un pierre c'est un corps. Mais qui presseroit: Et corps qu'est-ce? – Substance. – Et substance quoy? ainsi de suite, acculleroit en fin le respondant au bout de son calepin. On eschange un mot pour un autre mot, et souvent plus incogneu. Je sçay mieux que c'est qu'homme que je ne sçay que c'est animal, ou mortel, ou raisonnable.[194]

Such comments (which may well be directed against the training in law Montaigne received) show Montaigne to be completely out of sympathy with, for example, the *De interpretatione legis extensiva* of Caepolla in which, as we have seen, an initial definition of a key term (*extensio*) is subjected to further intensive definition (above 3.4.1). This may, of course, seem to be an extreme case: a textbook on interpretation defining its own terms; a modern equivalent might be an interpretation act in which in the preamble entitled 'interpretation' the term 'interpretation' itself was defined. But Caepolla was, as well as being a theorist, a practising lawyer and writer of *consilia*, concerned with the regulation of behaviour in the real world and with

---

[191] See e.g. Seneca, *De beneficiis*, v.19.8 ('sed ut dialogorum altercatione seposita tanquam iuris consultus respondeam, mens spectanda est dantis': (but to lay aside the bickering of dialogue I should reply like a jurist and say that the intention of the giver must be considered), cited by Hotman, *Iurisconsultus*, in *Cynosura*, i.114).

[192] See Rogerius, *De iuris interpretatione*, iii.64–78, in *Tractatus iuris universi*, i.389.

[193] For a modern use of this argument, see Davidson, 'A coherence theory of truth and knowledge', pp. 314 ff.

[194] *Essais*, iii.13, p. 1046: 'un mot . . . souvent plus incogneu' is to be conferred with the claims of etymology to provide a 'nomen notius': see above 3.3.2, and note 87.

the application of existing law to the specific circumstances with which, as a generally framed prohibitive, permissive, punitive or imperative statement, it is never precisely equipped to deal.[195] A much quoted example will serve to illustrate this. Bartolus cites a Bolognese statute which ordained that anyone who drew blood on the streets would be punished with the utmost severity: this was held by an act of interpretation not to extend to surgeon-barbers who open veins for medical reasons.[196] Such interpretation might adduce the intention of the legislator, the cause of the law (the mischief which provoked its enactment) the purpose enshrined in the law, even the intrinsic logic of the law's linguistic formulation; it would not do this in order to wallow in obfuscation, ambiguity or needless analysis, but rather to determine the scope and application of the law (D 1.3.10–12 and above 3.5.1–2). The Corpus Juris Civilis and canon law both make this point repeatedly:

D 1.3.17 (Celsus) Scire leges non hoc est verba earum tenere, sed vim ac potestatem.

To know the law is not to know the words of the law, but its force and power.

D 1.3.29 (Paulus) Contra legem facit, qui id facit quod lex prohibet, in fraudem vero, qui salvis verbis legis sententiam eius circumvenit.

Whoever does what is forbidden by law by fraudulently evading the sense but sticking to the words, contravenes the law.

D 50.16.6.1 (Ulpian) Verbum 'ex legibus' sic accipiendum est, tam ex legum sententia quam ex verbis.

The expression 'from the law' is to be taken to mean as much from its true sense as from its literal meaning.

---

[195] Du Moulin is his ally in this: see Gaspar Caballinus (alias Du Moulin), *De eo quod interest* (1546) in *Tractatus iuris universi*, v.24: 'leges autem non sunt ad sophisticum deducendae, nec tanquam magica quaedam carmina ex solo verborum praescripto tanquam ex nudo cortice tractandae, sed ex communi sensu usibus et commodis hominum accommod[and]ae' (for laws are not to be determined in sense by sophistical methods, nor to be treated like magic incantations according only to the prescriptions of words or, as it were, their mere surface, but are to be adapted to the customs and convenience of mankind through the application of common sense). See also Gammaro, *De extensionibus*, in *Tractatus iuris universi*, xviii.248; quoted by Kelley, *History, law and the human sciences*, ii.31.

[196] This is probably the classical example: it is cited by Bartolus (gl. ad C 1.14.5), Sapcote, Alciato, Rebuffi, Turamini and others: even Cross, *Statutory interpretation*, p. 18, refers to it. Decius (*Consilia*, lx) cites another example (the rule that one should not put to the sword all the relatives of an overthrown tyrant should be relaxed in the case of a relative who waged war to overthrow him), which is cited by Alciato, *De verborum significatione*, p. 19.

Decretum ii.64 In foliis verborum non consistit evangelium sed in radice rationis et in sensu.[197]

The Gospel consists not in the leaves of words but in the root of reason and meaning.

These *regulae*, which are frequently repeated, are reinforced by others stressing the dangers of logical or historical analysis, of definition, and of ambiguity:

D 1.3.20 (Julianus) Non omnium, quae a maioribus constituta sunt, ratio reddi potest.

It is not possible to determine the reason for all that which was laid down by our forebears.

D 1.3.21 (Neratius) Et ideo rationes eorum quae constituuntur inquiri non oportet; alioquin multa ex his quae certa sunt subvertuntur.

Accordingly it is not right to investigate closely the rationale for enactments; otherwise many settled certainties will be thrown into doubt.

D 33.10.7.2 (Celsus) etsi prior atque potentior est quam vox mens dicentis, tamen nemo sine voce dixisse existimatur, nisi forte et eos, qui loqui non possunt, conato ipso sono [voce inarticulata] dicere existimamus.

Although the intention of a speaker is prior to and more important than speech, yet nobody is thought to have said anything without having spoken, unless perhaps we reckon that those who cannot speak, speak by trying to form sounds, even if they are inarticulate.

D 34.5.3 (Paulus) In ambiguo sermone non utrumque dicimus, sed id dumtaxat, quod volumus: itaque qui aliud dicit quam vult, neque id dicit quod vox significat, quia non vult, neque id quod vult, quia id non loquitur.

In speaking ambiguously we do not say both things which might be understood, but only that which we mean; thus, whoever says something different from what he intends to say, neither says what the words mean, because he does not intend them, nor what he intends, because that is not what he says.

D 50.17.96 (Maecianus) In ambiguis orationibus maxime sententia spectanda est eius, qui eas protulisset.

In ambiguous speech, the intention of the utterer is to be given greatest weight.

[197] This is a quotation taken from Jerome, *PL*, xxvi.322 (see above, note 101).

D 50.17.202 (Javolenus) Omnis definitio in iure civile periculosa est: rarum est enim, ut non subverti posset.

Definition in civil law is precarious: it is rare to find one which could not be subverted.

All of these *regulae* are repeatedly adduced, and attract long commentaries and disputations in which there is a large measure of agreement; as has been noted above (1.4.5), what apparently could be combined in an almost infinite number of ways is reduced to an anthology with one or two variations in contents and disposition. These commentaries and disputations turn on two principal questions: What do the words of the law mean? What did the legislator (or testator) intend when he set down the law (or his will) by choosing these words? This alternative resembles closely the terms of the modern debate about objective and subjective meaning, with one important difference: the subjective meaning is clearly conceived of in mentalist terms (see esp. D 33.10.7) and is thought to be in some sense recoverable, even if only in an alternative linguistic form. I have found in none of these texts any argument which disputes the priority of thought over language or the impossibility of thought without language.[198] It is of course open for a modern interpreter so to construe quotations on this topic as to derive Renaissance support for the notion of the materiality of language; but I believe that this can only be done by breaking the Skinnerian rule that the only senses which may legitimately be derived from texts of the past are those which plausibly might have been derived by contemporaries of the text.[199] Of course there is a logical problem arising from the radical alterity of the past and from the irrecoverable nature of the thought processes of another human being;[200] but this cannot by itself sanction any construction placed on textual evidence. This is not to say, however, that an interest in the past is not directed by ideological

---

[198] For a typical example of the affirmation of the priority of thought, see Gentili, *In titulum Digestorum de verborum significatione*, p. 20: 'dixi, verbis antestare sententiam, et verum est quod semper et Rhetores concludunt . . .' (I have said already, and it is true, that intention comes before words, as rhetoricians themselves always conclude).

[199] Quentin Skinner, 'Meaning and understanding in the history of ideas', *History and theory*, viii (1969), 3–53.

[200] For a strong statement of this view (with respect to the radical incomprehensibility of past linguistic systems) see Oswald Ducrot, 'Quelques implications linguistiques de la théorie médiévale de la supposition', in *History of linguistic thought and contemporary linguistics*, ed. Herman Parret, New York and Berlin, 1976, pp. 189–227, esp. 227.

concerns which the historian cannot master; merely, that even given such ideological concerns, there are still checkable linguistic and historical constraints on interpretation.

Both *mens* (*sententia, voluntas*) and *ratio* are, of course, complex terms: 'mens' can denote a bare intention, a bare intention to communicate, an intention to communicate a given message, an intention to communicate a desire (command, emotion etc.) as well as a given message; 'ratio' can denote a cause (*causa impulsiva*), a purpose (*causa finalis*), a rationale, a process, a faculty.[201] Commentators make explicit the complexity of these terms to different degrees: all agree that words embody both sense (*rationem*) and intention. But which *mens* is in question? The historical event which constituted intention of the legislator or testator? Or the intention of the legislator to regulate future action, i.e. the intention he would express if confronted with the facts of a case subsequent to the enactment of his law? By what means can either of these intentions be ascertained? And which *ratio* is in question? the cause of the law? universal reason? the purpose of the law? the coherence of the law? We shall consider these questions in turn.

The historical intention of the legislator or testator is evoked in a number of frequently cited *regulae* (D 27.1.13.2; D 31–3 *passim*; D 35.1.19; D 40.5.24.8; D 50.16.220; D 50.17.12, 17, 19; C 1.14.12; as well as those listed above).[202] Normally speaking, the proper signification of terms is that which determines historical sense;[203] if any sense other than the proper is to be understood, careful justification needs to be provided, usually by having recourse to arguments from pragmatics or from cultural or geographical variation (see above 2.5). A second strategy, suggested in the famous Aristotelian passage about equity quoted above (1.2.3), does not involve historical reconstruction but the fiction of a living legislator or testator, and asks the question: what would the legislator or testator say if he were now asked what his meaning was (or rather, would be in

---

[201] See G.E. Demers, *Les Divers Sens du mot ratio au moyen âge*, in *Études d'histoire littéraire et doctrinale du XIIIᵉ siècle*, i. Paris and Ottawa, 1932, pp. 105–39; Piano Mortari, *Dogmatica e interpretazione*, pp. 236ff. Turamini, *De legibus*, p. 48, analyses intention as the material cause of the law, and distinguishes between *materia remota* (the *nuda voluntas* of the linguistics) and a *voluntas imperandi*, which is translated into a *cogitatio praecipiendi*. This is the *proxima voluntas* which is enshrined in the law, which can be said then to have a *voluntas praecipiendi*.

[202] Gentili lists separately, but does not distinguish in subsequent discussion, the *mens legislatoris*, the *mens testatoris* and the *mens contrahentis*: *In titulum Digestorum de verborum significatione*, p. 2.

[203] Turamini, *De legibus*, p. 194.

the present circumstances).[204] This conjectural reconstruction of the meaning of the dead lawgiver or writer of a will poses considerable logical problems. Is an intention to forbid one practice or express one wish an intention to forbid one practice or express one wish an intention also to permit its contrary or exclude all other wishes? There are *regulae* on this topic also (D 50.16.124; D 50.16.142; also D 31–3 *passim*, D 50.16.237; D 50.17.3) which are much discussed by medieval and Renaissance jurists;[205] their application is determined by the rules of topical argument (see above 2.5). Most commentators and writers of monographs opt for a middle road in this matter, arguing that legislators' and testators' wishes are paramount and to be defined historically, yet conceding at the same time that the traces of their intention (*vestigia*) are only accessible in the form of words, which Cicero calls 'faint and feeble indications of intention'[206] and that these pose a range of well-defined problems which are ordered around the question: 'quomodo colligitur ista mens?' (how can this intention be inferred?) The form of this question links the recovery of intention to the *causae coniecturales* by treating it as a fact, although the *causae legales* more usually include issues about intention.[207]

De Federicis answers this question in six parts:

ex qualitate legis; ex qualitate eorum quae disponuntur in lege; ex qualitate eorum, quae adiuncta sunt his, de quibus disponitur; ex qualitate personarum, ad quas disposita in lege referuntur; ex qualitate legislatoris; ex omnibus locis, ex quibus lex ampliatur et restringitur[208]

from the nature of the law, or of the subject matter of the law, or of things associated with the subject matter, or of the persons to whom the subject matter refers, or of the legislator, or finally from extensive or restrictive constructions placed upon the law.

This division is congruent with the approach of the postglossators, as his frequent reference to them testifies: later jurists set out more ambitious answers. Rebuffi's of 1534 is described by him as a

---

[204] *Ibid.*, p. 96, quoting Aristotle, *Nicomachean Ethics*, v.10 [v.14], cited above 1.2.3.
[205] See Otte, *Dialektik und Jurisprudenz*, *passim*; Horn, *Aequitas*, pp. 28ff.; Turamini, *De legibus*, pp. 49ff., 140f.
[206] 'Tenues et obscurae notae voluntatis' (*De inventione*, ii.48.141). See also Turamini, *De legibus*, p. 176, citing Bolognetti, *De lege, iure et aequitate*, xxxiv.1.
[207] The question is Rebuffi's: *In titulum Digestorum de verborum et rerum significatione*, p. 55.
[208] *De iuris interpretatione*, i.5–51, in *Tractatus iuris universi*, i.219.

supplement to those of De Federicis; his seven rules, which all justify the adoption of the *sensus improprius*, develop those set down by the canon lawyer Pietro d'Ancarano (Petrus Ancharanus) (1333–1416):

(i) Si proprius sensus contineat iniquitatem, tunc accipiemus sensum improprium.

If iniquity flows from the proper sense, then we should accept the improper sense.

(ii) Quando ratio legis repugnat: nam ratio legis mens legis est (gl. ad D 24.3.47)

When the purpose of the law is inconsistent with [the proper sense]: for the purpose of the law is its meaning.

(iii) Si communis usus repugnat propriae significationi.

If common usage is inconsistent with the proper meaning.

(iv) Causa honestatis servandae receditur a propria significatione et attenditur mens ad honestatem tendens.

In the interests of decency, one may depart from the true sense and pay attention to the meaning which is consistent with good morals.

(v) Quando est unica ratio.[209]

When the purpose of the law is unitary.

(vi) Ex argumento sumpto a contrario

By inference from an opposite.

(vii) Inspiciamus mentem ad commodum reipublicae.[210]

The common good justifies an enquiry into meaning.

A third division of the subject is suggested by the more analytical approach of Bolognetti, which Turamini adopts and summarizes.

---

[209] This is usually expressed in a less elliptical way: cf. Turamini, *De legibus*, p. 51: 'si posset lex sine ratione consistere soli imperantium placito, ius aliquando esset latrocinari, ius adulterari, ius falso supponere testamenta. Hinc consequenter deduci videtur rationem legis unicam esse debere, quia forma unica sit. Ideoque quod dicimus rationem esse legis formam, ad rationem finalem est referendum' (if the law could exist of only the wishes of the ruler without any *ratio*, at times justice would consist in theft, adultery and false testimony. Consequently it seems from this reasonable to deduce that the *ratio* of the law must be unitary, because form is unitary. Thus in speaking of *ratio* as the form of the law, we must be referring to the purpose of the law). See also gl. ad D 1.3.17.

[210] Rebuffi, *In titulum Digestorum de verborum et rerum significatione*, p. 55: the *argumentum a contrariis* is, of course, a topical argument: see above 2.5.

This addresses the more precise issue of ambiguity and its resolution (see also above 3.4.3):

Albertus Bolognettus . . . triplicem verborum statum constituit. Aut enim verba iusque adeo dubia sunt, ut nihil plane sit, ex quo voluntas legislatoris colligi [*sic*] possit, ut non tantum de verbis, set etiam de sententia dubitetur; aut verba dubia quidem sunt, sed eorum talis est ambiguitas, quae non tollat certitudinem sententiae, neque prorsus impediat, quominus ad voluntatem, et sensum legislatoris aliquibus vestigiis perveniri possit: aut denique verba nulla ex parte dubia sunt, sed undequaque apertissima; ita ut, quod in ea lege ambiguitatis inest, id non ex verbis oriatur, sed ex eo tantum quod aperta legis scriptura a verisimili legislatoris mente videatur abhorrere. Et in hoc tertio capite . . . tres casus distinguendos censet: primus est, cum verba aperta sic sunt, ut illud de quo agitur, expresse decidunt atque determinent; secundus, cum prorsus illud omittunt. Tertius, neque prorsus omittunt, neque etiam speciatim decidunt, sed generalibus verbis illud item tantum complectitur.[211]

Bolognetti has worked out a tripartite scheme. Either the words themselves are doubtful to the point where there is no clear evidence of the legislator's intention, with the result that there are doubts about the text and the meaning; or the words are doubtful, but their ambiguity is such that it does not abolish all knowledge of the meaning, nor indeed prevent it being possible to determine through some clues what the legislator's intention was; or finally the text is altogether clear, so that the ambiguity in the law arises not from the words but only from the apparent inconsistency between the words and the legislator's intention. Bolognetti thinks that there are three cases to be distinguished under this last category: the first case is when the words expressly determine the matter in hand; the second is when they clearly omit any mention of it; the third is when they neither expressly determine it nor omit mention of it, but it is only included in the words in general terms.

Turamini goes on to point to difficulties in this scheme, but accepts its general disposition of problems.[212] In all these accounts, the priority of *mens* over *verba*, and the non-verbal and real nature of the *mens*, the will of legislator or testator, are accepted;[213] and the choice of

---

[211] Turamini, *De legibus*, pp. 176–7; citing, somewhat inaccurately, Bolognetti, *De lege, iure et aequitate*, xxxiv.1, in *Tractatus iuris universi*, i.321. There are similar schemes in the works of Hopper (in *Tractatus de iuris arte*, pp. 363ff.) and Förster, *Interpres*, pp. 219ff. Bolognetti attributes this method to the *rhetores* (i.e. Cicero and the author of the *Ad Herennium*) 'ex scripto et sententia'.   [212] *Ibid.*, pp. 177ff.

[213] See Sapcote, *Ad primas leges*, pp. 56ff.; Gallus, *Disputatio de legibus*, pp. 2–3; Treterus, *Distributio titulorum juris de verborum significatione et de regulis iuris*, pp. 61ff.; Turamini, *De legibus*, pp. 64ff.; Hunnius, *De authoritate*, pp. 232ff. See also Cicero, *De inventione*, ii.48.143.

historical or hypothetical-present intention disappears under the rules for extracting sense. Moreover, as the legislator, the *lex animata*, is taken to be both rational and consistent, the conjectures about his intention are determined by principles which belong not to the recovery of intention but to the discovery of the *ratio legis*.[214] Turamini, as we have seen, ingeniously distinguishes *mens* and *ratio* by describing them as the material and formal causes of the law; but he, like others, fails in the end to separate them except in so far as *mens* may be pursued through extraneous contextual matter to the law; and this contextual matter takes the form of historical information and inferences which belong to the category of *ratio legis*. Thus the opposition *mens/ratio* fails in the final analysis. This impasse is reached also by those of his contemporaries who attempt the same distinction: Hunnius ends up by equating the *mens legislatoris* with the *mens legis*, the intrinsic intention of the law recoverable from its verbal form; Corvinus confesses that 'ex legis verbis voluntas legislatoris cognoscitur'; in other texts, *verba, mens, sententia, ratio, voluntas* of the law are used synonymously.[215] Even the question whether the legislator or the testator meant what he said leads these commentators to collapse the categories of *verba* and *mens* together: if the *mens* is non-verbal, it is of course possible for it to be clothed in the wrong words, and it is of course crucial in legal contexts which rely on motive that meaning is distinguished from saying (D 34.5.3, quoted above); but in the end the admission is made that 'vix enim praesumi potest legislatorem aliud voluisse, quam quod locutus est'[216] (one can scarcely ever assume that the legislator intended something other than what he said). Indeed, even the facts of the case can come in certain circumstances to be supplanted by the words which describe them: D 33.2.19: 'interdum plus valet scriptura quam [quod actum] sit'.[217]

---

[214] Hunnius, *De authoritate*, p. 256; Bolognetti, *De lege, jure et aequitate*, xxxiv.9, in *Tractatus iuris universi*, i.322.

[215] Hunnius, *De authoritate*, p. 241; 'hinc aequitas non male definitur quod sit moderatio seu mitigatio legis scriptae, qua *mentem, sententiam, rationem et voluntatem* scrutamur et exequimur . . .' (hence equity is well defined as the moderation or mitigation of written law, by which we scrutinze and examine closely its intention, meaning, purpose and will). Cujas, *Ad titulum de verborum significationibus*, p. 23 ('ex legibus, id est *ex verbis, vel mente* legum'); Corvinus, *Ad titulum Digestorum de verborum significatione*, p. 14 (on the phrase *ex verbis*: ' . . . non minus ex mente legislatoris quam ex legis verbis voluntas legislatoris cognoscitur' (the intention of the legislator is known no less through his *mens* [!] than through the words of the law)). All italics are my own.   [216] Turamini, *De legibus*, p. 183.

[217] This is cited by Fournier, Turamini, Alciato and others: but Doneau treats this case as exceptional: see *Ad titulum Digestorum de rebus dubiis*, pp. 10–11.

The law, therefore, is the legal norm or intention it embodies;[218] if the words of the law represent this norm or intention incorrectly, rules are required to enable the norm or intention to be correctly expressed;[219] but the rules can give no better access to the non-verbal norm or intention than the words; they can merely supply additional or corrective material, that is, contextual material in the modern sense.[220] The threat of infinite regress, of the self-referential prison-house of words is clear here, unless recourse is had to the absurd argument (explicit in some of our texts) that intention can exist without *verba* and can communicate itself non-verbally in a written text.[221]

If we begin not with the *mens legislatoris* but the *ratio legis*, the same circularity emerges. The law is taken to be alive; it 'always speaks';[222] the *ratio* of the law is variously described as its vital principle, its soul, its virtue, its power, its essence: *anima, virtus, spiritus, vis, potestas, essentia* (D 1.3.17). The letter kills, the spirit gives life, as St Paul had said;[223] 'nec putamus in verbis scripturarum esse Evangelium, sed in medulla, non in sermonum foliis, sed in radice rationis' (nor do we think that the Gospel is in the text of the Scriptures but in their pith, not in leaves of words but in the roots of their sense) declared Jerome; 'mens se habet ad literam sicut anima ad corpus', (meaning is to words as the soul is to the body), writes the fifteenth-century jurist Andreas Barbatia.[224] The *ratio*, like the *mens* of the law, is not its *verba*; nor is the law known to them who only know the words of the law.[225] *Ratio* seems in most texts to refer to one of three things: first, the cause of the law (i.e. the mischief which the law is designed to remedy); second, the purpose of the law (the end to which it was enacted); third, the

---

218 Sapcote, *Ad primas leges*, p. 57; Turamini, *De legibus*, pp. 64ff.; also Cortese, *La norma giuridica*, ii.295ff.

219 *Ibid.*, p. 156, citing D 27.1.13.2 ('sed et si maxime verba legis hunc habeant intellectum, tamen mens legislatoris aliud vult': but even if the literal meaning of the words is such, none the less the legislator meant something else'.

220 Gallus, *Disputatio de legibus*, p. 2; cf. Cross, *Statutory interpretation*, p. 18.

221 See de Federicis, *De iuris interpretatione*, i.4, in *Tractatus iuris universi*, i.210: 'mens sine verbis esse potest' (there can be meaning without words). See also D 16.3.1 and D 44.7.38, cited below 3.6.5.

222 Cicero, *De officiis*, ii.48; Lefebvre, *Les Pouvoirs du juge*, p. 16, cites a canon law source gl. ad Decretal. 1.2.1; X 12 De constitutionibus n. 85). The phrase 'lex semper loquitur' is frequently cited.

223 Cited by de Federicis, *De iuris interpretatione*, i.5, in *Tractatus iuris universi*, i.210; and Rebuffi, *In titulum Digestorum de verborum et rerum significatione*, p. 55. See also note 101, above.

224 Gl. ad C 6.42.30, quoted by de Federicis and Rebuffi.

225 See notes 1 and 166 above.

rationality of the law, either that immutable component of universal reason vested in the law in general, or its logical coherence.[226] In the first and second senses, the *ratio* of the law may be said to be historical and even labile: laws are born to cure a certain social mischief, and can die *cessante causa*, as Hopper pointed out in a famous passage which described laws as having a natural life cycle.[227] Solon had already pointed out that laws should last only 100 years;[228] the Corpus Juris Civilis envisages their survival in much longer terms, and even argues that they should continue to have force even when their cause was no longer known and could not safely be conjectured (D 1.3.20–1, quoted above). This labile *ratio* which is sometimes associated with the *circumstantiae* of a law's application,[229] contrasts in nature with the *ratio legis* which embodies some part of eternal reason and which is one and universal: Bodin associates this with Stoicism, whereas Turamini and Coras recall the Neoplatonist context of this by describing the *ratio legis* as an 'idea' or 'λόγος'.[230] It is also associated with the law inscribed by God in our hearts (Rom. 2:15, 2 Cor. 3:3) and the 'naturalis ratio' referred to in D 1.1.9.[231] In these senses it is close to the meaning of 'conscience' or a 'natural sense of justice' (see below 3.8.1), and to Cicero's famous formulations 'Lex est ratio summa, insita in natura, quae iubet ea quae facienda sunt,

---

[226] See above, note 185, and 2.4, 3.1.3 and 3.4.1; D 1.3.14, 15; D 34.5.12 (the logical coherence of the law as the presupposition of its rationality); Cicero, *De republica*, iii.18 ('est vera lex recta ratio naturae congruens diffusa in omnes, constans, sempiterna': true law is right reason congruent with nature, instilled in all men, constant and eternal), cited by Hunnius, *De authoritate*, p. 5; Turamini, *De legibus*, pp. 49ff., who cites Franciscus Piccolomineus, *Universa philosophia de moribus in decem gradus redacta*, Venice, 1583, x.24, pp. 583–4; Coras in *Tractatus de iuris arte*, pp. 219–20; Gammaro, *De extensionibus*, cl, in *Tractatus iuris universi*, i.257, quoting Panormitanus ad Decretal. 4.14.8: 'licet lex mutetur, tamen ratio legis est aeterna et immutabilis' (although the law changes, its *ratio* is eternal and immutable); Lefebvre, *Les Pouvoirs du juge*, pp. 28ff.; Kelley, *History, law and the human sciences*, i.

[227] Hopper, in *Tractatus de iuris arte*, pp. 362ff., cited by Egerton, *A speech touching the post-nati*, 1609, p. 47, quoted by Thorne, in *A discourse upon the exposicion of statutes*, p. 166n. On *Cessante causa*, see D 3.1.1.5; D 37.14.6.2; Alciato, *De verborum significatione*, p. 16; and Cortese, *La norma giuridica*, ii.239f.   [228] Cited by Turamini, *De legibus*, p. 189.

[229] As by Lucas de Penna, cited by Walter Ullmann, *The medieval idea of law*, London, 1946, p. 57; see also Kelley, *History, law and the human sciences*, ii.31.

[230] Turamini, *De legibus*, p. 11; Coras, in *Tractatus de iuris arte*, p. 210; Bodin makes this connection with Stoicism explicit with a quotation from Diogenes Laertius, vii.128: τὸ δίκαιον οὐκ εἶναι θέσει ἀλλὰ μόνον φύσει (justice is not learned but derived from nature: *Iuris universi distributio*, p. 10).

[231] See Sapcote, *Ad primas leges*, p. 5; Turamini, *De legibus*, pp. 8–11; Nicolaus Hemmingius, *De lege naturae apodictica methodus concinnata*, Wittenberg, 1577, titlepage (quoting Rom. 2:15) and B8ᵛ.

prohibetque contraria' (law is the highest degree of reason set in nature which ordains those things which are to be done and prohibits those which are not to be done) and 'est enim lex nihil aliud nisi recta et a numine deorum tracta ratio, imperans honesta, prohibens contraria' (law is nothing other than right reason whose source is the will of the gods, ordaining what is right and prohibiting its opposite).[232] The law is not, however, coterminous with ethics; at least one (not very often cited) *regula* makes this clear: (D 50.17.144 (Paulus) 'non omne quod licet, honestum est'[233] (not everything that is allowed is moral). Agrippa takes delight in his *De incertitudine* in citing a list of *regulae*, many, apparently, relating to natural as well as positive law, which expose this distinction further:

Vim vi repellere licet. Frangenti fidem fides frangatur eidem: Fallere fallentem non est fraus. Dolosus doloso nullo tenetur. Culpa cum culpa compensari potest. Male meriti nulla debent iustitia, nec fide gaudere. Volenti non fit iniuria. Licitum est contrahentibus se decipere. Tantum valet res quanti vendi potest. Item, ut liceat sibi consulere cum damno alterius. Ad impossibile neminem obligari. Item, si te vel me confundi oporteat, potius eligam te confundi quam me.[234]

You may resist force with force. Break faith with him that breaks faith; to deceive the deceiver is not fraud. A deceiver is not liable to a deceiver; a fault may be recompensed by a fault; those that deserve ill should enjoy neither justice nor good faith; no injury can be done to the willing; it is acceptable for those engaging in contracts to deceive themselves. A thing is worth as much as it may be sold for. It is permissible to provide for one's own safety to the damage of another. No man is obliged to fulfil impossible conditions. If either you or I are to be ruined, it is better that you be ruined than I.

Law may specify that one must *honeste vivere* (D 1.1.10), and that jurisprudence is the *ars aequi et boni* (D 1.1.1), but its relationship to moral philosophy is far from simple, and moral philosophy cannot always be adduced as a principle of interpretation or even as part of

---

[232] *De legibus*, i.6.18; *Philippics*, xi.28. These topoi are sometimes cited from Ramus' edition of the first book of Cicero's *De legibus* (1554) (Basle, 1580, p. 305): e.g. by Coras, in *Tractatus de iuris arte*, p. 9.

[233] Most commentators simply refer D 50.17.144 (sometimes numbered 187) to D 50.17.197 (sometimes numbered 157) (Modestinus): 'semper in coniunctionibus non solum quid liceat considerandum est sed et quid honestum sit' (always in unions one must wonder not only what is lawful but also what is honourable); see *Commentarii de regulis iuris*, pp. 693–4, 741–2. See also Rogerius, *De legis potentia*, iii.2, in *Tractatus iuris universi*, i.403.

[234] *De incertitudine*, xci. His main attack here is on D 1.1.10 ('suum cuique tribuere'), but he includes a reference to D 50.17.185.

the law's purpose (*ratio*): take for example the adage 'mulier dum meretrix non est inhonestum facit, si quid inhonesti faciat, sed quando meretrix est honestum facit quia ea quae meretricis sunt facit' (a woman who is not a prostitute behaves indecently when she engages in any indecent act: but a prostitute doing the same thing is not acting indecently because she is only doing what is expected of a prostitute: cf. D 12.5.4.3).[235]

Ratio legis, therefore, contains its potential internal inconsistencies: it is historical and yet perennial; it has a present force, but comes out of the past and, as Coras and others point out, also looks to the future; it is associated both with singular, the universal and omnitemporal, and with the plural, the particular and contingent; it is linked with a sense of natural justice, but is not identical to morality. Like *mens*, *ratio* is non-verbal, but accessible only through words: its non-verbal guarantor is logic. It is possible that the scholastically minded postglossators preferred *ratio* to *mens* for this reason;[236] for Renaissance jurists, *mens* is said to be preferable: some go as far as to claim that the public good (*utilitas*) overrides both.[237] Those who try to distinguish *mens* and *ratio*, however, have a hard time of it. Turamini's brave attempt to distinguish them as the material and formal causes of the law collapses, because the relationship of both causes to words is effectively the same; Gentili's commentary on D 50.16.6.1 begins by expounding Baldus' distinction between *mens* and *ratio* but ends up by defining both by the same metaphor (the *anima legis*); Doneau's account ends by conceding that 'rationem legis ipsam [esse] sententiam legis: ipsum id quod lex voluit consequi, et propter quod lex lata est' (the *ratio legis* and the meaning are the same, as are the mischief, which the law set out to remedy and the purpose of the law).[238] In this sentence of a *mos gallicus* systematizer, we have rejoined the post-

---

235 *Axiomata legum*, p. 179; also Laurentius Arnoldus, *Tractatus in quo sit collatio philosophiae moralis cum iure scripto*, Frankfurt, 1606. On the need for ethical training for lawyers because of the non-coincidence of law and morality, see Hopper, in *Tractatus de iuris arte*, p. 570, and Kelley, 'Iurisconsultus perfectus'.

236 See below 3.7.1 and Baldus, cited by Rebuffi, *In titulum Digestorum de verborum et rerum significatione*, p. 55.

237 See Thorne, introduction to *A discourse upon the exposicion of statutes*, pp. 57ff.; Hunnius, *De authoritate*, p. 3 (citing D 1.3.20 and D 9.2.51).

238 Turamini, *De legibus*, pp. 47ff.; Gentili, *In titulum Digestorum de verborum significatione*, pp. 19–20; Doneau, *Commentarii de iure civili*, ii.6, in *Opera*, i.110. Cf. the collapse of Goeddaeus' distinction between *voluntaris sensus* and *naturalis sensus* (*Commentarius*, pp. 10–11); and Caepolla's admission that signification can be identical to usage (*In titulum de verborum et rerum significatione doctissima commentaria*, pp. 134–6).

glossators and their declaration that 'ratio legis mens legis est':[239] the wheel has come full circle in the opposite direction, as it were.

The separation of *ratio* and *mens* and the insistence that both can be identified and described even though the words by which they are expressed are the only objective evidence of them is reminiscent of impasses in other areas of Renaissance thought, notably the attempt to prove the true sense of scripture from the words of the text, of which Waswo has perceptively said: 'in the face of all the equally good . . . arguments that "this is my body" is to be interpreted literally or figuratively, the universal insistence that scripture interprets itself is farcical'[240] ('equally good' here embodies of course a modern judgement, which the opponents in the debate could not possibly have accepted). The interesting question is why medieval and Renaissance jurists were able to rely on a distinction between intention and sense which could not be proved logically even in their own terms. Several tentative answers might be put forward. First, as has been said, the law relies on intention and the distinction between intended and unintended words and acts, without which it could not function. *Mens rea* and *mens legislatoris* must, therefore, be preserved as discrete phenomena. Moreover, even if unable to give a satisfactory codification of it, jurists must be able to rely on the distinction between error and deception, mistaken interpretation and deliberate misinterpretation, being upheld *de jure*. Third, additional contextual material can alter materially the interpretation placed on a text or an event: appeal to *ratio* (and parallel or contrary laws) and to *mens* (the pragmatic event of legislation and its historical or geographical circumstances) provides this.[241] Fourth, the rôle of interpreter which the allegation of additional material makes necessary is in the institutional interests of lawyers, whose philosophical and legal training places them in a powerful position with respect to their clients and pupils. The law has an exterior (*cortex, superficies*) in the form of words: it has an interior, its *mysterium* which the student and jurist must penetrate, and which is its *medulla*, or in Rabelais's words, its 'substantificque mouelle': namely its *mens* and *ratio*.[242] The true sense and meaning are, in the end, determined institutionally by the agreed procedures of argument and the accepted corpus of evidence

[239] Gl. ad D 1.3.17, gl. ad D 24.3.47, cited by Turamini, *De legibus*, p. 51; also Cortese, *La norma giuridica*, i.285.   [240] *Language and meaning*, p. 190.

[241] For an amusing example, see below 4.3, note 52.

[242] Caepolla, *In titulum de verborum et rerum significatione doctissima commentaria*, p. 13: 'mysterium verborum ponit mysterium intellectus' (citing Baldus, Gl. ad D 1.7.2).

(which turns out in most cases to be the relevant anthology of *regulae* from the Corpus Juris Civilis and their accompanying glosses). This is perhaps best exemplified not by a quotation from a Renaissance legal text but by one from a document written in 1893 (the encyclical Proventissimus Deus) which recalls explicitly the authorities cited above in order to make in unusually plain terms the point about the institutional determination of meaning:

The sense of Holy Scripture can nowhere be found incorrupt outside the [Roman Catholic] Church and cannot be expected to be found in writers who, being without true faith, only gnaw at the bark of sacred Scripture and never attain its pith.

The true faith on which this encyclical turns is determined not by words but by an institution (the Roman Catholic Church) which validates one interpretation and invalidates others.[243]

Both *mens* and *ratio* are not only beneath and behind the words of the law: they are also prior to the words. They are used to invoke a posteriori the origin of the law, either in the historically situated mind of the legislator, or in the mischief for which a remedy is needed, or in the general purposes served by the law as defined in D 1.1.9. This genetic account is in accordance with Aristotelian philosophy.[244] It has echoes in modern Continental philosophy in its attribution of an origin which the practice of the jurist shows to be not so much this as an effect of his operations on the text. This is clearest seen in the case of extensive interpretation, characterized, as we have seen, as that in which the *mens* exceeds the *verba* (above 3.4.1). By appeal to the *mens*, the law can be extended without new law being made: 'nulla enim verborum extensio est; sed extensio eorum ex sententia legis; quod si non corriguntur verba sed porriguntur, aequitas correctio est, non porrectio, vel productio verborum' (the words are not extended, but rather the meaning; for if words are not corrected but expanded (porriguntur) this is rectification by equity, not verbal expansion or production).[245] The rôle of the interpreter, according to all these commentators, is to make the text clear; it can never be to add to the law or supplement it in any way. Only the Emperor (legislator) can

243 *Enchiridion Biblicum*, 4th ed., Rome, 1964, no. 113; see also Agrippa, *De incertitudine*, xci, quoted above, note 14; J.K.S. Reid, *The authority of scripture*, London, 1957, p. 121, citing the Tridentine decree on canonical scriptures, fourth session, 8 April 1546: 'Holy Scripture can say, and by interpetation can be made to say, nothing that conflicts with ecclesiastical doctrine': cited by Waswo, *Language and meaning*, p. 211.
244 *Politics*, i.1.3, 1252a26.   245 Turamini, *De legibus*, p. 97.

do this since he alone can interpose himself between the law and equity (see above 3.1.3).[246] But if the *sententia* which exceeds the law is obtained by appeal to *mens* or *ratio* or both, then the words of the law are indeed being added to: even the use of the verbs *ampliare*, *extendere*, *porrigere* indicates this. A similar distinction to that between *mens* and *ratio* is made here between *interpretari* and *corrigere*; in a similar way, it collapses.[247] All interpretation becomes supplementation or correction. There is no originary *ratio* or *mens* to be recovered; because the law always speaks, each act of legal interpretation determines *de novo* and *de jure* the source of its authority; it may even be dispensed from so doing (D 1.3.20,21).

Derrida has described the lexicographers who juxtaposed the two meanings of supplement – to add to a whole; and to complete – as 'sleepwalkers' who failed to grasp the undecidability of the term.[248] This description would not be appropriate for Renaissance jurists. As Turamini and others show, especially in deploying arguments about extensive interpretation, they were highly sensitive to the question of authority in interpreting, which from the very inception of the school of Bologna had played a prominent part in discussions by interpreters and teachers of their rôle (see above 1.5.2). As in the case of principles or ἀρχαί mentioned above (3.1.2), it seems that jurists can articulate the problem without either being able to solve it or necessarily being interested in doing so. Provided that the distinctions they deployed could be used meaningfully in given contexts and lead to practical results, their logical or consequential failings could be ignored.

ILLOCUTIONARY AND PERLOCUTIONARY FORCE: PERFORMATIVES

3.6.2
We have not, however, exhausted the powers of words by determining their relationship to subjective and objective meaning, to *mens* and *ratio*. Two much quoted *regulae* make this clear:

D 1.3.7 (Modestinus) Legis virtus haec est: imperare, vetare, permittere, punire.

---

[246] Hopper, in *Tractatus de iuris arte*, p. 363; see also above, 1.5.1 and 3.1.3. D 1.3.12, 13 are *regulae* which allow judges to apply the law, but they may be read historically to relate to a pre-Justinian state of affairs.   [247] Turamini, *De legibus*, p. 99.
[248] *L'Ecriture et la différence*, Paris, 1967, p. 314.

The force of the law is this: to command, to prohibit, to permit, to punish.

D 1.3.17 (Celsus) Scire leges non hoc est verba earum tenere, sed vim ac potestatem.

To know the law is not to know the text of the law but its force and power.

To investigate this *virtus, vis, potestas*, we shall have to reverse the process of recovering meaning from words, and begin with thought in order to move towards meaning; and this will involve a detour into natural philosophy and theology. In a little known (and perhaps rightly uncommemorated) thesis, a seventeenth-century German doctoral student called Christophorus Bremerus set down the following map of knowledge:

Pulchro cohaerent ordine, Res, Conceptus, Verba, Scripta. Primas tenent res, quas conceptus sequuntur, quicquid rerum ullibi est, animae nostrae ingreditur ergastulum per species, per simulachra. Ac cum politicum animal homo sit, conceptus in plurium emittere tentat notitiam. Hinc lingua profert, quod in ima cordis latet profunditate. Verborum vero vicariae literae sunt. Quod enim verba praesentibus, id literae absentibus. Unde cum literarum, tum librorum honos ac dignitas. In quibus loquuntur absentes, imo et qui e vivis discessere. Securius saepe et confidentius viventibus. Sane sic species, et orationes, et scripta antecedunt. Conceptus sunt rerum: verba et literae conceptuum.[249]

Things, concepts, words and texts hang together in a beautiful order. Things have the first place; they are followed by concepts. Anything anywhere enters the prison-house of our mind through perceptions or simulacra. Because man is a political animal, he tries to bring concepts to the knowledge of others. Whence the tongue gives forth what lies in the very depths of the heart. Letters then take the place of words. What are words to those present are letters to those absent; whence the honour of dignity of letters and books. In these, those who are absent speak, even those who have departed this life, in a way which is more secure and bolder than the living. Thus perception precedes speech and the written word. Concepts relate to things; written words and letters relate to concepts.

Bremerus gives this account of the sequence *res, conceptus, verba, scripta* to confirm the correctness of Scaliger's *Exercitationes contra Cardanum*

---

[249] *Disputatio e Julii Caesaris Scaligeris Exotericis exercitationibus II et III . . .*, Wittenberg, 1645, A4ᵛ. This is, of course, a scholastic commonplace: see Magee, *Boethius on signification and words*, pp. 69ff.; Heath 'Logical Grammar', p. 57 (citing Eck's *Elementarius* of 1517). It persists a long time: see Louis de Lesclache, *Les Véritables Regles de l'orthograf francèse*, Paris, 1668, p. 5: 'Comme nos consepsions sont le portrait des choses que nous pouvons conétre, ét que la parole ét celui de la pansée, il ét aûsi trés certain que l'écriture ét le portrait de la parole.'

(1557); it is an amplification of Scaliger's claim that 'veritas est orationis adaequatio cum ipsis speciebus' (truth is the correspondence of discourse with perception).[250] Bremerus wishes to demonstrate the orthodox point that falsity is in concepts when they do not coincide with their objects (*res*), but not in propositions (*orationes*) which give a correct account of perception (*species*) even if the perceptions are false. Truth is a function, therefore, of intention as well as of things: 'veritas in sermone affectus orationis est, conveniens menti: veritas in conceptu affectus mentis est, conveniens rei' (discursive truth is an affect of speech, which must agree with the mental intention: conceptual truth is an affect of the mind, which must agree with its object). It is possible, according to Bremerus, to tell the truth logically, but lie ethically, and to lie logically, but tell the truth ethically. Thus (in his example), a Jew saying 'non serio, sed ore tantum' (not seriously, but only with his lips) that Christ was the Messiah would be telling what Bremerus calls the 'logical' truth (*conveniens rei*), but lying ethically; whereas if he denied that Christ were the Messiah, he would be telling the ethical truth (*conveniens menti*) but lying logically.[251]

3.6.3

This short excursus into the relationship of things, words, intention and truth has many echoes in Renaissance jurisprudence. *Res, verba, veritas, mens* (*voluntas*), *intellectus*, as we have already seen, are frequently encountered and difficult terms in law. All law is said to pertain to *personae, res, actiones* (D 1.5.1 and I 1.2.3.2); of these, *res* are the most wide-ranging category, including both corporeal and incorporeal entities, among which intentions and other mental events are numbered (see above 3.3.2). *Verba*, according to Aristotle and Cicero, are mental symbols or tokens (*notae animi*) representing concepts which are common to all men;[252] they consist in a material sound (*vox*), a semantic content (*sensus, intellectus*) and may have a referent (*res, intentio, suppositio*) as we have seen (2.2). By the late Renaissance, on the authority of the Corpus and of writers on forensic rhetoric, the definition of *verba* has been extended to read 'notae rerum declarantes animi voluntatisque passiones et motus' (symbols

---

[250] See above 2.4, and note 27.
[251] *Disputatio*, B2ʳ; for a different account of the articulation of *res* and *conceptus*, see Piano Mortari, *Diritto, logica, metodo*, pp. 114–264.
[252] *De interpretatione*, i (16a4f.); *Topica*, viii.35.

of things which express the passions and movements of the mind and will).[253] The introduction of subjective meaning is significant. It seems to make of intention a *res* which is not the *res* of signification, but can yet be signified and is part of *verbum*. Its apparent exclusion in the medieval period permitted the elaboration of a logic which treated only *intellectus* or thoughts and ignored the word as an expression of feelings (*motus animi*) or perceptions (*sensus, species*).[254] Signification is taken to be active on the part of the utterer and unproblematically passive on the part of the receiver;[255] terms and propositions are taken to signify naturally in a sort of universal mental language (*qua* mental event) and conventionally (*qua* spoken and written words); in this sense, signification is an effect of feelings, perceptions and thoughts, but the complex causal connection itself is not subjected to enquiry; rather, the possibility of a conscious subject investigating himself is rendered unproblematic: 'intellectus humanus seipsum intelligit et in se convertitur'[256] (the human intellect comprehends itself and is self-sufficient). Attention instead is given to propositions which, when asserted, become more than acts of signification, and can be treated as judgements. Propositions can refer to things at the universal level or can descend to particulars.[257] All of this is, and was, suitable for the investigation of theological problems; but it is not a particularly helpful model for law. There is no representation in it of intention in any of its guises: *generalis* (a desire to communicate), *particularis* (a desire to communicate a given *conceptus*), *verbalis* (the translation of this desire into the code of language);[258] nor of the *mens rea* which can have a presence in words (e.g. the *animus iniuriandi* of a slanderer: see below 4.3). There is no distinction made between objective and subjective meaning, although this is crucial to the understanding of both the words of the lawgiver (*mens legislatoris*) and the words of those involved with the law (*mens testatoris, contrahentis*, etc.); a *regula* (D 34.5.3) which, as we have seen (3.6.1), distinguishes between saying

---

253 Goeddaeus, *Commentarius*, p. 6; Cicero, *Partitiones oratoriae*, xxxix.136; D 32.25 (Paulus) 'cum in verbis nulla ambiguitas est, non debet admitti voluntatis quaestio' (where there is no verbal ambiguity, the question of speaker's intention should not arise); cf. also D 31.64–7, 69–80 and D 33.10.7.   254 Brinkmann, *Mittelalterliche Hermeneutik*, p. 25.
255 See *ibid.*, and *De interpretatione* iii, 16b19 ('he who speaks [names] establishes an understanding, and he who hears them rests [i.e., acquiesces in it]'); Spade, in the *Cambridge history of later medieval philosophy*, pp. 188f.; Magee, *Boethius on signification and words*, p. 75.
256 See Johannes Fridericus Schroterus, *Quaestio utrum Aristoteles intellectus nostri immortalitatem cognoverit et ad eandem responsio*, Jena, 1585, ci^r. This is a standard view: see *De animo*, iii.15–16; *De partibus animalium*, i.1.
257 *The Cambridge history of later medieval philosophy*, pp. 188ff., 197ff. (Nuchelmans).
258 On this see Turamini, *De legibus*, pp. 47ff., and above, note 201.

and intending, makes this clear. But in terms of medieval logic, *velle* here is equivalent to *dicere*, and no analysis could be made of the *regula*, which appears as nonsensical (that is, in breach of the rule of non-contradiction). While the distinction *velle/dicere* can be stated without absurdity in law although not in logic, it cannot easily be established, as we have seen (3.6.1), since words are taken to be the most important, if not in certain circumstances the only, source of information about intentions.

It is also generally presupposed that thoughts cannot be ambiguous and obscure, even if words can be, and are often so. Even thoughts about non-existents (the goathorse, the chimera) are not lacking in clarity and distinctness, even if they have no referents.[259] The mind is taken as having a universal language, as in the *De interpretatione*. Prior to this, there is the 'vox cordis' or the 'verbum cordis': this is the 'real word of cognition', which precedes the 'vox conceptus' (sometimes called 'cogitatio') or universal language of the mind, which itself precedes the 'vox articulata' or spoken word of which it is the efficient cause.[260] In this tripartite scheme, three languages are distinguished: the language of the heart or of faith, which cannot lie and cannot be ambiguous; the language of intellectual life which can be deceptive, but which is unambiguous; and the fallible, fallen language of human communication which can be both deceptive and ambiguous. This scheme is authorized by theology, as Rebuffi concedes:

Et licet theologi aliquando accipiant verbum pro mentis conceptu, qui de voce formanda et emittenda concipitur, antequam ulterius ad labia producatur: et sic dicitur cogitatio, quae adhuc in conscientiae secreto continetur: tamen hic [i.e. in jurisprudence] communiter sumitur pro verbo iam prolato vel scripto: alioqui si pro cogitatione, nullus potest eam

---

[259] See E.J. Ashworth, 'Can I speak more clearly than I understand?', in *Studies in medieval thought dedicated to Geoffrey L. Bursill-Hall*, ed. Konrad Koerner, Hans J. Niederehe and R.H. Robins, Amsterdam, 1980, pp. 29–38: also *Physics*, iv.1 (208a31) and *Prior Analytics*, i.28 (49a24).

[260] See Hans Arens, 'Verbum cordis: zur Sprachphilosophie des Mittelalters', in *Studies in medieval thought*, pp. 14–27; Brinkmann, *Mittelalterliche Hermeneutik*, pp. 26, 37 (where the loci in Augustine and Anselm are given); Nuchelmans in the *Cambridge history of later medieval philosophy*, p. 197, and Spade, in *ibid.*, p. 189. The causal relationship of 'vox cordis' to 'cogitatio' or 'vox conceptus', and of this to the 'vox articulata' is complicated by the parallel of the 'vox cordis' and 'vox conceptus' with the natural and the spoken or written word with the conventional: on this, see Nuchelmans. The tripartite system is reminiscent of the *modi essendi, intelligendi, significandi* of the 'modistae': see above, chapter 2, note 10. On the survival of this doctrine, see Pascal, *Œuvres complètes*, ed. Louis Lafuma, Paris, 1963 (Penseé 968), p. 634.

declarare praeter Deum Opti[ficem] max[imum] qui solus est cordium scrutator.[261]

Although theologians sometimes take 'verbum' to mean a concept of the mind which is conceived for the voice to form and enunciate before it is brought forth by the lips, and hence 'verbum' is said to be a thought which is contained up to this point in the secrecy of the conscience; jurists, however, normally take 'verbum' to mean the word that has already been uttered or written: besides, if it is taken to be a thought, none can declare it other than almighty God, who alone sees into men's hearts (1 Cor. 4:1–5).

The jurist is obliged to stop short of assertions about the *verbum cordis* or even the *cogitatio*; his realm, unlike that of the theologian, is the fallen language and diseased will of men.

As Rebuffi hints, speech has also a medical dimension ('antequam ad labia producatur'); it raises questions about the nature of perception and the processes of the mind, which are known as *intellectio*, and which require 'applicatio animae et intentio' as well as an object of perception. One of the most subtle discussions of these questions in the Renaissance is the dialogue of Girolamo Fracastoro (1483–1553) entitled *Turrius*; one of the most wideranging and polemical is that of Scaliger in his 307th exercise against Cardano.[262] The questions which arise – How does the will relate to the intellect? Is the intellect eternal? where is it? Does it contain anything which was not previously channelled through the senses? (i.e. are universals outside the intellect?)? How does it act? How is it related to the soul? Is it both active and passive? Is it universal? Is it immortal? – are not germane to jurisprudence, and thus the theological and medical dimensions of the enquiry into mental acts and states are seen to be

---

[261] Rebuffi, *In titulum Digestorum de verborum et rerum significatione*, p. 3. Deceit can, of course, exist in the heart of man as a natural disease or perversion of his will or perception: cf. Jeremiah 17:9 and medieval commentaries thereon. It is therefore possible for the 'vox conceptus' to represent faithfully a deceitful 'vox cordis'. Even if man is credited with total self-knowledge (i.e. if self-deceit is taken to be a form of 'moral' lying), it is difficult to view as anything but naïve Erasmus' often quoted optimistic affirmation in *Ecclesiastes*: 'Sermo hominis vero imago est mentis sic oratione quasi speculo reddita' (human speech is indeed the image of the mind just as if it were reflected as in a mirror); but Erasmus (if not those who quote him) qualifies this view with the rider 'qualecunque est cor hominis talis est oratio' (as is the heart of man so is his speech) which allows for the corruption of language by desire: *Ecclesiastes*, i, in *Opera*, Basle, 1540, v.645. Cf. Cicero, *De oratore*, iii.59.221: 'imago animi vultus'.

[262] Fracastoro, *Opera*, Venice, 1584, fols. 121–48 (cf. Aristotle, *De anima* iii.15–16); Scaliger, *Exotericae exercitationes*, cccvii, pp. 917–97; Draudius, *Bibliotheca classica*, p. 1396, cites other texts. Caepolla makes some allusion to these debates in distinguishing *intellectus hominis* (*universalis*) from *intellectus verborum* (*multiplex*), with reference to Aquinas, *Summa theologiae* 2a 2ae 8.1 and *Nicomachean Ethics*, vi (*In titulum Digestorum de verborum et rerum doctissima commentaria*, p. 27).

beyond the discipline of the law and to mark one of its frontiers. But in one clear respect the law adopts the common opinion of theologians and doctors, namely that thought precedes speech, and that the things (whether *realia* or not) that are the objects of thought precede thought. This leads in legal terms to the argument that law precedes crimes; as Jacobus Raevardus declares, Remus was not murdered, nor were the Sabine women raped, because crimes cannot occur before the law which defines them (cf. Rom. 9:15); *nulla poena sine lege*.[263]

3.6.4

The uncontested priority of reality and thought over language does not, however, solve the problem of intention in speech, subjective meaning, and the effects of speech which are not accounted for in Bremerus' traditional schema. The language of the law, particularly, has an important performative function which the scheme given above cannot account for: 'verba debent agere et aliquid operari in ea, qua situm erit, materia'[264] (words must act and do something to the matter of which they treat), says Breche. Justice is, as D 1.1.10 has it, a 'constans et perpetua *voluntas*'; in a somewhat puzzling formula, the law is said to be a 'mens sine appetitu'[265] (cf. Aristotle *Politics*, iii.11.4 (1287a35) 'law is wisdom without desire'); it acts disinterestedly (without desire) but intentionally (*cum vi imperandi*); it 'always speaks' (see above 3.1.3 and 3.6.1). As an imperative it is neither true nor false, but falls rather in the domain of rhetoric or poetics than of logic (see above 2.5); it belongs, therefore, to a category of utterance other than the assertoric or declarative.[266] According to D 1.3.17, the words of the law have *vis* and *potestas*: some commentators treat these words as synonymous (together with *potentia, virtus, anima, effectus, utilitas*);[267]

---

[263] *De auctoritate prudentium*, Antwerp, 1566, p. 7; cf. also Rom. 3:19–21, and Cicero, *De legibus*, ii.4, who argues that rape is a crime even before the law imposed penalties on rapists. There is also an echo here of the debate about the disputed precedence of *ius* and *iustitia*: see Alciato, *Parerga*, i.29, Isidore, *Etymologiae*, xviii.15.2 and chapter 1, note 105, above. Cf. also the question of the relationship of *lex* to *regula* (D 50.17.1: 'non ex regula ius sumatur, sed ex iure quod est regula fiat') and Cortese, *La norma giuridica*, i.321ff.

[264] *Ad titulum Pandectarum de verborum et rerum significatione*, p. 4.

[265] Turamini, *De legibus*, p. 35.

[266] *Ibid.*, p. 77 (on infelicity as well as error in language use); and Brinkmann, *Mittelalterliche Hermeneutik*, p. 33.

[267] Baldus gl. ad C 1.1.1, which he called a *repetitio de vi et potestate statutorum*, on which see Horn, *Aequitas*, p. 4; Rogerius, *De legis potentia, passim*; Coras, in *Tractatus de iuris arte*, pp. 162ff.; Fournier, *In titulum de verborum significatione*, p. 21; for a theological approach, see Claudius Carninus, *Tractatus de vi et potestate legum humanarum*, Douai, 1608.

others distinguish *vis* ('causa quae intelligatur alicui effectui, etiamsi non exprimatur' (a cause which is understood through a certain effect, even if it is not expressed)) from *potestas* ('effectum quem leges exercent in foro'[268] (the effect of words in the courtroom)); others define *vis* as the connotative senses of a word or its entailments (the *vis comprehensiva*); yet others associate *potestas* not with the perlocutionary effect of words in the courtroom ('I sentence you . . .') but to their quasi-magical generative powers: 'verbis inesse potestatem vimque admirabilem ad res ipsas inducendas fides sacrosancta docuit'[269] (the Catholic faith has taught that words contain a marvellous power of bringing things about). What is here described is the performative force of words which cannot be given a place in Bremerus' sequence *res–conceptus–verba–scripta*: 'vis et potestas legis aut maior aut alia est quam verba prae se ferant'[270] (the force and power of the law is either greater or other than what the words show); this has a parallel outside legal studies in the power attributed to words to 'signify more than they say'.[271]

On this unspoken force of words much legally binding communication depends: indeed, for the communication of agreement to a contract, the words are not necessary, but the *consensus ad idem* is (D 44.7.2). In such cases, offensive gestures (see below 4.3), gestures such as nodding (see above 3.2.1) and words are performative; that is, they create obligations (e.g. promises) or legal torts (e.g. slander) by their nature.[272] Crucial to this is another feature of verbal production which escapes Bremerus' codification (though he slips it in in a revealing aside: 'non serio, sed ore tantum'):[273] namely bona fides. It is a condition of the use of conventional signs (and words, as we have seen, are conventional signs unlike the language of the heart) that

---

268 Oldendorp, *Paratitla*, in *Opera*, i.87.
269 Thireau, *Du Moulin*, pp. 170ff. (on 'vis compraehensiva'); Sapcote, *Ad primas leges*, p. 6; cf. Caepolla, *In titulum Digestorum de verborum et rerum significatione doctissima commentaria*, p. 20, quoting a canon law source which claims that not only words but also plants and stones have virtues or powers. The word 'potestas' has a different meaning for medieval grammarians, designating the phonetic value, as opposed to the *figura* (written shape) and the *nomen* (the semantic charge); see R.H. Robins, *Ancient and medieval grammatical theory*, pp. 13–14 (referring to Priscian, i.2).   270 Förster, *Interpres*, p. 222.
271 On this see Seneca, *Epistulae*, lix.5; Erasmus, *Adagia*, prolegomena, §1 ('aliud significatur quam dicitur'): Montaigne, *Essais*, iii.5, p. 851. The language of the Bible is said to be excessive in the sense suggested here: see Brinkmann, *Mittelalterliche Hermeneutik*, pp. 21ff.
272 Sapcote, *Ad primas leges*, p. 55.
273 On an analogous 'aside' in J.L. Austin, see Derrida, *Marges de la philosophie*, Paris, 1972, pp. 386ff.; on joking words in defamation, see Schneidewinus, *In quatuor Institutionum libros commentarii*, col. 1082 (referring to D 47.10.11).

they are capable of being used either to inform correctly or to deceive, since they are precisely conventional; in modern semantics, this feature of language has come to be known as prevarication.[274] Words are instruments for the representation of men's true intentions and beliefs: in legal tracts, one finds the expression of an ethical imperative to use words correctly, or rather not to counterfeit words, just as one should not counterfeit money, for the proper operation of society depends on the reliability of commercial and linguistic exchange: 'sunt enim instituta verba ut per ipsa res declarentur, et per ea quis in alterius notitiam suas cogitationes mittat, non ut homines se fallant'[275] (words are created to designate things and to communicate thoughts between men, not to deceive). In this way civil law 'obliget in conscientia': and yet *conscientia*, the *verbum cordis* are precisely inaccessible to the law, and are even said (as we have seen) not to be in its domain; as St Paul says, only faith can prove the existence of unseen realities (Heb. 11:2).[276] Cicero's imprecations against prevaricative uses of language, notably the popular passage in his speech *Pro Caecina* (see above 3.5.2) are often quoted, with or without acknowledgement;[277] bona fides is linked to truth, but it cannot be said to have a correspondence (an *adaequatio rei et intellectus*) with the surface manifestation of language, because it is a *res incorporalis*, 'quae oculis conspici et manibus palpari non potest'[278] (which cannot be seen by the eyes or touched by the hands).

The Renaissance jurist thus requires that bona fides be distinct from the words which express it, just as he requires that *verba* be distinct from *mens* and *mens* from *ratio*. What words are required to do is to 'show' truth (i.e. bona fides, *mens, ratio*), not in a Wittgensteinian sense, but in the sense that signification 'shows' 'veluti in tabella' (see above 3.2.1). This 'showing' resides simultaneously in a recognition of the prevaricative function of language, and in a refusal to allow bad faith or the intention to deceive to prevent the operation of law; thus, the effect (language) is attributed to a cause (intention, good faith) but the cause is determined by the effect. Just as smoke is a sign of fire, so are words of the mind; the jurist must interpret the smoke, even if it

[274] See John Lyons, *Semantics*, Cambridge, 1977, i.74–85.
[275] Rebuffi, *In titulum Digestorum de verborum et rerum*, p. 4 (referring to the gloss and postglossators); similar points are made by Fournier, Sapcote, Savius, Hunnius and Förster: see above 3.5.2. The poena falsi is inflicted on both counterfeiters and those who commit cavillation, as has been noted.   [276] Turamini, *De legibus*, pp. 12–27.
[277] See above, note 183.
[278] I 1.2.2; Joannes Borcholten, *Commentaria de verborum obligationibus*, Helmstedt, 1595, p. 609.

can be shown that the sign it gives of mental processes can be counterfeited, and that the words which are taken as signs – the smoke itself – can have a force which exceeds their significatory function.[279]

This predicament is detectable at two telling points in discussion: in attempts to define bona fides and in attempts to legislate for contracts of which bona fides is a necessary component. Baldus attempts on several occasions to define bona fides, but his formulas lack in his own terms the precision required from definition (see above 3.3.2): it is a 'bona mentis qualitas et conscientia' (this fails as a definition, having no *differentia*); a 'legalitas quae *potissime* requiritur in his quae *plurimum* negociantur' (this fails as a definition according to Cagnoli's rule about words such as those underlined); 'a *quaedam* adjectio *sive* qualitas contractus quae designat eius excellentiam'[280] (no definition can define by a particular premise; *sive* suggests that *adjectio* and *qualitas* are synonymous, which they are not in topical terms: *excellentiam* is not quantifiable; the formula is not convertible). Renaissance commentators come off no better.[281]

In attempts to legislate for contracts, the problem of determining bona fides appears again. C 4.10.4 ('bonam fidem in contractibus considerari aequum est' (it is equitable to consider bona fides in contracts)) was no doubt in the mind of the author of the following passage from canon law (X 2.11.1, n. 12):

> Ego puto quod de aequitate canonica omnes contractus mundi sint bonae fidei: non dico [quo ad] titulum actionis, sed quo ad mentem et substantiam intentionis: ideo si dolus dat eius causam, aliis non contracturis, quod contractus sit nullus ipso jure: quia Deus qui regulat et regit omnia inspicit cor hominum et in jure canonico non memini hoc notasse in text[o] aliquo differentiam substantialem inter contractum bonae fidei et stricti iuris.[282]

> I believe that all worldly contracts pertain to good faith according to the equity of canon law. I do not refer here to the title of the action but to the meaning and the substantial intention. Thus if deceit occasions parties not to enter into contracts with others, let the contract be void by the same law. For God who rules over all sees into men's hearts. I do not remember having seen noted in any text of canon law the substantial difference between a contract in good faith and contract *stricti juris*. – Cf. D 16.3.31 (Tryphoninus): bona

---

[279] Savius, *In Pandectarum titulum de verborum et rerum significatione*, pp. 11ff.; Brinkmann, *Mittelalterliche Hermeneutik*, p. 25. The smoke is, of course, a *probatio inartificialis* of the fire, and thus in traditional topics can only give rise to *coniectura*.   [280] Horn, *Aequitas*, p. 168.

[281] See the works of Bolognetti, Oldendorp and Coras; and the lexical entries in Brisson, Kahl [Calvinus] and others.

[282] X 2.11.1, n. 12. D 16.3.31 is cited and discussed by Turamini, *De legibus*, pp. 108ff.

fides quae in contractibus exigitur summam aequitatem desiderat (the good faith necessary to contracts requires the highest degree of equity).

The writer of this somewhat obscure passage wishes to distinguish between a *contractus bonae fidei* and a *contractus stricti iuris*, voluntarism and formalism, but to do so can only adduce *Deus scrutator cordis hominum*. In fact, the judge will decide peremptorily whether a disputed contract is void or binding, and effectively settle the issue of good faith; but he cannot appeal to certain knowledge of the motives of the parties in so doing; his decision determines these *de jure*, not *de facto*.

This discussion of the language of law is reminiscent of some of the problems encountered by J.L. Austin in his attempt to categorize and account for speech acts; this itself is noted by Austin himself who acknowledges that lawyers had long grappled with such problems. It is, therefore, not surprising to find that he has in some sense or other a predecessor in the Renaissance. Not only does Alessandro Turamini use the terms felicitously/infelicitiously on one occasion with apparently the same purpose as Austin (that is, to avoid the duality true/false) but he also elaborates a tripartite theory of speech acts in a commentary on D 1.3.17 which is worthy of comparison with Austin's locutionary/illocutionary/perlocutionary categories, and which he generously attributes to his tutor Gerolamo Benvoglienti:

speciosam in his tribus [sc. verba, vis, potestas (D 1.3.17)] explicandis Hieronymus Benevolentus comparationem afferre solet. Ignem, vel materiam quamcunque ignitam, si consideremus, tria quaedam respiciemus, quibus haec, in quibus scientia legum versatur, maxime respondent. Materiam ipsam nempe lignum, vel aliam quamlibet, tum ignem inhaerentem et in ea ardentem, tertio calorem, qui circum diffunditur. Verba legis materiae vicem gerunt, vis eiusdem igni comparatur, potestas vero calori. Calefacit ignis eam aeris partem, quam non attingit, sic sententiae legis Velleae aliquando iuvat casus Galli, qui ad eam non pertinet L. Gallus § et quid si tantum, & sequen. ff. de libro & post. id fieri videtur ex potestate legis, non ex vi ipsius. Quare non male Iacob, et Alberic. potestatem ipsam vim extensivam interpretantur; cum et enim sententiam legis in casu deciso manifestam ad casus non decisos producimus. Hoc est ipsius legis potestatem, tum intelligere, tum negociis congruenter aptare, quod quomodo fiat in L. non possunt & in L. nam ut ait, supra satis videtur explicatum, in quibus legibus non verba, non vim, sed potestatem legis consideramus, et ea praecipue utimur.[283]

[283] *Ibid.*, p. 173. It is interesting to note that Turamini generously acknowledges his unpublished tutor: other writers also do this (Gammaro acknowledges Joannes Campegius,

Gerolamo Benvoglienti is accustomed to adduce a brilliant analogy in explaining these three terms [*verba, vis, potestas*]. If we think about fire or something on fire, we notice three things, which correspond very well to these three words concerning legal analysis. They are the matter itself – wood or something else – the fire burning inside it and the heat which is diffused around. The text (*verba*) corresponds to the matter, the force (*vis*) to the fire itself and the power (*potestas*) to the heat. For as the fire heats that part of the air it does not reach, so the case of Gallus sometimes helps determine the meaning of the lex Vellea, to which it does not pertain (D 28.2.29.5ff.). This seems to be done by the power, not the force of the law. This is why Jacobus de Arena and Albericus de Rosate did well to render 'potestas' as 'extensive force' (*vis*); just as we extend the explicit meaning of a law in one resolved case to unresolved cases. That is to say, we understand the power of the law and then adapt it appropriately to the circumstances as has been sufficiently explained in the context of D 1.3.12 & 13, in which laws we do not consider the words, nor even the force, but the power of the law and use this above all else.

The use of the analogy of wood, flame and heat is not new; it can be found in medieval writing about the Trinity.[284] What is of interest here is the superficial likeness of Turamini's (or rather Benvoglienti's) categories to locutionary (wood: *verba*), illocutionary (flame: *vis*) and perlocutionary (warmth: *potestas*) forces. Benvoglienti's is a somewhat forced reading of D 1.3.17, as it is not at all clear that *vis et potestas* is anything more than an amplificatory expression; and my comparison with Austin is also fragile, if one places Turamini's words here in the context of his whole book. There, the four-cause model of the law is elaborated (see above 3.4.1): its material cause is said to be the will of the legislator, its formal cause the purpose of the legislation, its efficient cause the legislator himself, and its final cause the common good. There is no place in this analysis for the performative or perlocutionary functions of the text of the law, which are treated as effects, as are the *ipsissima verba*.

These are not the only problems with the comparison: no distinction is made between different sorts of *vis* (illocutionary force), (e.g. between the performative *vis* of the legislator and the secondary, derived, *vis* of judge and legal pedagogue speaking with the authority

Cagnoli Richard Vercellensis (who also appears not to have been published), and Gilkens Matthaeacius).

[284] See *Piers Plowman*, C-text xix.167–223, ed. D.A. Pearsall, London, 1978, pp. 313–14. Pearsall notes similar imagery in the *Legenda aurea* xxxvii.164–5 and Bartholomaeus Anglicus (Barthélemy de Glanville), *De proprietatibus rerum*, xix.63.10. See also Ps. 83:1–2 for a similar analogy. I am grateful to Richard Green for this information.

of the legal profession: see above 3.1.3). I do not think, moreover, that Austin would have subscribed to a causal account of the coming into being of a law of this kind; nor would he have wished to describe locutionary/illocutionary/perlocutionary forces all as effects. But his comment that 'lawyers have always known about infelicities . . . only the still widespread obsession that utterances of the law, and utterances used in, say, 'acts of the law', *must* somehow be statements true or false, has prevented many lawyers from getting this whole matter straighter than we [sc. philosophers] are likely to, and I would not even claim to know whether some of them have not already done so'[285] seems here to be borne out.

3.6.5

A further aspect of performatives in law is raised by the title D 44.7 *De verborum obligationibus*. According to Rogerius the full range of performative utterances (*potentiae*) in law are found in D 1.3; he lists these as [*potentia*] *praeceptiva, prohibitiva, permissiva, punienda, consultativa*. The first four are explicit in D 1.3.7; the last refers to laws offering advice only and to the juristic activity of *consilia*. Some of these categories can be broken down further: Turamini, for example, splits *permissiva* into active, passive and neutral modes.[286] This classification does not distinguish the making of contracts, which fall under several categories; yet the Digest makes clear that these are indeed performances:

D 44.7.1 (Gaius) Obligationes ex contractu aut re contrahuntur aut verbis aut consensu.

Contractual obligations are concluded either by a material act or by words or by consent.

D 44.7.38 (Paulus) Non figura litterarum, sed oratione quam exprimunt litterae obligamur.

We are bound not by the form of the written word but by the meaning it embodies.

---

[285] *How to do things with words*, ed. J.O. Urmston and Marina Sbisa, Oxford, 1962, p. 19.
[286] Rogerius, *De legis potentia*, i.8, in *Tractatus iuris universi*, i.395; Turamini, *De legibus*, p. 145. The example given by Turamini to illustrate the division of *permissiva* is marriage: the law permits marriage actively (implicitly ordaining procreation); passively (implicitly allowing marriage as a means to prevent fornication); and neutrally (cf. 1 Cor. 7:9: 'it is better to marry than to burn'). Rogerius (*ibid.*) subjects *consultativa* to a similar division (into *perfecta, reverentialis* and *simplex*).

In some cases considered in D 44.7 and D 45.1, the written or spoken word brings into existence a contract; in other cases (involving, for example, deaf people: D 45.1.1) the contract is brought into existence by a gesture or an act. The contract is what is expressed by the words or gestures; but it cannot be reduced to formulas, since it is a *res incorporalis*. Charles Du Moulin offers the most extensive Renaissance examination of this topic. Using *distinctio* (see above 2.4) he dissects obligations into categories (*dictum, pollicitatio, stipulatio, conventio* and *constitutio*) and shows how each may be objectively verified by a judge by recourse to its characteristic linguistic formula, which is, respectively, 'I will . . .', 'I promise . . .', 'We agree . . .', 'Will you?', 'I will . . . (in a matter of doing or giving)'. Only the last constitutes a full obligation in civil law: but it is not necessary that it be communicated in law to be binding. Conversely 'solemn words', although spoken in a ritual manner, are not binding because 'formulae non erant de iure gentium'.[287] Thus a linguistic rule of thumb is provided for the identification of different performative acts in which the element of bona fides, though essential, is not addressed at all: the law determines *de jure* the truth of the matter: 'res iudicata pro veritate accipitur' (D 1.5.25 and D 50.17.207). This occurs also in the case of slander, which is another form of performative speech (see D 47.10): a crucial component is intention (the *animus iniuriandi*), without which a word or deed cannot be deemed to be an *iniuria* (see D 47.10.11); and yet the intention can only be determined *de jure post factum*. The particular interpretative problems arising from this are most explicitly dealt with in an English context, and will be discussed below (4.3).

NONLINGUISTIC INTERPRETATION: CUSTOM AND EQUITY

3.7.1
There are two other, unwritten, guides to interpretation which have already been touched on but which require further examination: custom and equity. Both are specifically linked to interpretation in the Corpus Juris Civilis:

---

[287] *Nova et analytica explicatio rubricae et legum I et II Pandectarum de verborum obligationibus*, Jena, 1588, pp. 7ff.; Thireau, *Du Moulin*, p. 172, gives a more extensive list. See also above 3.6.2. On 'formulae non erant de iure gentium', see Papponius, *Interpretatio tituli Digestorum de verborum obligationibus*, p. 141.

D 1.3.37 (Paulus) Optima . . . est legum interpres consuetudo.

Custom is the best interpreter of laws.

D 1.3.38 (Callistratus) Nam imperator noster Severus rescripsit in am-
biguitatibus quae ex legibus proficiscuntur consuetudinem aut rerum
perpetuo similiter iudicatarum auctoritatem vim legis optinere debere.

Our Emperor Severus has issued a rescript saying that in cases of ambiguity
arising from [written] law the force of law ought to be given to custom or
to the authority of an unbroken line of legal decisions.

D 1.3.40 (Modestinus) Ergo omne ius aut consensus fecit aut necessitas
constituit aut firmavit consuetudo.

Every law has been made either by agreement or by necessity or established
by custom. (Cf. D 1.3.32)[288]

D 50.17.19 (Paulus) In omnibus quidem, maxime tamen in iure aequitas
spectanda est.

In all things, but particularly in the law equity must be considered. (Cf. D
1.3.10, 1.3.12, 1.3.25 and D 50.17.85.2)

What custom and equity have in common is that they are both part of
the *ius non scriptum* (D 1.3.6 and 1.3.35). This falls into two parts: that
which is non-verbal in nature, and that which is in the form of
articulated speech as opposed to writing. We have already encountered the general problem of incorporating non-verbal entities into
language; this is sometimes associated with the poverty of a given
language, or with difficulties of reference or ambiguity.[289] One view
expressed stresses the fact that the law is not the written text itself but
the 'rei natura et conditio quae prohibetur aut iubetur' (the nature

---

[288] Cf. Agrippa's cynical parody of this and D 1.3.32 (*De incertitudine*, xci):
   hinc Julianus ait leges non alia de causa nos ligare, quam quod iudicio populi receptae
   sunt, qui communi consensu omne imperium ac potestatem in principem contulit, unde si
   quid populo ac principi placuerit, hoc tum per consuetudinem, tum per constitutionem
   iuris habet vigorem, etiamsi error videatur vel falsitas: nam communis error facit ius; et
   res iudicata veritatem [D 1.5.25, D 50.17.207]

   Hence Julianus claims that laws bind us for no other reason than that they have been
   accepted by the judgement of the people, who by common consent transferred authority
   and power to the prince, so that whatever is pleasing to the people or the prince has the
   force of law partly by custom and partly by constitution, even if it should seem to be an
   error or falsity; for common errors make law and judicial decisions are taken as truth.
   – Cf. also *Politics* ii.5.13 (1269a15).
[289] *Magna moralia*, ii.1 (1198b24–30); Turamini, *De legibus*, pp. 95–6.

and condition of the matter in hand which is prohibited or decreed); i.e., that which now might be called a legal norm.[290] This view is attributed to Lycurgus and the legal norm it adduces is assimilated to natural law which is sited in men's conscience ('insitum cordibus nostris').[291] Against this view is adduced that of Baldus, who claims that written law is preferable either to unspoken norms or to spoken testimony, because its fixation in graphic form allows for stable meaning to emerge and for agreement to be reached from this as to the interpretation and application of the law or the testimony.[292] Yet he claims at the same time that speech is more powerful and of greater dignity than written language; and this argument lends support to those who wish to reinstate native oral traditions of law, from which the 'ius insitum cordibus nostris' might be more immediately recovered.[293] Their case is strengthened by those who attack the authority of the Pandecta florentina precisely because it is in that most corruptible of all forms: the written word (see above 3.1.3). The question of speech and writing also touches on the question of the omnitemporality of the law: the law 'always speaks', and its force is derived from the fact that it speaks to us, although it is couched in written form.[294]

Consuetudo is a somewhat imprecise term: it covers customary law, local mores, folk memory, popular consensus, even culture in general (custom as *altera natura*). It is said to consist of three elements: *consensus populi*; *morum frequentia* and *temporis diuturnitas*, but it can include

---

[290] Connan, *Commentarii iuris civilis*, i.7, fols. 26–8. On legal norms, see Turamini, *De legibus*, p. 23 ('lex naturae' as the 'totius legitimi iuris norma').

[291] *Ibid.*, pp. 99f.; see also D 1.1.1–3.

[292] See Bremerus, cited above 3.6.1; Peter of Ailly seems to be one of the very few medieval thinkers to prefer written to spoken language: see Spade, in the *Cambridge history of later medieval philosophy*, p. 189.

[293] See D 45.1, D 44.7.38, cited above 3.6.5; Baldus gl. ad D 2.15 (ad rubr.): 'nam dignior et estimabilior est vox viva quam mortua . . . acuitas enim vivae vocis fortius et efficacius monet animum auditoris . . . habet enim in seipsum removentem intellectum ex veritate ei data a natura . . . item multa erubescimus loqui quae non erubescimus scribere' (for speech is more worthy and more to be valued than writing; for the acuity of speech moves the mind of the hearer more strongly and efficaciously; it contains moreover a self-sufficient sense thanks to the truth given to it by nature. Also, there are many things we would blush to say which we would not blush to write). But gl. ad X 2.17.10.7 reads 'scriptura non potest mutari: sed lingua testium est satis mutabilis et labilis' (written words cannot be altered: but the tongue of witnesses is not a little changeable and labile). These views are taken up by Rebuffi, *In titulum Digestorum de verborum et rerum significatione*, p. 55, and Savius, *In titulum Pandectorum de verborum et rerum significatione*, p. 21.

[294] See above, note 222; on ius scriptum *vs* non scriptum in the medieval period, see Cortese, *La norma giuridica*, ii.355–62.

customary law, local mores and folk memory.²⁹⁵ It can interpret in the sense that it represents past practice based on consensus or legal decision, and can answer the questions 'what does the law mean?' and 'is this law just?' in the forms 'it has meant this in the past' and 'it is no longer applicable'. Bartolus places it in a hierarchy above *mens* and *ratio* (which are themselves above *verba* or literal meaning).²⁹⁶ It is clearly related to the *usus loquendi* (see 3.4.4) and can authorize changes in the meaning of words.²⁹⁷ But if it is itself written down, it becomes a *praeceptum* and loses its status as custom.²⁹⁸ Baldus (gl. ad D 1.3.32) analyses it using the four-cause model: its *causa materialis* (here *naturalis*) is 'frequens factum sive actus'; its *causa formalis* is 'consensus'; its *causa efficiens* is 'tempus' and its *causa finalis* is 'utilitas consuetudinis'. The efficient cause, time, is implicit in the Digest title D 1.3: *De legibus senatusque consultis et longa consuetudine*; as 'inveteratum ius', it has authority after either ten years, or thirty years, or as the judge thinks fit, according to various authors.²⁹⁹ It equates to precedent in non-statutory systems, with the difference that *consuetudo* can be bad, and be itself in need of correction; it may be silent ('tacito consensu': D 1.3.32), and it does not appear in written form.³⁰⁰ It is subject itself to historical change, even if it also constitutes evidence of continuity. But as Coras points out, it can only be used as a means of interpretation if

²⁹⁵ D 1.3.32; Horn, *Aequitas*, pp. 82–7; on custom as 'altera natura', see *Rhetoric*, i.11 (1370a), and *De memoria* (452a27): Erasmus includes 'consuetudo altera natura' in his *Adages*. Hunnius, *De authoritate*, pp. 157–62; Joannes Oestenius, *De iure non scripto*, Greifswald, 1590; Petrus Salazar, *De usu et consuetudine tractatus*, Frankfurt, 1600, pp. 215–16, also follows Jacobus de Arena in describing *mores* as the remote cause of *consuetudo*, and *populi consensus* as its immediate efficient cause. Baldus, gl. ad D 1.3.32, applies the four-cause model of analysis to custom (the efficient cause is time, the material cause is repeated actions, the formal cause is consensus and the final cause is the common weal).

²⁹⁶ Gl. ad D 1.3.12 ('consuetudinem vincere mentem, seu rationem, et mentem vincere verba').
²⁹⁷ Rebuffi, *In titulum Digestorum de verborum et rerum significatione*, p. 4.
²⁹⁸ Connan, *Commentari iuris civilis*, i.10, fol.28: 'sunt enim huius non scripti iuris partes duae, consuetudo et aequitas: quarum utraque literis obliteratur, et cum scriptura naturam legis assumit, et amittit suam' (there are two parts to this unwritten law; custom and equity: both of which are obliterated by writing, and lose their nature, assuming that of statutes, when they are set down on paper); also Turamini, *De legibus*, pp. 99f.

²⁹⁹ See Althusius, *Iurisprudentia Romana*, p. 3 (referring to the views of the gloss, Wesenbeck and Le Douaren); also Franciscus Zoannettus, *Tractatus de moribus maiorum et longa consuetudine*, Venice, 1565.

³⁰⁰ Turamini, *De legibus*, p. 100 makes this explicit: 'non enim emendatur ius naturale per se; sed tanquam in scripturam relatum . . . ubi ius naturale scribatur, scriptura ipsius emendationi subiacet, non ius ipsum' (natural law is not changed in itself, only as it were as it is carried over into writing . . . where natural law is written down, the written form is subject to emendation, not natural law). See also, on bad custom, gl. ad C 4.38.14.6 'malae consuetudines servandae non sunt' (bad customs are not to be preserved); cited by Horn, *Aequitas*, p. 85.

it takes on written form: he thereby creates the potentially absurd category of a written *ius non scriptum* (cf. the *aequitas scripta* cited below 3.8.1). It is subject, therefore, to the same problems of verbal incorporation as *mens* or *ratio*.[301]

3.8.1

Equity is discussed in somewhat different terms. It is often opposed to rigour or inflexibility (C 3.1.8, D 50.17.56 and D 1.3.18: 'aequitas est rigori praeferenda'; (equity is to be preferred to rigour)),[302] but its principal function derives from D 1.1.1, and the description of jurisprudence as the *ars aequi et boni*. In commentary it is associated with a broad range of near-synonyms: *aequalitas, paritas, gratia, misericordia, benignitas, humanitas, caritas, bona fides, conscientia, bonum publicum, publica utilitas, mediocritas, mitigatio poenae*, even *veritas*.[303] In the medieval period it was given four principal definitions:

(i) 'rectitudo iudicii naturalem sequens rationem' (correctness of judgement, following natural reason);

(ii) 'applicatio animi ad directum iudicium, intellectu non errante in substantia nec in circumstantiis facti' (application of the mind to direct judgement, there being no error in the understanding of the substance of the case and the attendant circumstances);

(iii) 'rerum convenientia quae in paribus casis paria iura desiderat et bona omnia aequiparat' (an equivalence which promotes the application of the same laws to the same cases and ensures justice and equality); and

(iv) 'quod videtur aequum omnibus' (what appears fair to all).[304]

Equity is also subject to various distinctions. It is divided into *aequitas generalis*, which legislators alone may exercise, and *aequitas specialis*, encompassing the definitions given above; the latter is identified with Aristotle's ἐπιείκεια (see above 1.2.3), which in the *Nicomachean Ethics* is described as a virtue beyond distributive and commutative justice.[305] Its function is to correct the procrustean tendency of the law (*strictum ius* and *rigor iuris*) enshrined in the much-quoted adage

---

301 See above, note 221; see also Coras, in *Tractatus de iuris arte*, ii.20 ('quomodo probetur consuetudo'), p. 160: 'potest probari consuetudo vel scriptura vel testibus' (custom may be proved by written testimony or by witnesses).

302 See e.g. Rebuffi, *In titulum Digestorum de verborum et rerum significatione*, p. 55; Freher, *Sulpitius*, *passim*.   303 Horn, *Aequitas*, pp. 95–116.

304 *Ibid.*, pp. 8–12 (also X 1.6.8, n. 6; gl. ad D 1.1.1, 9, 10).

305 *Nicomachean Ethics*, iii.4; Oldendorp, *De iure et aequitate forensis disputatio*, Cologne, 1573, pp. 37–8.

'summum ius summa iniuria'.[306] In most senses, equity is linked to natural and divine law and the law inscribed in men's hearts (Rom. 2:15); in its special application, although described as a universal virtue, it is linked to the contingent facts of particular cases.[307]

As the combination *aequum* and *bonum* suggests, equity is in part deliberative and in part moral. The deliberative element is sometimes referred to as *naturalis ratio* after D 1.1.9 (although D 50.17.85.2 seems to suggest that *naturalis ratio* may in certain circumstances be opposed to equity): Celichius describes equity as 'that which natural reason proves clearly is just in each and every civil law' ('quod naturalis ratio in unaquaquam constitutione civili iustum esse convincit');[308] equity is also equated with the *ratio legis* in so far as this is understood as the final cause of the law or the application of correct logical procedures to it.[309] Moral equity, which Hunnius calls *aequitas naturalis* is close to conscience (the *vox cordis*) in some accounts, and is syncretized not only with Christian thought (D 1.1.10 'alterum non laedere' being linked to Luke 6:3 'do as you would be done by'), but also with associations of mercy and *benigna interpretatio*.[310] But as we have already noted, the relationship of law to ethics is not simple, even if 'equity' in general can safely be linked to the mitigation in a quasi-moral way of the harsher aspects of the law.[311]

It has many other associations. In some accounts equity is equated with the *mens legislatoris*, and is defined as that act which adapts historical law to present circumstances.[312] It is closely linked to bona fides (D 16.3.31); like this, equity is non-verbal, and yet some commentators write of an *aequitas scripta*;[313] it is associated with natural law, which also is non-verbal in nature, and like custom and

---

[306] Cited by Cicero, *De officiis*, i.10.33; see also C 3.1.8 (Constantinus et Licinius): 'placuit in omnibus rebus praecipuam esse iustitiae aequitatis quam stricti iuris rationem' (in all things, it is our wish that the predominant consideration be justice and equity rather than the letter of the law).

[307] See Freher, *Sulpitius*; Oldendorp, *De iure et aequitate*; Turamini, *De legibus*, pp. 8ff.

[308] Johannes Celichius, *De aequitate quid et quantum praestet in legibus liber*, Wittenberg, 1602, p. 12. Cf. Oldendorp, *De iuste et aequitate*, pp. 14–15, and *Nicomachean Ethics*, v.3–4 (1130b30).

[309] Connan, *Commentarii iuris civilis*, i.11, fols. 47ff.

[310] See above 3.6.2; Celichius, *De aequitate*, p. 20 (conscience described as the efficient cause of equity); Oldendorp, *De iure et aequitate*, p. 93; Althusius, *Iurisprudentia Romana*, p. 1; also D 50.17.56, 192.

[311] See above 3.6.1, and Rogerius, *De legis potentia*, ii.1ff., in *Tractatus iuris universi*, i.395.

[312] Connan, *Commentarii iuris civilis*, i.11, fols. 47ff.

[313] *Ibid.*, fol. 51ᵛ; gl. ad C 3.1.8 (Odofredus), cited by Horn, *Aequitas*, p. 25; Oldendorp, *De iure et aequitate*, pp. 48, 84 (where the 'aequitas scripta' is equated with 'summum ius', and 'non scripta' with the application of the lead rule of Lesbos).

equity can never be stated except in a form which is not natural law.[314] It is even linked to *utilitas*.[315] It is finally identified with the jurist or judge himself, who by his office becomes a *lex loquens*, the embodiment of the flexible measuring rule of Lesbos. In this guise, equity as interpretation becomes also equity as application; the jurist or judge performs the law by deciding its relationship to an individual case and by dealing with *casus omissi*, and raises again the spectre of extensive interpretation as correction of the law or addition to it which, as we have seen, is a matter of dispute among Renaissance lawyers.[316] Interpretation thereby passes from a subservient to a dominant rôle vis-à-vis the text (see above 1.6.3). This passage is clearly detectable in the amendment in canon law (X 1.6.8 n.6) of the fourth definition of *aequitas*: 'quod videtur aequum omnibus' becomes 'quod videtur aequum omnibus, vel pluribus, vel saltem sapientibus' (to all, to some, or at least to the wise). As in 3.4.4 above, the *sapientes* or *prudentes* emerge as the determining force of that which of its nature should fall not to them alone, but rather in the public domain: common usage, a sense of natural justice.

This survey of the different aspects of interpretation theory in the Renaissance shows that at the level of linguistic analysis, a certain number of problems emerge which, if exposed to patient probing, threaten the distinctions on which the theory of legal interpretation rests. Signification turns out to be the same as interpretation; or to put it in a slightly different way, signification fails to provide for interpretation that undisputed access to the real and that uncontroversial basis for argument which is expected of it; indeed, it ends up by being defined in almost identical terms. Definition turns out to be inapplicable in its scientific form, but rather to represent no more than stipulative description. *Divisio* can lay claim only to the status of a heuristic device. The *ratio* of a law which is thought to be different from its *mens* ends up by being identified with it. Unwritten legal norms – custom and equity – can only be adduced, it seems, in a

---

[314] Turamini, *De legibus*, p. 100; Oldendorp, εἰσαγογή *seu elementaria introductio ad studium iuris et aequitatis*, p. 2, printed with its own pagination in vol. i of his *Opera*.

[315] Cicero, *Pro Caecina*, xvii.49.

[316] Cicero, *De legibus*, iii.1.2 ('vereque dici potest magistratum legem esse loquentem, legem autem mutum magistratum': for it can truly be said that the magistrate is a speaking law and the law a silent magistrate). Freher, *Sulpitius*; Turamini, *De legibus*, pp. 95ff., where the question of extensive interpretation is raised with reference to Bolognetti's arguments in *De lege, iure et aequitate*, xxix–xxxiv. See also Gilmore, *Arguments from Roman law*, p. 24, and D 1.3.10, 12, 14, 15, 18, 25; D 50.17.85.2, D. 50.17.90.

transgressive written form. No clear demarcation can be drawn between legitimate extension of the law to *casus omissi* and illegitimate correction or emendation of the law by judge or interpreter. Yet for all this, the law operates more or less to the satisfaction of those involved in it. Because this study has concentrated on the linguistic and philosophical aspects of interpretation, this obvious point has perhaps not emerged with the clarity and emphasis it deserves. The purpose of this chapter has not been to cast doubt on the operation of the legal systems of the Renaissance, but rather to situate them with respect to the discussion of linguistic and especially semantic issues. That the law can operate even with apparently contradictory maxims ('take all words in their most charitable sense' and 'take all words in their plain sense') is clear from legislation and practice in the area of slander. This, together with a brief discussion of parallels in canon law and in English common law, will be the subject matter of the next chapter.

CHAPTER 4

Parallels and examples

4.1

The account given in the preceding chapter of interpretative procedures was drawn from the corpus of writing on the subject which appeared between 1460 and 1630; it was organized according to issues which seemed to me to expose the general character of the writing. I wish now to turn to two parallel discussions of these issues which may throw further light on them. The first parallel is provided by a theorist – Francisco Suarez – who knew much of this corpus, but whose own writing was without any influence on it for reasons I set out above (1.4.3). In his *De legibus*, Suarez distinguishes between three forms of interpretation: *authentica*, or that which is undertaken by the legislator himself or by his express authority; *usualis*, or that which is informed by *usus et consuetudo* (see 3.7.1); and finally *doctrinalis*, or that which is the product of interpretation techniques, and has no special authority.[1] In the first and last cases (approximately the categories *necessaria* and *probabilis* of 3.1.3), the question of intention (*mens*) and *ratio* arises. Suarez points out that although intention and *ratio* are not verbal in nature, they can only be perceived through the word: 'homines non possunt mentem alterius hominis percipere, nisi ex verbis eius' (no man can perceive another's thoughts except through his words). Such words can, of course, be ambiguous; the same word(s) can be used to express various intentions. In order to grasp the intention of another, it is thus not sufficient to know the words by which he express it; one must also know the contextual material, the 'conjunctae omnes circumstantiae a quibus determinari possunt ad

---

[1] *Tractatus de legibus ac deo legislatore*, Lyon, 1613, vi.3.5ff., p. 369: 'doctrinalis' is sometimes described in canon law as 'probabilis' (see Panormitanus, *Commentaria super quinque libros Decretalium*, Lyon, 1524, i.1, fols.144ff.).

hanc mutationem potius quam aliam iudicandam' (the conjunction of all the circumstances which may predispose towards one rather than another understanding of the law). We can only know the *mens* of the legislator by conjecture; the words in which he has couched his intention have, however, properties which are certain and clear, and which are for the purposes of interpretation prior to the *mens*. These properties may give rise to an interpretation which can be reinforced by other material providing information about the intention of the legislator: the subject matter of the law; comparison or contrast with other laws; the rejection of any verbal property which would lead to injustice in the application of the law. All of this material gives access to the *ratio legis* which in turn leads to the *mens legis*[*latoris*]; but Suarez implicitly makes of this latter a notional or virtual intention arising out of the work of interpretation, rather than that which is recovered by it. Extensive interpretation, which Suarez links exclusively to the identification of the *ratio legis*, is acceptable only if the *ratio* discovered is identical (*adaequata*) to the *ratio* of a similar law; similarity of reason is not sufficient. Suarez fails, however, as do others, to lay down clear rules for distinguishing identity from similarity.[2] This account is strongly influenced by Aquinas' analysis of law (*Summa theologiae*, 1a 2ae 90-7); the notion of *ratio* is, however, extended and is close to that given by Gammaro which distinguishes between cause, purpose and rational restatement.[3] If a law states that no priest shall be assumed to be so if he crosses the Alps, one can distinguish *ratio* as cause (i.e. the *causa impulsiva* or mischief: excommunicates are passing themselves off as priests away from their home); *ratio* as purpose (the *causa finalis*: let us avoid danger to souls by the administration of sacraments by false priests); and *ratio* as formal restatement (let no priest be assumed to be so if he crosses the Alps). These *rationes* are clearly distinguishable if all the *travaux préparatoires* – the historical preparation for the enactment of the law – survive; but in most cases these are missing, or if available, not always enlightening. Suarez's solution is to take into account as much contextual material as possible (the *circumstantiae*); which failing, to resort to identical *rationes* (here, laws avoiding danger to souls from false priests). His account is remarkably clear for its day; it resembles quite closely that of Doneau, which is also much praised, and which also identifies the *mens legis*[*latoris*] with the *ratio legis*, and

---

[2] *Tractatus de legibus*, pp. 368–453.
[3] *De extensionibus*, xv–xxxv, in *Tractatus iuris universi*, xviii.248–9.

sets out to recover the latter 'ex aliis partibus eiusdem legis', 'ex contrariis', 'ex consequentibus' and 'ex ratione latiore legis'.[4] But the Catholic Suarez could not have acknowledged under the rules of the Inquisition his debt to the Calvinist Doneau, even had he wished to; whether Doneau is one of his sources must remain a matter of pure conjecture.

ENGLAND

4.2

England offers a parallel of a rather different sort to Suarez. Its legal institutions bear little relation to those found on the Continent; although civil and canon law were taught at the universities and practised in doctors' commons, the greatest part of legal business by the late fifteenth century was conducted in law French by the inns of court or by persons trained there; and that training bore the stamp of an apprenticeship far more than an intellectual education based on the trivium. There were hardly any pedagogical materials. Christopher St German's *Dialogues between a doctor of divinity and a student in the laws of England* (1523–30) is ostensibly an exposition of the law for the benefit of a theologian and in the main addresses issues of conscience; Coke's *Institutes*, which first appeared in 1628, refers to 'lawyer logicke' ('syllogisms, inductions, definitions, descriptions, divisions, etymologies, derivations, significations') as necessary to the 'compleat lawyer', but it forms no part of his text; rather, he concentrates on expounding the 'true sense' of particular cases, and allows the student (who is not even the principal addressee of the text) to build up a competence in the law through this form of vicarious experience.[5] Abraham Fraunce's *Lawiers logike* (1588), which is an adaptation of Ramus's *Dialecticae libri duo* and a proselytizing work on behalf of his method, is addressed to practising lawyers more than to students of the law.[6]

---

[4] *Commentarii de iure civili*, i.13–15, in *Opera*, i.87ff.
[5] See Richard J. Schoek, 'Rhetoric and law in sixteenth-century England', *Studies in philology*, l (1953), 110–27; also Coke, *Institutes*, ¢ 5ʳ.
[6] See Kelley, 'History, English law and the Renaissance', in *History, law and the human sciences*, xi (but cf. 'Jurisconsultus perfectus', 96–7, where Fraunce is wrongly described as an anti-Ramist); Fraunce, *The lawiers logike*, preface to 'the learned lawyers of England, especially the Gentlemen of Grays Inne'. Robinson, Fergus and Gordon, *Introduction*, p. 371, mention other introductory works of an innovating kind by Fulbeck and Cowell.

Such books as are written up to the end of the sixteenth century on issues concerning statutory interpretation are, like the year books, the reports and the commentaries, written by practising lawyers for the use of judges, 'the sages of the law' as Edmund Plowden and Sir Christopher Hatton call them;[7] and this characteristic of English jurisprudential writing persists up to the present.[8] The reports and commentaries, notably those of Coke and Plowden, contain much material relevant to this enquiry; there is also some monographical material, notably the relevant section of Sir Robert Brooke's *Graunde abridgement*, the anonymous *Discourse upon the exposicion and understanding of statutes*, and Sir Christopher Hatton's *Treatise concerning statutes*: all of these, together with Plowden's *Commentaries*, were composed between the late 1560s and the late 1570s, but only the first and last were published at that time.[9] Towards the end of the century, formularies and lexica appear, notably William West's *Symbolaegraphy* (1592) and John Cowell's *Interpreter* (1607); the latter also produced an ambitious *Institutiones iuris Anglicani ad methodum et seriem institutionum imperialium compositae et digestae* (1605); there are also works which deal with subjects which are on the boundary between politics and constitutional issues, such as Thomas Ashe's ἐπιείκαια (1607) and Sir Thomas Egerton's *Speech touching the post-nati* (1609). This last development is not surprising, as questions about the interrelationship of common law and parliamentary statute, and especially questions concerning sovereigns and sovereignty had been at issue implicitly or explicitly for a very long period, and had been revived by James I's exalted vision of justice-dispensing kingship.[10] Whereas on the Continent the will of the prince is given a 'necessary' rôle in interpretation and legislation (see above 3.1.3), in England one finds much more reference to the common weal and the general benefit of the enactment of remedies to social mischiefs; but, in the words of Kelley, England's insularity is 'self-proclaimed but only apparent',[11] and, as we shall see, many interpretative principles are recorded in

---

[7]   Plowden, cited by Thorne, introduction to *A discourse upon the exposicion of statutes*, p. 29; Hatton, *A treatise upon statutes*, London, 1677, p. 30.

[8]   See Cross, *Statutory interpretation*, p. 20 (on Blackstone); also p. 43 (where he sets out his own rules of interpretation, all addressed to judges).

[9]   See Thorne, introduction to *A discourse upon the exposicion of statutes*, p. 10; and note 6, above.

[10]   *Ibid.*, p. 92; also *The political works of James I*, ed. Charles H. McIlwain, Cambridge, Massachusetts, 1918, *passim*.

[11]   Kelley, *History, law and the human sciences*, xi.31; Thorne, introduction to *A discourse upon the exposicion of statutes*, p. 62.

English texts which bear a close resemblance to those discussed above in the context of the Corpus Juris Civilis.

Thorne has stated that in so far as a theory of law can be affirmed of the late sixteenth century, it would consist in the tripartite principle that parliamentary enactments cannot be supposed to do wrong or desire iniquity; that such statutes as it enacts cannot be destructive of long custom and the common law; and that in the construction placed upon such statutes, the intention of the legislators is a more potent principle of interpretation than the sense (*ratio*) of the law (the hierarchy of intention over *ratio* reversing the medieval tendency).[12] This theory addresses in the first instance the question of authority (see above 3.1.3); as in Roman law, the authority of the legislative body, which embodies the will of the sovereign which is its 'forma informans', is higher than the authority of the text, however this is construed.[13] Coke refers to authority and reason as the two faithful witnesses in matter of law, and places them in that order.[14] Grammar and logic are, of course, employed in the work of interpretation, but it is rare to find systematic exposition of their rôle: some chapters of the *Discourse* and of Hatton's *Treatise* mention them, and Egerton in his *Speech touching the post-nati* shows that he, as no doubt all other English common lawyers, was aware of Continental practice in this domain:

Words are taken and construed sometimes by extension, sometimes by restriction, sometimes by implication; sometimes by a disjunctive for a copulative; a copulative for a disjunctive; the present tense for the future; the future for the present; sometimes by equity out of the reach of words; sometimes words are taken in a contrary sense; sometimes figuratively, as *continens pro contento* and many other likes: And all of these examples be infinite as well in the civile law as common lawe.[15]

Egerton does not here mention the question of negative as opposed to affirmative statutes or customary interpretation (3.7.1) which both Hatton and the author of the *Discourse* discuss succinctly,[16] but most other issues which found a place in civil law treatises (see above 3.4.1–3.8.1) are alluded to.

A more revealing account of interpretation, and one which has enjoyed considerable quotation since it was written, is that given by Coke in his report on Heydon's case of 1584:

---

[12] *Ibid.*, pp. 57ff.   [13] Hatton, *A treatise concerning statutes*, p. 3.   [14] Coke, *Institutes*, ¢ 5ʳ.
[15] *Speech . . . touching the post-nati* (1609), pp. 49–50, quoted in *A discourse upon the exposicion of statutes*, p. 140.   [16] *Ibid.*, ch. 4; Hatton, *A treatise concerning statutes*, chs. 3–4.

And it was resolved . . . that for the sure and true interpretation of all statutes in general (be they penal or beneficial, restrictive or enlarging of the common law), four things are to be discerned and considered:

1st. What was the Common Law before the making of the act,

2nd. What was the mischief and defect for which the Common Law did not provide,

3rd. What remedy the Parliament hath resolved and appointed to cure the disease of the commonwealth,

And, 4th. The true reason of the remedy; and then the office of all the Judges is always to make such construction as shall suppress subtle inventions and evasions for continuance of the mischief, and *pro privato commodo*, and to add force and life to the cure and remedy, according to the true intent of the makers of the Act, *pro bono publico*.[17]

A number of issues arise here. Coke's reference to the 'true intent of the makers of the Act' is to the preamble of English legislation, in which the mischief (*causa impulsiva*) is named; the body of the act states the remedy (*causa finalis*), and it is succeeded by provisos which set down any exceptions. This form of enactment circumvents the problem of an unknown *causa impulsiva* envisaged in D 1.3.20–1 (see above 3.6.1); it also results in the context of the enactment being interior to the legal instrument itself. Thus some of the problems addressed by civilians concerning *mens, ratio* and *usus* are obviated by the form of legislation. Second, cavillation is specifically referred to (and is stressed elsewhere in Coke's reports) as a defect specific to the law and those engaging in the law:[18] an example is provided by statutes of Edward VI on the stealing of horses and benefit of clergy (see below 4.3). This fear of cavillation is reflected in the desire to control word usage excessively; the publication of formularies, the *mitior sensus* rule, and the quibbles over the designation of corporate bodies at the end of the sixteenth century are symptomatic of this (see below 4.3).

Third, Heydon's case is taken to be a classic statement of the so-called 'mischief rule' of interpretation by Cross, who claims that it was later supplemented by the 'literal rule' ('follow the letter of the law wherever reasonable': cf. 3.1.2) and the 'golden rule' ('avoid iniquitous or absurd consequences of a law by interpreting it appropriately': cf. 3.4.2).[19] The suggestion here of an evolution in

---

[17] 3 Co. Rep. 7a, quoted by Cross, *Statutory interpretation*, p. 9.

[18] See Thorne, introduction to *A discourse upon the exposicion of statutes*, p. 40, citing 6 Co. Rep. 40b.   [19] Cross, *Statutory interpretation*, pp. 13–15.

thinking about the interpretation of statutes is, I think, misleading, since the 'literal rule' and the 'golden rule' are both adduced by judges in our period, and appear as principles of interpretation in the *Discourse* and in Hatton. Indeed, nearly all (if not all) of Cross's rules have their precedents not only in English, but in civil law.[20] What is interesting about the English corpus of maxims on this topic drawn from common law at this time is that they repeat in approximately the same form well-known *regulae* from the Corpus Juris Civilis itself or maxims of the glossators and postglossators. These parallels are made all the more striking because they are translated back into Latin, and clothed thereby in the respectability of that ancient language.[21]

In English law, there is no need to stress the rôle of *consuetudo* in interpretation, since the common law itself precisely enshrines it: but equity (known in the earlier Middle Ages as 'lequity de lestatut') played an important rôle, and even had a legal institution – the Court of Chancery – whose sole function was to apply it to decisions from other courts. Thorne describes 'lequity de lestatut' as 'a vague penumbra of essentially similar cases surrounding the precise words of an act to which it must in justice apply':[22] the words 'essentially similar' and 'in justice' betray the logical problems of the doctrine *ad similia procedere* (D 1.3.12) which have been examined above (2.5, 3.6.1, 4.1). In practice, the Chancellor of the day determined *casus omissi* and protected private rights under common law from infringement by statute in a piecemeal way; but quite often these decisions were accompanied by more theoretical statements drawn from Aristotle's strictures in the *Nicomachean Ethics* and the medieval

---

[20] See also Coke, *Institutes*, i.381, who sets out a threefold rule which contains explicit reference to the rule of context, the literal rule and the mischief rule: 'it is the most naturall and genuine exposition of a statute to construe one part of the statute by another part of the same statute, for that best expresseth the meaning of the makers . . . secondly, the words of an act of parliament must be taken in a lawfull and right sense . . . thirdly, that construction must be made of a statute in suppression of the mischief and in advancement of the remedie – *et qui haeret in littera, haeret in cortice*'. See above 3.4.1, for citation of the absurdity rule (notes 118 and 147) *in pari materia* rule (D 1.3.12), literal rule (D 32.25) *melius valeat quam pereat* rule (D 34.5.12); the *exclusio alterius* rule is found in Gammaro, *De extensionibus*, xcvii, in *Tractatus iuris universi*, xviii.253. Many other parallels could be made with Latin maxims cited in Hatton and in *A discourse upon the exposicion of statutes*.

[21] See, for example, Coke's casual version of *Decretum* ii.64 (quoted above, note 20); Bracton's approximate quotation of Azo ad 1.1, n. 7 on equity, quoted by Thorne, introduction to *A discourse upon the exposition of statutes*, p. 46; the same work's evocation of Alciato's opening sentence of *De verborum significatione* (p. 140); and Hatton's reformulations of D 32.25 and D 50.17.188 in *A treatise upon statutes*, pp. 18–19.

[22] Introduction to *A discourse upon the exposicion of statutes*, p. 45.

definition of equity given above (3.8.1).[23] Even an example such as the Bolognese barber letting blood finds its way into the reports and monographs. As on the Continent, equity is seen as a corrective in individual cases to the inflexibility of the law; it is particularly appropriate in this version to a system based on the precedent afforded by prior judgements as much as written statute, in which decisions can be justified on each occasion by recourse to topical argument. Circumstances play a vital rôle in juridical decisions, as do the *loci a simili* and *a contrariis*; inference has a far greater rôle than analysis based on the verbal arts such as definition. Although in Hatton's *Treatise*, in the *Discourse*, and in the *disjecta commentaria* of Coke and Plowden one can find not only similar doctrines of interpretation but also (in the case of Hatton and the *Discourse*) a similar disposition of material to that of their Continental counterparts, there is a noticeable difference of emphasis: less stress is laid on grammatical analysis, more on applied logic; there seems also to be a greater explicitness about the social and political context in which interpretation takes place.[24]

SEMANTICS AND THE LAW OF SLANDER

4.3
These somewhat incautious generalizations are to some degree supported if one examines differences in approach to the law of defamation at this time. Defamation is an injury to the person effected by words, writings, gestures, images or ritual acts, rather than physical force; but the degree of violence suffered is no less great for all that, for as St Gregory points out, words can inflict greater distress than physical assault ('aliquando plus turbant verba quam verbera').[25] The words, acts or gestures of defamation are, therefore, performative in the same way as promises or contracts. What the words assail is the good name or honour (i.e. self-esteem) of the

---

[23] *Ibid.*, pp. 46ff. See also J.H. Baker, 'English law and the Renaissance', in *The reports of Sir John Spelman*, ed. Baker, London, Selden Society, 1977, ii.32ff.; St German, *Doctor and Student*, ed. T.F.T. Plucknett and J.L. Barton, London, Selden Society, 1974, 'Introduction', xliv–li.
[24] *Ibid.*, chs. 8–10 ('construction de statute stricte'; 'construction de statute conter les parollz'; 'statute extende al cases dont ne sont ascun parollz'): cf. Turamini, *De legibus*, p. 159 (*ex verbis*; *praeter verbis*; *contra verba*). See also Baker, 'English law and the Renaissance', pp. 34–6.
[25] *PL*, lxxv.514f., quoted by R.H. Helmholz, *Select cases on defamation to 1600*, London, 1985, p. xix: cf. the etymology of *verbum* from *verberum* often cited in legal texts: e.g. Savius, *In Pandectarum titulum de verborum et rerum significatione*, p. 10.

injured party; and nothing is more sacred to the individual than his good name.[26] *Infamia* can take one of a number of forms: *infamia iuris* (arising from being found guilty of a crime); *infamia canonica*, incurred by sin, which can be expunged by penance; *infamia facti*, arising from a base or unclean life, revealed to the *boni et graves*, that is, the morally sound and worthy section of society.[27] Defamation usually relates to the category of *infamia facti*, often taking the form of an imputation of a criminal or morally obnoxious act: it is related to, but not identical with, abuse (*convicium*), *calumniatio* (vexatious litigation) and false accusation (*contumelia*).[28] The crime of defamation is intentional; one component of any successful prosecution must in theory be proof of malicious intent (*animus iniuriandi*). It can relate to all sections of society; its remedy may be sought in civil, criminal or ecclesiastical courts, and involves the restitution of the good name of the injured party, as well as (in different contexts) monetary damages, and the punishment of the offender.

Defamation falls under the general heading of *iniuriae* in the Corpus Juris Civilis (see D 47.10, C 7.14.5 and C 9.36);[29] it may take the form

[26] See Henricus Bocerus, *Commentarius in legem in C de famosis libellis*, Tübingen, 1611, p. 3: grave scelus est, et atrox facinus honorem alicuius et famam depeculari. Quid enim honesto viro sanctius, quid antiquius esse posset, quam ut sartam tectam integramque existimationem suam retineat, ac conservet? Cum fama hominis omnium rerum preciosissima sit, et inaestimabilis 1. si in duabus 105 ff. de reg iur, omnia si perdas (ait Poeta) famam servare memento: qua semel amissa postea nullus eris: graviorque oculorum amissione censeatur honoris privatio 1 infamia C de decanonib libr. 10.

It is a grave misdeed and an atrocious crime to plunder the honour and reputation of anyone. What could be more sacred to a respectable man, what could be more honourable, than that he should keep and preserve intact his self-respect as he would his house from disrepair? As a man's reputation is the most precious of all things, indeed inestimable [D 50.17.104], remember (as the poet says) to hold on to your honour even if you lose all; you will be nothing once it has been lost: for the loss of honour is thought to be worse than the loss of eyesight [C 10.31.8].
Note here the reference to *honesto viro*: in fact, defamation of women is also actionable. Théodore Grellet-Dumazeau, *Traité de la diffamation, de l'injure et de l'outrage*, Riom and Paris, 1847, pp. 54f., distinguishes between *honor* (self-esteem) and *fama* (reputation), as here, following Baudouin, *Ad leges de famosis libellis*, pp. 40, 60.

[27] See Helmholz, *Defamation*, xxii; the reference to 'boni et graves' is in C 2.11.13: also Alexander de Imola ad D 28.2.3 (see Schneidewinus, *In quatuor Institutionum libros*, col. 1053).

[28] There are long excursuses in D 47.10.16 on *convicium*, *contumelia* and *maledictio*. See also Helmholz, *Defamation*, xix; Bocerus, *Commentarius*, p. 20, who also distinguishes defamation from blasphemy (p. 49).

[29] Other *leges* which are cited are C 9.46; D 3.6; D 48.10.9. D 47.10.18 deals with the question of publishing truth in the public interest. See Grellet-Dumazeau, *Traité*, pp. 321ff. (on C 7.14.5: 'defamari statum ingenuorum seu errore seu malignitate quorundam periniquum est': it is highly iniquitous to defame free men whether in error or maliciously); Georgius Mundius a Rodach, *De diffamationibus earumque remediis, commentarius theorico-practicus*, Hanau, 1628, pp. 35–71.

of a poem or song, picture, or a text (*libellus*) as well as a verbal assault.[30] A public act, indeed an outrage 'ad dampnum et ad pudorem' is a necessary element;[31] what constitutes 'public' is subject to several definitions.[32] Legal proceedings may be in camera or in public; the plaintiff must show the defendant's malicious intent (for this reason the accidental injury of being struck or insulted in the place of another does not fall under the law).[33] The precise insult must be specified; it is not altogether clear whether general words of abuse count as defamatory, as well as specific accusations.[34] The plaintiff may choose either a civil remedy (implicitly damages in the form of money)[35] or a criminal indictment, which opens up a wider range of punishments. Truth is admitted as a defence, although the text which deals with this point (D 47.10.18) is later subjected to differing interpretations.[36]

Canon law reproduces many of the features of Roman law: R.H. Helmholz's exhaustive account of English practice, which makes reference to the major parallels in the Decretals, may serve as a guide to the canonists' approach. According to Helmholz, the English practice derives from the papal constitution *Auctoritate Dei Patris* of 1222 which, among other grounds for imposing excommunication in accordance with the decrees of the Fourth Lateran Council of 1215,

---

[30] I 4.4.1 'iniuria autem committitur non solum cum quis pugna puta cum faustibus caesus vel etiam verberatus erit, sed etiam si cum convicium factum fuerit . . . vel si quis . . . libellum aut carmen scripserit' (an injury or outrage is inflicted not only when someone is struck with a fist, stick or whip, but even when an insult is proffered in prose or verse).

[31] Helmholz, *Defamation*, li.

[32] E.g. D 50.16.31 ('coram pluribus'), C 2.11.13 ('apud bonos et graves'): on the distinction between *plures* and *multi*, see Corvinus, *Ad titulum Digestorum de verborum significatione*, pp. 57–8: cf. also Grellet-Dumazeau, *Traité*, pp. 94ff, who distinguishes between publicity, publication and communication.

[33] D 47.10.4 (Paulus) 'si cum servo meo pugnum ducere vellem, in proximo te stantem invitus percusserim, iniuriarum non teneor' (if when I wish to punch my slave, I involuntarily hit you standing next to him, I will not be liable for an action for insult).

[34] See Schneidewinus, *In quatuor Institutionum libros*, col. 1054: 'dicitur verbum iniuriosum per quod, sive in genere, sive in specie obiicitur aliquod delictum commissum. Si quis dicat, tu fur, latre, homicide, licet non descendat ad speciem, exprimend[o] *cui furatus sit, vel quem occiderit*, per talia enim verba, quodammodo redditur quis infamis infamia facti cum eius opinio apud honos et honestos viros multum laedatur ac gravetur' (a word is said to be defamatory in that an accusation of some crime is made, whether in general or in particular. If anyone says 'you thief!' 'you robber!' 'you murderer!' although he does not enter into details of who was robbed or killed, he makes the accused person lose reputation by the *infamia facti* through such words, since his standing with good and worthy persons is greatly damaged and impugned).   [35] C 7.14.5.

[36] Grellet-Dumazeau, *Traité*, pp. 324ff., gives a bibliography of Renaissance texts on this 'vetus et quotidiana quaestio'. See also Coing, *Europäisches Privatrecht*, Munich, 1985, pp. 513–16.

includes a clause excommunicating 'omnes illos qui gracia odii, lucri, vel favoris, vel alia quacunque de causa maliciose crimen imponunt alicui, cum infamatus non sit apud bonos et graves, ut sic saltem ei purgatio indicatur vel alio modo gravetur' (all who for the sake of hatred, profit, favour or any other cause maliciously impute a crime to any person who is of good repute among good and worthy persons, with the result that he is obliged at least to resort to compurgation or he is harmed in some other manner).[37] The compurgation referred to here is the process of open ecclesiastical enquiry by which accused persons could seek to exonerate themselves from a crime or any other imputation of wrongful conduct,[38] at the same time as establishing a *prima facie* case for defamation. This clause of the *Auctoritate Dei Patris* seems to have regulated by far the greatest number of defamation cases in the medieval period (although some activity is recorded in local and royal courts). Helmholz sees the year 1492 as an important turning point, as it was then that Henry VII restricted the courts Christian to trying only those defamation cases whose content was 'wholly spiritual', reversing thereby the jurisdiction over the laity given in the writ of statute *Circumspecte agatis* of 1286.[39] But as ecclesiastical courts continued to argue that imputations of crimes were also imputations of sins, they continued to act in cases of defamation until well into the seventeenth century.[40] The standard of evidence was higher in proving defamation than in obtaining compurgation, but it was exacting in both cases; both plaintiff seeking the latter and defendant, whose malicious intent had to be established, had therefore advantages under the law. The remedies available were the imposition of penance, whipping and public apology; it seems that some Continental courts (although not English ones) offered monetary damages also. Truth was technically only a defence if publication could be shown to be in the public good, but in English practice, if the truth of any imputation was established, the

---

[37] Helmholz, *Defamation*, xlv.

[38] *Ibid.*, xxxvii: also Cicero, *De inventione*, i.9.15 (on the distinction between *purgatio* and *deprecatio*, as that between acknowledgement of a deed together with a plea of ignorance, accident or force majeure; and acknowledgement of a deed accompanied by a plea for forgiveness).

[39] Hatton, *A treatise concerning statutes*, p. 15; Helmholz, *Defamation*, xlviii; Cross, *Statutory interpretation*, p. 25.

[40] *The reports of Sir John Spelman*, ed. Baker, ii.236–48; Helmholz, *Defamation*, xliii–xliv; W.S. Holdsworth, *A history of English law*, London, 1903–38, v.205–12, viii.333–78; S.F.C. Milsom, *Historical foundations of the common law*, London, 1969, ii.332ff.

issue of subjective intent (i.e. why the imputation was uttered) did not arise; truth thus overrode malice. This does not seem to be the case on the Continent, where the defence that what was imputed was the truth was seen as a controversial point of law.[41] Other defences were *retortio* (provocation) (but not if the retort was proffered itself in a spirit of malice) and the absence of an *animus iniuriandi*.[42] A version of innuendo or imputation (e.g. the plausible identification of pronouns and nominal antecedents) was acceptable, but restrictions were placed on extracting implications from abuse in which no precise crime or disability was named: a priest, who proceeded against a woman in Norwich in 1417 for having said to him words to the effect (*talia verba seu consimilia*) 'ego nescio mingere aquam benedictam veluti tu scis' (I can't pee holy water like you), failed in his plea that she had publicly accused him of the socially demeaning condition of incontinence.[43]

Many of the features of civil and canon law are reflected in Continental practice. By the late sixteenth century, we find, in keeping with the *mos italicus* predilection for *distinctiones*, division of *iniuria verbalis* into seven categories: *contumelia, convicium, improperium* (rebuke), *detractio* (detraction), *susurratio* (whispering), *derisio* (derision) and *maledictio* (curse).[44] The religious sectarianism of the age and the increasing incidence of vituperative pamphlets caused legislation to be enacted in France and in the Empire to curb sectarian insults and the circulation of defamatory libels; defamation could thus give rise to either a civil or a criminal action, just as witchcraft; and as a criminal action, it comes close to actions for treason.[45] C 9.36 (*De famosis libellis*) was extended to allow for the

---

[41] See above, note 36: Schneidewinus, *In quatuor Institutionum libros*, cols. 1056ff; Julius Clarus, *Receptarum sententiarum opera*, (1559), Lyon, 1600, v.51.

[42] Helmholz, *Defamation*, xxii, xxx–xxxviii; also Schneidewinus, *In quatuor Institutionum libros*, col. 1056, citing Panormitanus. The presence of the *animus iniuriandi* is the proof of both crime and sin: see Aquinas, *Summa theologiae*, 1a 2ae 71.6. ad 1, cited by Mundius, *De diffamationibus*, pp. 44–5.

[43] Helmholz, *Defamation*, xxvii. For an exemplary range of English cases see J.H. Baker and S.F.C. Milsom, *Sources of English legal history: private law to 1750*, London, 1986, pp. 623–55.

[44] Ludovicus Gilhausen, *Commentarius . . . in titulum 10 libri 47 Pandectarum*, Lich, 1602, pp. 8of.

[45] J. Lecler, *Histoire de la tolérance au siècle de la Réforme*, Paris, 1955, ii.41, 48–9; Bocerus, *Commentarius, passim* (citing the *Constitutio criminalis carolina*); Baudouin, *Ad leges de famosis libellis*, pp. 5ff.; 5 Co. Rep. 125; Schneidewinus, *In quatuor Institutionum libros*, col. 1075; on the legislation in France in 1563, 1566 and 1626, see *Edict du roy portant defenses d'imprimer aucuns livres sans permission du grand sceau, et d'attacher et semer aucuns placards et libelles diffamatoires sur les peines contenuës*, Paris, 1626, and *Cardinalium, Archiepiscoporum . . . qui comitiis ecclesiasticis interfuerunt sententia de famosis libellis*, Paris, 1626, cited by Lipenius, *Bibliotheca realis Juridica* (1757), s.v. famosis libellus, who cites altogether, in all editions between 1679 and 1778, some twenty relevant tracts.

prosecution of writers, distributors, printers, owners and broadcasters of seditious, heretical and defamatory printed material.[46] Defamation could take the form of processions, songs, gestures as well as printed or spoken words. Over the century, lists of actionable and non-actionable words were produced in various localities: thus in Germany and German-speaking Switzerland 'Bastard', 'Hure', 'Schelm', 'Dieb', 'Lappi', 'Lööli', 'blööde Siech' are all actionable, whereas 'Stallbruder' is not. This is not in itself surprising, since it is to be expected that insults could possess a strongly local colour: Théodore Grellet-Dumazeau lists, among others, 'onion head', 'one horse man', 'three obols man', 'rhinoceros nose', 'pea merchant' and 'bonhomme' (i.e. cuckold).[47] The issue of privilege is discussed: if a judge refuses to admit a case for trial, does this constitute defamation? Is it defamatory for a priest to denounce a parishioner for a base and unclean life from the pulpit, or make public the fact that someone is excommunicate?[48] The latter case was found to be defamatory, the former not; this might be said to be in keeping with the privilege and protection accorded by the legal profession to its own. Some local customs, inconsistent with Roman law, survive in the Renaissance in Moravia, Bohemia and Poland: notably the public defaming of defaulting debtors, whose initial contract of debt often included a clause that such defamation would take place if they did not pay by a given date.[49] Remedies varied from court to court: in most civil actions, the remedy was solemn recantation before a judge or a *deprecatio Christiana* (a less formal plea for forgiveness), together with the restitution of any real damages; in criminal courts, although C 9.36 allows for capital punishment, it seems that exile, mutilation (excision of ears, tongue or slitting of nostrils), whipping and public

---

[46] Bocerus, *Commentarius*, p. 55; Sir James Fitzjames Stephen, *A history of the criminal law in England*, London, 1883, ii.311ff.; John Hawarde, *Les Reportes del cases in camera stellata 1593–1609*, ed. William Paley Baildon, privately printed, 1894, pp. 222–30.

[47] On these terms see Adalbert Erler, Ekkehard Kaufmann and others, *Handwörterbuch zur deutschen Rechtsgeschichte*, Berlin, 1971– , i, cols. 1451–4; Gilhausen, *Commentarius*, p. 132; Grellet-Dumazeau, *Traité*, p. 179; Clarus, *Receptae sententiae*, v.51 ('tu es bonus homo, quae verba communiter intelligentur quod est cornutus'). Joannes Baptista Baiardus, *Additiones et annotationes ad Julii Clari receptarum sententiarum librum quartum*, Lyon, 1600, p. 75 (reporting that 'tu es impudens' is not a slander, whereas 'tu falsum dicis' is). Lipenius (1757, p. 48) refers to a *Tractatus quadripartitus de conviciis et calumniis germanicis* by Joachim Gregorius von Pritzen, (Frankfurt, 1618), which I have not been able to locate. It is generally agreed that it is not possible to defame a prostitute (*ibid.*, p. 76; Grellet-Dumazeau, *Traité*, p. 65).

[48] Coing, *Privatrecht*, p. 514 (who refers to Chasseneuz, *Commentaria super consuetudinibus Burgundiae*, Lyon, 1543, vi.4 as the locus classicus); John Kaye, 'Libel and slander – two torts or one?', *Law Quarterly Review*, xci (1975), 530–1.

[49] D 47.10; *Handwörterbuch zur deutschen Rechtsgeschichte*, i, cols. 1451–4.

disgrace are more common penalties.[50] Truth is a defence only if in the public interest; other defences are *retortio* as in canon law, and the subsequent qualification of actionable words: thus, according to some authorities, it is not defamatory to say 'tu mentiris', provided that you add 'salvo honore tuo vel salva reverentia tua'; but if you say 'tu scienter falsum dicis' or 'tu mentiris per gulam' or 'du luegst wie ein ehrloser Mann' (even under provocation), you are guilty of slander. Others insist that only 'tu dicis falsum' is not liable to prosecution, because it cannot be demonstrated that the utterance was made with malicious intent.[51] Indeed, proof that one was not motivated by malice constituted a defence although in practice this was very difficult to establish. An example is provided in an anecdote recorded by Guillaume Bouchet in his *Sérées* of 1584; a fishmonger proceeded against a neighbour who had publicly thrown a dead cat out of a window close to the shop and cried 'this cat has died because it ate a herring'; but the neighbour conducted a successful defence by claiming that the cat was killed as a result of having stolen the herring, not because the herring in itself was bad.[52] If, however, one wishes to claim that the words were uttered in jest, the onus of proof fell upon the defendant; such a defence is envisaged in D 47.10.11 and C 9.35.5, as Baldus points out: 'sicut se habent verba ita praesumitur esse animus, adeo ut incumbat onus probandi reo, se non animo iniuriandi dixisse: sicut etiam praestito iuramento se liberare potest'[53] (the words are taken to indicate the spirit in which they were uttered; thus, as it falls to the defendant to prove that he spoke without malice, he can liberate himself from the accusation by oath). The defendant can also plead subsequent forgiveness; if the plaintiff and the defendant were seen after the alleged defamation to embrace, kiss or greet each other, then the case might be dismissed. Sometimes the context ('mit Spielen, Essen und Trincken', as Saxon law had it) disqualifies the action.[54] Nearly all commentators draw attention to

50 Bocerus, *Commentarius*, p. 100; Schneidewinus, *In quatuor Institutionum libros*, cols. 1065–9.
51 *Constitutio criminalis carolina*, §110; Bocerus, *Commentarius*, p. 130; Gilhausen, *Commentarius*, pp. 102f.; Coing, *Privatrecht*, p. 513; Schneidewinus, *In quatuor Institutionum libros*, cols. 1054ff. Baiardus, *Additiones*, p. 75 points out that the addition of 'cum reverentia' disqualifies an accusation of lying from slander in Naples.
52 Bouchet, *Les Serées*, ed. C.E. Roybet, Paris, 1873–82, ii.10–11. Grellet-Dumazeau attempts to distinguish between 'volonté' and 'intention' in utterance (*Traité*, p. 149).
53 Gl. ad C 9.35.5.
54 Schneidewinus, *In quatuor Institutionum libros*, cols. 1081–5 (giving a comprehensive list of defences); Mundius, *De diffamationibus*, p. 158; Cujas ad C 9.35.5: 'sic et si dicat se per iocum dixisse probet' (if the defendant claims that he spoke in jest, let him prove it).

the growth in incidence of defamation cases during the sixteenth century.

In England, the law develops in a parallel way: as on the Continent, it is important to distinguish criminal libel, most often tried in the Star Chamber,[55] and the tort of slander. Defamation, described by one English judge as 'that tout spiritual offense' in 1497,[56] passed in the course of the sixteenth century from ecclesiastical to secular courts, where it generated so many cases between 1580 and 1640 that it became the subject of a separate treatise (indeed the first treatise on any tort), published by Joseph March in 1648. Actionability was limited to the following categories, according to March:

All scandalous words which touch or concern a man in his life, liberty or member, or any corporall punishment; or which scandall a man in his office or place of trust, or in his calling or function by which he gains his living; or which tend to the slandering of his title, or his advancement, or preferment, or any other particular damage; or lastly which charge a man to have any infectious disease, by reason of which he ought to be separated by the law from the society of men: all such words are actionable.[57]

No distinction was made between written and spoken words, or between words and defamatory actions such as personations, skimmingtons or cuckoldings, although these last fell more often under the criminal law, and were tried in the Star Chamber. A number of important differences in the practice of criminal libel are worthy of note: general words were there actionable, as opposed to the precise categories set out above; no attention was paid to damages; words were construed only in their plain sense; there was no jury (and hence no need for a distinction of law and fact); prerogatory powers could be taken to suppress defamatory matter; publication to a third party was not necessary. This last condition pertained even after the fall of the Star Chamber in 1640–1; indeed, there is one celebrated case of a manuscript pamphlet which was never published or even circulated, but kept among the private papers of a prominent political activist, being the subject of a libel action for treason and libel.[58] In criminal

---

55 On which, see William Hudson, 'A treatise on the court of the Star Chamber', (*c.* 1630) in *Collecteana iuridica*, London, 1792, ii.1–240.

56 Fineux, quoted by Helmholz, *Defamation*, xlviii.

57 Quoted by Kaye, 'Libel and slander', p. 527.

58 Stephen, *Criminal law*, ii.313ff.; Holdsworth, *History*, v.207ff., viii.339ff.; the case referred to here is that of Algernon Sydney (1622–82), cited in William Blackstone, *Commentaries on the laws of England*, London, 1774, iv.6, p. 80. Blackstone refers also to 'one Peacham, a

cases, the punishment meted out usually took the form of fines, the pillory or the loss of ears. Truth was not a defence: indeed, it might even be an aggravation. Civil cases were different. General words of abuse – 'false piking knave', 'town bull', – were not actionable until the sixteenth century, and were again excluded after the 1580s.[59] Other allegations – imputations of crime, contagious diseases, unfitness for a trade or profession (i.e. accusations of cowardice addressed to a soldier, of immoral life to a priest, of deceitful practice to a weaver) – were subject to the *mitior sensus* rule ('verba accipienda in mitiori sensu'), by which all terminological and syntactical ambiguity was to be resolved into the most charitable way.[60] As on the Continent, the law was more favourable to the defendant in civil actions on the case for words because the plaintiff needed to establish first malice, second the non-applicability of the *mitior sensus* rule, and finally special damages. Damages in the form of money were the most common remedy; these were particularly generous in cases involving slandered lawyers, as one might expect.[61] The law of defamation exposes, moreover, an interesting (and persistent) illogicality in English law concerning perjury; technically, those found guilty having pleaded not guilty are guilty of this crime; there are cases where those found not guilty of debt in one court were slandered as perjurers by their alleged creditors, who thus provoke an action on the case for words and plead truth as a defence, enabling them to have

---

clergyman' who was convicted for treasonable passages in a sermon never preached (Cro. Car. 125). Blackstone distinguishes between 'the bare words' and 'the deliberate act of writing them': 'if the words be set down in writing, it argues more deliberate intention; and it has been held that writing is an overt act of treason; for *scribere est agere*. But even in this case the bare words are not the treason, but the deliberate act of writing them.'

[59] Slightly different dates are given by J.H. Baker, *An introduction to English legal history*, London, 1979, pp. 497–503.

[60] The origin of the phrase 'in mitiori sensu' is given by Schneidewinus, *In quatuor Institutionum libros*, col. 1055: 'succedit igitur optima theoria Bart. in consil. 108 quando verbum aliquod profertur, quod est indifferens et potest sonare injuriam vel non, tunc debere illud in mitiorem partem accipi alligatque Bart. . . . 2 cons. 22 quaest 2 ubi dicitur. Nemo mentiens judicandus est, qui dicit falsum quod putet verum, quia quantum in ipso est, non fallit ipse, sed fallitur.' (Bartolus' saying takes the place of the best theory when he avers that when a word is uttered which is indifferent and may or may not be slanderous, then it should be taken in the milder sense . . . and he links to this text another which avers that no one is to be judged to be a liar who tells an untruth which he believes to be true, because he is not deceiving others insofar as his utterance goes, but himself.) See also above 3.5.2 and 3.6.1, on the distinction between *mendax* and *fallax*.

[61] Helmholz, *Defamation*, xcviii, ingeniously argues that this is because courts of law are the very place in which lawyers' reputations are maintained or lost. See also R.E. Megarry, *Miscellany at law*, London, 1955, pp. 194–5.

the same action tried twice, against the custom of English courts. There are Continental parallels of this practice.[62]

By 1630, in very different legislative contexts (not only ecclesiastical, but also civil and criminal; not only England, but also France and the area of influence of the *ius commune*), a broadly similar approach to defamation may therefore be noted. It is generally agreed that defamation can take other forms than spoken words; that it has a criminal dimension when public order is threatened by it; that civil remedies should include the restitution of the good name of the victim and often monetary damages as well. Legislation has a clear socially regulatory rôle: tempers are allowed to cool (it was not infrequent for cases never to be brought to a conclusion); the importance of the forum of the *boni et graves* was established; means were provided for preserving and regaining reputation.[63] In England, and indeed throughout Europe, an increase in criminal and civil cases is noted in the course of the sixteenth century: one seventeenth-century judge went so far as to fear that 'the growth of these actions will spoil all communications' (i.e. social intercourse).[64] It is worthwhile reviewing the various reasons offered for this expansion in actions for slander.

Some explanations may be set aside *ab initio*, such as the growth in the population, or the claim by one sixteenth-century judge that 'the malice of men doth more increase in these times than in times past'.[65] More compelling is the decline of ecclesiastical actions after 1492, with a concomitant increase in actions in other courts; second, the increased litigiousness of the Elizabethan age, induced by the prospects of high damages awarded by royal courts; finally, the broadening of the scope of the action to include general words for a period in the middle years of the century ('drunkard', 'hypocrite', 'crafty old knave', 'heretic', 'adulterer', 'thief', 'whore').[66] The religious upheavals and divisions of the times and political causes such

---

[62] 5 Co. Rep. 125; Helmholz, *Defamation*, xxxix, lxxxvii, xlii; Bocerus, *Commentarius*, pp. 54ff.
[63] Helmholz, *Defamation*, xl; J.A. Sharpe, 'Such disagreement betwyx neighbours: litigation and human relations in Early Modern England', in *Disputes and settlements: law and human relations in the West*, ed. John Bossy, Cambridge, 1983, pp. 167–87; Michael Weisser, *Crime and punishment in Early Modern Europe*, Hassocks, 1979, p. 61. Grellet-Dumazeau, *Traité*, p. 9 identifies six elements in defamation: four intrinsic (the allegation or imputation; the deed; the person; the injury to the person), one extrinsic (publication) and one moral (the *animus iniuriandi*).   [64] Vaughan C.J. (1671), quoted by Kaye, 'Libel and slander', p. 534.
[65] Helmholz, *Defamation*, xlv; 4 Co. Rep. 15; Holdsworth, *History*, v.207, viii.333ff.
[66] Helmholz, *Defamation*, lxvi, xlv, ciii.

as government policy on duelling have also been adduced: in England, the more tolerant attitudes to the action of judicial personnel and their increased numbers after 1600 have also been noted contributory factors to the rise in the number of cases.[67] One may also point to changes in attitudes to language itself. Helmholz has pointed out (following Clanchy) that the transition from an oral to a written culture may help explain the decline of actions in local courts in the early fourteenth century:[68] there are also linguistic factors which may help explain changes in a later period.

Direct evidence comes from the application of the *mitior sensus* rule. It can be shown that judges employ this to restrict the number of successful actions in the period 1580–1640; whereas between 1660 and 1700 the rule is abandoned for precisely the converse reason, as one eighteenth-century judge makes clear: 'It has been by experience found, that unless men can get satisfaction by law, they will be apt to take it themselves. The rule therefore that now has prevailed is, that words are to be taken in the sense that is most obvious, and in which those to whom they are spoken will be sure to understand them.'[69] The 'sense . . . most obvious' here is manifestly determined *de jure*. It marks a shift from reliance on intention (i.e. speaker's meaning) as a criterion of construction to reliance on uptake (i.e. hearer's meaning), as determined by quasi-objective means. It is clear that for reasons of legal convenience or politics, judges can alter their attitude to the application of linguistic rules, and their assessment of the value of words: sometimes these are 'mere wind' or 'brabling',[70] sometimes the very stuff of sedition or social evil.[71] That this is possible is due to the ingredients of defamation which relate to central problems of sense-making and sense-determination which have been our concern in this study, and to which we shall return briefly here: What constitutes evidence? How does the context of an utterance contribute to its sense? What can be said to be the objective sense of an utterance? What is the nature of intention and how is it expressed?

---

[67] *Ibid.*, ciii.　　[68] *Ibid.*, lxii.

[69] *Ibid.*, cii; Kaye, 'Libel and slander', pp. 528–9 (quoting Holt C.J.).

[70] 9 Co. Rep. 59; Helmholz, *Defamation*, lxxvi.

[71] 5 Co. Rep. 125; Grellet-Dumazeau, *Traité*, pp. 19–20, cites later examples of the reverse of the mitior sensus rule, one of which demonstrates clearly its logical weakness: 'une ordonnance de Chrétien VII, roi de Danemark, porte que si dans un ouvrage imprimé, l'auteur a caché des expressions injurieuses sous le voile de l'ironie ou de l'allégorie, dont cependant le sens et les mauvaises intentions sont de toute évidence, il sera puni de la peine qu'il aurait encourue s'il s'était exprimé clairement et sans figures (ordonnance de 1779)'. How can 'expressions injurieuses *cachées*' be 'de toute évidence'?

What constitutes evidence? It is customary as we have seen (3.2.5) to distinguish between *probationes inartificiales* ('facts' or 'clues' – possession of stolen goods, a bloodstained dagger, the *ipsissima verba* of an altercation) and *probationes artificiales*: that is, legal argument, the construction of prosecution or defence by reference to existing law and logical or persuasive reasoning (the establishment of good name, etc.).[72] Legal systems at this time approach this distinction between fact and argument differently: in England, for example, points of law were a matter for the court; points of fact, for the jury. Thus, in slander cases, the matter of law for the court was whether the words were defamatory; the matters of fact for the jury were whether they were published; whether they referred to the plaintiff, and whether any damages had been incurred, and if so, what. I have already mentioned the fact that judges might or might not dismiss cases by the application of the *mitior sensus* rule; but this is not the only peremptory action taken by the court. By determining what were, or were not, the facts of the case, the jury effectively decided themselves what were the *ipsissima verba*. An example is provided by Gray vs. Derby in 1552;[73] in that case the jury decided (although on what grounds is not at all clear) that the defendant had said 'thou art a barratour' but had not said 'Walter Grey thou art an untrue gentylman and a barratour and I will not cease untylle I see thy confusion.' It is, therefore, in the nature of the legal approach to language to eliminate obscurity and ambiguity and to provide an account of an event which can then be submitted to judgement (in this case, dismissal, as 'barratour' is a general and non-actionable word). History is in this case decided *post factum*: or to put it in Modestinus' words 'interdum plus valet scriptura quam quod actum est' (D 33.2.19, quoted above 3.6.1). Wherever the law must decide, it must opt for one answer or another: no equivocation is possible except by adjournment *sine die*.

How does the context of an utterance contribute to its meaning? In one sense, it is crucial, as in the case of the herring, the cat and the fishmonger, cited above; in another, it concerns the question of loss of reputation through communication to a third party. We have seen that in all legal systems at some level publicity is an ingredient of defamation: especially *apud bonos et graves*. The consensus of good people is what determines reputation; language is in this instance a

---

[72] Helmholz, *Defamation*, cii; L. Jonathan Cohen, 'Freedom of proof', in *Facts in law*, ed. William Twining, *Archiv für Rechts- und Sozialphilosophie*, supplement 16 (1983), 1–12; Cicero, *De inventione* and *Topica, passim*.   [73] Helmholz, *Defamation*, lxxxiii.

social affair, not a matter of logic or individual intention. In cases concerning defamation, the law becomes the forum in which social regulation occurs by compurgation, by perpetual adjournment, by the restitution of good name and punishment of the offender. Such social regulation operates through the authority of the court and the status of the *boni et graves*; this configuration recalls modern theories of social ontology and dialogicalism.[74] It arises in sixteenth-century discussions in reference to the need for bona fide communication, for common commitment to mutual understanding and for the suppression of over-subtle interpretation, as we have seen.

But, as we have also seen, publicity is not a necessary element of criminal libel. This absolute nature of libel is in a sense already enshrined in C 9.36, where handling a libellous tract is itself a contamination of which one must purge oneself; and in the laws concerning seditious literature in the sixteenth century, the equal penalty attached to composing, printing, financing, possessing, distributing or causing to be distributed and consuming such works carries a similar implication.[75] One Continental commentator (Bocerus) asks whether a libel is a libel if never communicated to another, or, if communicated, immediately snatched back *ex poenitentia*; he concludes that it is because the defamation that it contains bears witness to an *animus iniuriandi* which is persistent (since the author took the trouble to write it down) and not mere 'passing anger'.[76] There is an implicit inconsistency here with the normal legal rule governing the fulfilment of necessary conditions for contract, promise or other public and performative acts of language: namely a *consensus ad idem* (see above 3.6.5). Bocerus' libel is equivalent to a promise uttered alone in a locked room and recalls the case of the libellous tract sent to James I in a sealed box for which the author (who was also the sender) was executed.[77] This would seem to suggest an undue intrusion of the state (in the form of criminal law) into the person but it may arise as much from the difficulty in proving *animus iniuriandi*. In public cases, verbal assault is not in doubt because there are witnesses (the *boni et graves*), and the perlocutionary effect of the

[74] See Michael Theunissen, *Der Andere*, Berlin, 1977; Francis Jacques, *Dialogiques*, Paris, 1979, and *L'Espace logique de l'interlocution*, Paris, 1985.

[75] See Hudson, 'A treatise on the Court of the Star Chamber': for a different view see Milsom, *Historical foundations*, p. 389.

[76] Bocerus, *Commentarius*, pp. 55ff.; Kaye, 'Libel and slander', p. 532 (on 'brabling'); Grellet-Dumazeau, *Traité*, p. 159; Blackstone, *Commentaries*, iv.6, p. 80 (see above note 58).

[77] Stephen, *Criminal law*, ii.306n.

defamation is the loss of reputation: it is still, however, incumbent upon the plaintiff to prove malicious intent. In the case of criminal libel, the defamation may never become public, but the written form of the words provides evidence of malice.[78]

What can be said to be the objective sense of an utterance? And what is the nature of the intention it embodies, and how is it expressed? These questions bring us back to the distinction *ratio legis, mens legislatoris* and *verba* which we have already exhaustively examined (3.6.1); but they are approached here from a slightly different angle. Because of the importance of *mens rea* to law, it is clearly in the interests of lawyers to subscribe to the doctrine of clear intentional meaning and to give priority to its determination: we may recall Andrea Alciato's opening words to his influential commentary on D 50.16: 'cum inventa sunt verba ut dicentis sententiam exprimant, merito eius voluntas in primis spectanda est'.[79] Yet in England the *mitior sensus* rule takes the diametrically opposed line in determining sense by the analysis of the 'linguistic facts', not the motive behind them. As one judge put it, 'the law will not support any strained constructions': thus, 'words that are too general or not positively affirmative' are disqualified, as are 'words of double or indifferent meaning', 'words that are doubtful in form or meaning or sense', 'words qualified by subsequent words not actionable' and 'words that are apparently impossible'. Syntax as much as words could give rise to the application of the rule, whose effect was to assume always on the part of the speaker the most charitable intention regardless of what the intention might historically have been: thus 'pox' is taken to refer to 'smallpox' rather than venereal disease wherever possible.[80] Thus also, as Megarry records of a case reported in 1639, 'where one says of a lawyer *That he had as much Law as a Monkey*, that the words were not actionable; because he hath as much Law, and more also. But if he had said, *That he has no more Law than a Monkey*, those words were actionable.' Not that the construction 'as much as' was always taken inclusively as here: other reports record cases where the exclusive interpretation (which is, of course, much

---

[78] Kaye, 'Libel and slander', pp. 531–2.
[79] *De verborum significatione*, pp. 10, 204; it is significant that a writer on slander (Mundius) insists on the importance of *mens rea* to law: *De diffamationibus*, pp. 44–5: 'quicquid faciunt homines, intentio iudicat omnes, intentio namque diriget opus' (whatever men do, their intention judges them all, for their intention will direct their actions).
[80] 4 Co. Rep. 13ff.; Holdsworth, *History*, viii.333ff. Baker and Milsom, *Sources*, pp. 623–55.

closer to the spirit of the utterance) triumphed.[81] Determination of innuendo or implication is another example of logic applied to the words of the case in a way which overrides intention.[82] This set of interpretative moves exemplify, in spite of Judge Wray's caution about 'strained constructions', a feature of legal practice evoked in the rules set out in Heydon's case (above 4.2): namely ingenuity and [over] subtlety in construing the law; or, to put it another way, obedience to the letter not to the spirit of the law (see above 3.5.1). Sensitivity in England to this problem can be gauged by the statute of Edward VI according to which 'those who stole horses should not have the benefit of clergy'; this had to be supplemented one year later by a statute which read 'he who should steal but one horse . . .'[83] One is obliged to postulate that between these two enactments, a successful defence was conducted by the clerical thief of a single horse, using 'arguments more logical than sensible',[84] but the judges' and counsels' use of the *mitior sensus* rule clearly condoned such use. Nor is this the only area of law in which logic overrides patent intention at this time. The many questions arising from the corporate style of schools, colleges and churches show a similar propensity among lawyers to demand formulaic accuracy and to disregard intention.[85] Further evidence of the same trend is found in the publication of formularies at the end of the sixteenth century (see above 4.2). In all these cases, something approaching strict liability or formulaic justice prevails over *mens rea* and commonsense construal of the expressive functions of language.

Yet, as has been mentioned several times, malicious intent, the *animus iniuriandi* is an indispensable ingredient of defamation. There seems here to be a legal impasse, and a profound problem for semantics, in the dual requirement of a logical analysis of the words of the action according to conventional rules of language and a

---

[81] Megarry, *Miscellany*, pp. 191–5; Milsom, *Historical Foundations*, p. 388.

[82] Helmholz, *Defamation*, xcvi.

[83] Cross, *Statutory interpretation*, pp. 25f., citing Blackstone; for an example of a Continental egregious misreading, see Fournier, *In titulum de verborum significatione*, p. 20 ('de damno a quadrupede'); see also 3.5.2 above, and Ian Maclean, 'Responsibility and the act of interpretation: the case of law', in *The political responsibility of intellectuals*, ed. Ian Maclean, Alan Montefiore and Peter Winch, Cambridge, 1990, p. 171.

[84] Helmholz, *Defamation*, xcii–ci. Conal Condren has pointed out to me that 'clerical' in this context and at this time may mean no more than 'literate'.

[85] Bocerus, *Commentarius*, pp. 3–4; 11 Co. Rep. 18; J.M. Kaye, *A God's House miscellany*, Southampton, 1984, pp. 38–41, where the question of corporate titles is comprehensively discussed with reference to cases between 1557 and 1612. In a recent unpublished paper on common law and publication in England in the sixteenth century, Professor J.H. Baker noted the growing importance of the letter of legislation over its spirit in this period.

determination of the intention behind their utterance. The first requirement is, of course, strongly reminiscent of the Old Law, by which guilt or innocence is technical and not related to motive: such formulaic justice which, as Fritz Schulz reminds us, disappears very early from Roman law, seems to reassert itself in the sixteenth century; it may even have its theological parallel in the doctrine of double predestination.[86] It may, more speculatively, be distantly related to the rise of lexica in legal studies, and the reduction of law to a certain species of definition (see above 3.3.2). It may finally be motivated by the self-interest of the legal profession, for in making the language of the law technical, the lawyer makes himself indispensable to the litigant and the testator.

The second requirement of defamation – malicious intent – is much more difficult of access than the first. Intention is, as we have seen, broken down by some Continental commentators into three elements: (a) a general intention to convey a sense, (b) an intention to express a given mental event (the *verbum cordis*), (c) an intention to convey as well as a given sense an attitude towards the sense or the recipient of the sense: pleasure, pain, hatred, love, etc. (see above 3.6.4). English commentators at this time do not proceed so analytically, but they are aware that by representing intention in the form of words, a possibility of infinite regress arises, as each conventional representation of intention can be subjected to an objective, logical analysis which is subject in turn to the prevaricative features of language: in other words, because we can express ourselves only through words whose sense is guaranteed only by other words and hence is conventional in character and, moreover, easily reproduceable by anyone who masters the relevant conventions, it is logically impossible to distinguish between an utterance which incorporates a given intention and one which uses the same formulas of language but does not: in saying 'I mean this', I might either mean it or not mean it.[87] Intention is, therefore, an essential but totally irrecoverable element of defamation: the law of slander, like the

---

[86] Fritz Schulz, *History of Roman legal science*, 2nd ed., Oxford, 1953, pp. 29f., 294–5; on double predestination, see Alister E. McGrath, *Reformation thought: an introduction*, Oxford, 1988, pp. 86ff. See above 3.6.1 on strictum ius; and for the possible influence of the fixed form of the printed words on sixteenth-century attitudes, Ong, *The presence of the word*, New Haven, 1967.

[87] Baiardus, *Additiones*, p. 75 suggests that intention can be recovered through what preceded the offending words and through the way they were said: but both of these are as conventional and as reproduceable as words conveying sincerity ('consideratis praecedentibus verbis et modo qua dicta fuissent, posset cognoscere, an lapsu linguae vel animo [verba] fuissent prolata'). See also above 3.6.1.

treatises on the interpretation of law and the meaning of wills, depends on distinctions between malice and good will, truth and deceit, words uttered *in malam partem* and *in bonam partem*,[88] but is wholly incapable of generating adequate rules for making such distinctions. Rules are, of course, produced: intention in words is decided by the general or particular social context, by accompanying signs such as laughter or gestures, by the application of jurisprudential norms (e.g. the prior presumption of guilt or innocence in the accused). But in the end none of them is watertight, although, of course, courts are always able to decide peremptorily the matter by simply passing sentence. We are brought back again to the interpretative rules of Heydon's case, and its last symptomatic paragraph: 'the office of all the judges is always to make such construction as shall suppress subtle inventions and evasions for the continuance of the mischief, and *pro privato commodo*, and to add force and life to the cure and remedy, according to the true intent of the makers of the Act, *pro bono publico*' – 'subtle inventions' and 'true intent' take us back to the predicament described in extenso in an earlier chapter (3.5.1–3.6.1).

The parallels provided by Suarez and English law and the example of the law of defamation indicate that the problems which were discovered in the theory of interpretation in chapter 3 are common to other sixteenth- and early seventeenth-century contexts which treat of law in relation to language. This is on the one hand not surprising, as Roman law provides a precedent for legal thinking for canonists and common lawyers alike and supplies many maxims to both; on the other hand, it leaves the modern historian with the question whether the similarities of approach arise out of a common legal outlook, or a common crisis about language which affected Renaissance thinkers at more or less the same time. Both possibilities are plausible, and such evidence as has been considered here offers support for a positive answer to both. They do not represent, of course, mutually exclusive hypotheses; but they may have different implications for the practice of intellectual history, especially as regards a theory of paradigms of thought and the general problems of acceding to the past which were adumbrated in the introduction to this book. The conclusion which follows will attempt to answer this question, and assess its implications for current research on Renaissance attitudes to language and meaning.

[88] Helmholz, *Defamation*, xciv; Gilhausen, *Commentarius*, pp. 102ff.

Conclusion

When you are criticizing the philosophy of an epoch, do not chiefly direct your attention to those intellectual positions which its exponents feel it necessary to defend. There will be some fundamental assumptions which adherents of all the various systems within an epoch unconsciously presuppose. Such assumptions appear so obvious that people do not know what they are assuming because no other way of putting things has ever occurred to them.

(A.N. Whitehead, *Science and the modern world*, New York, 1948, pp. 49-50, quoted by Kelley, *Foundations*, p. 14)

The principal aim of this study has been to investigate theories of interpretation prevalent in Renaissance legal texts, and to show what explicit and implicit conceptions of meaning they contain. Two broad contexts were first explored: the first, that which is constituted by aspects of the social, economic and institutional forces acting on the practice of legal interpretation; the second, that which is afforded by the propaedeutic disciplines of the law: grammar, dialectics and topics. The results of the enquiry into the first broad context were somewhat mixed; this was perhaps to be expected of the ambitious project to show how ideas are influenced by the material conditions out of which they emerge. It is much easier to discuss the contents of books in abstracto than to attempt to link them intimately with the physical object – the book – by which they have come down to us; and it is to be expected that the signs of the financial and institutional interests served by the production of books about the interpretation of law would not be prominently displayed in the texts. Similarly, the interests as opposed to the message of humanism – the displacement of a well-entrenched conservative academic body by a new style of learning with greater emphasis on communication proposed by those who could hope to succeed to lucrative posts and well-established chairs – are rarely expressed in bald terms, although such studies as Grafton's and Jardine's *From humanism to the humanities* have shown how they underlie much polemical writing in the fifteenth and sixteenth centuries. In the case of law, this clash of interests between a conservative institution and a radical movement intent on supplanting it is most apparent in the opposition between *mos italicus* and *mos gallicus*. There may be a political dimension to this opposition, as in the case of northern France, where the adoption of the *mos gallicus* expresses local hostility to the interests of the Holy Roman Empire; this is not, however, the case in Lutheran Germany where the *ius commune* remained authoritative. But although the distinction between the French and the Italian modes of law is clearly perceived and articulated by contemporaries, legal historians have come more and more to underline the ground common to both *mores*, and their common reliance on the work of their medieval precedessors. It is the solidarity of the legal profession more than their internecine divisions which emerges also from the present investigation.

Two aspects of legal writing, both closely connected with the sense of identity of the legal profession and its institutional interests, show its perennial nature particularly clearly. The first is the continued composition of texts promoting the dignity of legal studies. These writings reflect a well-documented aspect of the *mentalité* of the medieval and Renaissance period, namely, its preoccupation with questions of precedence; but they also bear on the issue of interpretation in that they claim a 'scientific' status (in Aristotelian terms) for the discipline of the law, and they may even reflect more crude financial concerns in the shape of demands for higher stipendary remuneration than that given to rival faculties. The second aspect is the reaction to Justinian's prohibition of interpretation: a prohibition which threatens the practice of the law in nearly all its forms. What emerges clearly as a common feature from the texts which grapple with this prohibition is the claim to authority in matters of language and meaning which jurists, as judges, interpreters and pedagogues, are constrained to make. This bears upon interpretation in so far as the legal interpreter takes the place of the authorities to which he should be subservient; in fulfilling his function, he becomes the voice of the legislator in declaring his intention, and the embodiment of right reason in declaring equity. Both the defence of the dignity of the profession and the apology for the practice of interpretation are found in the earliest medieval texts and in those being written after 1600; the case for perenniality is here very strongly supported. The authority or power inherent in the practice of legal interpretation is, of course, one manifestation of power inherent in the law; the others, which are often identified with the ideological or political interests represented by the law, are not our direct concern here.

The evidence of publishing practices and its commercial and financial underpinning clearly belongs to the post-Gutenberg era; it was adduced to show first that a strong case can be made for a 'universe of discourse' or 'paradigm' in legal studies stretching from 1460 to 1630. This is not so say that there was no evolution in legal thought in this period: clearly, the discussion of law in relation to the figures of sovereign and subject, for example, bears witness to a very marked change. But as far as issues of interpretation are concerned, the terms in which discussions are conducted and the texts which are repeatedly adduced suggest strongly that a writer in 1460 could have communicated coherently with one in 1630, just as the latter was able to refer to the former in an argument or proof, for many fifteenth-century jurists enjoyed republication in the course of the sixteenth century. Pedagogical materials offer more signs of evolution over the same period; but even if styles and set texts change, in broad terms the same ground is covered. The evidence of the formats in which legal works are printed – folio, 4to, 8vo for the most part – showed that for practitioners, the possession and display of large-format legal texts might have been as important as their use as reference materials: a well-lined study induces confidence in the competence and scholar-ship of its occupant. This may be one factor (as well as a significant rise in student numbers) which may have contributed towards the extraordinary explosion in legal publication (as in all forms of academic publication) towards the end of the sixteenth century; but there are other forces which underlie this phenomenon. One is the nature of the law governing licences to print, which made it profitable for German printers to produce copies of Italian works outside the jurisdiction in which they were protected; this may account in part at least for repeated editions of the same work. The licence itself specified that a book needed to be novel in some way to enjoy protection, and this provision encouraged the reproduction of revised editions incorporating only the most minor alterations, which none the less qualified under publishing law as improvements; this can give the impression to a modern reader that Renaissance scholars suffered from an almost pathological desire for precision and accuracy. The co-existence of these different editions was itself a spur to other writers to produce reconciliations (or even simultaneous publication of several competing editions or commentaries of a work) which helped to perpetuate the process of re-editing. All of this bears on interpretation in so far as it encouraged the production of new accounts of hermeneutic practices whose claims to novelty may not be very strong.

A final aspect of the publication of legal texts which was investigated was their visual presentation. One reason for doing this was to present in their least mediated form the texts which are the object of this study, and to make manifest their anthologistic nature: that sewing-together of quotations, half-quotations, allusions and argument that might well be described, in Montaigne's words, as a 'marqueterie mal jointe'. The second reason for discussing these illustrations was to offer an evaluation of Ong's thesis about the visuality of Renaissance philosophy as this applies to law. It cannot be denied that humanists such as Alciato do much to make the text more elegant and even reduce the obtrusive presence of gloss; but in the domain of legal studies, the prevalence of *distinctiones*, which operate discursively as Ramist dichotomies do visually, weakens the case for a paradigm shift. The reader of 1630, less well versed in the manuscript tradition, may not have been able to manage the full panoply of legal abbreviations known to his homologue in 1460, but the standard edition of the Digest – that of Godefroy – has exactly the same layout on the page as the earliest productions of the text in print.

The second broad context adduced in this investigation was that of the propaedeutic disciplines of the law. These were to some degree in competition with legal studies, as the debates about the relative dignity of faculties make clear; but there is a broad consensus that they were all considered to precede jurisprudence in the curriculum. It is not surprising that the theory and practice of legal interpretation was deeply impregnated with elements drawn from grammar, logic and forensic rhetoric. What has emerged also, however, is that from the time of the postglossators, and possibly even earlier, the characteristic mode of legal argument – topics – was widely practised, and that the humanist discoveries of the fifteenth century and the pedagogical developments which flow from them, notably in the work of Agricola and Ramus, do not bring about a profound shift in juristic attitudes to language and signification, except perhaps in the codification of subjective meaning. A face-lift was undoubtedly given to text books, and it is certain that the text of the Corpus Juris Civilis itself underwent a strenuous philological examination, but this did not change its nature in any fundamental way. It retained its authority as a source of positive law even after its subjection to vigorous historical investigation. Nor did the relationship of juris-prudence to theology and medicine, its rival faculties, undergo a profound change. Continuity rather than radical change again emerges as the dominant phenomenon; this may well be ascribed to the general Aristotelian intellectual context which Charles Schmitt and others have argued to persist alongside, if not subjacent to, the effervescent humanist developments of the Renaissance. It cannot be denied that the publicity campaign about the merits of the new education and the intellectual benefits accruing from the recovery of antiquity was a strident and successful one; the success of the humanists in imposing their style on academic life in the late fifteenth and sixteenth centuries is impressive; but at the level of the theory of language and of logic rather less seems to have happened. Historians of philosophy (notably Bocheński) have argued that formal logic went into decline in the course of the fifteenth century, and that Agricola's reforms replaced the medieval concern for the correctness of logical conclusions with a preoccupation with the content, organization and construction of argument. But jurists still cited the same scholastic core texts from the Organon as propaedeutic to legal studies. It may be that in this respect they are as a body more conservative than other faculties, although it should not be forgotten that Agricola and Ramus were promoted by jurists such as Hegendorf and Frey.

The third chapter of this book addressed the issues of interpretation and meaning directly. It would be fastidious here to repeat all its findings, but pertinent to point to the major features of legal thinking on these questions. Interpretation is a form of mediation which should never be engaged in for its own sake. The totally unambiguous and wholly explicit legal utterance of course does not require interpret-ation; but this may be no more than an unattainable ideal. Even the law of conscience which is written in all men's hearts is mediated through language, and runs the risk of misrepresentation. When the interpreter is constrained to intervene to dispel obscurity or ambigu-ity, or to make explicit how a law is to be applied, he may do this by having recourse to authority, or to theories of signification, or to definition, or to the determination of meaning through etymology, or usage, or historical or geographical context; he should follow a set procedure designed especially for the elucidation of law, and be aware that his interpretation may fall into different modes – in broad terms, those which are declarative, extensive or restrictive of the literal sense or the legislator's intention. In nearly every individual concrete case of interpretation, all this makes sense and works; but the *distinctiones* on which the practice is built – between *necessarius* and *probabilis, interpretatio* and *significatio, definitio* and *descriptio, mens legislatoris* and *ratio legis,* legal fiction and cavillation, legitimate application of the law by extension and illegitimate extension constituting effectively legislation – are logically precarious. This last distinction exemplifes the 'logic of the supplement', as we have seen. The extralinguistic principles of interpretation – custom and equity – are also both as effective in particular instances in settling points of law, and as difficult to codify logically. That this is a general phenomenon, and not one restricted to the interpretation of the Corpus Juris Civilis, was suggested by the investigation of the parallel cases of Suarez and of England; and that the law worked in spite of its difficulties with the determination of meaning emerged from the discussion of the treatment of defamation by English courts in the latter part of the period under discussion here. Some suggestions as to why Renaissance jurists were able to tolerate the inadequacies of their founding hermeneutic principles have already been put forward: the necessary reliance of an uncodifiable *mens rea*, the possible recourse to context as a means of minimizing the risk of error in interpretation; the *de jure* determination of sense which allows for the system to operate by treating 'probable' premises as apodictic. These are all shared to some degree or other with postglossators, and are even implicit in the Corpus Juris Civilis itself. We are brought back again to the question: in what ways does Renaissance jurisprudence differ in its perception of meaning and interpretation from what went before it, and what succeeded it? Was there a widespread crisis in the Renaissance about the analysis of language and meaning of the kind described by Waswo which is reflected in legal interpretation? Or does this investigation indicate rather that there is a perennial 'legal' view of language and its problems which unites in a common professional outlook Bartolus and Baldus with the most recent writers on the interpretation of law?

In what ways did Renaissance jurisprudence differ from what went before it in its perception of language? There is evidence both of continuity and of change. On the one hand, there is a common commitment, in the Middle Ages as in the Renaissance, to a mentalist approach to language. In legal terms, this means furthermore a commitment to bona fides, *mens*, and *ratio* as significant mental events which occur before any utterance or act, the presence or absence of which can alter radically the interpretation to be placed on an act or an utterance. In the Middle Ages as in the Renaissance, things (*res*) are accorded an extralinguistic status which is not called into question, and particulars are taken to be knowable objects which can be discussed in terms of general laws. This is not the position of medieval logic, in which minor premises did not imply the existence of the particular objects there named; thus it would be possible, but misleading, to show a development from medieval philosophy, with its preoccupation with formal logic, to Renaissance law, with its deployment of topics. Although Thorne claims to detect a movement from *ratio* (rational coherence) to *mens* (the historically situated intention of the lawgiver) in English law, and although it has been argued here that postglossators share the Aristotelian view that genera were more knowable than species or individuals, it remains true that medieval lawyers were committed to a referential view of the objects with which they dealt, and conformed more to topics than to the exigences of apodictic syllogisms. Furthermore, they were aware that ideas as well as words could change; it was the humanists rather more than they who insisted on the decadence of language.

If there was an area in which Renaissance lawyers radically altered the positions taken by the postglossators, it was in the area of subjective meaning and of the performative or illocutionary force of words. By adopting incidental remarks of Varro and Fortunatianus for their own purposes, they were able to adapt the traditional schema relating the objects of thought to thoughts, and thoughts to words, in order to accommodate intention; and by introducing intention into linguistic analysis, they were able to consider separately aspects of words which their predecessors had recognized but not considered closely; namely the force of words independent of or supplementary to their objective semantic content. Turamini's theory of speech acts is very close to that of Austin's, although it emerges from a quite different intellectual context; it shows an interest in expression and in reception of words which belongs traditionally to the discipline of rhetoric. In this sense it is true to say that the Renaissance lawyers followed the trend of their humanist counterparts in preferring rhetoric to logic, expression to formal coherence; but it is at the same time misleading. Turamini did not think of his suggestion about the force or performative functions of language incompatible with the claims of jurisprudence to be an art subjected to dialectical rules of argument; rather he saw it as a way of limiting the indefinite nature of the law and articulating the areas in which it might be said to lie beyond the scope of logical notation.

The preoccupation of Renaissance jurists with the limits to be placed on extensive interpretation betrays a similar desire to draw the frontiers of law in such a way as to permit the deployment of topics but not to get embroiled in the task of establishing the apodictic status of their premises. The justification of the 'rectification of the law' by equity, which operates both as a principle of justice and as one of moral parity, requires that the law be extended to encompass the *casus omissi*, but does not require that the topical arguments *a simili* and *a contrariis* which are invoked to bring this about be supported by discussions of identity and difference such as are found in Aristotle's *Metaphysics*. This separation of topics from the logical foundations on which it rests does not emerge unscathed from a thoroughgoing sceptical critique; nor does the marriage of justice and ethics suggested by the formula 'ars aequi et boni'. Heinrich Cornelius Agrippa is able to demonstrate both the trace of the profession's self-interest in its interpretative procedures and the tenuousness of the connection between law and ethics; more damagingly, Montaigne, a trained lawyer himself, is able to show that definition is an inconclusive procedure trapped within the prison-house of language, that juristic claims to knowledge are weak, and that the law's reliance on such topical arguments as *a simili* is ill-judged, since all claims to certain knowledge which rest on topics are ill-founded and under-mined by the contingent *circumstantiae* which are an indispensable part of legal argument. These and other, earlier, critiques show that even in the Middle Ages, it was possible not only to articulate some of the ideological commitments in the practice of the law (e.g. the self-interest of the profession), but also to point to the radical inadequacy of such distinctions as *mens legislatoris* and *ratio legis*. Both of these insights are, however, dependent on a mentalist approach to language and the Aristotelian hierarchy of sciences into apodictic and more or less 'probable' disciplines. Even the Renaissance speculations about rhetoric and performance in language do not seem to disturb these fundamental assumptions, in Whitehead's terms. I can myself find little evidence in the law to support Waswo's claim that Renaissance thinkers were groping towards a notion of relational semantics.

Logic in the form of topics was seen, as has been said, as a coherent and rigorous procedure built on uncertain foundations: it is thus possible to find in legal tracts such phrases as 'non omnino absurdum', which in strict logical terms could have no sense, but which show the effect of non-apodictic premises on subsequent argumentation. But did the Middle Ages and Renaissance also harbour the view that not only topical argument but the language system in itself was radically imperfect? This possibility is often expressed in terms of the fall; the story of the tower of Babel, and hence the myth of the loss of a perfect Edenic language, are popular in Renaissance imaginative literature. They are, however, rarely encountered in legal texts. This is not to say that jurists were not aware of certain limitations of the language system. They allude to the shortage of words to name the infinite (or rather indefinite) particulars of the real world, referred to in *De sophisticis elenchis*, 163a; they also discuss ambiguity in all its syntactical and nominative forms, and show how it may be an ineradicable feature of language. They are, moreover, aware of the danger of literal translation, and the risks of communicating the spirit and not the letter. The possibility that language may be separated from its essence – good faith, intention, even objective sense – is also envisaged, and the same impotence shown in considering this problem as is evident in the writings of modern philosophers; in Gadamer's unsubstantiated insistence on the 'Verhältnis zur Wahrheit', in Davidson's explicit 'principle of charity', in Habermas's 'ideal speech situation', in Grice's 'co-operative principle' and so on. Equally, the recognition that both words and concepts have a history and cannot be treated as logical constants betrays the awareness of Renaissance jurists of the logical inadequacy of the system of language.

But there are also legal systematizers (such as Bodin) and theorists of language (the precursors of the seventeenth-century English enthusiasts for the idea of a universal language) who believe that the state of law and of language is not necessarily fallen, and that *recta ratio* is a universal and infallible mental tool. They ignore the weaknesses of the *loci a circumstantiis, a simili, a contrariis, a correlativis* on which so much of the law rests, and are not deterred by the prevaricative feature of language, or the irreducible problems of usage, history, ambiguity and the determination of subjective as opposed to objective meaning. From a modern perspective, they seem both to be in a minority, and to be less perceptive than many of their contemporaries. Those who oppose them are not only sceptics such as Montaigne, whose attack on the inadequate semiosis of good faith and intention is made in the terms of the law itself: 'il n'y a que vous qui sçache si vous estes lâche et cruel, ou loyal et devotieux; les autres ne vous voyent poinct; ils vous devinent par conjectures incertaines' (*Essais*, iii.2, p. 785). They are attacked also by those jurists who argue that the law is at best an art, committed to regulating an unknowable universe in Aristotelian terms (the contingent, the particular, the potential) with insufficient logical and linguistic tools. The law in its application needs 'rectification' by equity; in its linguistic form, it requires furthermore declaration, restriction and extension. In Renaissance discussions of this last phenomenon, there are many avatars of what Derrida has called 'the logic of the supplement': the law is both sufficient to itself and simultaneously requires something to be added to it to make it complete. But it seems to me that this does not indicate blindness or naïvety on the part of Renaissance jurists: they are explicit about the limitations of the systems they employ, and are not dismayed by the fact that these systems do not provide apodictic knowledge of the real. Their position is a subtle one, and is paralleled by other subtle positions taken by Renaissance thinkers. Ramus' attack on Aristotle, for example, is based on the same inadequacies as those perceived and tolerated by jurists, since it is topical in character; it is also parasitic on the same assumptions about mentalism and about the hierarchy of knowledge. And for all its visual brilliance and claim to exhaustiveness, his dichotomizing system is no more necessary than the legal *distinctio*, to which it is closely related, as Frey, Fraunce and others recognize.

Was there a widespread crisis in the Renaissance about the analysis of language and meaning of the kind described by Waswo? It certainly seems tenable to claim, as does Waswo, that it was possible to articulate, if only implicitly or allusively, a relational view of semantics, that is, a view on which words are said to have meaning in relation to other words, and the real is a product of the language system in so far as it is knowable at all. But it also seems that the evidence produced from legal writings in this book would support Waswo's opponent Monfasani in his claim that Valla and his contemporaries were speaking within an Aristotelian paradigm with respect to mentalism and to word usage. The claim made by Waswo and others that Renaissance thinkers could argue or envisage that linguistic categories actually structure the world is inimical to mentalism; it makes mental conceptions secondary phenomena or even epiphenomena of the language system. I do not myself believe that this was the case for Renaissance lawyers, nor even that it could be the case for lawyers today. The prior existence of the world, of classes of objects and individuals in that world, of intentions and mental states, of the distinction between perception and reality are indispensable assumptions for the operation of the legal system, even if the epistemological foundations of these categories are less than secure. And even if it could be shown that it was only by a posteriori operations on the contents of consciousness that knowledge could be obtained about the world, or, to put it in Renaissance juridical terms, that the decision of a lawsuit determined its facts rather than the facts the decision (see D 33.2.19), it remains a necessary presupposition of the decision that it was preceded by facts, or of the contents of consciousness that the world had in some way and to some degree determined them. In the precise case of the language system, this results in a firm and explicit commitment to mentalism on the one hand, and on the other to a *de jure* determination of the relationship of words to the world.

We may finally ask whether this investigation supports the view that there is something like a perennial 'legal' view of language and interpretation, a common professional outlook which transcends the divisions between Middle Ages and Renaissance, and Renaissance and the present. The importance of this question for the intellectual historian lies in the implication that disciplines possess a character born of their peculiar preoccupations which can be used as a means of approach to the texts of the past. On the one hand, it is possible to be struck by similarities in outlook and approach, especially where the terms of a problem remain approximately constant: in the case of law, the nexus of written statute, individual case, changing circumstances, supposed legislative intent and the requirements of equity presents something like a perennial configuration of issues which have common conceptual problems. I have attempted to suggest this before in a general study of the problems faced by interpreters of the law from Justinian to the present day; and one may sense the problems in such commonplace assertions as that recently uttered by an American President on declaring the nomination of a conservative to the judiciary: 'I want a judge who will interpret the law as it is, not one who engages in new legislation.'

But on the other hand, Renaissance jurists, like their philosophical, medical and theological counterparts, were eclectic, and while recognizing that their discipline was encompassed by certain frontiers, did not feel that their competence was limited in the same way, or that they were excluded from the speculations of other disciplines and the fruits of humanistic learning. Tiraqueau, Nevizzani, More, Bacon were all lawyers whose writings extend over the whole range of human intellectual enquiry, and who in different ways characterized the complex patterns of thought of their contemporaries as much as they reflect the perspective peculiar to the 'legal mind', if there is such a thing. But it is not implausible to suggest that a given configuration of intellectual concerns may offer a privileged access to past thinkers preoccupied by similar problems; and the example of eclectic thinkers of the past may embolden modern scholars to attempt to grasp the particular configuration of their intellectual concerns. This study may not offer an answer to the question whether access to past modes of thought may be obtained by adopting a given disciplinary outlook, but if it brings this possibility to the attention of historians, it may yet have served a useful purpose.

Bibliography of primary sources

This is not a full descriptive bibliography, nor an exhaustive list of law books of the period 1460–1630, but rather a finding list of the principal sources of this study and a record of those books germane to it that I have been unable to locate. In the latter case, the citation source is given: either as D (=Georgius Draudius, *Bibliotheca classica*, Frankfurt, 1625) or L (=Martinus Lipenius, *Bibliotheca realis juridica*, Frankfurt, 1678: supplement, Leipzig, 1757). In the case of rare items I have indicated the location (BL=British Library, London; HAB=Herzog-August-Bibliothek, Wolfenbüttel; PBN=Bibiothèque Nationale, Paris; OB=Bodleian Library, Oxford). Dates in brackets after titles indicate the earliest edition that I have been able to trace, or, in the case of fifteenth-century authors, the date of composition. I have recorded the details of other editions where this has seemed relevant. Cross-reference is made to latinized and vernacular forms of the surname where this diverges significantly. In listing books under one or the other form, I have not sought consistency, but I have used the surname most commonly found in library catalogues. I have standardized, where appropriate, i and j, u and v, omitted accents, and expanded abbreviations and contractions. All references to Frankfurt and to Frankfurt am Main.

Agustín, Antonio, *De legibus et senatusconsultis liber. Adiunctis legum antiquarum et senatusconsultorum fragmentis, cum notis Fulvii Ursini*, Rome, 1583, 4to.

Albericus de Rosate, *Dictionarium iuris*, Venice, 1573, fol.

Tractatus de statutis, in *Tractatus iuris universi*, ii.2–85.

Alciato, Andrea, *Opera*, 4 vols., Basle, 1582, fol.

De iuris interpretis iudicium, in Lagus, *Methodica iuris utriusque traditio*, p. 1022; *Clarissimorum iurisconsultorum tractatus*, pp. 146–7; and *Cynosura iuris*, iii, 29–30. See also *Opera*, iv.346 (*Parerga*, ii.42).

De praesumptionibus, Cologne, 1580, 8vo (D records an edition containing treatises of this title by Alciato, Henricus Boich, Guido Papa and Joannes Oldendorp, Frankfurt, 1580, 8vo).

De verborum significatione libri quatuor, Lyon, 1530, fol. A much-published treatise and commentary on D 50.16; most sixteenth-century reprintings are recorded in the *Index aureliensis*. A compendium of commentaries entitled *Commentarii ad tit[ulum] Dig[estorum] de verborum significatione trium illustrium interpretum, Alciati, Brechaei, Forneri* appeared in Lyon in 1589, fol. HAB. See also s.v. Langenbeck.

Althusius (Althaus), Joannes, *De iniuriis et famosis libellis*, Basle, 1601, 4to. L.
Iurisprudentiae Romanae methodice digestae libri duo (1589), *editio altera*, Herborn, 1592, 8vo. HAB.

Alvaradus, Didacus Rodericus, *De coniecturata mente defuncti ad methodum redigenda*, Frankfurt, 1599, 8vo. HAB.

Appellus (Apel), Joannes, *Dialogus de studio iuris recte instituendo, exercendo*, in *Cynosura iuris*, i.179–214 (see also below, s.v. Cantiuncula).

Arnoldus, Laurentius, *Iurisprudentia ethica*, Frankfurt, 1615, 4to. D.
Tractatus in quo sit collatio philosophiae moralis cum iure scripto, Frankfurt, 1606, 4to. HAB.

Axiomata legum, ex receptis iuris utriusque libris, et interpretum commentariis, ordine certo, et in literas alphabeticas distincta . . ., Lyon, 1547, 8vo. HAB.

Baiardus, Ioannes Baptista, *Additiones et annotationes ad Julii Clari Receptarum Sententiarum librum quintum*, Lyon, 1600, fol. PBN.

Banvinus, Fridericus, *De famosis libellis et calumniatoribus*, Paris, 1562, 4to. L.

Baron, Eguinarius, *De ratione docendi discendique iuris civilis ad iuventutem [commonefactio]* (1546), in *Clarissimorum iurisconsultorum tractatus*, pp. 141–5, and *Cynosura iuris*, i.37–40. See also s.v. Lagus.

Baudouin (Balduinus), François, *Ad leges de famosis libellis et de calumniatoribus, commentarius*, Paris, 1562, 4to. HAB.
De optima iuris docendi discendique ratione fragmentum epistolae (1545?), in *Cynosura iuris*, i.62–6.

Bayro, Petrus de, *De nobilitate facultatis, utrum medicina et philosophia sint nobiliores utroque iure: et qui doctores earundem facultatum nobiliores ac digniores existant: quomodoque incedere ac invicem praecedere debeant?*, Turin, 1512, fol. D.

Bello, Joannes, *Communes iurium sententiae*, Lyon, 1549, 8vo. HAB.

Beroa, Joannes Andreas, *Iurisconsultus sive de principiis et rationibus iuris*, Venice, 1615, fol. D.

Besold, Christoph, *Ad titulos I.III.IV.V et VI libri I Pandectarum commentarii*, Tübingen, 1616, 4to. HAB.
Templum iustitiae, sive de addiscenda et exercenda iurisprudentia dissertatio, Tübingen, 1616, 4to. HAB.

Bocerus, Henricus, *Commentarius in titulum unum Codicis de famosis libellis*, Tübingen, 1611, 8vo. HAB.

Bodaeus, Stephanus, *Prosopopoeia iurisprudentiae: qualis esse bonus iurisconsultus debeat*, in *Cynosura iuris*, iii.33–7.

Bodin, Jean, *Iuris universi distributio*, Cologne, 1580, 8vo.

Bolognetti, Alberto, *De lege, iure et aequitate disputationes* (1570): *postrema editio*, Wittenberg, 1594, 8vo; also in *Tractatus iuris universi*, i.289–323.

Bolongninus, Joannes, *De iuris et facti significatione multiplici, differentia, etc.*, Lyon, 1547. L.

Bona Cossa, Hippolytus, *Aureum repertorium alphabeticum de praesumptionibus*, Venice, 1580, 4to. D.

Borcholten, Joanne, *Commentaria de verborum obligationibus*, Helmstedt, 1595, 4to. HAB.

Breche, Jean, *Ad titulum Pandectarum de verborum et rerum significatione commentarii*, Lyon, 1556, fol. (see also above, s.v. Alciato), OB.

Aphorismi iurisprudentiae: opus advocatis atque ideo omnibus qui in foris iudicialibus versantur seu pragmaticis utile et pernecessarium, Paris, 1552, 8vo. HAB.

Brederodus, Petrus Cornelius, *Thesaurus dictionum et sententiarum iuris civilis*, Lyon, 1585, fol. OB.

Brismannus, Paschasius, *De recte ineunda studii iuris ratione iudicium*, Helmstedt, 1594, fol. HAB.

Brisson, Barnabé, *De formulis et sollemnibus populi Romani verbis libri viii* (1583), Frankfurt, 1592, 4to.

Lexicon iuris sive de verborum quae ad ius pertinent significatione (1559), Frankfurt, 1587, fol. OB.

Bronchorst, Everardus, ἐναντιοφανῶν *centuriae duae*, Hanau, 1597, 8vo. HAB.

Budé, Guillaume, *Opera*, 4 vols., Basle, 1557, fol.

Busius (Buis), Paulus, *Subtiliorum exercitationum legalium libri vii*, Cologne, 1626, 12mo. PBN.

Caepolla (Cipolla) Bartholomaeus, *Opera omnia*, Lyon, 1577, fol.

De interpretatione legis extensiva, ed. Gabriel Sarayna, Venice, 1557, 8vo.

In titulum de verborum et rerum significatione doctissima commentaria (1460), ed. Vincentius Porticus, Lyon, 1551, fol. HAB.

Cagnoli, Girolamo, see s.v. Decius.

Calvinus (Kahl), Johannes, *Lexicon iuris*, Frankfurt, 1600, fol.

Cantiuncula (Chansonnette), Claudius, *De ratione studii legalis paraenesis*, in *Clarissimorum iurisconsultorum tractatus*, pp. 72–119; Lagus, *Methodica iuris utriusque traditio*, pp. 973–1008; and *Cynosura iuris*, i.89–98.

Topica legalis, Basle, 1545, fol. This volume contains also the commentaries of Apel and Gammaro.

Carbone a Costacciaro, Lodovico, *Bellum legale inter leges et consuetudines*, Bologna, 1592, 4to. L.

Carninus, Claudius, *Tractatus de vi et potestate legum humanarum*, Douai, 1608, 4to. HAB.

Carolis, Jacobus de, *Gemmatus pavo, coloribus seu capitibus distinctus, in quo iuris canonici et civilis, variae per modum etymologiae, quaestionis, diffinitionis, declarationis et distinctionis tanguntur materiae*, Venice, 1594, 8vo. D.

Celichus, Johannes, *De aequitate quid et quantum praestet in legibus liber*, Wittenberg, 1602, 8vo. HAB.

Chansonnette, see Cantiuncula.

Charonda (Caron, Le Caron), Ludovicus, *De verborum obligationibus scholia*, Wittenberg, 1601, 8vo. HAB.

Chasseneuz, Barthélemy de, *Catalogus gloriae mundi* (1528), Paris, 1546. Many reprintings.

Clarissimorum et praestantissimorum iurisconsultorum, tam veterum quam recentium, varii utilissimi diu multumque desiderati tractatus: partim de iuris studio recte instituendo, partim etiam de utriusque pontificii et caesarei iuris oeconomia, Cologne, 1585, 8vo. HAB. Contains the works of twelve authors.

Claro, Guilio, *Receptarum sententiarum opera* (1559), Lyon, 1600, fol. PBN.
Colerus, Christopherus, *De ratione discendi ius civile diatribe*, Frankfurt, 1603, 8vo. D. Printed with Cujas's *Oratio* (q.v.).
Concenatius, Jacobus, *Epitomes oeconomicae artis iurisprudentiae*, Basle, 1562, fol. HAB.
Coke, Sir Edward, *The reports*, ed. John Henry Thomas and John Farquhar Fraser, London, 1826.
The first part of the institutes of the lawes of England, or a commentarie upon Littleton, not the name of a lawyer onely, but the law itself, 2nd ed., London, 1629, fol.
Connan (Conan, Connat), François de, *Commentarii iuris civilis*, 2 vols., Paris, 1553, vol. PBN.
Constitutio criminalis carolina: die peinliche Gerichtsordnung Kaiser Karls V., ed. J. Kohler and Willy Scheel, Halle, 1900.
Contius (Le Conte), Antonius, *Methodus discendi iuris elegantissima*, in *Cynosura iuris*, i.169–73. (See also below s.v. *Corpus*.)
Copius, Bernhartus, *De studio iuris oratio*, in *Cynosura iuris*, iii.3–28.
Coras, Jean de, *Tractatus de iuris arte* (1560), in *Tractatus de iuris arte duorum clarissimorum iurisconsultorum Ioannis Corasii et Ioachimi Hopperi*, Lyon, 1591, 8vo.; also in *Tractatus iuris universi*, i.59–81.
Corpus iuris civilis iustinianei [cum commentariis Accursii, scholiis Contii et Dionysii Gothofredi ad Accursium], ed. Joannes Felius, Lyon, 1627, fol.
Corvesius, Petrus, *Methodicus sive de ratione artis, in quo disseritur, an civilis scientia methodo tractari possit*, Lyon, 1547, 8vo. HAB.
Corvinus, Arnoldus, *Ad titulum de verborum significatione commentarius*, Amsterdam, 1646, 12mo.
Cowell, John, *Institutiones iuris Anglicani ad methodum et seriem Institutionum imperialium compositae et digestae*, Cambridge, 1605, 8vo. BL.
The interpreter, London, 1607, 4to.
Cranius, Henricus Andreas, *Dissertatio de gravi et frequentissimo iniuriarum et famosorum libellorum delicto*, Helmstedt, 1600, 8vo. L.
Cujas, Jacques, *Opera*, 5 vols., Lyon, 1606. fol.
Ad titulum de verborum significationibus [sic] commentarius, Frankfurt, 1595, 8vo.
De ratione docendi iuris oratio, Strasbourg, 1600, 4to. See also s.v. Colerus.
Cynosura iuris, see s.v. Reusner.
Dannhauerus, Johannes Conradus, *Idea boni interpretis et malitiosi calumniatoris quae obscuritate dispulsa, verum sensum a falso discernere in omnibus auctorum scriptis ac orationibus docet, et plene respondet ad quaestionem unde scis hunc esse sensum et non alium. Omnium facultatum studiosis perquam utilis*, Strasbourg, 1630, 8vo. PBN.
a (von) Dassel, Hardewigus, *Idea boni iurisconsulti, hoc est, de optimo genere docendi interpretandi iuris civilis . . .*, Hamburg, 1589, 8vo. HAB.
Decius (de Dexia) Philippus, *In titulum Digestorum de regulis iuris [commentarius] (1525) cum additionibus Hieronymi Cuchalon, et cum recente et perutili*

auctario et annotationibus Caroli Molinei (Du Moulin), Lyon, 1545, 8vo. Reprinted in a compendium of commentaries on D 50.17 which includes those of Philippus Francus (de Franchi) (1499), Johannes Ferrarius (1541), Girolamo Cagnoli (1576) and Jacobus Raevardus (Reyvaert) (1568), and which appeared in Lyon in 1593, fol.

Delrius, Marcus Antonius, *Elementorum sive principiorum iuris eptiome ex commentariis Ioachimi Hypperi* [sic] *compendiose concinnata*, in Cynosura iuris, ii.166–212.

Dhumbert, Joannes, *In omnes titulos novem primorum librorum Codicis Justiniani.. . explicationes*, Lyon, 1558, 8vo. HAB.

A discourse upon the exposicion and understanding of statutes, with Sir Thomas Egerton's additions, ed. and introd. Samuel E. Thorne, San Marino, 1942.

Doneau (Donellus), Hugues, *Opera omnia*, 12 vols., Lucca 1762–70, fol.

Ad titulum Digestorum de rebus dubiis commentarius, Bourges, 1571, 8vo. PBN.

Duarenus, see s.v. Le Douaren.

Du Moulin (Molinaeus), Charles, *Nova et analytica explicatio rubricae et legum I et II Digestorum de verborum obligationibus* (1566), Jena, 1588, 8vo. HAB. See also s.v. Decius.

Egerton, Sir Thomas, *A speech touching the post-nati*, London, 1609. See also s.v. *A discourse.*

Ehemius, Chrstopherus, *De principiis iuris* (1568), Hanau, 1601, 8vo. HAB.

Elenus, Hieronymus, *De optima facilimaque perdiscendi iuris civilis ratione*, in *Cynosura iuris*, i.73–87.

Enchiridion titulorum aliquot iuris, videlicet, de verborum et rerum significatione, ex Pandectis, de regulis iuris, tum ex Pandectis, tum ex Decretalibus et Sexto. De gradibus affinitatis ex Pandectis. Ad haec, rubricae omnes caesarei et pontificii iuris, Lyon, 1567, 12mo. HAB.

Enchiridion titulorum iuris, quibus universum pene ius summatim continetur: de verborum obligationibus, de verborum significatione, de diversis regulis iuris antiqui, rubricae iuris. Omnia secundum editionem Florentinam, et cum brevibus ac novis annotatunculis, Louvain, 1554, 12mo. HAB.

Everardus (Everaerts), Nicolaus, Amsterodamus, *Ordo studendi in iure civili*, in *Clarissimorum iurisconsultorum tractatus*, pp. 254–61, and *Cynosura iuris*, i.160–1.

Everardus (Everaerts), Nicolaus, Mitelburgus, *Consilium de legibus praecipuis in Codice et Pandectis iuris studioso perdiscendis*, in *Cynosura iuris*, 162–4.

Topica seu loci legales, Louvain, 1516, fol. OB. Also Basle, 1544, fol., and Lyon, 1579, 8vo.

de Federicis, Stephanus, *De interpretatione iuris commentarii IIII iam recens studiosis restituti et a mendis, quantum fieri potuit, repurgati* (c. 1495), Frankfurt, 1535, fol. HAB. Also Cologne, 1577, Frankfurt, 1615, Lyon, 1636, and *Tractatus iuris universi*, i.208–25.

Ferrarius, see s.v. Decius.

Finckelhusius, Laurentius, *Commentatiunculae, sive orationes duae de praestantia [iuris]prudentiae et causis mutationis legum*, Rostock, 1597, 4to. D.

Floridus, Franciscus, *In M. Actii Planti aliorumque Latinae linguae scriptorum calumniatores apologia, nunc primum ab auctore aucta atque recognita. Eiusdem de iuris civilis interpretibus liber, itidem auctus et recognitus*, Basle, 1540, fol. HAB.

Forster or Förster, Valentin Wilhelm, *Interpres sive de interpretatione iuris libri duo*, Wittenberg, 1613, 8vo. HAB.

Fournier (Fornerus), Guillaume, *In titulum de verborum significatione commentarii*, Orléans, 1584, 4to. OB. See also s.v. Alciato.

Francus (de Franchi), see s.v. Decius.

Fraunce, Abraham, *The lawiers logike, exemplifying the praecepts of logik by the practise of the common lawe*, London, 1588, 8vo.

Freher, Marquard, *Sulpitius sive de aequitate commentarius ad legem I Codicis de legibus*, Frankfurt, 1608, 4to. HAB.

Freigius (Frey), Joannes Thomas, *Idea boni et perfecti iurisconsulti*, in *Cynosura iuris*, iii.D1–D3.

De logica iurisconsultorum (1582), *editio postrema*, Basle, 1590, 8vo. HAB. Another edition in 1587, D.

Partitiones iuris utriusque, hoc est omnium iuris tam civilis quam canonici materiarum in tabulas apta et illustris digestio, Basle, 1571, fol. OB.

Freytag, Laurentius, *Oratio de praestantia et laudibus templi iustitiae iustinianae*, Tübingen, 1603, 4to. D.

Frischlin, Nicodemus, *De studio iuris ac legum elegia*, in *Cynosura iuris*, i.215–16.

Froschius, Franciscus, *Isagoge in iuris civilis studium*, Strasbourg, 1554, D.

Gail, Andreas, *Practicae observationes*, Cologne, 1580, fol. L. Subsequent editions in 1595, 1601 and 1616.

Gallus, Georgius, *Disputatio de legibus et longa consuetudine, deque iuris et facti ignorantia, praeside Scipione Gentili*, Altdorf, 1591, 4to. HAB.

Gammaro, Pietro Andrea, *De extensionibus* (*c.* 1510), in *Tractatus iuris universi*, xviii.247–60.

De veritate ac excellentia legalis scientiae (1540), *ibid.*, i.132–47.

[*In Topica Cantiunculae commentarius*], see s.v. Cantiuncula.

Gentianus, Franciscus, *De conciliatione legum . . .*, Venice, 1574, 4to. D.

Gentili, Alberigo, *De iuris interpretibus*, London, 1582, 8vo.

In titulum Digestorum de verborum significatione commentarius, Hanau, 1614, 4to. OB.

Gilhausen, Ludovicus, *Commentarius novus et singularis, legum atque praxeos studiosis pernecessarius, in titulum decimum libri 47 Pandectarum qui est de iniuriis et famosis libellis. Interiecta est materia legis diffamari Codicis de ingenius manumissis*, Lich, 1602, 8vo. HAB.

Gilkens, Peter, *Iurisprudentiam, nedum constare ratione, sed esse scientiam proprie dictam contra calumnias Angeli Thii et Iacobi Zabarellae philosophiae doctorum . . .*, 1605, 4to. HAB.

Goeddaeus, Johannes, *Commentarius repetitae praelectionis in titulum xvi libri 1 Pandectarum de verborum et rerum significatione* (1591), Nassau, 1614, 8vo (5th ed.).

Goina, Gianbattista, *Dialogus, quod philosophi iurisconsultos dignitate praedant*, Venice, n.d., 8vo. PBN.

Goltstenius, Chilianus, *De praecipuis materiarum iuris sedibus epistola*, in *Cynosura iuris*, i.158–60.

Grasecius, Paulus, *Conclusiones de consuetudinis natura, causis, effectis*, Strasbourg, 1591, 4to. L.

Grégoire (Gregorius), Pierre, *De iuris arte methodo et praeceptis*, Lyon, 1580, 12mo. HAB. A précis appeared in *Clarissimorum iurisconsultorum tractatus*, ii.120–6.

Gribaldus alias Mopha, Matthaeus, *De methodo ac ratione studendi [in iure]*, Cologne, 1553, 8vo. HAB. Editions in 1556, 1582 and a précis in *Cynosura iuris*, i.110–30.

Hase, see s.v. Lagus.

Hatton, Sir Christopher, *A treatise concerning statutes* (*c.* 1590), London 1677, 12mo.

Hawarde, John, *Les Reportes del cases in Camera Stellata (1593–1609)*, ed. William Paley Baildon, [London], 1894.

Hegendorf (Hegendorphinus), Christoph, *Dialectica legalis, sive disserendi, demonstrandi ars, ita iuri civili accommodata, ut et nihilominus sit omni studiorum generi usui futura*, Lyon, 1536, 8vo. HAB.

Epitome tyrocinii iuris civilis (1540), in *Clarissimorum iurisconsultorum tractatus*, pp. 148–97 (a fragment in *Cynosura iuris*, i.98–109).

Rhetoricae legalis libri duo, Frankfurt, 1541, 8vo. HAB.

Hemmingius, Nicolaus, *De lege naturae apodictica methodus concinnnata* (1562), Wittenberg, 577, 8vo.

Holosten, Arnoldus, *De privilegiis statutorum et consuetudinum*, Cologne, 1566, 8vo. L.

Hopperus, Joachimus, *Eduardus, sive de vera iurisprudentia, ad Regem libri 12 . . .*, Antwerp, 1590, fol. D.

Tractatus de iuris arte, in *Tractatus iuris universi*, i.81–103. See also above s.v. Coras and Delrius.

Hotman, François, *Opera*, 3 vols., Geneva, 1599, fol.

Iurisconsultus sive de optimo genere iuris interpretandi (1559), in *Cynosura iuris*, i.106–65. Other editions in 1566 and 1569, L.

Hunnius, Helfrich-Ulrich, *Tractatus de authoritate et interpretatione iuris tam canonici quam civilis*, Marburg, 1630, 8vo. HAB.

Ilovius, Stanislaus, *De laudibus iurisprudentiae oratio*, Bologna, 1565, 4to. HAB.

Kahl, see s.v. Calvinus.

Lagus (Hase), Conradus, *Methodica iuris utriusque traditio*, Lyon, 1562, 8vo. HAB. Contains also treatises by Cantiuncula, Le Douaren, Baron and Alciato. 'Ex ore Conradi Lagi annotata, una cum summariis et scholiis Justini Gobleri'.

Langenbeck, Detlev, *Andreae Alciati libri de verborum significatione in gratiam studiosorum in perutilem et iucundam tabulam contracti*, Cologne, 1555, 8vo. PBN.

Le Douaren (Duarenus), François, *De ratione docendi discendique iuris conscripta epistola*, in *Clarissimorum iurisconsultorum tractatus*, pp. 120–40; Lagus, *Methodica iuris utriusque traditio*, pp. 1008–19, and *Cynosura iuris*, i.17–37.

Lersner, Jakob, *Oratio de dignitate utilitate iuris civilis, verum eius usum, contra misonomos ostendens*, Cologne, 1542, 8vo. HAB.

Mantica, Francisco, *Tractatus de coniecturis ultimarum voluntatum in libros duodecim distinctos* (1580), Geneva, 1611, fol. PBN. Editions in 1587, 1605, 1607, 1612, 1615 and 1620.

Maranus, Guilielmus, *De iustitia et aequitate*, Toulouse, 1622, fol. L (Lipenius also records an edition in 1628).

March, John, *Actions for slander, or a methodical collection under certain grounds and heads of what words are actionable in the law*, London, 1648, 4to.

Martinus, Fridericus, *Conclusiones de consuetudine*, Ingolstadt, 1589, 4to. L.

Massa, Antonius, *De exercitatione iurisperitorum seu de iuris arte liber*, Frankfurt, 1600, 8vo. D.

Masson, Jean Papyre, *Philocalia sive de recta iuris interpretandi ratione*, Paris, 1605, 8vo. L.

Mathesilanus, Matthaeus, *Tractatus extensionis ex utroque iure elucubratus*, in Caepolla, *De interpretatione legis extensiva*, fols. 57–67.

Matthaeacius (Matteacci), Angelus, *De via et ratione artificiosa iuris universi libri duo*, Venice, 1591, fol. HAB.

Medices, Sebastianus, *De legibus, statutis et consuetudine tractatus*, Cologne, 1574, 8vo. HAB.

Menochio, Jacopo, *Consilium de legendis interpretibus super principaliores iuris tractatus*, in *Cynosura iuris*, i.167–8.

De praesumptionibus, coniecturis, signis et indiciis commentaria, Cologne, 1595, fol. OB.

Mercier (Mercerus), Jean, *Conciliator, sive ars conciliandorum eorum que in iure contraria videntur*, Bourges, 1587, 8vo. PBN. Other editions in 1597 and 1610.

Metzner, Leonhard, *Disputatio de iniuriis et famosis libellis*, Copenhagen, 1613, 4to. L.

Modus legendi abbreviaturas in utroque iure occurrentes. Cui accesserunt legum flosculi, item brocardica iuris seu communes iurium sententiae, Cologne, 1577, 8vo. D.

Molinaeus, see s.v. Du Moulin.

Mommerus, Aegidius, *De ratione legendi discendique iura* (1554), in *Tractatus tres de modo discendi, docendi et exercendi iura*, ed. Otho Melander, Lich, 1605.

Mundius a Rodach, Georgius, *De diffamationibus, earumque remediis commentarius theorico-practicus*, Hanau, 1628, 8vo. PBN.

Muret, Marc-Antoine, *Commentarius in quattuor titulos e primo Digestorum Iuris Civilis, de origine iuris, de legibus, senatusque consultis, de constitutionibus principum, de officio eius cui mandata est iurisdictio*, Ferrara, 1581, 8vo. HAB.

Neideccerus, Laurentius, *Dialectica iuris civilis et disserendi, imo iudicandi ars*, Mainz, 1601, 8vo. HAB.

Nevizzani, Giovanni, *Utrum expediat multos habere libros*, in *Clarissimorum iurisconsultorum tractatus*, pp. 277–83.

Oestenius, Johannes, *De iure non scripto* . . ., Greifswald, 1590, 8vo. HAB.
Oratio de iure scripto ac aequo bono, utrum plus valeat, Greifswald, 1589, 8vo. HAB.

Oldendorp, Joannes, *Opera*, 2 vols., Basle, 1559, fol.
Interpretatio privilegiis duplicis, quod Friderichus primus . . . *concessit bonarum literarum studiosis*, [Marburg], 1543, 8vo. HAB.
De iure et aequitate forensis disputatio, Cologne, 1573, 16mo. HAB.
Iuris naturalis gentium et civilis εἰσαγωγή, Antwerp, 1539.

Olingerus, Paulus, *Iuris artis totius atque methodi absolutissimae vera et principalissimae divisionis* . . . *singularis et brevissima quaedam elucidatio*, Strasbourg, 1555, 8vo. HAB.

Pacius (Pace), Julius, *De iuris civilis difficultate ac docendi methodo, oratio*, Heidelberg, 1585, 8vo. BL; also in *Cynosura iuris*, ii.81–105.
Synopsis seu oeconomia iuris utriusque . . ., Strasbourg, 1620, fol.
Tituli tractatusque iuris civilis studio in primis necessarii. De origine iuris. De verborum significatione. De diversis regulis iuris antiqui. Annotationibus delectis et Julii Pacii argumentis illustrati, 3rd ed. Geneva, 1589, 8vo. HAB.
Tractatus de iuris methodo libri duo, Speyer, 1597, 8vo. D.

Papponius, Hieronymus, *Interpretatio tituli Digestorum de verborum obligationibus*, Venice, 1604, 4to. HAB.

Pelleus, Ludovicus, *Confutatio eorum qui ius civile artis aut scientiae titulo non esse donandum assumere*, in *Tractatus iuris universi*, i.103–5.

Phreislebius, Christophorus, *Paratitla seu annotationes ad iuris utriusque titulos, legitimae scientiae studiosis, praesertim tyronibus non minus necessaria quam utilia*, Lyon, 1544, 8vo. HAB.

Pistor, Modestinius, *Index locorum communium totius iuris*, in *Cynosura iuris*, i.131–58.

Ponte, Olradus de, Laudensis, *Consilium iv utrum expediat multos habere libros*, in *Clarissimorum iurisconsultorum tractatus*, pp. 262–77.

de Praetiis, Simon, *De ultimarum voluntatum interpretatione tractatus*, Lyon, 1587, fol. OB.

von Pritzen, Joachim Georg, *Tractatus quadripartitus de convitiis et calumniis germanicis*, Frankfurt, 1618, L.

Questiones de iuris subtilitatibus, ed. Hermann Fitting, Berlin, 1894.

Raevardus (Reyvaert), Jacobus, *De auctoritate prudentium liber singularis*, Antwerp, 1566, 8vo. HAB.
[*Commentarius in titulum De regulis iuris antiqui*], see s.v. Decius

Rebuffi, Pierre, *In titulum Digestorum de verborum et rerum significatione commentaria* (1576), 2nd ed., Lyon, 1586, fol. OB.

Reusner, Nicolaus, χειραγωγία *sive cynosura iuris, quae est, farrago selectissimorum libellorum isagogicorum de iuris arte, omniumque rationum docendae discendae iurisprudentiae, a summis et praestantissimis saeculi nostri iureconsultis conscriptorum*, 3 vols. Speyer, 1588–9, 8vo. PBN.

a Riberteria, Joannes, *Topicon iuris libri quatuor quibus ad civilis philosophiae studium facilis patet aditus*, Paris, 1575, D.

Rodericus Alvaradus, see s.v. Alvaradus.

Rogerius, Constantinus, *Singularis tractatus de iuris interpretatione* (1463), Lyon and Turin, 1550, 8vo. HAB. Also in *Tractatus iuris universi* i.386–94. *Eruditus tractatus de legis potentia*, Lyon and Turin, 1550, 8vo. HAB. Also in *Tractatus iuris universi*, i.395–403.

St German, Christopher, *Two dialogues in English, between a Doctor of Divinity, and a student in the laws of England, of the grounds of the said laws and of conscience* (1532), ed. T.F.T. Plucknett and J.L. Barton, London, 1974.

Salazar, Petrus, *De usu et consuetudine tractatus*, Frankfurt, 1600, 8vo. HAB.

Sapcote, Jerome, *Ad primas leges Digestorum de verborum et rerum significatione*, Venice, 1579, 4to. PBN.

Savius, Aurelius David, *In Pandectarum titulum de verborum et rerum significatione tractatus isagogicus*, Lyon, 1546, 8vo. HAB.

Scappius, Antonius, *De iure non scripto*, Venice, 1586, fol. L.

Schardius, Simon, *Lexicon iuridicum*, Cologne, 1593, fol. L.

Schefferus, Iohannes Reichardus, *Dicaeopaedia, hoc est, iurisprudentiae institutio*, Basle, 1579, 8vo. HAB.

Schickhardus, Martinus, *Logica iuridica*, Herborn, 1615, 8vo. HAB.

Schmugk, David, *Apologeticus contra iuris studiosorum obtrectatores*, Frankfurt, 1630, 8vo. HAB.

Schneidewinus, Johannes, *In quatuor Institutionum imperialium . . . libri commentarii* (c. 1568), 9th ed., Strasbourg and Frankfurt, 1677, 4to.

Scribonius, Volckmarus, *Introductio ad iurisprudentiam, in qua natura eius explicatur, et germana eam docendi et discendi ratio demonstratur*, Leipzig, 1611, 12mo. D.

Speckhan, Eberhardus, *Tractatus brevis et succinctus de difficultate iuris Romani . . .* (1590), Helmstedt, 1600, 8vo. HAB.

Spiegel, Jacobus, *Lexicon iuris civilis* (1538), Basle, 1569, fol. HAB.

Steinmetzius, Joannes, *Oratio de nobilissima iurisprudentia, habita in inclyta [academia] Giessena*, Giessen, 1610, 4to. D.

Stephanus, Matthias, *Methodica tractatio de arte iuris*, Greifswald, 1615, 8vo. HAB.

Suarez, Francisco, *Tractatus de legibus ac deo legislatore* (1612), Lyon, 1613, fol. PBN.

Suffredus, Petrus, *De iuris arte et praestantia legum Romanarum fragmentum*, in *Cynosura iuris*, i.72–3.

Swinburne, Henry, *A briefe treatise of testaments and last wils* (1590–1), London, 1635, 4to. OB.

Teuberus, Michael, *Methodicus ordo operum iure dantibus necessarius* (1558), in *Tractatus tres de modo discendi, docendi et exercendi iura*, ed. Otho Melander.

Thesaurus tyrocinii legalis, id est, de iuris studio recte instituendo, utriusque tam civilis quam canonici iuris oeconomia, Cologne, 1607, 8vo. D.

Thomingius, Jacobus, *Modus et ratio discendae iurisprudentiae*, in *Cynosura iuris*, i.66–71.

Tituli in sequenti enchiridio contenti ii sunt: de verborum et rerum significatione ex Pandectis, de regulis iuris, tum ex Pandectis, tum ex Decretalibus et Sexto., de gradibus affinitatis ex Pandectis. Rubricae omnes caesarei et pontificii iuris (1542), n.p., 1590 8vo. HAB.

Tituli tractatusque iuris civilis studio in primis necessarii, Geneva, 1572, 12mo. HAB. Other editions 1589, 1597, 1598, 1601, 1604, 1622. Contains D 1.2, D 50.16 and D 50.17.

Tractatus universi iuris, 18 vols., Venice, 1584, fol.

Tractatus tres de modo discendi docendi et exercendi iura, ed. Otho Melander, Lich, 1605, 8vo. HAB. Contains treatises by Teuberus, Vulteius and Mommerus.

Treterus, Jacobus, *Distributio titulorum iuris de verborum significatione et de regulis iuris ad Institutiones iustinianeas*, Frankfurt, 1625, 12mo. HAB.

Tuldenus, Diodorus, *De principiis iurisprudentiae*, Louvain, 1621. HAB.

Turamini, Alessandro, *De exaequatione legatorum et fideicommissorum disputatio paradoxica*, Naples, 1593, 4to. PBN.

Omnes iuris interpretationes habitae, dum in humanis agebat, in titulos Digestorum de legibus, de legatis, de acquirenda possessione, et de iure fisci (1592), Venice, 1606, 4to.

de Vergeriis, Aurelius, *Ad quaestionem de famosis libellis tractatulus*, Strasbourg, 1564, 4to. HAB.

Vigelius, Nicolaus, *Compendiosa discendi iuris et de iis respondendi ars*, Frankfurt, 1598, 8vo. D.

Examen iurisconsultorum . . . cum adiunctis testimoniis, quibus authoris iurisprudentia pro vera agnoscitur, Venice, 1593, 8vo. HAB.

Iuris civilis universi absolutissima methodus, Basle, 1561, fol. OB.

Methodus iuris controversi, Basle, 1606, fol. HAB.

Viviennus, Georgius, *Enchiridion de verborum ac rerum significatione titulis xvi libri Digestorum quinquagesimi per ordinem alphabeti*, Cologne, 1570, 8vo. HAB.

Vulteius, Hermannus, *De studio iuris* προλεγόμενον, in *Tractatus tres de modo discendi, docendi et exercendi iura*, ed. Otho Melander.

Tractatus tres. I Idea iuris logica . . . II Diatribe de causis iuris constituentibus III expositio xvi posteriorum libri ii Institutionum ad ultimas voluntates pertinentium, Frankfurt, 1586, 8vo. HAB.

Wesenbeck, Matthäus, *Exempla iurisprudentiae*, Basle, 1573, 8vo. HAB.

Oeconomia iuris canonici, in *Clarissimorum iurisconsultorum tractatus*, pp. 48–120.

Prolegomena iurisprudentiae, Leipzig, 1584, 8vo. HAB. Excerpted in *Clarissimorum iurisconsultorum tractatus*, pp. 198–253, and *Cynosura iuris*, i.41–53, with the title *Prolegomenon de iuris arte et scientia comparanda*.

West, William, *Symbolaeography*, London, 1592, 4to.

Zazius (Zäsy), Udalricus, *Opera omnia*, 6 vols., Lyon, 1549–51, fol.

Zoannettus, Franciscus, *Tractatus de moribus maiorum et longa consuetudine*, Venice, 1565, 8vo. L.

Index of citations from the Corpus Juris Civilis

In the following index, no distinction has been made between references to the Corpus and to the glosses on the Corpus. References to whole titles or title rubrics precede references to laws and paragraphs. The few references to Canon law are found on pp. 115 (Decretal. 5.40.8), 145 (Decretum ii.64), 152 (Decretal. 1.2.1, X 12. n.85), 167–8 (X 2.11.1 n.12), 175 (X 16.8. n.6) and 188–9 (*Auctoritate Dei Patris*). The Theodosian Code is cited on pp. 58, 93 (1.4.1) and 117 (6.21.1).

226

Index of names

Index of terms

236

IDEAS IN CONTEXT

Edited by Richard Rorty, J.B. Schneewind, Quentin Skinner
and Wolf Lepenies

Forthcoming titles include works by Martin Dzelzainis, Mark Goldie, Noel Malcolm, Roger Mason, James Moore, Nicolai Rubinstein, Quentin Skinner, Martin Warnke and Robert Wokler.

Titles marked with an asterisk are also available in paperback